RACE IN ANOTHER AMERICA

RACE IN ANOTHER AMERICA

THE SIGNIFICANCE OF SKIN COLOR IN BRAZIL

Edward E. Telles

PRINCETON UNIVERSITY PRESS · PRINCETON AND OXFORD

Library of Congress Cataloging-in-Publication Data

Telles, Edward Eric, 1956–
Race in another America : the significance of skin color in Brazil / Edward E. Telles.
p.   cm.
Includes bibliographical references and index.
ISBN: 0-691-11866-3 (cl : alk. paper)
1. Brazil—Race relations. 2. Racism—Brazil—History. 3. Miscegenation—
Brazil—History. 4. Blacks—Race identity—Brazil. 5. Race discrimination—Law and
legislation—Brazil.   I. Title.
F2659.A1T45 2004
305.896'081—dc22   2004044288

British Library Cataloging-in-Publication Data is available

This book has been composed in Sabon Typeface
Printed on acid-free paper. ∞
pup.princeton.edu

Printed in the United States of America

10   9   8   7   6   5   4   3   2   1

CONTENTS

ACKNOWLEDGMENTS

Although I began writing this book in 2001, I have been thinking and writing about race in Brazil for at least a decade before that. Along the way, I have accumulated many debts to people who have influenced my thinking, many more than I can possibly thank in these pages. They range from academics to black-movement leaders to everyday Brazilians. Although I was previously interested in migration and urban poverty, I first gave the issue of race in Brazil serious thought in 1989–1990 when I went to Brazil as a Rockefeller Foundation Fellow at the invitation of Vilmar Faria in Population Studies at the State University of Campinas. At that time, I began reading and discussing these issues with Octavio Ianni and Elide Ruggai Bastos in Campinas and on a couple of occasions, when I could escape to Rio, with Carlos Hasenbalg and Nelson do Valle Silva. By the end of my stay, I decided I would begin analyzing the Brazilian government's newly available microdata on race.

Although I returned to teaching at UCLA in late 1990, I often returned to Brazil, mostly because of my binational relationship with Ana Maria Goldani. Of course, research reasons were also important. My research included a trip in 1993, when Ianni, Hasenbalg, Antonio Sergio Guimarães, and I met to plan a national survey of racial attitudes in Brazil, and another in 1994 as a Fulbright Fellow at the Federal University of Bahia. The Fulbright posting brought me into contact with the emerging Bahian school of race relations.

From 1997 to 2000, I was fortunate to be at the Ford Foundation in Rio de Janeiro. My position as program officer in human rights gave me a bird's-eye view of the tremendous changes in Brazilian racial politics, where I had tremendous access to black-movement and other civil-society leaders throughout Brazil, as well as to leading government officials and academics. I thank the black-movement leaders who often opened up their world for me to see and taught me to see their own Brazilian experience. Prominent among them were Sueli Carneiro, Ivanir dos Santos, Romero Rodriguez, Abdias do Nascimento, Sergio Martins, Edson Cardoso, Hedio Silva Jr., Maria Aparecida Bento, Helio Santos, Gilberto Leal, João Carlos Nogueira, Dora Lucia Lima de Bertulio, Ivair Alves dos Santos, Diva Moreira, and Samuel Vida. When I could steal time away from my bureaucratic duties, sporadic discussions with scholars at various Brazilian universities, including the Federal University of Rio de Janeiro and Candido Mendes, also enriched my understandings of Brazilian race relations. Chief among these scholars were Antonio Sérgio

Guimarães, Livio Sansone, João Reis, and Jocélio Teles dos Santos, my former colleagues in Bahia. I also owe thanks to a wonderful set of colleagues at the Ford Foundation in Rio de Janeiro, which included Nigel Brooke, Sarah Costa, Elizabeth Leeds, José Gabriel Lopez, and Ondina Leal, as well as my New York friends at the foundation, particularly Alan Jenkins and Anthony Romero. Janice Rocha, my secretary at Ford, deserves special mention for much needed help in organizing my professional life and putting up with me. Special thanks go to Brad Smith, who brought me into the Ford fold and gave me a grant upon my departure to help free up some teaching time at UCLA to work on this book and relieve the trauma of returning to academia.

Having little knowledge of formal human rights before I took my position as the human rights program officer, I owe lots to James Cavallaro, who taught me about the state of human rights abuses and the law in Brazil and internationally. He continues to help me understand human rights issues, and he and his family have become dear friends. On the leisure side, special thanks to Jim, Gabe, and other friends for engaging me on the squash and basketball courts and then toasting to those games. Special thanks go to Joaquim Barbosa Gomes, whom I befriended in Rio and who later came as a visiting scholar to UCLA. He explained the intricate Brazilian legal system, but to avoid embarrassment, I refused his invitations to play *futebol*. Our comradeship in Los Angeles was abruptly but happily cut short when he suddenly departed to Brasília, where he became the first *negro* justice of the Brazilian Supreme Court in its 174 years. My family and I are especially grateful to Eduardo and Luche Slerca and their kids for opening up their own family lives to us, helping to make Rio de Janeiro genuinely home.

While in Brazil, I was fortunate to have a National Science Foundation grant to help me with my research on Brazilian racial classification, which I began at UCLA before going to Rio de Janeiro. Although I completed the research I had planned on racial classification, the grant also helped me to begin thinking and do some preliminary research about a more ambitious project on Brazilian race relations, which would turn into this book. At the time, my own work on the project was mostly scribbling down ideas inspired by conversations with my grantees and occasional reading. Later, as I better defined my analyses, Antonio Duran helped me generate the necessary data. He was extremely knowledgeable about the intricacies of manipulating IBGE data, and his results were extremely reliable.

When I began writing the book after returning to the United States again, Sam Cohn was especially important for making me rethink my assumptions about how to produce a workable book. Walter Allen, Jorge

Balán, Harley Browning, David López, Peter Lownds, José Moya, Alejandro Portes, and Mark Sawyer read earlier versions of this manuscript and gave me valuable suggestions on drafts that I was later embarrassed to have given them. Michael Hanchard, Tom Skidmore, Roger Waldinger, and Howard Winant gave me especially detailed comments, which I greatly appreciate. Somewhere during those revisions, I translated and published a version in Portuguese, which has become a reference in Brazil's current social policy debate (*Racismo à Brasileira: Uma Nova Perspectiva Sociológica*. 2003. Rio de Janeiro: Relume Dumará). The English version has come a ways since then, thanks largely to the patience, professionalism, and enthusiasm of my Princeton editor, Ian Malcolm.

Other colleagues that stimulated my thinking at several points include Paulo Sergio Pinheiro, Michael Mitchell, Michael Turner, Anani Dzidzenyo, Bryan Roberts, Charles Wood, Mark Fosset, Aziza Khazoom, Ray Rocco, Seth Rascussen, Stan Lieberson, and Michelle Lamont. I also thank Ciro Biderman for the map of São Paulo, Luis Cesar Ribeiro for the map of Rio de Janeiro, and the Leroy Nieman Center at UCLA for getting them into publishable format. Aida Verdugo Lazo also made some last-minute calculations of IBGE data for me. Humberto Adami and Katia Mello have kept me apprised of Brazilian events since my return.

I was especially fortunate to have a graduate research assistant, Cristina Sue, who worked beyond the call of duty, crunching numbers, creating tables, editing, typing, and retyping my endless corrections. Another graduate student, Stan Bailey, graduated shortly after my return but I thank him for our lively conversations in Brazil and upon my return. Overall, I have been lucky to have excellent graduate students and colleagues at UCLA, who have further stimulated my thoughts.

Unfortunately, my mother and father passed away in recent years and were not able to see the outcome of my (and thus their) efforts. I thank them for raising me and always being extremely supportive. My wife, Ana Maria, forced me to clarify my thinking, cast aside my North American blinders, and think big. She had left her university position in Brazil to come to Los Angeles, after our daughter Julia was born. For this, I am forever grateful. My daughter Julia has always encouraged me to get plenty of playtime with her, although I am sure it was never enough. I hope that someday she will read this book and perhaps find it interesting. To Ana Maria and Julia, I dedicate this book. I hope that in some small way it helps to improve human relations in their native Brazil.

RACE IN ANOTHER AMERICA

Chapter One

INTRODUCTION

RECENTLY, the president of the United States asked the president of Brazil, "Do you have blacks, too?"[1] Unbeknownst to President Bush and many other North Americans, that South American country currently has more than three times as many inhabitants of at least partial African origin as the United States. Both the United States and Brazil were colonized by a European power that dominated militarily weaker indigenous populations and eventually instituted systems of slavery that relied on Africans. In the Brazilian case, European colonists and their descendants enslaved and imported eleven times as many Africans as their North American counterparts. In the late nineteenth and early twentieth centuries, both countries also received millions of immigrants from Europe as they sought to industrialize. Since then, the light-skinned descendants in the United States and Brazil have come to dominate their darker-skinned compatriots through discriminatory practices that derive from a racial ideology, creating what sociologists call racially stratified societies. Both societies have experimented with affirmative-action policies to promote blacks and members of other disadvantaged groups, beginning in the 1960s in the United States and only recently in Brazil. However, the major similarities between these two large multiracial countries regarding race may end there. For one, the vast majority of persons in the United States with any African origin are categorized as black. In Brazil, large numbers of persons who are classified and identify themselves as white (*branco*) have African ancestors, not to mention the brown (*pardo, moreno*), mixed race (*mestiço, mulato*), and black (*preto, negro*) populations. Unlike in the United States, race in Brazil refers mostly to skin color or physical appearance rather than to ancestry. This difference, and many others regarding race matters, between the two countries derives from two distinct ideologies and systems of modern-day race relations. Although both racial systems are rooted in the ideology of white supremacy, their respective racial ideologies and patterns of race relations evolved in radically different ways as they responded to distinct historical, political, and cultural forces.

W.E.B. Du Bois arguably set the stage for the study of race relations in the first decade of the twentieth century when he declared the color line as the problem of the century. However, that assertion was clearly based on the bifurcated U.S. model, where blacks and whites were understood to be clearly separate groups. Had Du Bois witnessed the Brazilian case, he may have perceived that racism and discrimination were important social problems there, but he is unlikely to have identified the color line as the central problem. Also, Du Bois noted that blacks were exceptionally excluded from North American democracy; but for most of the twentieth century, there was no democracy in Brazil. Most of the population, including many whites, was excluded from access to even basic rights and subject to authoritarian domination.

Since Du Bois, the relation of blacks and whites in the United States has continued to serve as the paradigmatic case for the sociological understanding of race. Theories derived from the U.S. case are often then illegitimately applied to interpret other cases. In particular, mechanisms affecting race relations in the United States are often assumed to exist in other places like Brazil. But that is clearly not the case, as I will demonstrate in this book. Race is an important organizing principle in both Brazil and the United States but in very different ways. In the interest of building a universal *sociology* of race relations, I hope that this study will encourage a reexamination of sociologists' common conceptions of race relations, which too easily get translated into general knowledge despite their narrow empirical base.

In the last several decades, race relations have become a central area of sociological study which has uncovered a considerable body of evidence for understanding them. However, comparable evidence for Brazil continues to be relatively weak, largely because the small Brazilian social-science community considered the subject unimportant for that country. While a history of blatant and legal racism has undoubtedly contributed to making race an important area of study in the United States, racism in Brazil has generally been more subtle, and legal racial segregation has not existed since slavery. Indeed, the dominant assumption from Du Bois' time until recent years has been that race does not really matter in Brazil.

Such differences and similarities about race in the two countries have become common knowledge, but analysts are less certain of how other features of the two race systems compare. For example, analysts often note the existence of racial inequalities in Brazil as in the United States, but these are too easily explained as simply a product of racist practices that exist despite the absence of formal segregation. On the surface, that may be true, but there is much more to it than that. While it is becoming increasingly clear that racism is a universal phenomenon, it is less accepted that its manifestations may vary widely. Are the nature and levels of racial inequalities the same? Surely, history, politics, class structure, culture, and ideology are very distinct between the Brazil and the United States. Should these not have also affected the development of a distinct system of race relations?

Most notably, racial ideologies between the two countries contrast sharply. How did such distinct ideologies come about? Do they affect the social manifestations of race relations or merely their interpretations? A special problem in comparisons of race in Brazil and the United States has been the disentangling of ideology from social analysis. To what extent is research on race simply a reflection of the ideology? Do ideologies not have elements of truth? How much do they distort reality? Ideology also affects interpretations of sociological analysis. In other words, how do analysts present comparisons in ways that are compelling and make sense to both Brazilian and North American readers?

North American sociology has developed evidence-based theories for explaining the persistence of racism and racial inequality despite the end of formal segregation. For example, a key sociological text argues that racial residential segregation, which continues today in practice despite civil-rights reforms, forms the major basis for contemporary black disadvantage and other dimensions of race relations in the United States.[2] It posits that the physical and social distance between blacks and whites, along with the strong social norms that maintain that distance, accounts for high levels of racial inequality. Conversely, it hypothesizes that without extreme segregation, racial discrimination and inequality will subside. Segregation is thus thought to be the linchpin of U.S. racial domination.[3] The same may not be true for Brazil, at least if we are to believe its racial ideology. According to that ideology and to most of the research on the subject, residential segregation in Brazil is believed to be simply class based, and race is simply not an independent factor.

RACE MIXTURE AND EXCLUSION

Segregation between blacks and whites is a well-known fact in the United States. Segregation was long formalized through the legal and policy apparatus, and as many scholars have pointed out, urban residential segregation continues to demarcate rigid boundaries between blacks and whites. At least prior to the civil-rights reforms, segregation was the dominant ideology behind race relations. Whites dealt with blacks largely by maintaining considerable social distance from them, whether through avoidance in residence, marriage, friendships, or elsewhere. Just as importantly, the practice and ideology of racial segregation came to be known in Latin America as a defining feature of North American culture.

Latin Americans—especially Brazilians—thought that their culture made them morally superior, at least regarding issues of race.

Rather than segregation, race mixture or miscegenation (in Portuguese, *mestiçagem* or *miscegenação*) forms the foundational concept of Brazilian racial ideology. Race mixture represents a set of beliefs that Brazilians hold about race, including the belief that Brazilians have long mixed across racial lines, more so than in any other society, and that nonwhites are included in the Brazilian nation. Miscegenation has long been a defining metaphor of the Brazilian nation, although it initially provoked anxiety and fear among the elite, as in the United States. Although race mixture may not necessarily reflect the reality of Brazilian social behavior, the concept has been fundamental for understanding Brazil's race relations, on Brazilian terms. As Da Matta (1991) claims, understanding Brazil requires U.S. or other non-Brazilian readers to dismiss notions that Western societies are generally guided by ideas of purity. For him, Brazilians celebrate ambiguity, whereas North Americans seek to define clearly. In this sense, miscegenation represents the former and segregation the latter.

Like Brazil, many other Latin American countries hold dearly to their ideologies of *mestizaje*, the Spanish equivalent of race mixture. Those nations have melded racial differences into a single homogenous entity, creating an improved hybrid race of Mexicans, Dominicans, Venezuelans, and so on. However, accounts of Latin American race mixture tend to be romanticized versions that often became widely accepted as state-sanctioned visions of nationality or peoplehood in Latin America. Latin American elites have long prescribed their form of mestizaje as the formula for a positive system of human relations, free of the racial cleavages found in North American society. Even well-known Latin American scholars have been known to proclaim the virtues of presumed miscegenation in the region. In the United States, Latino scholars have also prided themselves on their racial mestizaje, as if their own histories provide a positive example for U.S. race relations. However, these supporters of mestizaje often fail to note that throughout Latin America it was built on white supremacist ideologies and has been unable to prevent the racial injustices that are increasingly uncovered throughout Latin America. Today, many sociologists have come to a consensus that race mixture represents little more than metaphor.

Brazilian academics and journalists have increasingly used the term "exclusion" to refer to the status of blacks and poor persons in their society. Exclusion is a well-known term in Latin America, with origins in Europe where it is also widely used. Exclusion, or social exclusion, refers to the "lack of social integration which is manifested in rules constraining the access of particular groups or persons to resources or limiting their access to citizenship rights."[4] Social exclusion is thought to be particularly appropriate for describing Brazilian society because one-third of all Brazilians live in poverty, and most are not white.

The exclusion of blacks has thus become an important counterideology to the positive interpretation given to race mixture. Like Brazil's black social movement, which has long promoted the counterideology, a new generation of scholars largely holds that racism is pervasive throughout Brazilian society. Like the race-mixture ideology, that counterideology is dangerous to social analysis because it may also blind analysts to reality. Some have wholly accepted the counterideology and go as far as to say that segregation is similar to that in the United States in practice, despite the lack of any postslavery history of its formal manifestation. However, rejecting the ideology hypothesis does not require us to accept the counterideology. Accepting ideology or counterideology is especially tempting where the evidence about race relations is weak.

Like ideologies and counterideologies generally, racial ideologies often reduce our understanding of race relations to simple unidimensional assumptions. According to ideology, at least, exclusion is the antithesis of miscegenation. Rather, miscegenation in Brazil connotes racial inclusion, not exclusion. Latin American concepts of race mixture hold that blacks, Indians, and whites socialize, reside together, and biologically mix to the point that racial distinctions become unimportant. But is there any truth to this? If so, how can there be both exclusion and miscegenation? Exclusion and inclusion refer to extreme points on a continuum of bad versus good societies; in the case of race, bad versus good race relations. But it is common to hear Brazilians speak of their country as being the world's most miscegenated country and the world's most unequal country, in the same breath. Does that imply that there has been so much mixture that only class is important, whereas race no longer makes a difference? Or does it mean that Brazilian society is racist and stratifies by race, and miscegenation is merely ideological or characteristic of an earlier historical period? What about those white Brazilians who claim to find blacks and mulattos in their family albums? How common is this? Are such ancestors merely historical remnants? Or are such findings overstated to project a culturally desirable pedigree of miscegenation?

Contemporary analysts of Brazilian race relations seem to have discarded the possibility that race mixture and racial exclusion can coexist. If white Brazilians are so racist, then why would they mix with nonwhites? Scholars argue that racial inequality and racism are so ubiquitous that they pervade all dimensions of Brazilian life. Miscegenation, some argue, occurred only among social unequals during slavery, and today occurs only for the sexual pleasure of whites but not in serious relationships. But what of all that common wisdom that miscegenation is widespread? Does it have no basis in fact? What of the earlier academic literature based on careful fieldwork which argued that Brazilian society was clearly more inclusive than the United States? Were those scholars completely wrong? Or did any inclusiveness that existed then disappear? Why would they make such an argument? Is there any evidence to support the existence of social inclusion for nonwhites anywhere, or were those scholars merely overtaken by the powerful ideologies of race mixture?

Today's social analysts have arrived at surprisingly distinct conclusions about Brazilian race relations compared to those of an earlier generation. Current scholars emphasize exclusion; past scholars emphasized race mixture. These two generations of scholars accepted either racial exclusion or inclusion as truth while ignoring or discrediting the other. Rather than considering the possibility that both racial inclusion and exclusion may coexist, the current generation of scholars has treated that possibility as the confusion of reality with popular beliefs. Those who have argued that Brazilian society is more racially inclusive and characterized by race mixture or hybridity, have also theorized that racial inequalities and discrimination are leftover from slavery but are transitory. On the other hand, the current consensus defends the exclusivity argument and asserts that racial inclusivity, or miscegenation, is merely a popular belief that is not supported by reality.

The evidence used by the current generation is based largely on official statistics that have demonstrated high levels of racial inequality. Furthermore, these academics have marshaled plenty of evidence of discrimination to support their view. But have current scholars examined race relations widely enough and asked all the right questions? Has all the proper evidence been brought to bear? For an ideology of inclusion to be so pervasively accepted for so many years would seem to require some evidence, however limited, of its existence. What is it about the Brazilian system that supported arguments about racial inclusivity? And if there is any support for them, how can inclusiveness coexist with exclusiveness? For me, this remains the enigma of Brazilian race relations.

Two Generations of Race-Relations Research

A common categorization in the history of thought about Brazilian race relations maintains that there have been three main stages of thinking about Brazilian race relations. Roughly speaking, these three respective currents claimed that (1) there is little or no racial discrimination but rather great fluidity among races; (2) racial discrimination is widespread but transitory; and (3) racial discrimination is persistent and structural.[5]

While most authors are easily categorized into one of these three schools of thought, others present a mixture of these ideas or have changed their views over the course of their careers. Also, the chronological order of important contributions is not always linear but often the outcome of multiple academic debates, partially determined by the nationality of the scholars. For the purposes of this book, I generally accept this division but collapse the latter two stages into one. Thus, I characterize scholarly perspectives on Brazilian race relations as comprising two generations. The first defended racial democracy, in which Brazil is uniquely inclusive of blacks; the second challenged racial democracy, arguing that Brazil is characterized by racial exclusion. According to the first school of thought, there is little or no racism in Brazil; for the second, racism is pervasive.

The idea of miscegenation as a positive aspect of Brazilian race relations was fully developed by Gilberto Freyre in the 1930s, and some form of this perspective was defended by North American Brazilianists, including Donald Pierson, Marvin Harris, Charles Wagley, and Carl Degler, until the 1960s, and in the case of Degler, as late as 1972. Freyre and his followers believed that any existing racial inequality was an artifact both of the enslavement of blacks and their adherence to traditional cultural values, but they predicted that it would soon disappear. For them, racial differences were fluid and conditioned by class, and racial discrimination was mild and largely irrelevant. Specifically, Harris (1952) and Wagley (1952) concluded that class, rather than racial, discrimination underlies Brazil's hierarchical social relations, even though racial prejudices and stereotypes were often voiced. In general, these scholars agreed with Freyre that "being" Brazilian implied a metaracial character, which muddled racial distinctions through extensive miscegenation.

This view would be radically challenged in the late 1950s, when Brazilian sociologists, led by Florestan Fernandes, would conclude that racial democracy was a myth. Funded by the United Nations Educational, Scientific, and Cultural Organization (UNESCO) to document, understand, and disseminate Brazil's presumed secret of racial harmony in a world then marked by the horrors of racism and genocide, Fernandes would surprise his sponsors by sharply disagreeing with Freyre and his North American counterparts on the UNESCO project. Fernandes concluded that racism was widespread in Brazilian society, although he blamed slavery and its social and psychological effects on blacks themselves for their inability to compete with whites in the newly industrializing labor market. Moreover, he believed that even though racial prejudice and discrimination were functional to slave society, they were incompatible with the competitive order established by a capitalist class society. As a result, he predicted racism would disappear with capitalist development, although whites would seek to maintain their privileged positions for as long as possible.

I attribute most of the disagreement between the two generations of race-relations scholars to their separate research emphases. The first generation focused on sociability and social relations, mostly among class equals, while the second generation emphasized inequality and discrimination. I refer to these two dimensions as vertical and horizontal social relations, respectively. The North American scholars in particular tended to follow Gilberto Freyre's emphasis on horizontal relations. Many of these scholars, including Wagley and Harris, were anthropologists, but they also included sociologists like Donald Pierson (1942). For Pierson, a student of the emerging Chicago school of sociology, segregation and intermarriage were believed to be appropriate indicators of adaptability or integration of minority groups in society. This was the dominant tradition in North American sociology. They assumed that integration would lead to eventual assimilation, where the dominant and previously subordinate racial groups would become similar and racial differences would disappear. Researchers of this school found horizontal relations to be harmonious and integrative compared to the United States, thus predicting an optimistic future for the descendants of Brazilian slaves. These scholars found any racial hierarchy, conflict, or exploitation in Brazil to be unproblematic or transitory.

By contrast, Fernandes and his Brazilian UNESCO contemporaries focused mostly on the vertical relations of racial inequality. To the limited extent that Fernandes and his followers mention horizontal relations in their work, they emphasized the distance between whites and blacks. The subjects of miscegenation and the mulatto, which were of major interest in the earlier literature, are generally ignored by Fernandes. Guimarães (1999) claims that, like other *Paulistas* (residents of São Paulo state), Fernandes never saw miscegenation as a value but rather was motivated by social equity and development concerns. Southern Brazilians held the notion that true Brazilians were mostly white and valued being part of a European, rather than a *mestizo,* nation. As the primary destination of mass European immigration, São Paulo had become an ethnic mosaic and blacks were a stigmatized minority. Moreover, a disdain for miscegenation and for mixed racial categories may have come from Fernandes's close association with the black movement. Like Abdias do Nascimento, a black activist writer, Fernandes associated miscegenation with a whitening campaign to eliminate blacks from the Brazilian population. Thus, Fernandes not only ignored any practice of miscegenation, but he rejected it as simply an ideology for legitimizing racial discrimination.

Carl Degler's explicit comparison of race relations in Brazil and the United States was especially influential in the latter. As the winner of a

Pulitzer Prize, Degler's work influenced North American understandings of race in Brazil more than any other source. Writing in 1972, during the more optimistic days of the U.S. civil-rights movement, Carl Degler (1986) mixed first- and second-generation interpretations in his book. Although Freyre and his followers were already in disrepute, Degler, a self-described follower of Harris, concluded that race made little difference for mulattos but generally agreed with Fernandes that the smaller number of Brazilian blacks suffered the burdens of racism. Thus, Degler claimed that the primary difference regarding race relations between the two countries was the existence of a "mulatto escape hatch" in Brazil, which allowed mulattos to overcome racial disadvantage by avoiding classification as black but also weakened the possibility of black solidarity.

After a fifteen-year hiatus in Brazilian race research due to repression by the military government, the study of race resurfaced with the completion of Carlos Hasenbalg's 1978 Ph.D. dissertation at the University of California, Berkeley. Unlike Fernandes but like the thinking emerging within Berkeley's department of sociology, Hasenbalg concluded that racism was compatible, not incompatible, with the development of Brazilian capitalism. Hasenbalg believed that racial domination and the subordinate status of blacks would persist because racism had acquired new meanings since abolition and would continue to serve the material and symbolic interests of dominant whites through the disqualification of nonwhites as competitors. By relying extensively on government statistical data, Hasenbalg and Nelson do Valle Silva produced a series of studies about racial inequality in income, education, occupation, and infant mortality throughout the 1980s. With their studies, there remained little academic doubt about the existence of racial inequality and discrimination in Brazil. Interestingly, Silva also produced several statistical studies on intermarriage and racial classification. Some of Silva's findings seemed to support the first generation's findings, but he downplayed any such support as his body of work was neither comparative nor integrated into their general theoretical conclusions. Rather, Hasenbalg and Silva's work is remembered for greatly strengthening the dominance of the second-generation perspective.[6] Unfortunately for North Americans, little of this second generation of work would become available in English, and thus Degler's 1972 book would continue to be the standard reference in the United States for nonspecialists in their understanding of race in Brazil.

In sum, the stages of Brazilian racial ideas were not discrete but overlapping, with elements of previous stages sustained in subsequent stages. Racial democracy had been seriously challenged beginning in the 1950s by São Paulo academics, while some form of the racial-democracy concept continued to be defended by U.S. academia well into the 1970s.

Popular and elite support for the idea of racial democracy ended in the 1990s. Although some of its elements continue to survive in current discourse and indeed are held by some members of society. Much of the old popular discourses become grafted into the new. Surely, many of these discontinuities can be explained by differences in academic contexts, ideology, and political interests in maintaining or challenging the racial-democracy discourse. Differences between U.S. and Brazilian scholarship could also be explained by distinct conceptions of what constitutes racism and discrimination in the two countries. Additionally, a significant language barrier and limited translation prevented satisfactory mutual appreciation and awareness of a growing literature by academics in both countries.

BRAZIL ON THE AGENDA OF AN INTERNATIONAL SOCIOLOGY OF RACE

This issue of race in Brazil has recently gained a prominent place in the work of internationally eminent sociologists Herbert Gans and Pierre Bourdieu. Interestingly, their respective interpretations of Brazil are nearly contradictory. While this may largely be due to their misunderstanding about a reasonable range of the literature, it is also unfortunately due to the literature itself, in which serious analysts of Brazil have reached opposite conclusions. Despite very limited comparative evidence, Gans (1999) confidently argues that sociological outcomes between the United States and Brazil are similar:

> Brazil has not passed civil rights legislation; racial stratification, discrimination and segregation have persisted but only through the class system; a high rate of illiteracy has enabled whites to virtually monopolize the higher class; intermarriage has taken place mainly among blacks and black-white "biracials"; "biracials" gain little socioeconomic advantage from their lighter skins; and the darkest-skinned blacks are forced into slums and prisons as in the United States. (377)

On the other hand, French sociologist Pierre Bourdieu and his U.S.-based colleague Loïc Wacquant (1999) argue that, unfortunately, analysts have merely transposed U.S. conceptions of race onto Brazil, despite the empirical realities:

> Carried out by Americans and Latin Americans trained in the USA, most of the recent research on racial inequality in Brazil strives to prove that, contrary to the image that Brazilians have of their own nation, the country of the "three sad races" . . . is no less racist than others. (44)

They go on to discredit an influential book by a North American scholar for misunderstanding Brazilian race relations and blame U.S. foundations for exporting the U.S. model.

Although Gans and Bourdieu reach distinct conclusions, both are guided by the question of whether Brazilian race relations are better or worse than black-white relations in the United States. While they both agree that U.S. black-white relations are deplorable, Gans believes that things are no better in Brazil, while Bourdieu and Wacquant strongly imply that Brazil is less racist. Their contrasting results do not derive from a careful or systematic understanding of the Brazilian racial system. Indeed, there seems to be little familiarity with Brazil, as far as I can tell. What seems clear is that both sets of authors, in the absence of a clear understanding, project their own alternately pessimistic or optimistic image of Brazil onto their sociological analysis. Unfortunately, the literature on race relations in Brazil allows them to have their choice.

Although we might expect more from such notable sociologists, perhaps one cannot blame Gans and Bourdieu for errors of fact because neither is a student of Brazilian society. One might wonder why they took a stab at trying to interpret race in Brazil. Apparently, they both recognized that Brazil was an important case for understanding race. For whatever reason, it is interesting that these authors based their poorly founded conclusions on particular stages in the debate on Brazilian race relations. Judging from their citations, Bourdieu and Wacquant rely on the early generation of scholarly work that largely defended racial democracy. They use this work as their gold standard from which to judge all subsequent literature. Gans, by contrast, bases his observations on more recent work that reduces racial democracy to being merely ideology or myth and claims that racism is widespread in Brazil. Thus, Bourdieu and Wacquant apparently find the first stage of research more compelling and choose to use it to discredit the second stage, misreading (or failing to read) key texts and imputing false conclusions.[7] By contrast, Gans selectively uses the second stage of research while ignoring the first stage.

Toward an Integrated Analysis
of Brazilian Race Relations

My goal in this book is to reexamine the arguments presented by both generations of scholars. To this end, I examine a wider range of interracial relations and behaviors in Brazil in comparative and historical context. I thus attempt to provide a more integrated and wide-ranging account of Brazilian race relations than has been presented in the past and try to flesh out the contradicting interpretations of two generations of scholars. By taking advantage of Brazil's excellent data on race and a host of socioeconomic measures, I employ a set of well-developed social science methodologies and indicators of interracial behaviors to examine a broad range of race-relations issues. Unlike my predecessors, I approach these issues by acknowledging the possibility that some form of both inclusion and exclusion, however limited, may exist.

The idea of racial exclusion reflects a consensus position in the contemporary analysis of race relations in Brazil. That consensus holds that Brazilian race relations are not much different in practice than in the United States and South Africa, even during formal segregation or apartheid. Based on the limited available evidence, I find this hard to believe. My interest in this book is thus to describe race relations at various levels by making systematic international comparisons, particularly on those dimensions that are measurable and address key sociological issues regarding the importance of race and the salience of racial boundaries. Although the terms "miscegenation" and "exclusion" may be well understood as common sense in the Brazilian context, they are often vague notions that are therefore of limited analytical value. On the other hand, they capture the central tensions in Brazilian race thinking that I seek to confront in this book.

Analytically, I find that the concept of exclusion is inadequate because it expresses a dichotomy in which persons or categories of people are either entirely in or out. Such a perspective would seem to preclude the possibility of inclusion coexisting with any exclusion. I do not believe race relations are necessarily unidimensional in this sense. Also, the reference for the term "exclusion" is unclear: included or excluded from what? Similar terms such as "marginalization" or "informalization" are problematic for similar reasons. Although they have the advantage of linking poverty and inequality to the social processes of development, I prefer the more neutral concept of "vertical relations" to capture the dimension of economic exclusion. Miscegenation suggests little or no social distance among persons of different color, although it connotes a different understanding outside of the Latin American context. Similarly, segregation is used analytically in U.S. sociology to refer to great social distance, but for Latin Americans it also connotes an abhorrent and explicit system of racial division and separation. Therefore, I use the more neutral concept of "horizontal race relations" to refer to miscegenation, or more precisely, levels of sociability, which can then be used to analyze cross-national differences.

Vertical race relations are often viewed as cause or consequence of the nature of horizontal relationships. Many U.S.-based sociological theories assume that as long as social distance remains high, particularly in intermarriage and residential segregation, prejudice and discrimination will persist.[8] However, the extent and nature of discrimination at each of these levels, while not fully independent of the other indicators, may have separate logics. One cannot, for example, assume that discrimination at one level implies equal discrimination at all levels. Even if this is the case for black-white relations in the United States, it is not necessarily the case for other instances of race relations, in the United States or elsewhere. While racial injustices of any kind on any dimension are morally wrong, it is insufficient to say that Brazilian society is racist; that kind of thinking might make for good activism at some level, but it makes for poor sociology at any level. The intensity and manifestations of racism and the interrelationships between different dimensions need to be understood in order to accurately understand Brazilian reality.

I believe we can better understand the Brazilian system by separating out horizontal and vertical dimensions of race relations. This strategy permits locating and distinguishing those points in which Brazilian race relations may be more or less exclusive than previously believed or in comparison to the United States. This distinction allows us a reexamination of hypotheses about horizontal relations by the early generation of research with current data and more sophisticated methodologies. We can also use more current empirical study and theory to inform our analysis of vertical relations. To present a fair and accurate depiction of race relations requires strong, empirically based indicators that can address race relations on both the horizontal and vertical dimensions. The intensity of racism at both these levels can be further understood when we compare Brazil's indicators on both dimensions to those of a society that stands out for its troubled race relations and for being the dominant model for the study of race.

COMPARISONS TO THE UNITED STATES

In addition to trying to make sense of the internal logic of the Brazilian race system, another main reason for writing this book is to compare Brazil with the United States (and, to a lesser extent, South Africa). As the articles by Gans (1999) and Bourdieu and Wacquant (1999) reveal, systematic comparisons of race in Brazil and the United States are seriously in need. In these countries, race has been important throughout the past five centuries or more, from the time Europeans first set foot on American (or African) soil. At the very least, the important case of Brazil needs to be understood to develop a global theory of race relations. Brazil and the United States are the two largest countries in the Western Hemisphere, both in terms of total population and African-origin population. Brazilians claiming to be black or mixed race number about 80 million, constituting nearly half of Brazil's 173 million people. A large percentage of whites in Brazil also have African ancestors, raising the number of African-origin persons to perhaps over 100 million. This compares to about 30 million blacks in the United States, or about 12 percent of a total population of approximately 270 million.[9]

Comparisons to the United States have often served as a backdrop for understanding Brazilian race relations, as the work of many North Americans and Brazilians alike reveals. Historians of slavery have long sought to explain differences between the United States and Brazil since Freyre (1933) and Tannenbaum (1947). Explicit and implicit comparisons to the United States are prevalent throughout the literature on Brazilian race relations, probably due to the former's economic, political, and cultural hegemony. Also, many analysts of Brazilian race relations have been North Americans (e.g., Donald Pierson, Charles Wagley, Marvin Harris, Carl Degler, George Reid Andrews, and Michael Hanchard) or Brazilians that studied in the United States (e.g., Gilberto Freyre, Nelson do Valle Silva, and Antonio Sergio Guimarães).[10]

The Brazil-U.S. comparison in this book relies mostly on quantitative indicators, which have been used in abundance to understand U.S. race relations. Despite strong ethnographic and historical evidence, comparisons of Brazil and the United States using quantitative indicators are rare. Also, the substantive reach of both qualitative and quantitative research has been confined to mere parts of the entire racial system. Anecdotal evidence has often been used to fill in gaps where strong evidence is lacking, leading to many misconceptions and myths in the comparisons. Carl Degler's *Neither Black Nor White* is a good example. Although it may provide the best comparative account even thirty years after its publication, it was unfortunately sustained on weak and often anecdotal data, not to mention that it is now greatly outdated, as race relations have changed markedly in both countries.[11]

I believe statistical indicators can be used for the study of race in any society, provided data are available and interpreted in the context of the particular case. They convey condensed information on various dimensions of race relations and, in this case, permit U.S. and Brazil comparisons with a greater degree of confidence than was previously possible. I expect that these indicators will help to either validate or invalidate previously held assumptions. While many of the findings based on such indicators may seem obvious, others may challenge strongly held truths or bring light to our sociological uncertainties.

On the subject of comparative indicators, a careful consideration of the issue of racial classification is fundamental. The ambiguity of Brazilian race data has led to some questioning of its reliability for capturing "real" racial differences. However, previous research that relies on large data sets has used them uncritically. In contrast, I question the reliability of race data in a context where race is thought to be ambiguous and subject to social factors. Where reliability is most questionable and where data permit, I examine race relations outcomes using two recent data sets that classify race according to both interviewer- and self-classification. Although inequality between whites and nonwhites may be so great that ambiguity is unlikely to account for the racial gap, brown-black differences may be less so and thus require more careful examination. Because racial classification cannot be taken for granted in Brazil, I dedicate an entire chapter to this issue and emphasize matters of classification where appropriate in subsequent chapters.

Ultimately, I seek to reexamine the adequacy of race-relations theories. To what extent can sociological theories account for race relations in Brazil? How can an understanding of the Brazilian case help to build better race-relations theories? What does the U.S.-Brazil comparison say about the construction, maintenance, and manifestations of racial boundaries in contemporary society? To what extent, where, and why do societies as different as Brazil and the United States set racial boundaries?

As the focus of this book is clearly the Brazilian case, my comparisons to the United States are not systematic, but instead are brought in at key moments to highlight contrasts between the two countries. Due to the fact that the U.S. literature on race is large, often hotly contested, and enters into many debates, I decided to limit the interpretation of that case to dimensions where fairly objective indicators can be found and to those areas in which there is considerable consensus. I hope that the comparisons in this study using basic sociological indicators for both the United States and Brazil will overcome misinformation and stereotypes of race relations in the United States for Brazilian readers, just as I hope it will overcome the same assumptions about Brazil for North American readers.

The dynamics of race relations in the United States are far from universal and, in many ways, they may be an exception to the more common cases of racism without racist laws. Rarely have states enforced segregation laws as strict as those in the United States (and South Africa), although many more societies—including about twenty Latin American countries, including Brazil—have had little or no formal segregation, while racializing large segments of their populations. On the other hand, for readers whose principal interest is in the U.S. case, Brazil may provide some valuable lessons about the newest phase of U.S. race relations, which has been referred to as laissez-fare racism, postracism, or discrimination with a smile for its absence of legal racism and general acceptance of antiracism.

BRAZIL'S NEW ERA OF RACIAL POLICY

A final reason for reexamining Brazilian race relations is to discuss them in the context of the sudden and dramatic changes in Brazilian race thinking. This new phase is reflected mostly in the new acknowledgment of racism and government attempts to redress it. The issue of race in Brazil has moved to the center of the social-policy agenda. As a result, public interest in race has skyrocketed. For the first time in Brazilian history, social policies have begun to explicitly promote social integration of blacks and mulattos. Such policies do not merely seek to eliminate or alleviate material poverty but also strive to eliminate or reduce class, racial, gender, and other discriminations that bar citizens from access to social justice. This includes both universal policies that encompass the entire population or the poor population, as well as particularistic policies that combat discrimination and promote categories of people that have been excluded on the basis of particular characteristics, including race. The designs of these policies vary widely, but together they seek to address a broad range of social exclusions that are manifested economically, psychologically, politically, and culturally. This change is a milestone in Brazilian racial thought, much like Brazil's earlier ideological transition from white supremacy to racial democracy.

Indeed, the idea of affirmative action or policies specifically designed for blacks and mulattos sounds quite odd and out of place in the Brazilian context. In fact, the whole idea sounded preposterous and highly unlikely just a few years ago. Brazil had been one of the first multiracial states to go beyond race, but it had become apparent that its racial democracy continued to privilege whites at the expense of nonwhites, just as it did during most of its history of white supremacy. Now that these policies are actually being implemented, Brazilian policymakers are accused of imposing U.S. policies. Why would Brazil want such policies? Opponents claim that the Brazilian context is different from the United States and such policies would be of limited effectiveness. But does Brazil have an alternative to U.S.-style race-conscious policies? As the Brazilian state begins to use race explicitly to promote blacks for the first time in its history, what consequences can be expected?

These recent changes have engendered a backlash of scholarly thinking on race in Brazil. Although largely schematic and anecdotal, it has had much influence on the policy debate, mostly because it has been advocated by several well-known senior Brazilian scholars. They argue that rather than dismiss racial democracy as mere myth, it should be used to fight against racism. Myths are not mere falsities to be discovered and discarded but rather represent a popular way of thinking, which makes

Brazil unique or at least different from the United States. Prompted by the federal government's plans to implement affirmative action, they believe that the belief in racial democracy provides an ideal of racial egalitarianism, which will help Brazilians to overcome racism. Furthermore, they argue that U.S.-style affirmative action will produce negative consequences for Brazilian society, making its race relations more like those of the United States.

Finally, although recent decisions to implement affirmative action may represent the most explicit intervention ever by the Brazilian state on issues of race, I also seek to show how the Brazilian state has been very actively involved in shaping race relations throughout its history. This has included the explicit importation of European immigrants to whiten its population as well as the promotion of racial democracy through a series of actions by elites, including representatives of the Brazilian government.

ORGANIZATION OF CHAPTERS

In my quest to present an integrated and comparative analysis of Brazil as well as to provide a historical context and an analysis of policy, I organize the book into ten chapters. Chapters 2 and 3 provide a history of politics and ideology, which serves as background for understanding race in Brazil, followed by five chapters on contemporary race relations. Chapter 4 examines the complex system of Brazilian racial classification. Then I explore vertical relations, specifically, racial inequality in chapter 5 and discrimination in chapter 6. These chapters are followed by analyses of horizontal race relations of intermarriage in chapter 7 and residential segregation, a less intimate indicator of interracial sociability, in chapter 8. I then summarize the main points of the previous chapters and draw out the theoretical implications in chapter 9. Finally, I examine the implications of the Brazilian system for designing social policy in chapter 10.

DATA

The Brazilian censuses, annual national household surveys, and two attitudinal surveys provide a treasure trove of data on race, enabling me to map out the form and nature of race relations across large sectors of the population. These largely unexplored data are based on random sampling techniques, so that all sectors of Brazilian society are represented in their rightful proportions. The importance of such data cannot be underestimated. Unlike the majority of Latin American countries, Brazil has collected race data in a majority of its censuses and has been able to document racial inequalities. Most Latin American countries do not collect population information about race. As a result, they can more easily deny racial inequality, given the inability to prove its existence. Brazil sought to do the same in the 1970s, when it did not collect data on race. However, the proof of racial injustice in Brazil since then has come largely through such government data.

Data for chapters 4 through 8 rely mostly on the analysis of survey and census data, primarily supplied by the Instituto Brasileiro de Geografia e Estatistica (IBGE). These include the 1960, 1980, and 1991 censuses, as well as the national household surveys, Pesquisa Nacional por Amostra de Domicilios (PNAD), from 1976, 1981, 1986, 1996, and 1999. Particular chapters rely more on one or another data set, depending on the substantive appropriateness and availability of the data. All of these sources inform the time-series charts in chapter 5, which span the period of 1960–1999. Where possible, I use either the 1991 census or the 1996 or 1999 PNAD to represent a fairly current depiction of the situation. I use the 1991 census when I need a large number of cases for analysis. Unfortunately, microlevel data for the 2000 census were not yet available at the time of this writing.

Moreover, I examine residential segregation, intermarriage, and the cross-sectional effects of industrialization on inequality, using a special 1980 data set of urban areas, that was specially created by the IBGE. In the case of residential segregation, the IBGE does not make their census data available by census tracts, but they graciously agreed to calculate these indexes for the forty largest urban areas in 1980. At a later point, they calculated intermarriage, inequality, and other indexes for the seventy-three largest urban areas. I worked closely with the IBGE in producing these summary indicators, including examining computer programs to ensure that formulas for computing indicators were correctly applied. District-level maps of São Paulo and Rio de Janeiro were created using the 1991 census and the 1990 PNAD, respectively. Finally, I use two independently developed surveys, including a 1995 national survey and a 2000 survey for the state of Rio de Janeiro, in the chapters on racial classification and for occasional references to racial attitudes.

Chapters 3 and 10 focus on the new era of race consciousness and policies designed to revert racism and racial inequalities. They draw largely on information I gathered as the program officer in human rights for the Ford Foundation's Brazil office. There, I was fortunate to witness closely the dramatic changes occurring in Brazilian society, with ready access to influential academics, policy makers, and leaders of the black movement. My perspective of the sudden changes in Brazilian politics of race during the past decade and the black movement is thus largely an insider's view, which would be difficult to access from traditional sources such as meeting records, official documents, and interviews. The largely demographic analysis of the other chapters has important implications for the ways in which I understand the structural sources and the implications of those changes.

A NOTE ON REGION

Regional differences are fundamental to understanding Brazilian society. In a country with a landmass larger than the continental United States and levels of development that vary from the highly industrialized São Paulo to the very poor Northeast, regional differences need to be considered before generalizing local findings to describe "race relations in Brazil." My own experience of having resided in Bahia, Rio de Janeiro, and São Paulo, as well as frequently visiting my wife's family in Rio Grande do Sul on many occasions, is that racial classification is distinct and race relations have a different feel in these different contexts. For one thing, the white proportion of the population in each of those places is roughly 20, 55, 75, and 85 percent, respectively. While the South and Southeast have been described as class societies marked by massive European immigration, industrialization, and early urbanization, the Northeast and North have been characterized by their especially great status differences and a castelike system, inherited from slavery but not transformed by industrialization or immigration. Throughout this book, I either directly examine regional differences or indirectly through its correlates of racial composition or industrialization. For theoretical reasons that I explain later, I tend to examine horizontal relations as they relate to racial composition (e.g., percent white), and for hierarchical relations, their correlation with industrialization.

Economist Edmar Bacha once described Brazil as "Belindia," comprising a small Belgium, reflecting a high level of development, and a large but poor India.[12] Although he meant merely to describe regional differences in development, Bacha's statement could be interpreted as having racial implications as well. This is apparent in map 1.1, which shows the twenty-six Brazilian states coded by percentage of the population that is white and divided by levels of social development. Increasingly lighter shades on the map indicate states with higher proportions of whites. White majorities are found in the seven southernmost states while whites are a numerical minority in the other nineteen states. The bold line separating the large northern part of the country from the smaller southern half represents levels of social development, according to the human development index, as measured by the United Nations. The human

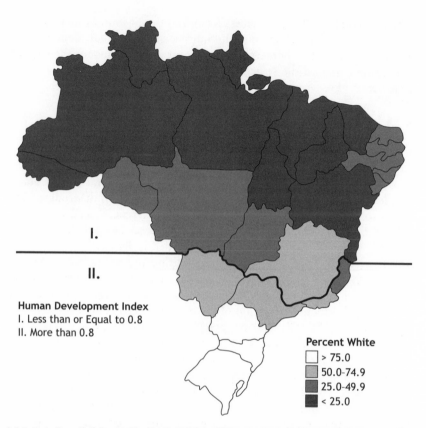

MAP 1.1 Brazil showing human development and percent white by state

development index measures health and educational development, encompassing levels of literacy, life expectancy and infant mortality. Social development coincides with racial composition in Brazil. All nineteen states north of the bold line have an index of human development that is less than or equal to 0.8, while the seven states below it are relatively highly developed. With the exception of Minas Gerais—in which whites are a bare majority (51.4 percent)—and Espiritu Santo—in which whites are a bare minority (47.9 percent)—all majority white states are highly developed, while the majority nonwhite states rank low on human development. Thus, whites are privileged by their location in the South and Southeast, while blacks and browns tend to reside in the less developed regions of Brazil.

The differences between the first and second generations of research were also regional. The classic studies of Brazilian race relations focused almost entirely on the northern half of Brazil, which were too often generalized to all of Brazil and may have partly accounted for differing conclusions about race in Brazil. For example, the importance given to miscegenation seems to be differentiated by region in the academic interpretation of race in Brazil. In the 1930s, Freyre (1937, 1986) reduced Brazilian society to the patriarchal family of the rural Northeast which he describes as the cradle of Brazilian civilization where miscegenation found its greatest expression. In the 1950s and 1960s, North American researchers of race in Brazil also focused on the northern regions and, like Freyre, noted high rates of racial fluidity there, especially when compared to their native United States. By contrast, their Brazilian contemporaries, such as Florestan Fernandes, focused on the white southern regions and emphasized racial discrimination and inequality, generally neglecting the issue of miscegenation.

A Note on the Concept of Race and the Use of Racial Terms

Because race is a controversial and sensitive topic, I prefer to define the concept early on. As is the consensus in sociology, race is a social construct, with very little or no biological basis. Race exists only because of racist ideologies. In the West, which includes Brazil, nineteenth-century scientific theories established that humans could be divided into distinguishable racial types, which were hierarchically ordered according to an ideology establishing that such characteristics are correlated with a person's intellectual and behavioral traits. Even though such theories are currently discredited by the vast majority of the scientific community, beliefs in the existence of races are embedded in social practices, giving the concept a great influence on social organization. By race relations, I believe that Robert Park's (2000) definition, which he wrote in the 1930s, of "relations that exist between individuals conscious of racial differences" continues to be applicable, even though he denied that race was important in Brazil and would sometimes invoke essentialistic or biological distinctions. This definition avoids the idea of race as based on a group identity that is common in the United States but is often inappropriate for Brazil.

Race is important because people continue to classify and treat others according to societally accepted ideas. The idea of race has had enormous influence in the evolution of modern societies, including Brazil's, and it has had negative consequences for its victims. I can empathize with a concern that the use of the term "race" reifies social distinctions that have no biological value, but race continues to be immensely important in sociological interaction, and therefore sociological analysis must take it into account. As sociologists have long discovered, ideas or beliefs, like those about race, can have powerful real-world consequences. W. I. Thomas's (1922) classic sociological formulation succinctly stated "if men define situations as real, they are real in their consequences."

Concepts like race vary in their connotations in different languages, as they evolved out of distinct cultural contexts. For example, color is more commonly used in Brazil, while race is more common in the United States. Choosing race instead of color is understandable in English but clumsy in Portuguese and Spanish. Nevertheless, I find race and color in Brazil to be analytically similar and derived from similar racial ideologies. I thus decide to use the term race, which underlies both concepts. I further describe my thinking on this at the beginning of chapter 4.

The choice of English translations of racial categories is more problematic. The Brazilian system uses multiple and overlapping terms, which cannot be precisely translated into English. Since I rely greatly on data that uses the census categories white, brown, and black (*branco, pardo, and preto*), I will usually employ these terms in this book. Unfortunately, the common terms *moreno* and *negro* also translate as brown and black, respectively, so when I refer to these terms, I often leave them in Portuguese to avoid confusion. Because much of the literature uses the term "mulatto" to refer to mixed-race persons of black and white descent, I occasionally use it as well. Certainly, the choice of one or another term may annoy some readers but almost all the terms (except perhaps white) are problematic. However, such choices are inevitable.

A special problem is choosing a term that aggregates browns and blacks. Although it is important to sometimes make the distinction between browns and blacks as this book will show, the white-nonwhite distinction is generally the most important racial cleavage between Brazil's haves and have-nots. Although the black-movement classification system recommends that the term *negro* include blacks and browns, I prefer to use "nonwhite" to avoid the conceptual confusion between that use of *negro* and its more restricted popular use. Occasionally, I use the Portuguese *negro* as analogous to nonwhite, especially when I refer to government, black-movement, and journalistic uses of the term, which is the term they prefer. However, it is not always clear if *negro* is being used to refer to only those at the dark end of the color continuum (blacks) or if it includes intermediate color categories. Examples are the *movimento negro* (the black movement), social policies for negros or popular attitudes about negros. This ambiguity is discussed further in chapter 4.

In seeking to respect the black movement's attempt and right to self-identify, I could also have used the term "Afro-Brazilian" or "Afro-descendant," translations of *Afro-Brasileiro(a)* and *afrodescendente*. Although these are not commonly used in the discourse of ordinary Brazilians, they are increasingly used by college-educated persons and activists in the black movement. According to some black-movement leaders, *afrodescendente* has gained currency because their Spanish-speaking allies can easily use it, whereas *negro* is extremely demeaning in some Latin American countries. Also, black-movement leaders prefer *afrodescendente* because it clearly identifies the descendants of enslaved Africans, which is critical in the current reparations (for slavery) movement.[13]

Admittedly, the term "nonwhite" should include the small and regionally concentrated Asian and indigenous population, the other two race categories in the census, but I exclude them in my analysis. This study examines the white-to-black color continuum, which encompasses the vast majority of all Brazilians. The experiences of the small and regionally concentrated Asian and Indian populations are distinct from the regionally diverse and larger white, black, and brown populations. Other ethnic groups, including Jews and Arabs, who are largely assimilated and considered white Brazilians in the Brazilian census, as well as those of Japanese and indigenous origin, are the subjects of separate scholarly treatments, to which I defer.[14]

Chapter Two

FROM WHITE SUPREMACY TO RACIAL DEMOCRACY

> We are a mestizo country . . . if not in the blood then in the soul.
> —*Silvio Romero 1888*[1]

To interpret Brazil's current system of race relations, we need to understand the social, cultural, and intellectual context within which Brazilian ideas of race emerged and evolved. In this chapter, I show how distinct ideologies in Brazil were formed around elite concerns about Brazil's apparently high rates of miscegenation. I begin with the belief in miscegenation as degenerate and leading to Brazil's backwardness (most of the nineteenth century), proceeding to whitening through miscegenation and as a genetic solution to its backwardness (late nineteenth and early twentieth century), and then to miscegenation as a positive value and proof of Brazil's "racial democracy" (1930s to 1980s). I pay particular attention to scholarly thinking and to the related state actions around issues of race, whether they were explicit or implicit, discriminatory or anti-racist. Finally, I examine Brazil's changing racial composition from its first census in 1872 to its most recent in 2000.

The Origins: Portuguese Colonization and Slavery

The Portuguese first landed on Brazilian shores in 1500, and soon after they began to enslave the native population for its growing sugar economy. With the decimation of the indigenous population through wars and disease brought by the Europeans, the Portuguese colonizers looked to Africa for an alternative labor supply. Beginning in the mid-sixteenth century, Africans began to be brought to Brazil as slave laborers for the expanding sugar economy. Roughly three hundred years later, when the slave trade ended in 1850, 3.6 million Africans had been brought to Brazil as slaves, mostly to labor in the production of raw materials for export to the North Atlantic. At first, Brazil produced mostly sugar, then the economy shifted to mining and cattle raising in the eighteenth century and finally to coffee growing in the nineteenth century.[2] In 1888, Brazil became the last country in the Western Hemisphere to abolish slavery, although a series of government reforms gradually emancipated slaves before then. Just as independence in 1822 had been a smooth transition from colony to state, the transition from slavery also did not involve war or rupture in local values or the social structure, as it did in the United States. According to Carvalho (2004), the colonial aristocratic system remained fairly intact and a Brazilian national identity was thus slow to develop. Elite doubts about its large nonwhite population further impeded the formation of a positive national self-image.

As early as 1755, the king of Portugal had encouraged his subjects in Brazil to "populate themselves" and "join with the natives through marriage."[3] In the same year, the Marquis of Pombal rose to power in Portugal as the war minister, eventually becoming prime minister, and during his twenty-two-year reign went to great lengths to encourage such intermarriages.[4] However, the Portuguese crown did not encourage intermarriages of the white colonists with blacks and mulattos, and the Catholic Church condemned miscegenation in general, but that meant that interracial marriages were simply not recognized by the church. Such prohibitions against race mixture were easily ignored, especially given such a highly uneven sex ratio among the colonizers.[5] The Portuguese colonizers in the early historical period were mostly males in search of wealth rather than settlement (as in the U.S. case) and Portuguese women were often forbidden to migrate, creating a very high gender imbalance among the white colonial population. This led Portuguese colonizers to seek out Indian and African mates, and the number of progeny of these mixed unions grew throughout most of the colonial period.

However, given the racial hierarchy imposed by the slave-based economy, relationships between the white colonizers and nonwhite Brazilian women were highly unequal. White men frequently raped and abused African, indigenous, and mixed-race women. Indeed, mixed-race Brazilians were largely spawned through sexual violence throughout the period of slavery, although cohabitation and marriage between whites and nonwhites was not uncommon.[6] Thus, a tradition of race mixture was established in Brazilian society through both violent sexual relations as well as informal and formal unions. Although the relative frequency of the different forms of miscegenation is not clear from the historical record, by the 1872 census—when the male-female balance had been largely restored but before slavery was completely completely abolished—5.1 percent of marriages in the federal district of Rio de Janeiro were between whites and mulattos, and another 0.8 percent involved whites and blacks.[7]

WHITE SUPREMACIST VIEWS OF MISCEGENATION

As slavery was being abolished throughout the Americas in the nineteenth century, science would validate racial domination by claiming that Caucasians were inherently superior to nonwhite people.[8] Prior to that, when race mostly described one's descent rather than a hierarchy of biological types, the subjugation of Indians and Africans proceeded on the basis of moral and religious reasoning rather than on scientific argument. Scientific interest in the issue of race in Brazil began in the late nineteenth century, and concern grew over how race would affect Brazil's future development. This was especially true in in the emerging science of eugenics, which set out to discover "the social uses to which knowledge of heredity could be put in order to achieve the goal of better breeding."[9] Eugenics, at that time, viewed blacks as inferior and mulattos as degenerate. Furthermore, eugenicists believed that tropical climates like Brazil's weakened human biological and mental integrity, and therefore the Brazilian population exemplified biological degeneracy.

A notable example of this thinking was by Count Arthur de Gobineau, who published *L'Essai sur l'Inégalité des Races Humaines* in 1856, and from 1869 to 1870, he was appointed to serve as the Representative of France in Brazil.[10] He would come to deplore Brazil, commenting that its miscegenation had affected all Brazilians (except the emperor whom he befriended) across all classes and even "in the best families," making them ugly, lazy, and infertile.[11] His obsession would lead him to openly identify ministers and other members of the Royal Court as mulattos. For him and other Europeans, as well as for North Americans of the time, Brazil typified the perils of miscegenation by producing a degenerate people that would doom the new country to perpetual underdevelopment. Such a view of the Brazilian population by highly respected Europeans would leave its mark for many years to come.

In the 1880s, Raimundo Nina Rodrigues, a professor at the prestigious medical school in Bahia was perhaps the first Brazilian scientist to examine the subject of race. As a follower of European eugenics and particularly Italian criminologist Cesare Lombroso, famous for measuring cranial capacity to determine intelligence, Rodrigues similarly feared that miscegenation would lead to degeneracy. He predicted that Brazil's future, especially in the north, would become ethnically black or mestizo.[12] In his well-known ethnographic study of the African-origin population in Brazil, Rodrigues declared unequivocally that Africans were inferior. Rodrigues died at a young age in 1906, when he was in the midst of developing his ideas. He had advocated for separate criminal laws by race, which was about as close as any influential Brazilian had ever come to proposing legal racial segregation.[13] Whereas a principle of *livre arbitrium* was part of the Imperial Penal Codes, Rodrigues proposed to eliminate the principle for blacks because he believed that they were not free to choose crime because of their diminished capacities.[14] However, reflecting his uncertainty about mulattos, he encountered difficulty in placing them into his conceptual scheme. He decided to divide the mulatto population into superior, ordinary, and degenerate or socially unstable types.

Rodrigues's uncertain classification of the mulatto may have reflected his own mixed-race identity,[15] as well as the general sentiments of the Brazilian elite, since many of them could be classified as mulatto. Miscegenation had presented a dilemma, and consequently Brazilian eugenicists and other intellectuals had begun to waver in their conclusions about mulattos. Mulattos were clearly perceived as distinct from pure-blood blacks and Indians, and there was often an optimistic sense that they were more like whites. Rodrigues's ambivalence about the status of the mulatto and the need to distinguish them from whites may have kept him and other members of the elite from taking the extreme segregationist route chosen by the United States and South Africa in the late nineteenth and early twentieth centuries. Moreover, it would have been difficult to determine who was white in Brazil, so the imposition of segregation was impractical, as it would have potentially excluded many influential members of the Brazilian elite, as Gobineau had disparagingly described them. Although most members of the Brazilian elite are likely to have been classified as white in their own country, their status as whites in the eyes of Europeans and North Americans was not so certain. This fact is likely to have influenced their own visions of race mixture and their development of a national project.

In addition, persons that were classified as mulattos in nineteenth-century Brazil had also occupied important positions in the Council of the State, the Chamber of Deputies, the Senate, or stood out in letters and arts. Some of the more prominent figures were José de Patrocinio, Luiz Gama, Afonso H. de Lima Barreto, André Rebouças and Tobias Barreto. Even Brazil's greatest writer, Machado de Assis, was a mulatto. Certainly these mulatto members of the elite had very privileged lives at the time and were often treated as whites were, but their racial origins were not completely forgotten. Although the flexibility of the Brazilian system had allowed them to sometimes escape the stigma of race, they sometimes suffered for having African origins. For example, the personal histories of André and Antonio Rebouças reveal that, while they were members of the upper echelons of Brazilian society, their African origins would be used to discredit them in debates about the emancipation of slavery.[16] In addition, Aluisio Azevedo's (1973) classic *O Mulatto*, although fictional, relates the experiences of a mulatto doctor in the late nineteenth century.

He is apparently able to socialize freely in elite society, generally being treated as and perceiving himself as white, until he encounters the racially sensitive domain of marriage.[17]

Literary critic Silvio Romero, an important Brazilian intellectual of the time, equivocated in his response to the determinist dilemma posed by Gobineau and other Europeans, and to a large extent by Rodrigues. Although Romero agreed that blacks and especially Indians were inferior to the Portuguese, who themselves were inferior to the "Germano-Saxons," he also considered the possibility that miscegenation produced vigorous growth, and thus that Brazilians might be racially benefited in their future development. Romero's uncertainty about the consequences of Brazil's miscegenation would certainly add to the Brazilian elite's climate of racial insecurity, although by 1888 he began to be more confident in his optimism about miscegenation and Brazil's future.[18]

WHITENING AS THE SOLUTION

Eugenics promoted social policies which would apply the new scientific understandings of heredity to improve the human population. Brazilans developed their own brand of eugenics and subsequently influenced ideology and social policy.[19] North American, British, and German eugenicists closely followed Mendelian eugenics, which strictly adhered to genetic inheritance and its racial implications. However, most Brazilian and other Latin American eugenicists followed the neo-Lamarckian strand, which was the dominant view among the French, with whom they maintained strong intellectual ties. Neo-Lamarckianism argued that genetic deficiencies could be overcome in a single generation. Although neo-Lamarckianism would be short-lived, its predominance among Brazilian eugenicists at the turn of the century had enormous implications for Brazilian interpretations of race in the ensuing decades.

These scholars accepted the racist predictions of black and mulatto inferiority but thought this inferiority could be overcome by miscegenation.[20] Based on their interpretation of eugenics, and their own sensitivities to theories about racial and tropical degeneracy, Brazilian scholars used a theory of constructive miscegenation and proposed a solution of "whitening" through the mixing of whites and nonwhites.[21] Based on the higher white fertility rates and their belief that white genes were dominant, these eugenicists concluded that race mixture would eliminate the black population, eventually resulting in a white or mostly white Brazilian population. Brazilian eugenicists also successfully countered scientific claims that tropical climates were unhealthy for whites, which originally had limited their ability to import European laborers.

Whitening, as prescribed by the eugenicists, became the major basis of Brazil's immigration policy. To accelerate the whitening goal, Brazilian elites and policy makers looked for workers in Europe, where a demographic transition was producing surplus labor. In Brazil, as in other Latin American countries, the elite sought out and subsidized European immigrants to "improve the quality" of its work force and replace the former slaves.[22] In particular, the state of São Paulo, in collusion with coffee planters, encouraged, recruited, and subsidized European immigration, while the federal government restricted available Asian immigration until 1910. This new supply of labor supplanted the former African slave population in places like São Paulo and at the same time acted as a "civilizing agent" by whitening the Brazilian gene pool. These white settlers were expected to mix eventually with the native population, thereby diluting Brazil's large black population.[23]

Population History of 1872–1940:
Whitening the Black out of Brazil's Population

The large number of Europeans immigrating to Brazil, coupled with ongoing miscegenation, made several Brazilian eugenicists confident that their country was successfully whitening. For example, in 1912, João Batista Lacerda believed that miscegenation would eventually produce whites and predicted that by 2012, the Brazilian population would be 80 percent white, 3 percent mixed (mestiço), 17 percent Indian, and there would be no more blacks.[24] The extent to which the whitening process actually occurred can be gauged through a review of Brazil's racial composition across its censuses.

Figure 2.1 shows Brazil's changing racial composition from its first census in 1872 until its most recent in 2000. In 1872, the only year that a national census was taken during the period of slavery, Brazil's population consisted of roughly 10 million persons. The census enumerated 37 percent of the population as white, 44 percent as brown, and 19 percent as black. The brown category in 1872 consisted of *pardos* (42 percent) and *caboclos* (1.8 percent), the latter referring to persons of predominately Indian origin.[25] Since the slave trade ended in 1850 (and few blacks have migrated to Brazil since then), the percentage of the black population diminished in subsequent censuses. By 1890, in Brazil's first census after abolition, data began to capture the influence of massive European immigration. The white population increased as a share of the total Brazilian population from 37 to 44 percent between 1872 and 1890. The brown population decreased from 44 percent to 41 percent, and the black population fell from 19 to 15 percent.[26]

Percent

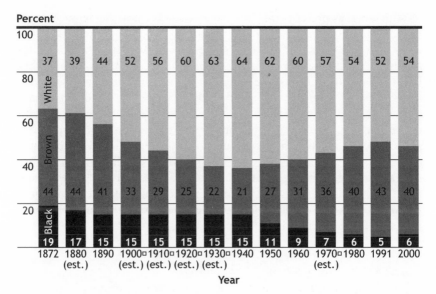

FIGURE 2.1 Racial composition: Brazil, 1872–2000. (1872, 1890, 1940, 1950, 1960, 1980, 1991, and 2000 censuses of Brazil. Based on estimates (est.) for remaining years.)

Figure 2.2, based on immigrant entry data, shows that European immigration began to increase significantly in the 1880s, reaching its peak in the 1890s. In the 1890s, more than 1.2 million European immigrants were added to a population of about 5 million whites. In the following three decades, more than 2 million more immigrants had come mostly from Europe. In the 1930s, as the Brazilian economy reeled as a result of faltering coffee prices and a world economic crisis, and clearly by the 1940s, with the war raging in Europe, mass immigration came to an end. Immigration recovered somewhat in the 1950s; but the relative impact of immigration on national racial composition greatly declined by then since the native population had already grown tremendously.

Figure 2.2 shows the trends in total immigration and immigration from the four largest sending countries from 1872 to 1969. In 1880, persons from Portugal, Italy, Spain, and Germany represented nearly all immigrants to Brazil, but by 1930, they constituted only half of all immigrants. Lesser (1999) notes that Brazil's eugenics-influenced immigration policy favored the entry of immigrants from these countries as agricultural laborers, but a fear of nonassimilation and social and labor activism among those groups led policy makers eventually to seek immigrants of other nationalities. The newer immigrant groups came largely

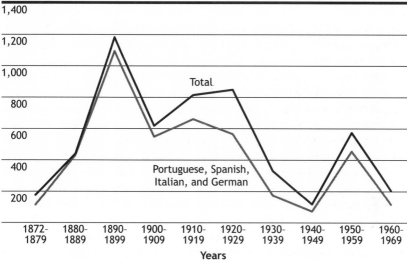

FIGURE 2.2 Immigrants into Brazil by decade and national origin: 1872–1969. (Merrick and Graham 1979.)

from eastern Europe, including many Jews, and from the Middle East. Immigrants from these other countries often negotiated to be in the "desirable" white category, leading to a significant shift in notions of Brazilianness and whiteness between 1850 and 1950. While Brazil's immigration policy had previously barred Asians from coming to Brazil, immigration from Japan began in 1910, and by the 1930–39 period, constituted 30 percent of all immigration to Brazil.[27]

Although Brazilian eugenicists expected that whitening would occur through both "natural selection" and European immigration, the actual extent to which the Brazilian population whitened could not be assessed after 1890 until 50 years later in 1940. There were no censuses in the intervening years with data on race, and no censuses were taken in 1910 and 1930. The question about color was omitted in the 1900 and 1920 censuses, although a 1920 census publication includes an article by Oliveira Vianna (1922) announcing the rapid reduction of the "inferior blood coefficient" in the Brazilian gene pool. The omission of race in those years was probably due to the elite's intent to downplay Brazil's racial composition, as well as the overall low level of resources given to census taking in the period.

SHIFTING VIEWS OF RACE: 1910S TO 1920S

With the ending of European immigration in the 1920s, concerns about miscegenation and Brazil's racial future resurfaced. By then, neo-Lamarckianism had become increasingly discredited in the eugenics community. A new generation of Brazilian eugenicists, often trained in the now more scientifically credible Mendelian line of genetics, had challenged the view of the neo-Lamarckians. However, unlike many of their foreign counterparts, most of Brazil's eugenics community after World War I had become critical of the simplicities of Mendelian implications on race and came to discredit the concept of race altogether.

However, faced with the proposal to restrict Japanese immigration and the planned immigration of Afro–North Americans to Brazil, the so-called eugenic problem of immigration would find its way back into policy and scientific discussions at the First Brazilian Eugenics Conference in 1929. There, a heated debate ensued about whether mixture with blacks would lead to degeneracy, in response to the restrictionist presentation of Congressman A. J. Azevedo Amaral at the scientific conference. The president of the conference, Edgar Roquette-Pinto, who was influenced by and had previously discussed his own ideas with Franz Boas, convincingly argued that miscegenation was normal and healthy rather than degenerative, and that race had nothing to do with eugenics. For him, Brazil's problem was "mostly that it lacked a realistic sense of self-confidence" as it seemed to fear treading out on an uncharted course, radically different from the growing racist state policies being implemented in the United States and Germany. Another eugenicist at the conference, Fernando Magalhães, reminded the attendees that "we are all mestizos and would therefore exclude ourselves," just as Silvio Romero had expressed forty years before. The turn to certain racist solutions found in the United States and Germany received little support in Brazil. According to Stepan (1991),

> The variant of eugenics identified with public hygiene and compatible with racial mixing and the myth of racial democracy gained support; extreme reproductive eugenics, or Nazi-style race hygiene, did not.

Influenced by increasingly aggressive eugenics-based policies in Germany,[28] Renato Kehl (1933) advocated for the sterilization of degenerates and criminals, compulsory prenuptial exams, and legal birth control. He had moved far away from the idea of constructive miscegenation. However, by then, Kehl had become fairly isolated as most of his colleagues had reached quite distinct conclusions. Much of the Brazilian elite and many eugenicists had for some time begun to extol the virtues of

Brazilian miscegenation, including the possibilities of racial harmony and unity.[29] In that same year, a highly influential book by Gilberto Freyre would close the door on Kehl's type of thinking.

GILBERTO FREYRE AND RACIAL DEMOCRACY: 1930S TO 1980S

Race mixture became a central feature of Brazilian national identity largely due to a single publication. Selected by leading academics as the most influential nonfiction book of twentieth-century Brazil,[30] Gilberto Freyre's *Casa Grande e Senzala* transformed the concept of miscegenation from its former pejorative connotation into a positive national characteristic and the most important symbol of Brazilian culture. Under the influence of his mentor, anti-racist anthropologist Franz Boas—who proposed that racial differences were fundamentally cultural and social rather than biological—Freyre effectively proposed a new national ideology.

Although he did not coin the term and elements of the concept were promoted well before him, Freyre fully developed, expressed, and popularized the idea of racial democracy, to where it dominated Brazilian race thinking from the 1930s to the early 1990s.[31] Freyre argued that Brazil was unique among western societies for its smooth blending of European, Indian, and African peoples and cultures. As a result, he claimed that Brazilian society was free of the racism that affected the rest of the world. Although the notion that Brazil had a more benign system of slavery and race relations than the United States was longstanding,[32] Freyre turned this contrast into a central aspect of Brazil's emerging national identity, granting it scientific, literary, and cultural status that would prevail at least until well into the 1980s.

Freyre characterized the extended patriarchic family of the large rural slave plantations (*latifundios*) in the sixteenth and seventeenth centuries as a cauldron for interracial mixing that harmonized differences and diluted conflicts, thus enabling extraordinary assimilation, creating a new "Brazilian people." In later publications, he would extend this argument into the modern period.[33] Although he had been obsessed with the idea that miscegenation had become Brazil's Achilles' heel,[34] Freyre came to believe that race mixture produced "a unity of opposites" among racial stocks, including white masters and black slaves. In the 1940s, he referred to Brazil as an "ethnic democracy," where he may have used the term "ethnic" to replace the scientifically false notion of race. By "democracy," he was referring to the Spanish connotation of the term, which referred to brotherhood or fluid social relations rather than to a type of political institution.[35]

According to Freyre, miscegenation was possible early on because of gender imbalance among the Portuguese colonizers and also because of a Portuguese predisposition to cultural and biological mixing. Freyre believed that the Portuguese possessed a high degree of plasticity that enabled them to conform to and blend with other societies and cultures, especially in comparison with the cultural rigidness, seclusion, and self-reliance found among other Europeans. Ruled by the Moors for more than five hundred years, the Portuguese had developed a culture that was accustomed to and welcomed darker-skinned peoples, Freyre alleged. Indeed, miscegenation with the Moors had long been practiced in Portugal. Like his Portuguese contemporaries, Freyre considered Portugal itself to be non-European and a bridge between Christian Europe and Islamic North Africa. Freyre's doctrine of "Lusotropicalism" justified Portuguese colonialization, arguing that they were the only European colonizers to create a new civilization in the tropics, an accomplishment attributable above all to their racial tolerance.[36]

Ironically, Freyre's antiracist vision of miscegenation was contingent on the process of whitening, as developed by the earlier generation. Freyre acknowledged that miscegenation could only occur in modern times because of the population's belief in the white supremacist ideology of whitening. According to this popular notion, ordinary black Brazilians believed their greatest chance for escaping poverty was to marry whites and light mulattos.[37] His whitening bias is revealed in his phrase "Negroes are rapidly disappearing in Brazil, merging into the white stock." However, Freyre would generally downplay whitening and rather focus on miscegenation's effects on diffusing racial differences and the contribution of African cultural influences on the white elite. This association of miscegenation and racial democracy with whitening would later lead black activist Abdias do Nascimento (1978) to accuse Freyre's ideas of promoting a campaign of genocide against Brazil's black population, through which the Brazilian elite sought to eliminate black people and black culture.

Freyre's optimistic analysis of Brazilian race relations was largely based on the contrast he repeatedly made with the racial situation in the United States. Freyre had grown up as the scion of a *latifundio* family in Brazil's Northeast and was educated in local North American missionary schools. He then became an undergraduate at Baylor University in segregated Waco, Texas, from 1917 to 1921, and attended graduate school at Columbia University. He later became a visiting professor at both Indiana and Stanford Universities and traveled extensively throughout the racially segregated South. Thus, it is not difficult to imagine how the contrast between the two systems of race relations in Brazil and the United States at that time may have led Freyre to conclude that there was little or no racism in Brazil.

The extraordinary influence of Freyre's work was due to many factors, including his use of anthropological logic and evidence and explicit treatment of sexuality, which were innovations in Brazil. Most importantly, his literary elegance, essayistic style, and vivid portrayal of Northeast tradition and life would capture the imaginations of readers for generations, although at the expense of scientific precision and the systematic use of evidence.[38] Moreover, Freyre's work had served to promote national unity in a country that was becoming increasingly divided between the traditional rural oligarchy and the new industrial elites exemplified by the expanding urban economies, particularly in São Paulo. According to Bastos (2001), Freyre had elegantly recovered, invented, and elevated Northeast regional traditions and values as truly Brazilian traditions in a society that had mostly copied and valued European and North American culture. Freyre's radical new ideas of racial and cultural fusion were consistent with a growing modernist movement in the Southeast region, which would greatly transform Brazilian culture and further promote national unity and "Brazilianness."[39]

ACADEMIC AND LITERARY SUPPORT FOR RACIAL DEMOCRACY

Freyre's theories received great attention and academic support in the 1940s. In 1942, sociologist Donald Pierson reported that race did not seem to affect social relations, based on his study of Salvador, Bahia. Like Freyre, Pierson believed that "bonds of sentiment" arose from a tradition of miscegenation, which attenuated racial prejudices and put mixed-blood offspring in a socially advantageous position through intermarriage. He concluded that racial groups did not exist and thus reasoned that racism could not either, and that it was class, not race, that created social barriers between whites and nonwhites.[40] For Pierson, existing color hierarchies simply reflected an incompleteness of the assimilation process—which had only begun with abolition a half century before—and the persistence of surviving African cultural practices among the darkest segment of the population.

Pierson's conclusions about Brazil stood in sharp contrast to the findings about U.S. cities by the early Chicago school, where Pierson had been a student of Robert Park. Through his study of Bahia, Pierson has sought to demonstrate that there was nothing natural about North American racism. He concluded that Brazil was a "multiracial class society," which was in the process of breaking down racial differences and assimilating the descendants of African slaves, and therefore was much more advanced than the United States. Sociology and anthropology were underdeveloped in Brazil at the time, and foreign scholars such as Pierson would become important in the development of those fields. His work would therefore have a great impact in the Brazilian academy, as well as in U.S. social science.

Freyre would also have a major influence in the development of the field of comparative slavery, which began with Tannebaum's *Slave and Citizen* in 1946. Building on Freyre's treatise, Tannebaum argued that the Catholic Church was able to influence Latin American slavery by extending greater humanity and legal citizenship to slaves in Latin America than they received in the United States, where slaveowners had greater autonomy over their slaves. He used Freyre's evidence of extensive manumission in Brazil to support a theory of a greater benevolence of slavery in Latin America. However, subsequent literature would point to counterevidence such as the greater mortality of slaves in Latin America, revealing a greater physical harshness and cruelty in colonial Brazil, where slaveowners could more easily purchase slaves, therefore diminishing their concerns about overworking them to death.[41] Later studies would also show that manumission sometimes made little difference for freed blacks and mulattos, who lived side-by-side and worked with slaves in similar and sometimes inferior socioeconomic conditions.[42]

In literature, perhaps no other writer projected Freyre's image of Brazil in popular culture as widely as Jorge Amado, whose novels have been translated into at least a dozen languages. His portrayal of Brazilianness exalted race mixture, racial harmony, and cultural syncretism. In Freyrean style, Amado encouraged miscegenation, believing that racial problems could only be solved by "the mixture of blood." But unlike Freyre, who spoke on behalf of the landed elite and its capacity for ensuring harmonious race relations, Amado wrote about the street-level experiences of his mostly mulatto characters. One of Amado's books, *Tenda dos Milagres* (Tent of Miracles), was made into one of Brazil's most popular films in 1977, further disseminating the idea of Brazil's miscegenation and racial democracy.[43]

RACIAL DEMOCRACY IN THE SERVICE OF THE NATION

As Brazil sought to recover from the world financial crisis, Getulio Vargas became president in 1930. Vargas received support from Brazilians of all colors as he sought to modernize the predominately agrarian Brazilian society. In 1937, he announced a new constitution that effectively gave him full dictatorial powers. During his tenure, Vargas instituted a series of modernizing reforms that led to greater centralization of the Brazilian government, regional integration, industrial growth, and improvement of the rights and conditions of many urban workers. Vargas remained in power until he resigned in 1945, when democracy returned to Brazil. Vargas was later elected again as president and took office in 1951, where he remained until his suicide in 1954. Vargas was followed by a series of democratically elected presidents until the military coup of 1964.

The Frente Negra Brasileira (FNB) was the most important black organization in the first half of the twentieth century. With its nationalistic and anti-immigrant tendencies, the FNB became a political party in 1930 and sought the integration of blacks into Brazilian society through social mobility. FNB members had supported Vargas's rise to power as they believed that he had destroyed the party of the rural oligarchy, which they regarded as the "bulwark of the aristocratic class of former slaveholders."[44] Although Vargas shut down the FNB in 1937, as he did with all political parties, he had acknowledged their support as he immediately began a series of reforms to protect native workers from immigrant competition, ensuring that large numbers of blacks and mulattos would enter its growing industrial labor force for the first time and be preferred for government employment.[45]

Since Vargas, Brazilians have become proud of their *Carnaval* and *futebol,* not only because of their high quality, but also because they represent Brazil's self-image of multiracial harmony and festiveness to the rest of the world. Members of Brazilian soccer teams often represent the entire color spectrum, as do Carnaval dancers, and racial differences seem to be irrelevant in both cases. Vargas appropriated this symbolism, thus integrating blacks and mulattos into Brazilian national culture, helping to diffuse black protest. By actively promoting national chauvinism among Brazilians of all classes and making Carnaval and soccer prominent symbols of national identity, Vargas enhanced his own prestige. Moreover, Gilberto Freyre's popular *Casa Grande e Senzala* was an added benefit, providing Vargas with a narrative of race and nation that was inclusive of the Brazilian masses and could substitute for the white-supremacist ideology of whitening.[46] Thus, Vargas would effectively add the consolidation of the racial-democracy ideology to his list of national unification and modernizing feats.

A notable exception to Brazil's growing self-promotion of its racial unity during that period was the passage of the Afonso Arinos law of 1951, which made racism illegal and punishable. However, the exception in this case clearly confirmed the rule as the Afonso Arinos law was drafted presumably in response to foreign influences that had triggered two discriminatory incidents. One involved a widely publicized complaint by Afro–North American dancer Katherine Dunham, who was not allowed to check into a prestigious São Paulo hotel. Gilberto Freyre, then a senator, attributed the Dunham case to the fact that it happened in São

Paulo, where U.S. industrialism and commercialism had taken over "with a vengence."[47] The sponsor of the bill, Afonso Arinos added his own complaint of discrimination suffered by his black chauffeur at the hands of Spanish immigrants, "ignorant of our traditions and insensitive to our old customs of racial fraternity."[48]

Through its constitution and by signing international laws, the Brazilian state endorsed other antiracist laws, but these were mostly thought of as unnecessary and pro forma responses to international conventions and expectations. The Brazilian Constitutions of 1934 and 1946 had stressed equality before the law regardless of race, although the 1934 document also restricted the immigration of persons of African descent.[49] In 1965, Brazil ratified the International Labor Organization's Discrimination Convention of 1958 (Convention 111), which interestingly required the promotion of victims of racial discrimination in the labor market. In 1968, it signed the UN's International Convention on the Elimination of All Forms of Racial Discrimination (ICERD), which prohibited all forms of racial discrimination and required the submission of biannual reports to the elected eighteen-member Committee on the Elimination of All Forms of Racial Discrimination (CERD), which monitors whether individual states are complying with the convention.[50] By accepting these conventions, such laws would be incorporated into domestic law. However, Brazil's racial democracy ideology had become so well accepted that the Brazilian government had generally convinced itself, its population, and the international community that its people were antiracist by culture and therefore did not need such laws.

THE 1940 CENSUS: RESUMPTION OF RACE COUNTING

As a part of Vargas's modernization efforts, Brazil established its first modern census in 1940. After an absence of fifty years, race was reintroduced in that census at the very same time that the racial-democracy ideal began to take hold. The new official belief that race was not problematic is demonstrated in the following quote from a Brazilian government publication in 1950:

> The preparation of the 1940 Census developed in a period in which racist aberrations appeared on the way to global predominance. Nevertheless, the national Census Commission not only wanted to remain faithful to the most honorable tradition of modern Brazilian civilization, the equality of the races, but it also sought to eliminate any suspicion that the question on color, introduced in the census purely with scientific objectives, was to serve as a preparatory instrument for social discrimination."[51]

If racial distinctions were no longer believed to be important, then why ask the race question? Despite the emerging belief in racial democracy, belief in whitening also persisted among some sectors of the Brazilian elite. Concerns about Brazil's racial composition surely remained and the 1940 census would be an opportunity to measure the effects of massive European immigration during the previous six decades. A government document published in 1961 claimed that as a result of the 1940 census

> Many educated Brazilians . . . were anxious to see the exact percentage of the progressive predominance of the white group in the national population, which, with triplicate impropriety, was customarily called aryanization, and according to the then widely diffuse ideas, seemed supremely desirable.[52]

The nomination of Giorgio Mortara as the director of Brazil's first modern census in 1940 was also important in making it a key analytic variable for differentiating the Brazilian population in the published 1940 and 1950 censuses. Mortara had been a prominent statistician and demographer in his native Italy, but as a Jew, the Facist regime forced him to renounce his prominent academic posts and he seized the offer to become director of the Brazilian census. Keenly aware of the implications of race thinking in fascist Europe, and despite the official line of the Brazilian government, Mortara would make race an important variable in the analysis of the new Brazilian census.

The results of the 1940 census revealed that mass European immigration had brought Brazil closer to its whitening goal. As figure 2.1 shows, 64 percent of Brazilians were white in 1940, a 20-percentage-point increase from 1890.[53] During the same period, the relative size of the black population hardly changed, while the proportion of the mixed-race population declined by more than half from 41 percent to 20 percent. In absolute terms, the Brazilian population more than quadrupled in size from 10 million in 1872 to 41 million in 1940. The white population grew by more than six times, the black population quadrupled, and the mixed-race population merely doubled. The decline in the percentage of the mulatto population was likely the result of little intermarriage because of the especially great marginalization of blacks and browns in this period (Andrews 1992) and relatively high levels of endogomy among the immigrant ethnics, whose social interactions must have been limited by their language, customs, and cultural institutions. Also, the changing categories for the mixed-race population from mestiço and caboclo to pardos may have led to the underestimation of the change in the brown and overestimation of the black population. A shift from ancestry to appearance may have also led persons who would have been classified as mestiços but were dark in appearance to be reclassified as black in the 1940 census. Although the growth of the white population and the decrease in the proportion of the brown population would have led to some optimism for whitening supporters like Lacerda and Roquette-Pinto, the fact that the proportion of the black population did not change during this period would have surely discouraged them.

THE MILITARY AND RACIAL DEMOCRACY

By 1962, Gilberto Freyre had become a self-proclaimed defender of Brazilian patriotism and the growing military presence in the Brazilian government. In that year, Freyre first used the term "racial democracy," which he would ardently defend.[54] The concept of racial democracy reached its peak as a dogma under the military governments from 1964 to 1985, which also encompassed the period of Brazil's greatest economic growth. The military governments turned Freyre's doctrine into an obsession and an uncontested principle of the Brazilian nation. In a 1977 speech to the National Congress, the year in which President Ernesto Geisel shut down that institution, its president proclaimed:

> We have all inherited common attributes and what we are building—socially, economically and culturally—proves the correctness of our rejection of the myths of racial superiority.[55]

The idea of racial democracy became incorporated into the emerging Brazilian religion of *umbanda,* with its African roots. Umbanda gained legitimacy during this period as white middle-class persons, including military officers, became leaders in *umbanda* federations.[56] Motivated mostly by economic causes, the Brazilian government also expanded its relations with Africa and established centers in Rio de Janeiro and Bahia to study Africa and its relations with Brazil.[57] Finally, Brazil's so-called economic miracle from 1968 to 1974 also helped diffuse resistance of any kind to the military. With the government's active intervention in the Brazilian economy, economic growth averaged 11 percent per annum. All social classes benefited from that growth, although income inequality grew as the middle class made the greatest gains.

At the height of military repression, the Brazilian national soccer team won the 1970 World Cup, dominating all of its opponents. Led by Pelé, a black player, who would be elevated by sports fans to godlike status, Brazil's team became known as the greatest team of all times. Under the command of General Medici, the Brazilian government showcased its heroes, thereby reforming its international image and sparking a new wave of nationalism. At the same time, the United States was ending a decade marked by civil-rights protests, the assassination of the major antiracist leaders, and urban rioting. Local and international observers could not help but notice the contrast with Brazil and its nationally celebrated and multiracial soccer heroes. All the while, though, hundreds of political protestors were being tortured and assassinated in Brazil, away from public view.[58]

Ignoring Brazilian realities, the military government confidently proclaimed that racial discrimination did not exist in Brazil in its 1970 report to the CERD. Brazil's foreign minister declared:

> I have the honor to inform you that since racial discrimination does not exist in Brazil, there is no need to take sporadic measures of a legislative, judicial or administrative nature to assure the equality of races in Brazil.

In the following six pages of the report, the minister of justice and the interior confirmed the foreign minister's proclamation by citing the extensive Brazilian legislation guaranteeing equality. In the first three paragraphs of the 1972 addendum to the report, the Brazilian government reported:

> 1. The climate of peaceful and friendly interrelations that is one of the outstanding features of Brazilian culture has not only been manifested but has been improved.
>
> 2. It is impossible to provide statistical data since the last [1970] census did not ask for indications of race.
>
> 3. It should be mentioned that miscegenation is rapidly increasing.

Even in the dark days of authoritarian rule from 1967 to 1974, the ideology of racial democracy was well entrenched and widely understood. The mere mention of race or racism was met with social sanctions, which would often result in one being labeled a racist for bringing up the issue. If such sanctions were not enough, any protest like those occurring in the United States at the time would surely have been met by the repressive power of the military government and the willingness to use it. I have been told by a reliable but confidential source, that Brazil's military government perceived black protest as a major threat to national security.

However, the mounting academic evidence of racism by leading Brazilian academics had not escaped the attention of the military governments, even at the height of repression. Brazil's authoritarian rulers were quite aware of racism and racial inequality in Brazil but were troubled by the prospect of racial conflict similar to that occurring in the United States. For at least the more astute military leadership, their actions in support of racial democracy were probably not cynical so much as a rather well-engineered strategy for staving off racial polarization. This was made clear in a book published by the Brazilian army in 1969 called *Brazil 2000: A Future without Fantasy.* In the second paragraph of the introduction, it states:

No, we have not become violent racial segregationists, but we cannot consciously pride ourselves on our "racial democracy." How will we react when blacks overcome social and economic disadvantages that segregate them, and the university educated among them are no longer only 448 out of 5,600,000 individuals? Today, blacks do not cause trouble, but what will happen when they have enough economic power to buy titles to private clubs or into the more expensive private schools or force their admission into important offices or positions, or live in first-class neighborhoods? Will we be mature enough to accept them as brothers in everything or are we headed for racial conflict?

Interestingly, the book widely cites the findings of the very scholars that the military would later exile. Skidmore (1985) believes that the forced exile of Abdias do Nascimento, Florestan Fernandes, Fernando Henrique Cardoso, and Octavio Ianni was largely due to their questioning of the nationalist consensus on race. The military had made research on race perilous to the personal safety of these scholars.

ACADEMIC CHALLENGES TO RACIAL DEMOCRACY

By the 1950s, Brazil had gained an international reputation for its racial democracy. As a result, UNESCO commissioned a series of studies to understand the secret of Brazil's racial harmony in a world marked by the horrors of racism and genocide. Florestan Fernandes of the University of São Paulo was commissioned as the primary Brazilian investigator in the UNESCO project. However, his conclusions stunned his sponsors by mounting the first major assault on the racial-democracy image of Brazil, leading to the first clear break with Freyre and to Fernandes's vehemently disagreeing with the findings of his Freyre-inspired North American counterparts on the UNESCO project, most notably Charles Wagley and Marvin Harris. Instead, Fernandes concluded that racism was widespread in Brazilian society. Fernandes directly attacked racial democracy, calling it a myth, and concluded that Brazilian whites were hostile to and prejudiced against blacks. Whites continued to benefit from the racial domination of blacks, long afer the end of slavery. However, he also blamed slavery and its social and psychological effects on blacks themselves for their inability to compete with whites in the newly industrializing labor market. Moreover, he believed that although racial prejudice and discrimination were functional to a slave society, they were incompatible with the competitive order established by a capitalist class society. For Fernandes, racism would therefore disappear with capitalist development, although whites would seek to maintain their privileged positions for as long as possible.

Much of the disagreement between Freyre and his predominately North American supporters, and Fernandes and the mostly Brazilian UNESCO scholars, about the extent of racism in Brazil may be attributed to differing emphases. The Freyreans tended to follow Gilberto Freyre's emphasis on sociability or horizontal relations rather than economic or vertical relations, presumably because they believed that indicators of the integration of minority groups in society like miscegenation and intermarriage best represented current and future race relations. In their optimistic intepretation that Brazil's racial system was more benign than that of the United States, they dismissed racial inequality as merely the result of the recent abolition of blacks from slavery rather than from current racial discrimination.

Guimarães (1999) argues that the research agendas of Pierson, Wagley, and Harris were shaped by the comparative concerns of assimilation and integration. In the spirit of Chicago School theory, they assumed that the distinct racial groups would eventually assimilate and structural differences would disappear, as dominant and previously subordinate groups would become similar. Researchers of this school found social relations among the races to be harmonious and integrative compared to the United States, thus predicting an optimistic future for the descendants of Brazilian slaves. The conflict and exploitation found in the labor market and in the naturalized racial hierarchy in which blacks were subordinate, on the other hand, were either unproblematic or transitory for them.

By contrast, Fernandes and his Brazilian UNESCO colleagues focused mostly on the vertical relations of racial inequality and the racial discrimination that produced it. Guimarães claims that, like other *Paulistas* (residents of São Paulo state), Fernandes generally ignored race mixture, which was valued in the more traditional Northeast. Rather, southerners like Fernandes held the notion that true Brazilians were mostly white and valued being part of a European rather than a mestizo nation. As the primary destination of mass European immigration, São Paulo had become an ethnic mosaic, and blacks were only one of several minorities, although they were the most stigmatized. Moreover, a disdain for race mixture may have come from Fernandes's close association with Abdias do Nascimento, who associated the elite's support for miscegenation with a whitening campaign to eliminate blacks from the Brazilian population. Instead, social equality and development concerns motivated Fernandes and his followers to investigate race relations.

Although Fernandes had become a central figure in the Brazilian social sciences, he eventually abandoned research on race upon his return from exile, as did his student, Fernando Henrique Cardoso. Fernandes and Cardoso returned from exile and wrote about other sociological issues, including dependency theory, and both became politicians in the 1980s. Cardoso eventually became president of Brazil. Otavio Ianni, unlike his mentor Fernandes and his earlier co-author Cardoso, continued to write about racism, among other subjects. Despite such academic challenges beginning in the 1950s and modern black protest beginning in the mid-1970s, most sectors of Brazilian society would continue to believe in racial democracy throughout the 1970s and into the 1980s.

THE BROWNING OF THE BRAZILIAN POPULATION: 1940–1991

From 1940 to 1991, census findings began to show that miscegenation became the primary force driving changes in Brazil's racial composition. The whitening goal was greatly advanced from 1940 to 1991, in the sense that the black population fell from 15 to 5 percent. However, the white population also continued to decline from its recorded peak of 64 percent in 1940 to 52 percent by 1991, with an increase to 54 percent in 2000. The brown population was the only population to grow, more than doubling its proportion from 21 to 43 percent during the same period. Thus, the second half of the twentieth century was characterized by browning, rather than whitening, *strictu sensu*.

As a result of rapidly declining mortality levels in the early part of the period without correspondingly sharp declines in fertility until the latter part of this period, Brazil's total population nearly quadrupled from 41 million in 1940 to about 153 million in 1991. Whereas previous population growth was mostly through immigration, these decades witnessed unprecedented natural growth, encompassing the "Brazilian demographic transition." From 1940 to 1960, women had, on average, more than 6 children each, and life expectancy increased from 44 to 59 years.[59] Fertility declines began to occur sharply in the 1960s for white women, well before similar declines for browns and blacks.[60] Although racial differences in fertility decline were partly offset by earlier mortality declines among whites as well, the differences could account for greater natural growth among the nonwhite population since about 1960.

Changing racial classification rather than actual race mixture may also account for the growth of the brown population. Miscegenation affects racial composition from one generation to the next, while racial classification may change for individuals over the course of their lives. Demographer Charles Wood (1991) finds that 38 percent of 10- to 19-year-olds classified as black in the 1950 census, reclassified as brown in the 1980 census, when they became 40 to 49 years of age. Thus, at least part of the reduction in the size of the black population in the second half of the twentieth century is probably due to a growing tendency of blacks to reclassify as brown. If we assume that these estimates are roughly similar for all age groups, then such reclassification would account for most of the decline in the black population and about one-third of the growth in the brown population from 1950 to 1980.[61] In any case, the period from 1940 to 1991 has been marked by the growth of the brown population, which can primarily be attributed to miscegenation.

Results from the 2000 census reveal a reversal from the previous five censuses. Proportionally, the brown population began to decrease, while the white and black populations increased. Specifically, the black population increased from 5.0 percent in 1991 to 6.1 percent in 2000, and the white population went from 52.1 percent in 1991 to 53.4 percent in 2000. By contrast, the brown population decreased from 42.1 to 38.9 percent. Asians and Indians combined went from 0.7 to 0.8 percent. These changes could reflect the changing quality of data collection or demographic factors such as a greater decline in mortality within urban areas, where whites and blacks are more likely than browns to reside, but it more likely suggests changing racial classification with growing preferences for the polar categories of black and white, as I will suggest in chapter 4.

Conclusion

Whitening and racial democracy, the twin pillars of Brazil's racial ideology, have been rooted in a profound belief that miscegenation is a historical fact that makes Brazil unique. Whitening took a negative view of Brazil's miscegenation, and racial democracy promoted miscegenation as Brazil's solution to racism. Brazil's ideology of whitening sought to rectify scientifically based fears of the nineteenth century that its extensive miscegenation would doom Brazil to perpetual underdevelopment. However, Brazilian elites, backed by a small scientific community, decided they could eliminate the large black population through a process of whitening through miscegenation, accompanied by massive immigration. Whitening became accepted as popular ideology, which ranked individual worth or quality on the basis of race, and the Brazilian state directed immigration policies to admit only Europeans.

As scientific racism waned and biological concerns about racial determinism ended, the Brazilian elite chose to promote the idea of racial democracy. Racial democracy denied that there was any racism in Brazil. Once again, miscegenation became a central feature of this ideology and served as a global counterpoint to the horrors of race-based genocide and segregation. Although troublesome for elites at one time, miscegenation in Brazil became a source of national pride as the fiction of racial superiority began to be uncovered. While whitening was a development strategy of the Brazilian state in the context of scientific racism, racial democracy would become a centerpiece of a consolidating national identity. In particular, Brazilians especially gained a sense of moral superiority over its powerful but unabashedly racist neighbor to the north, where miscegenation was associated with degeneracy, mongrelization, and sexual terror and prohibited for three centuries.

To use David Goldberg's (2002) phrase, the Brazilian state "fashioned the terms of racial expression . . . as well as racist exclusions and subjugation." At first, it created racial conditions and representations through slavery and whitening but then denied them through racial democracy. Unlike the United States and South Africa, which sought the clear separation of whites from nonwhites, Brazil began to develop a soft racial state in the 1930s, which celebrated biological and cultural hybridization. Like these other societies, the Brazilian state used race to promote its particular form of nationalism, but rather than create exclusionary policies, it would take a very different route. The Brazilian state instead denied racism and diffused racial divisions while ignoring the racial hierarchy, thus constructing a multiracial nationalist image to serve its modernizing project.

In addition, Brazilian and mostly North American academics came to support some form of a racial-democracy argument from 1933 or earlier to the late 1950s, and North American academics endorsed it until into the early 1970s. Racial democracy was analytically supported on evidence concluding that race was of little relevance to sociability or horizontal human relations in Brazil, making them far superior to those of the United States. However, racial democracy would begin to face challenges by Brazilian sociologists, largely on evidence that vertical race relations in Brazil were deplorable by their near total exclusion of blacks. The disagreements between the two generations of scholars thus largely hinged on their respective emphases on horizontal or vertical race relations. In studying one or the other dimension, they were somehow able to ignore or explain away the other.

Despite the challenges by Brazil's leading academics to racial democracy, it survived as the dominant ideology for roughly another thirty years, as a military government was able to suppress ideologically and forcibly counterhegemonic thinking and activism. Although democratization and antiracist movements had begun a decade before, racial democracy had become well entrenched in the Brazilian mind and continued serving the maintenance of Brazil's civil and economic order. It was only in the mid-1990s, that the Brazilian state began to recognize racism and implement racial reforms. Despite the end of racial democracy, its legacy nevertheless continued to shape social relations in the following years.

Chapter Three

FROM RACIAL DEMOCRACY TO
AFFIRMATIVE ACTION

> It is not enough to end slavery. It is necessary to destroy the
> work of slavery.
> —*Abolitionist Joaquim Nabuco (circa 1890), and cited by*
> *Marco Maciel, vice president of Brazil (1996)*

The shift from racial democracy to affirmative action represents a dramatic moment in Brazilian history. Occurring mostly in the 1990s, this transition consisted of an acknowledgement of racism by the Brazilian government and society generally, the consolidation of black-movement organizations, their limited incorporation into the democratic process, and finally, the implementation of race-based affirmative action in many Brazilian institutions. These changes occurred in the context of Brazilian democratization in general, which was characterized by the retreat of the military, a strong rejection of their rule by Brazilian society, the rapid expansion of civil-society organizations, decentralization involving civil-society participation at the local level, and the strengthening of democratic political institutions. As a validation of the vigor of Brazilian democratization, 95 million Brazilians freely and orderly elected a socialist candidate as president in 2002. In this chapter, I examine this momentous shift in Brazil's racial politics from about the beginnings of that country's democratization to the initiation of large-scale affirmative action in the early 2000s. I thus focus on the changing black movement and their growing access to spaces inside the Brazilian state.

Beginnings of Democratization

Brazil returned to democratic rule in 1985, although the resumption of some constitutional guarantees had been reestablished as early as 1978. Although it occurred slowly and unevenly, democratization would begin to yield political space to social-movement activists representing a variety of concerns and ideologies. The demands of some social movements received higher priority than others. Especially intense resistance to black-movement demands persisted, because their cause seemed to threaten central tenets of Brazilian nationalism. The racial-democracy ideology, in particular, limited the black movement's ability to resonate with the Brazilian elite, especially during the 1980s when it continued to be advocated. At the same time, Brazil had grown enormously and consistently in the previous five decades, but the 1980s saw economic decline. This would limit social-movement gains as the government focused on the economy and on granting basic political and civil rights.

Before the late 1970s, black associations in Brazil tended to have culturalist and assimilationist goals and were engaged in the politics of patron-client relations and corporatism. However, with the beginnings of redemocratization, such goals and the political methods used to pursue them were becoming discredited by a new generation of black activists. The mostly young and often college-educated black leaders of the 1970s and 1980s pursued a confluence of race and class politics, emphasizing black identity and relentlessly denouncing racial democracy as a myth. In 1974, blacks in Salvador, Bahia, founded Ilê Aiyê, an exclusively black (preto) Carnaval school, in response to their racial exclusion in previous Carnavals.[1] Ilê Aiyê's actions in favor of negritude signaled a bridge from the cultural mobilizations of the past to the beginning of modern black protest. Although not explicitly political, the Black Soul movement similarly marked the beginnings of change in Rio de Janeiro and São Paulo in the same year. Black Soul was characterized by ostentatious expressions of black identity in fashion, music, and dance, which Gilberto Freyre himself came to denounce as un-Brazilian and a product of U.S. imperialism.[2] The transition to modern black politics was completed in 1978 with the formation of the Movimento Negro Unificado (MNU). In July of that year, about 2000 blacks rallied together in front of the Teatro Municipal in São Paulo to demonstrate against the existence of widespread racial discrimination in Brazil.[3] By the mid-1980s, the small but growing black movement began to exert a limited influence on the federal and a number of local governments.

EARLY PUBLIC-POLICY ATTEMPTS

In response to growing black-movement demands, some states established special councils or *conselhos* on the status of blacks in the 1980s. Created in 1984, the first of these was the Council for the Participation and Development of the Black Community in the state of São Paulo. Its purpose was to monitor legislation that defended the interests of the black population, suggest projects on their behalf to the state legislature and executive branches, and investigate complaints of racial discrimination and police violence. With the beginnings of democratization, the council's government and civil-society members were optimistic that the historical moment would provide an opportunity to reunite currently divided black leaders to work together to create "real emancipation" for blacks. By 1988, the council's civil-society members were selected to represent a diversity of political parties, particularly from the Left, reflecting the need to create a united front among the divided and ideologically diverse black organizations. In the end, it encountered many political and operational problems, but the former president of that council, Helio Santos, credits it with improving the image of black Brazilians through its effects on the educational system and in advertising, and activist Sueli Carneiro believes that the experiences of black activists in the São Paulo conselho awakened them to possibility of democratic participation. The São Paulo experience provided a model for similar councils in several other Brazilian states, including Bahia (1987), Rio Grande do Sul (1988), and Rio de Janeiro (1991), and in many smaller municipalities, although they often tended to focus on cultural issues.[4]

In 1985, despite his wavering support for racial democracy, President José Sarney proposed, but never implemented, a Black Council for Compensatory Action (Conselho Negro de Ação Compensatória) at the federal level, following a meeting with Afro-Brazilian leaders. However, on May 13, 1988, the centennial of abolition, President Sarney announced the creation of the Palmares Cultural Foundation (Instituto Fundação Cultural Palmares). In his radio address on that day, Sarney vacillated between the official interpretation of Brazilian abolition as peaceful and consensual and a perspective critical of racial democracy. Aiming to get the support of the black population, Sarney expressed that the foundation would "make possible a black presence in all the sectors of leadership in this country."[5]

According to its home page, the Palmares Cultural Foundation seeks to "promote and preserve cultural, social and economic values that come from black influences in the formation of Brazilian society," as guaranteed in the Brazilian Constitution (article 215 of the 1988 Constitution). Moreover, it seeks to "create and implement public policies that may create the possibilities for participation by the black population in development, arising from its history and culture."[6] While the foundation has served as an important intermediary between the black movement and the Brazilian government, its emphasis on culture and cultural rights and its location under the Ministry of Culture reflects the government's traditional concern with Afro-Brazilian culture and history. For some analysts, the emphasis of the foundation, as well as by several other black-movement activities of the time, on culture distracted it from addressing the more important socioeconomic needs of black people in work, education, and health.[7]

On another front, Brazilian rights advocates began making significant progress in securing legislative and constitutional reforms to expand the democratic rights of all citizens and create new rights for historically disadvantaged groups. Black and feminist groups in particular were successful at including important antiracist and antisexist laws in the 1988 Constitution. The 1988 Brazilian Constitution revolutionized the legal basis of the defense of human rights. The Constitution also recognized principles of tolerance, multiculturalism, and individual dignity, rights and identities, and became the basis of hundreds of antiracist laws at various jurisdictional levels.[9] Specifically, Article 5 (paragraph 42) made the practice of racism an unbailable crime, subject to imprisonment.[10] The Constitution also mandated some important structural changes in the judiciary in the direction of expanding individual and collective rights. These included the strengthening of the constitutional role of the Federal Supreme Court and major reforms in the functions of the Public Prosecution (Ministério Publico). By increasing the number of institutions that could petition for unconstitutionality and creating new social and economic rights, the Public Ministry also became the state's adjudicator for members of society that had little or no political power.[11] Since then, the 1989 Caó law defined practices of racism, and similar laws have also been implemented at the state and municipal levels.

On the street, the voices of the black movement were becoming increasingly heard as they used the occasion of the centennial of abolition in 1988 to mobilize Brazilians in defense of racial justice. On May 11, Brazilian army units in Rio de Janeiro blocked a march that condemned abolition as a farce and arrested several of its participants. The Army spokesman alleged that the marchers sought to degrade the image of a famous Brazilian military figure by marching past it, although the organizers had agreed to march far from it. For the black movement, that demonstration would become a historical benchmark for the future of black consciousness and organization in Brazil.[8] Although the Brazilian state considered issues involving race to be extremely marginal to its social priorities at the time, activities such as these were helping the black movement begin to capture public attention.

The elections of increasing numbers of blacks to prominent posts began to challenge their perceived status in public minds and raise the hopes of much of the black population. Unlike the past, black elected officials now often recognized their blackness and made race an important issue, as noted by Johnson (1995). In the 1980s, Abdias do Nascimento, a backup (*suplente*) senator and a longtime black activist from Rio de Janeiro, became the first black legislator to defend explicitly the Afro-Brazilian population in Congress. Since about 1991, with the 49th legislature and the election of Benedita da Silva, a poor black woman who raised racial issues in her grassroots campaign as early as 1989, blacks in Congress began to speak out openly and regularly on behalf of race issues. Since then, black deputies such as Paulo Paim of Rio Grande do Sul, Ben-Hur Ferreira of Mato Grosso do Sul, and Luiz Alberto of Bahia—all members of the Worker's Party—have taken firm stands on behalf of black rights. Although vastly underrepresented, there had been black deputies and senators in the past, such as Nelson Carneiro, who served in the Senate for nearly thirty years but never defended the black population.[12] In the early 1990s, Albuino Azevedo, Alceu Collares, and João Alves were elected as state governors for Espirito Santo, Rio Grande do Sul, and Sergipe, respectively. Elected to one of Brazil's most powerful civil-society positions in 1994, Vicente Paulo da Silva (Vicentinho) became president of the Central Unica de Trabalhadores (CUT), Brazil's largest labor union. Benedita da Silva later became vice-governor and then governor of the state of Rio de Janeiro.

Democratization offered the hope of including previously excluded groups, especially to the extent that they were able to organize themselves. During this period, the black movement was also involved in extensive grassroots campaigns to organize on the basis of race. Despite cultural focus of many black-movement organizations in the past, increasing numbers of activists began to focus on racism and racial inequality. Black-movement leaders were beginning to gain national and international attention through campaigns highlighting that blacks were the primary victims of Brazil's poverty and human-rights abuses, which included street children, trafficking in women, and the violence from the growing drug trade.[13]

Like other social movements and with the support of international foundations, particularly the Ford Foundation, several black leaders formed nongovernmental organizations (NGOs) that employed highly trained professionals and support staff.[14] For example, Geledés—The Institute for Black Brazilian Women was created in São Paulo in 1990, and CEERT (Center for the Study of Racial Inequality in the Workplace) in São Paulo was later formed and began to sensitize Brazil's trade unions to issues of race. CEAP (Center for Marginalized Populations) was formed under that name in 1989 in Rio de Janeiro and evolved into a primarily black-movement organization by 1994. With European funding, it actually began to organize in 1979 as the Association of Ex-Students of FUNABEM around street children issues, focusing largely on the fact that street children were predominately black. By the end of the 1990s, black-movement NGOs of varying sizes, resources, and professional capacity had been created in many Brazilian states. The NGOization of the black movement mirrored changing Brazilian social movements generally, in which these organizations increasingly became their institutional representatives.

Civil-society organizations were beginning to recognize that, at least in theory, injustices in a democratic state should be resolved through legal mechanisms and institutions. Black-movement organizations thus set up legal branches to seek redress for victims using the new antiracist clauses of the 1988 Constitution. In particular, some black-movement NGOs hired attorneys, drawn mostly from the small number of black law-school graduates, to meet the growing demands of constituents that had become increasingly conscious of racism and wanted to file their grievances. At first, these organizations established SOS Racisms to defend victims of racial discrimination, mostly through cases in which plaintiffs suffered from racial insults. The first SOS Racism was begun at the Research Institute of Black Cultures (IPCN) in Rio de Janeiro in 1992 as a newspaper, modeled after the French newspaper of the same name and funded by the French. In 1993, Geledés established the first SOS Racism with legal assistance, and by 1997, SOS Racisms existed in NGOs in several Brazilian states including Rio de Janeiro, São Paulo, Santa Catarina, Sergipe, and Pernambuco. While some of these cases proved to be important for highlighting the sometimes explicit and long-denied nature of racism in Brazilian society, cases that decided in favor of plaintiffs were rare and had little effect on redressing Brazil's racism. Researchers from the *Folha de São Paulo* could identify only three convictions handed down from 1988 to 1998.[15]

An important exception was the legal victory in 1992 at the Labor Court (Tribunal Superior do Trabalho) of Vicente Paulo Espirito Santo, a worker for the Santa Catarina Electrical Company, who was fired because of his supervisor's desire to whiten the department. This was the first case of racism ever to reach a high court in Brazil. According to Nilo Kaway, the attorney representing Espirito Santo, the plaintiff was ultimately victorious, despite setbacks in the first hearing and in an appeal, due to a combination of strategic planning, dedication to the case, and luck. In addition to vigilant and competent legal representation, Kaway cites the importance of political pressure from the local black-movement NGO, which was able to gain the attention of the leading national news program. He also notes the persistent attention and emotional support given by that NGO and local labor unions so that the plaintiff would not back down, despite offers of monetary compensation from the company, and, serendipitously, the momentary media attention given to racial issues because of the 1992 Los Angeles riots.

With the organizational and professional support needed, black-movement leaders were able to carry out and sustain their antiracist strategies, including the launching of public education campaigns and the use of media to expose the prevalence and perniciousness of racism in Brazil. Black-movement organizations were able to get national television and print-media coverage of events such as the case of Espirito Santo in 1992 and the March of Zumbi in 1995. Additionally, black-movement organizations used the national media to accuse high-profile institutions and personalities of racism, such as Brazil's media giant, TV Globo, about an episode of a popular soap opera ("Dono do Mundo") in which the protaganist shouts racial epithets at his gardener. In addition, these organizations denounced Sony Music and Tíririca of recording a racist children's song (1996) and the federal transportation minister for declaring that Pelé and asphalt were Brazil's most admired blacks (1997). These actions often prompted offers from the perpetrators to compensate for their aggressions, when they were recognized. For example, TV Globo ran a television series about a middle-class black family soon after, and the minister met with black-movement leaders, vowing to hire more blacks in the Transportation Ministry. More recently, black-movement NGOs secured national media coverage of their Campaign against Racism in the Bahian Carnaval (2000), accusing Samba schools of preventing blacks from participating, and of a boycott of a middle-class shopping center in Rio de Janeiro (2001), accusing storeowners of failing to hire black employees.

Such activity seemed to be affecting public opinion. The term "racial democracy" was beginning to fall out of favor in the popular Brazilian lexicon. By 1995, a national survey by Brazil's major newspaper revealed that the vast majority of Brazilians believed that Brazilian whites held racial prejudices, as shown in table 3.1. The black movement made racial democracy a hopelessly inappropriate concept. Despite challenges from the most important academics in Brazil throughout the period, Freyre's way of thinking had taken the day for more than fifty years, but a new way of thinking finally took its place in the 1990s.[16] This new period was marked by the recognition of racism by various sectors of Brazilian society and emerging pressures on the state to extend real democratic citizenship and human rights to its black population. To speak of Brazilian race relations would now require major attention to the issue of affirmative action, reflecting the government's recognition of racism in Brazil and the end of racial democracy. However, as table 3.1 further demonstrates, roughly 90 percent of Brazilians of all colors and in all regions in

TABLE 3.1
Percent supporting race mixture and recognizing racial prejudice
by color and region: Brazil, 1995

Percent agreeing that "whites hold prejudices against negros"				
	Brazil	Northeast	Southeast	South	North/Central West
White	89	83	91	90	87
Brown	88	85	91	87	89
Black	91	89	94	82	93
Percent agreeing that "race mixture is a good thing"				
White	88	76	88	85	90
Brown	87	87	87	89	91
Black	89	90	90	88	88

Source: Data Folha Survey, 1995.

1995 agreed with the statement "race mixture is a good thing."[17] Thus, thinking about race shifted from denying racism to recognizing it, but at the same time, it would sustain the racial-democracy value of race mixture.

THE NEW SCHOLARSHIP ON RACE

As the military governments began to relieve their repression of academics, scholarship on race resurfaced. With the completion of his Ph.D. dissertation from UC-Berkeley in 1978, Carlos Hasenbalg returned to Brazil and initiated a new phase of race research in the Brazilian academy. Hasenbalg's work, like that of Florestan Fernandes before him, focused on the effect of capitalist development and industrialization on racial inequality. Like Fernandes, Hasenbalg found widespread racial discrimination and inequality, and believed that whites benefitted mostly by disqualifying nonwhites as competitors and restraining the aspirations of nonwhites. However unlike Fernandes, he concluded that racism was compatible with the development of Brazilian capitalism, arguing instead that racial inequality would thrive rather than disappear with capitalist development. Hasenbalg's treatise mirrored larger debates in the U.S. academy concerned with race, class, and capitalist development.

The work of Hasenbalg and his University of Michigan–trained colleague, Nelson do Valle Silva, was critical to debunking the belief in racial democracy, mostly because it convinced Brazilians of vast racial inequality and discrimination in their country. Their work relied largely on newly available racial statistics[18] and Silva's empirical bent and sophisticated statistical skills, which he brought to the study of race and class in Brazil. Another important contribution to changing Brazilian ideas about race was a book on racial inequality in the labor force, *O Lugar do Negro na Força de Trabalho,* published in 1983 by the IBGE, the Brazilian equivalent of the Census Bureau and the Department of Labor Statistics put together. The importance of this work was enhanced because it was produced by the governmental statistical agency.[19]

In the 1990s, race would begin to be accepted as a legitimate field of study in the Brazilian social sciences, reflecting the new consensus that race and racism were important. Scholarship on race proliferated in a wide variety of disciplines and made much broader research inquiries than it had in previous decades. This change signaled an important transformation in Brazilian academia, where research on race went from being considered a marginal area of research from the 1960s until the mid-1990s to becoming one of its fastest-growing topics of scholarly interest. This was revealed quite clearly in the number of panels on race at Brazilian scholarly meetings, particularly ANPOCS [Associação Nacional de Pos-Graduação em Ciencias Sociais (National Association of Graduate Studies in the Social Sciences)]. Most notably, leading economists, political scientists, and policy analysts became interested in the topic for the first time, and a growing number of young Brazilian social scientists developed their research agendas around race.

Quantitative studies of Brazil's racial inequalities continue to be produced as a constant reminder of Brazil's racial injustices, providing important fodder for black-movement demands. Indeed, the Brazilian government's Research Institute for Applied Economics (IPEA) was commissioned in 2001 with conducting studies on racial inequality. However, statistical research on racial inequality seems to have lost its academic prominence because of its inability to produce innovative findings, although it continues to make news headlines and sustain social-movement claims about the need to redress the inequalities this research continues to uncover. On the other hand, a growing number of ethnographic, historical, and other methods have been used to provided important new findings about Brazilian racism. Most notably, two scholars, Antonio Sergio Guimarães and Livio Sansone, have produced research on a broad range of topics for the past decade and have occupied important institutional positions, which have allowed them to influence greatly the debate on race in Brazil and train many young scholars, including a number of Afro-Brazilians.

THE EMERGENCE OF BLACK-MOVEMENT DIALOGUE
WITH THE FEDERAL GOVERNMENT

Political elites began to respond to the claims of the black social movement only to the extent that activists could make their presence known. On November 20, 1995, thousands of marchers commemorated three hundred years since the death of Zumbi dos Palmares, the legendary leader of the marooned slave community (*quilombo*) that resisted the Portuguese for nearly one hundred years. The march in Brasilia culminated with black-movement activists, along with labor leaders, voicing their claims to the National Congress and meeting with President, Fernando Henrique Cardoso to demand concrete measures to combat racial discrimination. On the same day, the president announced the creation of the Interministerial Working Group (Grupo de Trabalho Interministerial or GTI) for the Development of Public Policies to Valorize the Black Population. Notably, a head of the Brazilian government had recognized racism for the first time and announced the possibility of measures to promote racial justice, breaking with decades of official denial of racism. The GTI was charged with creating ideas for how to include blacks in Brazilian society, which it published in a 72-page document.[20] Unfortunately, the government did not create a similar group or mechanism for operationalizing these ideas, and government ministries sought to boycott implementation of the GTI's recommendations.

The possibility of affirmative action–like policies was debated at the Multiculturalism and Racism conference sponsored by the Ministry of Justice and sanctioned by President Cardoso in 1996. In that seminar, he declared that "[racial discrimination and prejudice] must be unmasked and counter-attacked, not only verbally, but also via mechanisms and processes that can bring about a transformation of a more democratic relation among races, social groups and classes."[21] Later that year, President Cardoso created the National Program for Human Rights (Program Nacional de Direitos Humanos), which prescribed short-, medium- and long-range goals for women, disabled persons, and indigenous and black persons. For the short term, the program mandated the study of public policies that "valorize negros." For the medium term, it sought to "develop affirmative action policies that give negros access to professional training, to universities and to high technology areas." For the longer term, its goals were to repeal all discriminatory laws, improve policies and regulations that seek to combat racial discrimination, and create "compensatory policies that socially and economically promote the negro population." The federal government thus endorsed the idea of explicit race-based public policies in support of nonwhites.

According to Helio Santos, the director of the GTI, the black movement held high hopes for change in the government's historical attitude about race because of the president's own academic history.[22] Early in his career, as a student of Florestan Fernandes, Cardoso conducted research on race relations in Brazil's South region, from which he wrote two books.[23] This would explain much of his own commitment to race issues. However, the president's early commitment to the black movement seemed to fizzle out during the five years after the program's unveiling, although it reignited with the World Conference on Racism in 2001. At that time, less than two years before the end of Cardoso's second consecutive four-year term, many of the goals of the National Program for Human Rights concerning blacks had yet to be implemented. The government's dialogue, according to Hedio Silva, had turned into a monologue in which the black movement persistently made its claims, while the government listened but no longer responded.[24] The beginnings of the first Cardoso administration was a movement of guarded optimism for some black-movement activists, and their reservations turned out to have merit. The Brazilian elite, as many expected, continued to resist any real attempt to incorporate blacks and mulattos in their country's development schemes.

Although Cardoso himself may have wanted to implement affirmative-action policies, he needed his peers to design and support them. Cardoso often relied on the opinions of a small community of senior social scientists and economists, some of whom served as his ministers. At the 1996 conference, he called in a handful of prominent Brazilian academics and international race scholars to weigh in with their opinions about the possibility of social policies for promoting the black population. The invited Brazilian scholars were stars in their fields but had mostly ignored race throughout their careers prior to the presidential summons. Rather, their analyses often reflected their knowledge of popular notions of race and their penchant for class-based analysis. The international scholars, by contrast, were mostly experts on racial issues, but their analyses seemed to resonate less in the policy-making community, perhaps because they were less attuned to Brazilian politics at the time, and they were not involved in subsequent discussions. Incidentially, black-movement leaders were also invited to the conference but were mostly relegated to the audience.

While recognizing racism in Brazilian society, the senior Brazilian scholars, whose opinions mattered most for Cardoso and his administration, reinforced the belief that racial democracy's values are deeply cherished in Brazil, thereby placing Brazilian society in an advantageous position for improving its prospects for abolishing or attenuating racism, especially when compared to countries like the United States. Although they recognized that racial democracy is not a descriptor of Brazilian society, they believed it should be viewed as a national project or goal to promote racial justice. They also expressed the ideas that race-targeted policies would solidify racial boundaries and perpetuate the idea of race itself. For them, Brazilian popular culture celebrates ambiguity and miscegenation rather than the conceptual separateness of groups, as required to identify beneficiaries of affirmative action. Rather than providing light about how to design policies to include nonwhites, these scholars voiced oblique opposition to affirmative-action policy, denouncing it as an inappropriate replication of U.S. policy.[25] At the same time, President Cardoso, credited for controlling Brazil's hyperinflation, was riding a long wave of popularity that would last from 1995 until December 1998, when the national currency was devalued.[26] For nearly four years, then, his administration must have surmised that the implementation of a controversial program like affirmative action would have been politically risky. As a result, the Cardoso government hesitated to pursue actively the goals it had earlier set out. However, the president's earlier proclamations seemed to have accelerated a rhythm of antiracist activities, including experiments in affirmative action.

BEGINNINGS OF AFFIRMATIVE ACTION

Despite the resistance by the federal government to implementing large-scale policies to combat racial inequality and discrimination, various sectors of Brazilian society began to develop a limited set of affirmative-action policies, including initiatives established by progressive local governments and demonstration projects of various sorts by the government and private sector. In her study of ten large metropolitan areas between 1995 and 1999, Heringer (2000) identified 124 programs intended to combat racial discrimination. Forty were specifically for negros, while seventy others sought to combat racial discrimination generally, valorize black culture and history, or promote members of disadvantaged groups including negros, and still another fourteen sought to combat racial discrimination without mentioning race. Twenty-nine of these programs were sponsored by the federal, state, or municipal governments, forty-two by NGOs, another seventeen by government-NGO partnerships, and the rest by universities, churches, political parties, and businesses. The federal programs included professional, administrative, and computer training and education about the government procurement system for negro small businesses in an effort to increase their efficiency at securing public contracts.

Initiatives to promote and support nonwhites in the university were particularly noteworthy. Among the nongovernmental initiatives were courses in several Brazilian cities to help blacks (sometimes "the disadvantaged and blacks") pass the college entrance exams, which alone determine acceptance into particular universities and fields of study. These were begun in Rio de Janeiro in 1994 by a Catholic priest with support from the Church, local neighborhood organizations, and the contributions of participants, and continues to serve as a model. The Rio course is directed to "negros and the disadvantaged [*carentes*]," which reflects a compromise in a debate about whether it should be for the poor in general or blacks in particular.[27] Most of these initiatives were private, although the city of Belo Horizonte created a similar course in 1999, and public universities began to sponsor such courses. Additionally, Geledés, a black women's NGO in São Paulo, with financial backing from Bank Boston, chose several promising black adolescents from poor families to support financially and academically over several years until they are able to finish college and enter the labor force. This project, known as "Generation XXI," is meant to be a model to demonstrate how poor black youth can succeed with the proper support.[28]

Two local governments, led by leftist parties, implemented policies to combat racism. For the first time in any large city, Belo Horizonte, Brazil's third-largest city, established the Municipal Department for Black Community Affairs (SMACOM) in 1998, but it became caught in a political crossfire and was dismantled in 2000, as described by Diva Moreira (2002), the former SMACOM director. As mandated by executive law in that municipality, the secretariat sought to develop social policies in poor areas, especially in housing and professional training. Participation in its programs was not limited to negros, although SMACOM included programs to combat racial discrimination and valorize black culture and people, particularly women.[29] In 1999, Brazil's sixth-largest city, Porto Alegre, responded to accusations of racism by establishing that 5 percent of the work force of all contractees with the city be negro.

A São Paulo–based black-movement NGO, the Center for Research on Race Relations in the Workplace (CEERT), has sponsored several seminars to examine diversity in the private-labor market. These began in 1995 when several black-movement leaders alerted the Ministry of Labor that U.S. multinationals that had racial and gender diversity policies in the United States discriminated against women and especially negros in their Brazilian affiliates. This led the ministry, in association with the secretary of human rights under the Ministry of Justice, and the International Labor organization, to organize several meetings among the North American company's representatives, labor unions, and black and women's social-movement organizations. Subsequently, CEERT has sponsored meetings with the human-resource administrators of these and Brazilian companies to share experiences and discuss programs that promote race and gender equality and diversity. They found that the few companies that had diversity programs involved women and the physically disabled but never negro workers. As a result of CEERT's efforts, panels on racial diversity were held at the meetings of the Brazilian Association of Human Resources and the Instituto Ethos's Conference on Business Social Responsibility in the Americas, both of which brought together hundreds of business leaders.[30] An Instituto Ethos publication (2000) asserted that diversity may improve productivity and corporate image, enhance worker satisfaction, reconcile the firm to client profiles, lower turnover, and decrease legal vulnerability.[31]

In the area of media, well-known actress Zeze Motta created the Brazilian Center for Information and Documentation of the Black Artist (CIDAN) in 1984 to promote negro actors and other artists. Responding to media, film, and theater executives claiming that there are few black artists available, CIDAN created a Web site in 1999 with the photographs and vitas of more than 1,000 black artists, which major media and advertising companies subsequently consulted and used to hire black artists, including those in major television productions.[32] Legislatively, a state law in Bahia, where nonwhites constitute about 75 percent of the population, requires that in state publicity at least one-third of all models or actors in advertising be negro.[33] Attempts at similar legislation at the federal level have met with little success. The Statute of Racial Equality, as proposed by Deputy Paim, is more stringent than the Bahian law, requiring that television stations air only programs and films in which at least 25 percent of actors are negro, and that producers of films and advertising hire negros for at least 40 percent of their artists and models.

The one area in which the federal government was active in explicit support of the negro community during the 1990s was in allowing the recognition of historically black rural communities or *quilombos*. Recognition of quilombo lands followed the precedent set in recognizing indigenous lands. Since runaway slaves organized to resist slavery on many of these lands, the descendants of these slaves today represent historical and symbolic continuity from the time of resistance to slavery, making them central to black-movement struggles throughout Brazil. Many of these communities have been isolated for decades or even centuries and thus conserve elements of African religious, linguistic, and other cultural traditions. More practically, quilombo lands often permit the economic survival of their residents in an environmentally sustainable manner, contrasting sharply with the widespread deforestation by encroaching private enterprises of nearby lands.[34]

Despite widespread support of quotas for nonwhites in work and in college entrance, federal affirmative-action laws continue to be delayed in Congress. On social issues, not to mention racial issues, Congress is especially sluggish in passing legislation. As of March 2002, up to 130 bills that deal with racial issues are pending in the National Congress. The two most notable bills were introduced in Congress by Senator (and former president) José Sarney and by Federal Deputy Paulo Paim. Sarney's bill proposes that 20 percent of admissions to all Brazilian universities and employment positions in public service go to blacks and browns. Paim's bill, the Statute for Racial Equality, also introduced in 2000, is much more ambitious: it establishes 20-percent quotas for negros in public universities, medium and large firms, and municipal, state, and local governments. It also requires similar quotas of at least 30 percent for party candidates, 25 percent for television and film actors, and 40 percent for publicity campaigns, as well as the payment of 102,000 reis as reparation to all African descendants in Brazil, the teaching of African history in all schools, an ombudsman for racial equality in Congress, and a guarantee of legal ownership for residents of quilombos. In 1999, a Senate bill by Antero Pães de Barros required that at least 50 percent of all admissions to federal universities go to public-school graduates. The idea of quotas or targets for the poor rather than for negros seemed to stand a greater chance of approval by the federal legislature, given the historic opposition of the Brazilian elite to race-specific actions. So far, the National Congress has balked at passing race-specific affirmative-action legislation. Brazil's executive branch, on the other hand, is much more agile and responsive to social-movement pressure, although executive policy actions are often less stable than the laws that Congress passes.

THE BLACK MOVEMENT GOES GLOBAL

Brazil's black movement gained greater influence on the Brazilian government by reaching beyond national borders. Although globalization presented new problems, such as the spread of racism on the Internet and a greater vulnerability of poor populations to the decisions of international capital, the transnationalization of human rights provided new opportunities for social movements generally. Informally, through the Internet, e-mail, and expanding international media, the work and visibility of international human-rights networks expanded greatly. The black movement, often in cooperation with other human-rights organizations, seized on these new opportunities and established ties with black-movement organizations throughout Latin America, the United States, and South Africa. In particular, globalization has helped in the consolidation of a

United Nations Human Rights System including the San Salvador Protocol and the Interamerican System. This includes international courts that try human-rights cases that previously exhausted judicial processes in member countries and allegedly received unjust outcomes. More generally, the globalization of human rights has enhanced the idea of universal human rights and the need to protect disadvantaged members of society, such as nonwhites in Brazil.

The black movement's growing attention to the UN System includes the monitoring of Brazilian government reports to the international conventions on racism, such as the Committee for the Elimination of Racism (CERD). The Brazilian government's 1996 CERD report declared, "the Federal Government, as determined by President Cardoso, has acted with absolute transparency in this area" (7).[35] While earlier reports promoted Brazil's racial-democracy ideology, that report began to report on Brazilian racism and racial inequality. Prepared in consultation with the Center for the Study of Violence at the University of São Paulo, the report pointed to national legislation and administrative measures that prohibit racism and racial discrimination. Although it attributed racial inequalities to historical racism and the concentration of nonwhites in poor and rural regions, it stopped short of blaming contemporary discrimination. This was consistent with the declarations of Rubens Ricupero (1993), the Brazilian ambassador to the United States, who claimed "this undeniable inequality is the product not of racism but of distinct historical causes." However, in the 2001 report, released just prior to the UN World Conference against Racism, the Brazilian government admitted to contemporary racism, disclosing its many dimensions, and demonstrated how the Brazilian judiciary responded.

Concerned that black communities in Latin America had not gotten their fair share of development funds, black-movement leaders also began to participate in meetings with such hallmarks of global capitalism as the World Bank and the Interamerican Development Bank (IDB).[36] Perhaps as a result of a growing black-movement presence, these institutions have become increasingly concerned about social issues in their work in Latin America and have listed aid to the victims of racism among their priorities since the late 1990s. The first time that a Brazilian black-movement leader participated in one of these meetings was in New York in January 1998, when an IDB representative from Brazil considered Ivanir dos Santos's proposal to invest in Afro-Brazilians as preposterous, boldly expressing, "I don't think you should bring up that issue. That's a problem of the United States, which doesn't exist in Brazil."[37] However, the Uruguayan president of the IDB was sensitive to the issue of racism, therefore overriding the protest of his Brazilian representative, and the IDB's dialogue with Brazil's black movement began. These meetings represented a powerful challenge to Brazil's racial-democracy ideology because the decisions of these institutions would condition much-needed foreign aid for Brazil's social development on race-conscious considerations.[38]

Domestically, Brazil's black movement has also become part of a wider and growing human-rights movement within Brazil that now recognizes that blacks and mulattos are the major victims of most human-rights violations because of persistent discrimination and their subsequent position in the economic and social structure. The general Brazilian human-rights movement has also increased its ties to the international human-rights community itself in a way that parallels and sometimes works together with the black movement. Although Brazil's modern human-rights movement began mostly with middle-class opposition to the military government and its denial of political and civil rights, the human-rights movement of recent years has brought these same activists together with grassroots activists that fight social injustice on economic, social, and cultural grounds. The black movement has finally been able to put race issues on the national human-rights agenda for both the government and civil society in general. The National Movement for Human Rights (MNDH), which grew out of the struggle for political and civil rights during the military dictatorship, reflects this. Although it began in the 1970s in opposition to the political and civil-rights abuses of authoritarian rule, it now brings together more than six hundred mostly grassroots NGOs, including black-movement organizations from throughout Brazil, with a growing concern for economic, social, and cultural rights. Their publications regularly note that negros are disproportionately victims of nearly every type of human-rights abuse in Brazil.

THE ROAD TO DURBAN

One of the most apparent consequences of social-movement transnationalization has been the growth and consolidation of an international human-rights system, consisting of international conferences and legal conventions. International conferences, beginning with Rio de Janeiro's Conference on the Environment in 1992, served as strong examples to Brazilians about the power of a global civil-society involvement regarding social justice and human-rights issues. Through the presence of social-movement NGOs and countries with progressive human rights, these international conferences and their conventions serve to pressure countries to position themselves with respect to human rights in the eyes of the international community, declare their support (or not) by becoming signatories, and thus commit to international human rights laws. While core countries, particularly the United States, often disregard these treaties, arguing that their rule of law and democratization are well established in their own countries, peripheral countries are concerned that their position regarding these treaties affects their international reputations, especially regarding their level of democratization. The UN Race Conference in 2001 and the activities leading up to it are typical and coincided with changing activities inside of Brazil's organized black movement.

The year 1997 marked a new stage in black-movement activities as the black movement began to step up its efforts to use the institutional mechanisms of law and social policy. Recognizing an increasingly democratic context in which it perceived that laws might be used for social change and that government would seek civil-society proposals to help design social policy, the black movement shifted from simply denouncing racial injustice to becoming increasingly solutions oriented. Its new focus was initially demonstrated by its organizing of legal professionals in that year. In a meeting in Aracajú, black-movement organizations, attorneys, and leaders interested in antidiscriminatory law formed a national multiracial network comprising attorneys, prosecutors, and judges. They subsequently held other meetings across Brazil, with as many as one hundred participants, featuring national and international legal scholars and jurists as well as the national secretary of human rights. Of particular note, Nelson Jobim, a former minister of justice who is now on the Brazilian Supreme Court, met several times with this association and became an important interlocutor with the government. Aside from the technical discussion of strategies to improve antiracist law, find better ways to implement it, and extend its benefits, the network sought to begin an active debate about how best to promote the status and the economic, social, and cultural rights of the black population. Not satisfied with the efficacy of the law in reverting Brazil's racial status quo, black-movement attorneys and other leaders increasingly strategized on how to make their work more efficient.

In the same year, the UN General Assembly decided to convene the Third World Conference against Racism, Racial Discrimination, Xenophobia and Related Forms of Intolerance as international concern grew about increasing incidents of racism, and as the UN recognized the challenges and opportunities for combating these phenomena in an increasingly globalized world. The national network of antiracist attorneys now resolved to prepare its participation at that conference. Specifically, they enlisted the assistance of the International Human Rights Law Group (IHRLG), which had taken the lead in organizing the World Conference for the United Nations. The IHRLG would meet with black activists and relevant policy makers and lead several training sessions for participation in the World Conference.[39]

Prior to the international conferences, black-movement dialogue with the government had nearly always been channeled through the Palmares

Cultural Foundation (PCF), since its founding in 1988. Several black-movement leaders attended the first preparatory conference to the World Conference against Racism in Geneva on May 1–5, 2000. There the PCF monopoly as the representative of the Brazilian government to the black movement was broken, and higher-level sectors of the Brazilian government soon showed signs of wanting serious dialogue with the black movement. Although the Brazilian government committed itself to hosting the regional meeting of the Americas in preparation for the World Conference, the representative of the PCF announced that Brazil would no longer be the host, claiming that black leaders did not want the conference in Brazil. This was an insincere statement considering the efforts of black-movement leaders to inform their constituents about the conference. It was especially startling given the presence of black-movement leaders. Although the head of the Brazilian mission in Geneva later cited cost factors as the reason for not hosting the regional meeting, this was an equally unconvincing claim considering that these conferences were mostly subsidized, and that the poorer countries of Senegal and Iraq were to host the African and Asian conferences.

The real reason lay in the government's concern over their rapidly crumbling international image of racial tolerance and their belief that such a conference would bring undue attention to Brazilian racism. Just ten days earlier on April 22, Brazil had celebrated five hundred years since Portuguese navigators first landed on its shores, with a ceremony by leading dignitaries, including President Cardoso, on the beach where the historic event occurred. Peacefully protesting this celebration of five hundred years of European exploitation, landless workers, blacks, and indigenous protesters were held back from the celebration site near Porto Seguro in Bahia for several days. Despite permission granted by a judicial decision, when they sought to parade onto the site on the day of the celebration, they were detained, and several were beaten by the police, an event widely aired in the international media.

With Brazil steadfastly maintaining its decision not to hold the regional conference—despite pressure from Mary Robinson, the UN's high commissioner for human rights—Chile was finally chosen as the new site. At least two important meetings involving Brazil's black movement were held prior to that conference. The first was a national meeting by the national Coordination of Black Entities (CONEN), which set goals for the black movement's participation in Chile. At the same time, Gay McDougall, executive director of the International Human Rights Law Group—the organization largely responsible for assembling the Third World Conference—and Ariel Dulitzky, the Law Group's attorney for Latin American affairs, made several visits to Brazil and trained black-movement organizations in several cities of Brazil, as well as participating in the CONEN conference. In its visit to Brazil, as well as two prior trips by Dulitzky, the Law Group trained attorneys and activists on technical, substantive, and political issues that would be discussed at the World Conference and at its preparatory conferences.

Mostly preceding the official preparations for the World Conference, the Southern Education Foundation held a series of four international meetings to discuss "human relations" in Brazil, South Africa, and the United States between 1997 and 2000, and propose actions to overcome the consequences of racism. The conference organizers produced a series of publications, many with Portuguese translation, and brought together black-movement leaders and government officials of the three countries to discuss common issues and possible solutions. It was noteworthy because it brought together important black leaders from the three countries with government officials and academics. The Brazilian delegation felt marginalized in the first three conferences, partly for linguistic reasons but also because they felt that the organizers and delegations from the United States and South Africa perceived Brazil to be unimportant and Brazilian racism to be less serious than in their countries.[40] All of these conferences were important for Brazilians in that they established close ties between government officials and the black movement, but the Brazilians also perceived that their race problem was of little international interest. However, by the fourth conference, which occurred soon after the Geneva Preparatory Conference in Capetown in May 2000, the Brazilian delegation sparked the interest of the South Africans and North Americans. Indeed, Brazil became central to the proceedings, further propelling the influence of Brazil's black activists.

Provoked by the absence of a Brazilian on a panel considering solutions to racism, eighty-five-year-old Abdias do Nascimento shouted from the audience, questioning the conference organizers' integrity in seriously including Brazil.[41] Other Brazilian activists joined in, also questioning the historical absence of blacks among Brazilian government representatives. A young diplomat from the Brazilian embassy, sent specifically from Pretoria to monitor the proceedings, repeatedly proclaimed that the Brazilian Foreign Service and the Brazilian government did not discriminate. As expected, Brazilian black activists reacted, and a lively exchange took place, provoking the attention of the North Americans and South Africans to the Brazilian case. They finally realized that their countries, freed of legal segregation and apartheid, and beginning to face the color-blind defense, had much to learn from Brazil. The Brazilian diplomat's denial of racism resonated with the South Africans and North Americans, who suddenly realized that their relatively brief experience with postformal racism had long characterized Brazil. Wade Henderson, executive director of the Leadership Conference for Civil Rights of the United States, remarked to Rio's vice governor, Benedita da Silva, Brazil's highest-ranking black official, that "we [North] Americans and many South Africans finally were able to recognize that Brazil was not that racial ideal that we had." As a result, International alliances were strengthened, and the Brazilian government was increasingly concerned.

The dialogue established at the preparatory meetings for the World Conference and at the Southern Educational Foundation between black-movement leaders and members of the Ministry of Foreign Relations was unprecedented. Also known as Itamaraty, the name of its historic building in Rio de Janeiro, Brazil's Foreign Service is often considered to be especially elitist and particularly closed to civil society. Among its foreign colleagues, Itamaraty continued to proclaim the idea of Brazil as especially tolerant well into the late 1990s, after the idea of racial democracy no longer had popular support in Brazil. The Foreign Ministry was perhaps the last branch of government that continued to proclaim openly Brazil's racial tolerance and even racial democracy, comfortable in its belief that such claims would continue to resonate among some foreigners, and that it was immune from black-movement and civil-society vigilance. At the same time, it had almost no nonwhites among its more than 1,000 diplomatic professionals.

Itamaraty officials continued to spout Brazil's moral superiority on race to foreign governments without challenge. In what may have been the last gasp of racial democracy among Brazil's Foreign Ministry, a high-level Brazilian ambassador announced his country's offer to host the regional UN World Conference against Racism in March 2000. He stated, "I need not insist on the significance of this event for Brazil, whose very essence as a nation is expressed through the affirmation of multiethnicity and tolerance."[42] While his peers commonly hailed Brazil's racial democracy, in this case the Brazilian diplomat did not mention racial democracy, although he seemed to be aware that the image of Brazil he projected would continue to be accepted in the international community.

Preparations for these international conferences provided a catalyst for Brazil's black movement, unlike any other in recent years. Most importantly, these meetings allowed them to discuss directly issues of racism with the undivided attention of high-level Brazilian government officials, an event that would rarely, if ever, occur in Brazil. This dialogue was further ensured by the presence of international peers, particularly diplomats, and NGO leaders committed to human rights. Also important, these conferences rallied together black activists from throughout the country with a renewed optimism about the possibility of black progress, especially in light of an unprecedented—although suspicious for many—dialogue with the federal government.

Brazil's black movement played a central role in forming La Alianza Estratégica de Afro-Latinoamericanos (La Alianza), an organization based in Montevideo, which has brought together Afro–Latin Americans and Afro-Caribbeans since 1998 through leadership training, the exchange of information, the discussion of common problems, and the development of regional strategies. Brazilian black-movement organizations worked closely with La Alianza in preparation for the Third World Conference on Racism. With black-movement representatives from at least ten other countries from the region, La Alianza met in San Jose, Costa Rica, on October 2000 and signed a document to be presented to the Latin American governments in Chile.[43] The document known as "El Documento de Santiago" provided a diagnosis of historical and current discrimination in the region and recommendations for overcoming its consequences. It also affirmed that denying the existence of discrimination and racism at the level of the state as well as society contributes directly to the practices of racism, discrimination, xenophobia, and related forms of intolerance. Finally, the document demanded the designation of effective antiracist policies that "can include" affirmative action. In that same month, twenty-six black women's organizations from Brazil, Peru, Ecuador, and Uruguay met to discuss strategies to further influence the World Conference.

The Latin American regional meeting was held in Santiago, Chile, in December 2000. That meeting was a turning point for the black movement in that the Brazilian government for the first time showed a resolve to do something about the issues the activists raised. Much to the surprise of Alianza members, the Latin American governments decided to accept "El Documento Santiago" in its entirety and make it part of their official platforms. Romero Rodriguez, a black-movement leader from Mundo Afro in Uruguay, proudly proclaimed that the "Documento de Santiago" had become the most important document for Latin American blacks since Abolition.

In June and July, a series of preparatory meetings were held in almost all of the twenty-six Brazilian states. The Brazilian government funded at least eighteen conferences for regions and states, including special topics such as one on the Afro-indigenous population. Additionally, fifteen states funded their own preparatory conferences.[44] Most of the funding for these conferences was by the Brazilian government, which signaled a strong commitment to the UN Race Conference. Government attention to the black movement was reaffirmed and consolidated at the National Preparatory Conference in July 2001 in Rio de Janeiro, which was attended by approximately 2,000 black-movement supporters from throughout Brazil. Government officials could not help but notice that the black movement was no longer based on a small cadre of activists but rather had developed widespread support. Moreover, they were confronted with many testimonials about race-based injustices and suffering personally endured by those present. Government officials, for the first time, had opened themselves up, in a public forum, to accusations that they had long ignored the deeply harmful racial discrimination of Brazilian society, and that it was high time for them to seek the proper correctives.[45]

Also prompted by the Brazilian government's sluggishness in addressing black-movement demands, black parliamentarians met in Salvador in July 2001 for the first time ever to form a black congressional caucus. Despite representing a diversity of parties and ideologies, they recognized the black movement's claim of persistent racial discrimination and inequality and the need to develop policies to promote equality. Among their priorities, they vowed to coordinate their efforts to promote a "National Reparations Fund to support public policies with lawfully determined funding"—that is, "a percentage of federal, state and local budgets for ten years"—and policies for "the well-being of the black population" and to "preserve the self-esteem of the black population."[46] Such a caucusing of black elected officials would have been unthinkable only a few years earlier.

THE WORLD CONFERENCE

The much-awaited World Conference finally occurred in late August 2001. The black movement was able to send between 150 and 200 activists to Durban as part of an NGO delegation, with the financial support of various private foundations and local governments as well as some self-financing, which involved great personal sacrifice. It also counted on representatives from other human-rights NGOs, including those representing indigenous peoples, women's rights, and economic, social, and cultural rights. The importance of the Brazilian delegation was heightened as a Brazilian black-movement activist and director of a São Paulo NGO, Edna Roland, became the general rapporteur for the official World Conference. The Brazilian government delegation consisted of about fifty representatives, which included the minister of justice, the secretary of human rights, several congressional delegates, local officials, and the national committee on race and racial discrimination with both its government and civil-society delegates.

According to Guacira Cesar, a feminist active at Durban and at the previous UN conferences on women and human rights, the Brazilian government had never invested this level of support to address any social-movement demands.[47] The Brazilian government had sent its secretary of human rights along with several ambassadors to the Chile conference. Along with the minister of justice and the secretary of human rights, it sent five diplomats to the Durban conference, which was more than it had sent to any other UN conference, including those in Vienna

(Human Rights, 1993), Cairo (Population and Development, 1995), Beijing (Women and Development, 1995), Copenhagen (Social Summit, 1995), and Beijing Plus 5 (Women and Development, 2000). The federal government's participation demonstrated an unprecedented seriousness about racial issues that continued to amaze even some of the most skeptical black-movement leaders. Itamaraty would no longer ignore or deny racial issues as it had in the past but rather it would commit major efforts and resources to Durban.

One event in particular was indicative of the growing cooperation between the government and the social activists. On the day before the beginning of the official conference, the minister of justice invited the civil-society activists to a meeting at his hotel so that they could share their concerns about the conference and he could brief them about the government's strategy. What followed was an interesting mix of nationalism and racial grievance making. After the brandishing of a Brazilian flag and a rousing bout of the Brazilian national anthem, in which everyone that I could see jubilantly participated, each of the attendees introduced themselves. Even though the activists had shown themselves to be patriots and nationalists, their often lengthy introductions also revealed high levels of black consciousness and their grievances and lamentations about the government's failure to act on their behalf. A few days later, the same black-movement activists and their international and domestic allies held a demonstration for the international press in front of the UN meeting hall in Durban, denouncing Brazil's failure to implement antiracist policies.

During the conference, the Brazilian government and Latin American governments turned out to be progressive on race issues, especially when compared to the government delegations from other world regions. By contrast, the United States and Israel eventually withdrew from the conference, leaving thousands of U.S. NGO activists disappointed and demoralized. The conference was politicized by two issues, both of which caused the United States to exit: the demand for reparations for centuries of slavery (and colonization), and the proposed sanctioning of Israel for its treatment of the Palestinians. The all-powerful Bush administration thus saw the conference as contrary to its interests. To stay and face the prospect of having its domestic race issues raised for discussion in a world forum, or to have their closest ally chastised and sanctioned would not be tolerated by an increasingly isolated and arrogant United States. Additionally, the nations of the European community, acting in unison, failed to support reparations for colonialism and slavery, and India denied that the caste system was racist.

Perhaps the greatest sign of change was what happened in Brazil itself rather than at the conference. While scores of black-movement activists attended the NGO conference in Durban in the days preceding the official UN conference, their friends at home witnessed a transformation in the Brazilian media's historical neglect of race. To literally translate a phrase used by black activists at the time, "the race question was catching fire." In the week preceding and during the first week of the conference, the major newspapers in Brazil ran stories on race, racism, and the World Conference daily. The five major newspapers in Brazil ran 170 news articles, editorials, letters, and opinion pieces during the week of August 25–31, an unprecedented event in Brazilian journalistic history, where the subject of race was thought to be of little public interest, and articles ran only occasionally.[48] Part of the reason for the media's interest may have involved its exploitation of a rift in the government between the president's support for racial quotas and the minister of education's opposition, which was occurring in the wake of the forthcoming elections, in which the minister was expected to be a leading candidate. However, it undoubtedly also reflected a growing interest in the race issue by the Brazilian public.

The World Conference in Durban raised much optimism among black-movement leaders. Itamaraty appeared to have reversed its position, to now support the black movement. The government's promises, which included the implementation of affirmative action, were unprecedented and represented a new discourse that flew in the face of opposition from both the Left and the Right. But were these merely words? Despite the belief by many that policy was about to be revolutionized, many skeptics remained. Joaquim Barbosa, quoted in several newspapers, represented this view well, noting

> I don't see any political or institutional conditions. This is a government at the end of its term with difficulties of getting approval for even items that form part of its political agenda. How are they going to pass affirmative action? The government is going to play to the public, saying it's going to happen, knowing well that it doesn't have the slightest chance of doing anything.[49]

He also noted that the legal-philosophical principle of affirmative action is the search for the effective implementation of the principle of equality. Affirmative action implies setting aside formal equality and seeking real and material equality. It means breaking the logic by which we are all equal, when in fact, we are not. Such doubt seemed to be widespread. Although Brazil began experimenting with small-scale forms of affirmative action, both in the public and private spheres, large-scale government affirmative-action programs were, prior to the Durban conference, merely plans.

THE POST-DURBAN TRANSFORMATION

The Durban conference ended on September 8, 2001, with continuing debate and interest on racial issues in the Brazilian media. Regardless of the failure of Durban for the United States, the results were unequivocably positive for the black movement in Brazil. On September 5, the Brazilian government seemed to be well on its way to initiating race-specific affirmative action on a large scale. In response to the demands of the World Conference, the minister of agrarian development, Raul Jungmann, announced a "Program of Affirmative Action for Black Men and Women."[50] The program would strive to reduce the inequalities of opportunity among civil servants (*servidores*) and beneficiaries of agrarian reform and family agriculture by mandating race-based quotas for the participation of black men and women in administrative positions and positions in public exams (*concursos publicos*); guaranteeing black communities access to rural financing; and promoting seminars, research, and programs that focus on gender, race, and ethnicity. Specifically, 20 percent of all administrative positions in the ministry was to be reserved for negros, with this number increasing to 30 percent by 2003; and 30 percent of the ministry's budget allotted to predominately black rural communities. The program also mandated that all quilombo lands on federal and state lands should be recognized and titled.

However, the events of September 11, 2001, in the United States suddenly sidelined Brazilian media attention and public discussion of race in Brazil for at least one month, slowing the momentum and political payoff of Durban. Then on October 9, the State Legislative Assembly of Rio de Janeiro announced that 40 percent of admission slots in state universities would be reserved for blacks and browns.[51] Unlike the federal actions, the Rio action was legislative and therefore not subject to administrative modification or the likelihood of change or repeal with a new administration. Earlier that year, the same Rio de Janeiro state government body had reserved 50 percent of its university slots for public-school graduates. Also, at about the same time, a judge ruled in favor of a case brought forth by the Public Ministry, stipulating that public universities in the state of Minas Gerais should constitutionally be required to reserve 50 percent of its slots for students from public schools.

In December, the Ministry of Justice and the Federal Supreme Court followed suit, the former mandating that at least 20 percent of its high-level staff and consultants, as well as the staff of subcontractors, be black, and the latter that 20 percent of the employees of subcontracting firms be negro.[52] The president also announced a program of affirmative action in the virtually all-white Foreign Diplomacy School (Instituto Rio Branco), providing twenty scholarships annually for black students.[53] As Benedita da Silva had announced in Durban on March 24, 2002, the minister of labor directed that 20 percent of the budget of the Worker Assistance Financing (FAT) be directed to professional training for negro workers, particularly black women. The federal actions spawned a series of related actions in early 2002 by local governments, including the states of Matto Grosso do Sul and Santa Catarina, the municipalities of Jundiaí and Uberlandia, and universities in several Brazilian states.[54] Other localities instituted actions specifically for indigenous peoples. Most notably, the Federal Senate approved a bill by Senator Sebastião Rocha that supplanted the Sarney bill and would mandate a 20-percent quota for all public employment, all public and private universities, and federal subcontractors, for a period of fifty years.[55]

In May 2002, President Cardoso signed the National Program for Affirmative Action, which was presented to him by seven of his twenty-one Ministers. It proposed federal administrative mechanisms to promote disadvantaged populations but did not set any quotas or goals. The administration's candidate for president, Health Minister José Serra, did not sign the plan, but promised to "create mechanisms that increase the participation of *negros* in businesses that transact with the federal government," without mentioning quotas or anything similar.[56] However, Serra eventually lost in the general elections in November to Luiz Inácio "Lula" da Silva of the Worker's Party (Partido dos Trabalhadores or PT). Near the end of Cardoso's term, his administration initiated the Diversity in the University program with the assistance of the InterAmerican Development Bank. That program seeks to create educational materials on diversity for secondary schools, establish a clearinghouse for sharing experiences and providing information on building college student diversity, and fund college-prep courses for mostly nonwhite students.

LULA'S FIRST YEAR

Lula began his presidency in January 2003. Lula's election signalled further progress in increasing black representation. Soon after his election, he chose three blacks or mixed-race persons to head ministries, an unprecedented act in Brazilian history. These included Gilberto Gil, a prominent singer and composer of Brazilian popular music, to head the Ministry of Culture; Benedita da Silva, a former senator and governor from Rio de Janeiro, to be the minister for social assistance and promotion; and Marina Silva, a mixed-race environmentalist and former senator from the Amazon region, to be the minister of the environment. He later created a secretariat for Promoting Policies of Racial Inclusion

(SEPPIR) and installed a black woman, Matilde Ribeiro, in that position. The Senate elected Paulo Paim as their first vice president shortly after Lula's inauguration. Most importantly, President Lula nominated forty-eight-year-old Joaquim Benedito Barbosa Gomes to the Brazilian Supreme Court, thus becoming the first black person in that position in the 174 years of that court. While the ministerial positions are temporary positions at the disposition of the president himself, the position of Supreme Court minister is particularly important because of its influence, and the term of office is guaranteed until the holder is seventy years old.

Since Lula's election, affirmative action seems to be gaining a hold in Brazilian policy circles. Affirmative action continued to be extended to other local governments and universities, including the National University of Brasília. Through SEPPIR the current administration has laid out extensive plans for "promoting racial equality." It supports racial quotas and other forms of affirmative action, including the continuation of the Itamaraty fellowships and the diversity in the university program, and Lula signed into law a plan that introduces African culture and history into the curriculum for elementary and secondary schools. Most importantly, he made the "overcoming of racial inequalities" a priority in his multiyear government plan. The black movement–federal government dialogue is at unprecedented levels. The future of real government action in combating racism will surely depend on the political will of the new PT administration and the black movement's ability to negotiate and influence the new government. Most of Brazil's black-movement leadership seems to be from the Worker's Party, as is the leadership of most social-movement organizations, and Lula apparently recognizes this.

By 2003, affirmative action began to suffer a backlash. In particular, the Federation of Private Schools has brought legal action challenging the constitutionality of Rio de Janeiro state laws that mandate quotas requiring 40 percent of admits to state universities be reserved for blacks or browns and 45 percent for public secondary-school graduates.[57] There have also been more than 100 writs seeking injunctive relief (*mandatos de segurança*) by white students demanding admission because of discrimination and displacement by the quotas. The Brazilian media—which had earlier supported the new racial quotas—and much of the white middle class now seem solidly positioned against the quotas. Meanwhile, the Rio de Janeiro state's public prosecution and black-movement attorneys have begun to prepare defenses of the state laws. This case is expected to reach the Brazilian Supreme Court in the coming months. However, in 2003 the Rio state legislature considerably reduced the number of admission slots reserved for quota students. The new quotas became 20 percent for public school students, 5 percent for the physically disabled, and the racial quota became 20 percent for blacks (negros) as opposed to the previous 40 percent for blacks and browns (negros and pardos).

CONCLUSIONS

Brazilians' belief in racial democracy has become a thing of the past. Through its perseverance over the last twenty years during a period of democratization, the black movement had already turned public opinion around in Brazil. There is now widespread recognition of racism by Brazilian society, and the Brazilian government has begun to search for ways to deal with racism. After several fits and starts, Brazil surprisingly ushered in an era of affirmative action. Aside from the real change in the position of blacks that it is likely to create, Brazil's affirmative action has forced the issue of race on the national social agenda. Whether or not they agree with the racial quota systems that have been adopted so far, Brazilian policy makers and public opinion no longer ignore Brazil's racial hierarchy.

The end of the widespread belief in racial democracy was not revolutionary in the same sense as the end of legal segregation in the United States or apartheid in South Africa. After all, racial democracy was an ideology of nonracialism and thus, for many, essentially antiracist. As sociologist Howard Winant (2001) claims, Brazil had anticipated by several decades the transition to nonracialism that the United States and South Africa followed. However, the Brazilian elite under racial democracy had been silent or ambivalent when it came to issues of race, considering it a nonissue and discussion of it as un-Brazilian and racist. The end of racial democracy unveiled a facade that had long blinded Brazilians to deep-seated racism in their society. It also meant a coming to terms with racial exclusion as a central feature of Brazil's notorious social inequality. For the first time, Brazilian elites, academics, media, and policy makers began openly discussing racism and racial inequality. In comparative perspective, while some in the United States and South Africa came to believe that they had recently transcended race and racism through their new experiences of color-blind societies, the irony was that Brazil had done the same decades ago but without the racial reforms instituted by those two countries.

Unlike in the United States and South Africa, Brazil's black-movement victories were not dependent on mass social movements. Attempts at mass movements in Brazil have generally been failures. Rather, the black movement has used international forums and a receptive international human-rights regime to denounce the Brazilian government for its record on racial justice despite an international reputation as a racial democracy. Black-movement NGO leaders went around their own elected representatives and sought the assistance of multilateral development institutions and international human-rights organizations. Additionally, they benefited from a common identity with black-rights leaders and organizations in the United States, with whom they shared valuable political and legal strategies. By acquiring the attention and commitment of these relatively powerful organizations the Brazilian black movement was able to secure its own place on the Brazilian government's agenda and pressure it for reform. At the same time, the Brazilian government had sought to improve its own standing in the international community and so needed to protect its reputation of being especially tolerant. Rather than risk being a new pariah of race relations, the international interests of the Brazilian government prompted steps toward real reforms at home.[58]

The international human-rights community was particularly receptive to issues of race as preparations were being made for the UN Conference in Durban. The Third World Conference on Racism in Durban in 2000 granted legitimacy to the struggles against racism "and related forms of intolerance" in Brazil, throughout Latin America and other regions of the world, where such had long been denied. While North Americans may rightfully believe that the Third World Conference was doomed by the actions of the United States, important gains were made in not-so-powerful countries like Brazil that faced international and domestic protest over racist policies and their failures to combat racial intolerance. Media attention to the issue of race during the days of the conference was unprecedented in Brazil, as were government actions soon after. The idea of developing social policy to redress racism and racial inequality seems to have become well entrenched in Brazil's political life. Thus far, the Brazilian government seems to take issues of race seriously, although the extent to which it will seek to practice appeasement rather than pursue real reform remains to be seen.

At best, racial democracy continues to be a dream for Brazil's future. Many Brazilians seem to still believe that elements of racial democracy are at the core of Brazilian values. There also seems to remain an underlying sense that human relations in Brazil, at some level, are superior to those of segregated countries, particularly Brazil's perennial referent, the United States. Notably, the longstanding value given to race mixture, which sustained ideas of racial democracy, continues to be valued by Brazilians. Unfortunately, an ideology of whitening, which derives from a yet earlier stage in which miscegenation was considered degenerate, also continues to guide popular beliefs about the worth of others. Ironically, miscegenation has also come to frame opposition to affirmative action. Like racial democracy had been in previous decades, a belief in the positive value of miscegenation remains relatively uncontested, a sort of commonsense truth that continues to represent beliefs about Brazilian race relations. Ideas about racial hybridity and syncretism continue to predominate in popular culture. The exact form that racial thinking will take in this postracial-democracy period is not yet clear.

This chapter focused mostly on political and ideological change, both essential for understanding the changing context of race in Brazil. The ultimate goal of these changes, however, should be real social change. Social exclusion, including discrimination, poverty, and violence, continue to be persistent problems in Brazilian society, disproportionately affecting blacks and mulattos. Whether or not Brazilian democratization and changing racial politics change that state of affairs remains to be seen. However, Brazil's new recognition of racism and increasingly proactive stance in combating it requires us to at least understand its nature. Much of the remainder of this book will seek to do just that, beginning with the important issue of how Brazilians classify by race.

Chapter Four

RACIAL CLASSIFICATION

> *Deputy Gerson Peres:* Your Excellency slanders the fatherland
> when you say there is racism in Brazil. Not only does it not
> exist but your excellency is at this tribunal representing the
> negro people.
> *Deputy Abdias do Nascimento:* I want to respond to Your Ex-
> cellency saying that the noble Deputy has slandered more
> than seventy million Afro-Brazilians. Your Excellency per-
> petuates your [white] privileges and impedes negros from
> equal participation at all levels of society.
> *Deputy Peres:* My origin is negro, Honorable Deputy.
> —*House of Deputies debate about international
> sanctions against The Republic of South Africa, 1985*

THE STATISTICAL representation of race relations depends on classification, and this needs to be understood on Brazilian terms. Given the extensive debate about the ambiguity in defining race in Brazil and the
implication that such data are unreliable, this chapter pays particular attention to the validity of the race variable in official statistics. I pay particular attention to differences in racial identity and ambiguity by region
and class. I demonstrate how ambiguity in Brazilian racial classification
comes from the categories themselves, by the way in which persons are
labeled in particular categories and through the use of distinct classification systems. Since data can be based on self- or other-classification, I
describe the divergences between forms of classification and discuss their
implications for data analysis, rather than taking these data for granted.
Finally, I explore the extent to which cultural characteristics, which are
often associated with black ethnicity, actually align with racial distinctions.

COMPARATIVE PERSPECTIVES ON CLASSIFICATION

In 1968, the U.S. State Department sponsored a group of about eighty
young Brazilian college students for a tour of various North American institutions. As part of their agenda, the Brazilian contingent met with two

black student leaders at Harvard University, who spoke to them about recent U.S. civil-rights gains for blacks. In the ensuing discussion, some of the Brazilian students opined that the U.S. reforms did not affect capitalism, the central problem plaguing most modern societies. Radically distinct conceptions of fundamental social problems emerged, but at one point, realizing their ideological impasse, the two North Americans noted that among the roughly eighty Brazilians, only seven or eight were black. Where was their racial democracy if blacks were so underrepresented in their group? After the meeting had finished, the Brazilians met and began to self-reflect, but rather than raising concerns about black under-derrepresentation, they were mostly bewildered about how more than one or two persons in their delegation could be considered black. Given Brazilian connotations of blackness, the individuals they referred to must have felt insulted and embarrassed.

Above all, the incident demonstrated how blackness is differently understood in Brazil than in the United States.[1] A person considered black in the United States is often not so in Brazil. Indeed, some U.S. blacks may be considered white in Brazil. Although the value given to blackness is similarly low everywhere, who gets classified as black is not uniform. Also, the notion of who is black, mixed, or white in Brazil may change greatly within Brazil depending on the classifier, the situation, or the region. The black or negro category is much more elusive in Brazil. Brazilians generally seek to escape from it if they can but occasionally, as in reasons of political expediency as the chapter epigraph demonstrates, may seek to be included in it. Stuart Hall's idea of race as the "floating signifier" is thus particularly appropriate, where meanings about race are not fixed but relational and subject to redefinition in different cultures.

Another difference between the two countries is in the use of the term "race." In Brazil, rather, the term côr ("color") is more commonly used than race. Color is often preferred because it captures the continuous aspects of Brazilian racial concepts in which groups shade into one another, whereas race in Brazilian Portuguese (raça) is mostly understood to mean "will power" or "desire." Relatedly, the idea that each individual belongs to a racial group is less common in Brazil than in the United States. However, côr captures the Brazilian equivalent of the English language term "race" and is based on a combination of physical characteristics including skin color, hair type, nose shape, and lip shape.[2] More importantly, as with race, one's color in Brazil commonly carries connotations about one's value according to the general Western racial ideology.

These differences in racial classification between Brazil and the United States derive from distinct histories, particularly from their respective decisions about how to classify mixed-race persons and whether or not to institute legal segregation. Although the so-called races could have been easily delimited when Europeans, Africans, and Indians first met, the strategies for classifying the progeny of race mixture varied widely. After slavery, mulattos in the United States were often recognized as a distinct category, and the U.S. census used a mulatto category from 1850 to 1910.[3] However, with the legalization of segregation, the more common "one-drop," or hypodescent, rule became law, thus largely overriding local traditions of recognizing mulattos.[4] Depending on the state, blacks were legally defined as those that had at least one-eighth, one-sixteenth, or one-thirty-secondth of African ancestry, thus mandating that all racially mixed persons with any significant African admixture be categorized as black. Although those laws were abolished in the 1960s, such ancestry rules continue to influence the classification of U.S. "blacks." South Africans adopted other racial-classification rules for apartheid, which combined descent and appearance criteria, although their laws created a tripartite system with a separate classification for the intermediate colored category.[5] Nonetheless, race-based laws in both the United States and South Africa required highly specified classification systems to eliminate or reduce uncertainty about who belonged in which category. Despite the end of legal segregation or apartheid, a tradition of following those rules keeps racial classification fairly rigid in those two countries. That tradition has been so internalized that North Americans and South Africans often still believe that those classification systems represent an essential or natural division of the human species, even though their definitions were constructed according to particular social and cultural contexts.

Unlike the United States and South Africa, Brazil has never had laws defining racial-group membership, at least in the postabolition period. The decision by Brazil's elites to promote whitening through miscegenation, rather than to segregate, precluded the need for formal rules of classification, and thus classification was left to individual perception. Whitening centered on a relational system with tensions that were often situationally resolved about who would be classified as white or as whiter than others, thus leading to a large amount of ambiguity. As a result, racial classification in Brazil became more complex, ambiguous, and fluid than in those countries with segregatory legal traditions.[6] According to Harris (1963), the ambiguity of Brazilian racial classification is apparent in how particular persons are classified and in the racial categories themselves.

This ambiguity is further complicated by the presence of at least three major systems of classification, as Sansone (1997) notes. These systems employ different conceptions of race, each implying different levels of ambiguity, and where they use the same terms, their conceptions vary depending on the system. Currently, three major systems of racial classification are used to characterize the vast majority of Brazilians along the white-to-black color continuum, each with a set of categories that vary in number and degree of ambiguity. The systems are (1) the census system which uses three major categories—branco, pardo, and preto—along the continuum; (2) the popular system, which employs an indeterminant number of categories, including the popular, but especially ambiguous, term moreno; and (3) the newer classification system—which I call the black-movement system, since that is where it originated, which uses only two terms, negro and branco. I describe each of these in the following sections.

RACE IN THE BRAZILIAN CENSUS

The Brazilian Institute of Geography and Statistics (IBGE) is the governmental agency responsible for designing and collecting the decennial population census. Since 1950, the IBGE has employed the categories white (*branco*), brown (*pardo*), black (*preto*), Asian (*amarelo*), and since 1991, indigenous (*indígena*). These categories are often used in the data-collection efforts of various other Brazilian institutions, although the collection of race data is mostly new outside of the census and vital statistics systems. Since Asians and indigenous peoples constitute less than 1 percent of the national population, the three categories along the black-to-white continuum account for more than 99 percent of Brazilians. While white and black refer to the ends of the continuum, the census's brown category (pardo) serves as an umbrella category for the various mixed-race terms used in popular discourse. Pardo, which translates as brown, actually refers to a grayish brown color. Although often used as a proxy for mulattos or persons with white and black admixture, it may also include other categories including caboclos, i.e., assimilated Indians or persons of mostly indigenous ancestry.

Like censuses in general, the Brazilian censuses are believed to pattern national views of race. Aside from maintaining counts of a country's population, national censuses are important because they establish and institutionalize categories that may become templates for social differentiation, thus structuring race relations and shaping popular understandings of race. State decisions about which racial categories to use and whether and how to collect such data are known to vary over time and across societies, depending on ideologies, racial practices, and state responses to social and political demands.[7] As I described in chapter 2, Brazilian racial categories in the census have remained fairly stable, except for the intermediate categories chosen in the nineteenth century.

By comparison, the U.S. census questions about race have historically changed more than those in Brazil, as exemplified by the former use of mixed-race terms, followed by their elimination.

RACE IN POPULAR DISCOURSE

The second classification system refers to racial classification in popular Brazilian discourse and is characterized by a plethora of race or color terms, although there is evidence that the number of popular terms and the ambiguity of their use may be declining.[8] A commonly cited finding is that a national survey in 1976 revealed the use of more than 100 terms in an open-ended question about color. However, the fact that 95 percent of those respondents used only 6 terms is often ignored.[9] In my reanalysis of that 1976 data, I found that 135 terms were used in the sample of 82,577 Brazilians. However, 45 of these terms, such as "purple," "dark chocolate," or "Pelé-colored," were used by only one or two persons. Eighty-six, or nearly two-thirds (64 percent), of those terms were used by only 279 of the 82,577 respondents (0.3 percent of the population). Thus, Brazilians do use a large number of racial terms, but the vast majority of them use a few terms.

Analysis of a 1995 national survey yielded similar results. In that survey, the interviewers asked respondents their color, using an open-ended format as they did in the 1976 survey. Results are shown on table 4.1. The top row shows that white was the most common category chosen, at 42 percent. However, the second most popular category was the unofficial moreno category, chosen by 32 percent of all Brazilians. Moreno also translates as brown, like the census term pardo, but is much more commonly used in everyday discourse. Pardo was employed by only 7 percent of the population. *Moreno claro* (light moreno) was used by another 6 percent of the population. Five percent of the population classified themselves as preto, the census black term, while only 3 percent of the sample classified as negro, which also translates as black. Finally, the remaining 5 percent used many terms, including 2 percent who classified as claro (light), but no other term was used by a full 1 percent of the population.[10] Thus, 97 percent of the non-Asian and non-Indian population used only seven color terms in 1995, and 54 percent chose the three official census terms.

One term is particularly noteworthy for the high frequency of its use and for its extreme ambiguity. Moreno and its variant moreno claro were used by 38 percent of the population. Ethnographers have found the term ambiguous enough to substitute for almost any other color category.[11] Its

TABLE 4.1
Frequency of respondent's preferred color label in open-ended format:
Adult population in urban Brazil, 1995

	Percentage	Cumulative Percentage
Branco	42	42
Moreno	32	74
Pardo	7	81
Moreno Claro	6	87
Preto	5	92
Negro	3	95
Claro	2	97
All Others[a]	3	100
Total	100	—

Source: Data Folha Survey of Racial Attitudes, 1995.

[a] All others less than 1 percent each including mulatto (0.8), escuro (0.7), and moreno escuro (0.5).

connotations encompass (1) light-skinned persons with dark hair, (2) persons of mixed race or parentage with generally brunet hair, and (3) black persons.[12] The widespread use of moreno is remarkable when one considers that it has never once been officially used in the more than one hundred years of Brazilian censuses. However, its centrality in the popular Brazilian classification may be due to its tie to the racial-democracy ideology because it downplays racial differences and emphasizes a common Brazilianness.[13] Gilberto Freyre proclaimed that it represented the fusion of blacks, Indians, and Europeans into a single Brazilian "metarace," making it, as Maggie (1991) describes, the Brazilian race category par excellence, because it permits discussion of race through inclusion by subverting opposition.

Harris and his collaborators (1993) found that if the moreno category were substituted for the pardo term in the census, 63 percent of residents of a small town would be classified as moreno compared to 32 percent using the pardo category. These authors went on to argue that a society's preferences should be respected by democratic states, and thus open-ended social categories should be used in Brazil's official data collecting. Given that open-ended categories for race are unlikely to be accepted by the census, they argued for a compromise in which the more popular

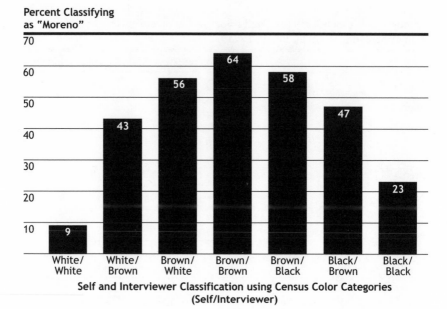

**Percent Classifying
as "Moreno"**

FIGURE 4.1 Percent classifying as "moreno" by self- and interviewer classification using census color categories: Brazil, 1995. (Data Folha Survey, 1995.)

moreno would be substituted for the official pardo category. They argued that, because the decision to use moreno in an open-ended question has the effect of including many persons that identified themselves as white in the census format, changing the "brown" term would result in a larger nonwhite and smaller white population than the census currently counts. In a reply to this article, I contended that, given its vast ambiguity, the use of moreno rather than pardo would preclude any reasonable measurement of inequality by categories that represent racial differences that are salient in social interactions. After all, this seems to be the point of continuing to collect biologically invalid, but sociologically important, race data in any modern multiracial democracy. Such a consideration would seem to outweigh the right to classify as one desires.[14]

The ambiguity of the term moreno is illustrated in figure 4.1, which uses data from the 1995 Data Folha survey of Brazil. Survey interviewers categorized respondents using the census categories and then asked them to identify their color (1) in an open-ended question, and (2) by selecting one of the five census categories. Based on the open-ended question, figure 4.1 illustrates how persons identifying as moreno are distributed along a color spectrum comprised of the combined interviewer- and self-classification categories using the two census format questions. Among those who were consistently classified as white by interviewers and themselves, only 9 percent chose moreno, but the choice of moreno was more frequent at all other points, roughly distributed along a bell-shaped curve, with the highest frequency in the middle of the color continuum. Fully 64 percent of consistently classified browns chose the term moreno in the open format compared to 23 percent of those who described themselves and were described by interviewers as black. Persons who called themselves brown in the census format were more likely to reclassify as moreno in the open-ended format than those who were classified by the interviewers as brown but identified themselves as white or black. These results reveal the ambiguity of the moreno term as Harris and his colleagues (1993) showed, but they also show that persons in the middle of the color spectrum are especially likely to choose the term.

THE BLACK-MOVEMENT SYSTEM OF RACIAL CLASSIFICATION

The black movement has long used a third classification system, which has now become widely accepted by the government, media, and academia. This system of classification uses only two terms, negro and branco. Thus, it is distinguished from the other two systems because of the prominence of the term negro, just like moreno is typical of the popular system. The term negro, like moreno, has never been used in the census. While the term was highly offensive in the past and in some situations may continue to be so, negro has now largely become a term for ethnic pride and affirmation as black-movement activists have made the term negro into a political category since at least the 1930s.[15] In contrast to moreno, which represents a Brazilian tradition of universalism through racial ambiguity, the term negro represents the polar opposite. Negro, in the modern sense is employed by those who seek to diminish ambiguity and destigmatize blackness. Black-movement activists maintain that, unlike in the United States, the official and popular Brazilian use of multiple color categories and the unofficial hierarchy in which brown is superior to black have inhibited the formation of a collective black identity around which African Brazilians may mobilize in response to shared discrimination and exclusion.[16] Thus, they claim that Brazil's informal one-drop rule holds that one drop of white blood allows one to avoid being classified as black, a tradition that they seek to revert.

The use of the black-movement system was consolidated among government officials when President Cardoso and the Ministry of Justice

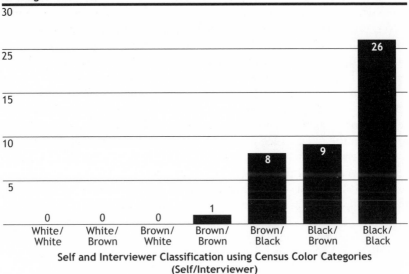

FIGURE 4.2 Percent classifying as "negro" by self- and interviewer classification using census color categories: Brazil, 1995. (Data Folha Survey, 1995.)

broke with Brazilian government tradition by beginning to use negro in 1996. At the 1996 conference called by President Cardoso, Dora Lucia Bertulio (1996, 204) stated, "My suggestion to be proposed to the IBGE is the unification of the *negro* category to encompass the *pretos* and the *pardos* in the present-day official forms." Soon after, President Cardoso and the Ministry of Justice through the National Human Rights Program endorsed Bertulio and other black-movement activists through its recommendation to "instruct the IBGE to adopt the criterion of considering *mulattos, pardos* and *pretos* as members of the *negro* population."[17] The IBGE has yet to adopt the black-movement system, although they considered proposals to in 1991 and 2000.[18] This institutionalization of the negro category infuriated some scholars of Brazil because, for the first time, the government set criterion for membership in a racial category and violated popular (emic) notions of negro by including many persons (especially pardos as defined by the census) who would never consider themselves as such. The Brazilian government had sought to dichotomize, or worse, (North) "americanize," racial classification in a society that used and even celebrated intermediate terms.

Negro in the popular system, like preto, refers only to those at the darkest end of the color continuum. Thus, while the black movement has

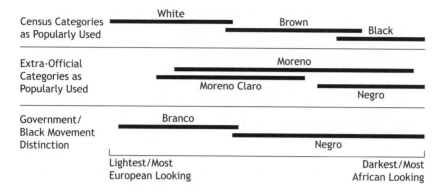

FIGURE 4.3 Use of Brazilian racial categories along the color continuum

succeeded in giving negro wide currency in the government and the media, the popular use of the term continues to be limited.[19] However, in her study of a poor community in Rio de Janeiro, Sheriff (2001) reported that the negro-white system is well understood and used among the general population when discussing issues involving racial discrimination, even though residents used relational and descriptive color terms in most social situations.

Based on the 1995 national survey, figure 4.2 shows how negro, as popularly used, is distributed along the continuum; it demonstrates that self-identification as negro is preferred mostly by those at the darkest end of the continuum. While only 1 percent of consistently classified browns preferred to call themselves negro, 26 percent of consistently classified blacks preferred this term. Those inconsistently classified as brown and black were intermediate in their use of the term. Among the three categories in which persons were classified, either by self-identification or classification by others, not one person classified as negro. Thus, despite the black-movement and government discourse that all blacks and browns are negros, the street-level usage of the term is limited to only those at the darkest end of the color spectrum.

To summarize, figure 4.3 schematically illustrates how the racial categories used in the three classification systems are distributed along a color continuum that runs from the lightest and most European-looking persons on the left to the darkest and most African-looking persons on the right. The census system is illustrated at the top, showing the three terms and the extent to which they overlap along the continuum. As I will show later, the extent of overlap between browns and blacks in the census is significantly greater than between whites and browns. The middle shows the categories most used by ordinary Brazilians. Most notably, the commonly used term moreno refers to a range of persons occupying nearly the entire color continuum. The bottom shows that the black-movement system conflates browns and blacks as defined by the census into a single negro group.

AMBIGUITY IN CLASSIFICATION
USING BRAZILIAN CENSUS CATEGORIES

One's racial classification therefore depends largely on what system of classification is used. Moreover, it depends on who makes the classification. This includes whether one classifies oneself or is classified by others. In addition, different others may make distinct classifications of the same person, and these may vary among the same individual depending on the situation. Racial classification in Brazil is thus far from being an exact science.

Racial discrimination thus depends on how others are classified in the first place. One's self-identity, which may not necessarily mirror classification by others, does not affect whether or not one will be discriminated against. Nonetheless, analysts of racial inequality often rely on race data, which is presumably based on self-responses. Sociologists rarely question such data, thus assuming race is essential or constant, much like being male or female. The current theory of race as a social construction with attendant ambiguities is widely accepted in sociology but rarely incorporated into sociological analysis. Given the ambiguity that others have found regarding race in Brazil, I believe this is an important consideration for this or any other study that uses race for analysis.

Census data on race limit analysts to preordained racial categories and official methods of data collection. Thus, my analysis of race data is limited mostly to the official classification system. Following international practice, the IBGE instructs interviewers to code race in the decennial census of Brazil according to the respondent's declaration. However, interviewers sometimes respond themselves, either because they assume they know the correct response category, they feel uncomfortable in asking about race because they think it may be rude, or they rush interviews and provide cursory responses to questions they feel are not critical.[20] Moreover, a single respondent in each household provides the racial classification of all other household members, which may or may not reflect how each individual member would self-classify. The decision about how to classify other members may be based on the respondent's knowledge of that person's self-classification or simply their perception. Thus, the Brazilian census actually uses a combination of self-reports and classifications by others in collecting race data.

When census interviewers categorize respondents themselves, they do so based on first impressions. Thus, they must rely strictly on appearance, since they do not have prior knowledge of other characteristics (e.g., descent, culture). Aside from phenotype, appearance may include status markers like dress, language, and perceived level of education.[21] Also, persons who are being categorized can also influence their categorization by intentionally conveying particular information about themselves in order to manage the impression that others have of them.[22] When respondents to the census classify other members of the household, racial categorization may also be influenced by factors that are well known to the respondents, including how the classified would self-identify.

When census respondents identify themselves, a distinct process occurs. Self-identification in a color or racial category is often a more thought-out and reflective process involving one's socialization, rather than merely a refraction of categorization by others.[23] Certainly, humans learn about the society in which they are born, how its members are categorized, and that others treat them as members of particular categories. However, identification in particular categories may also reflect descent, culture, and other characteristics transmitted during socialization. Additionally, self-identification may involve the rejection or acceptance of the symbols, traditions, and lifestyles associated with particular categories.[24] In Brazil, this includes the avoidance of nonwhite, and especially black, categories because they are often associated with negative characteristics. On the other hand, affirmative-action policies may now provide incentives for classification as nonwhite.

Given the importance of both methods of classification, I examined the extent of consistency between them with data from a 1995 national survey.[25] Table 4.2 shows how the entire sample was distributed according to self-classification and classification by interviewers. The cells along the center diagonal show persons who were consistently classified by interviewers and respondents as white (49 percent), brown (23 percent), or black (8 percent), while all others were inconsistently classified. Taking the sum of the three diagonal cells, 79 percent of the sample was consistently classified. In other words, just over one-fifth of Brazilians (21 percent) were inconsistently classified.

While the official census estimates of Brazil's racial composition suggest precision (e.g., 55.3 percent of the population is white), table 4.2 also shows that national percentage figures by color depend on whether racial classification is by interviewer, respondent, or both. If one includes all persons who self-classify or are classified as white by members of the white population, then the sample would be 61 percent white while the percent nonwhite would be only 39 percent. Conversely, if the criteria restricted whites to only those who were consistently classified as white,

TABLE 4.2
Percent distribution of sample across interviewer-classified and self-classified race cells: Adult population in urban Brazil, 1995

	Interviewer classification			
Self-classification	White	Brown	Black	Total
White	49	6	0	55
Brown	6	23	3	31
Black	0	5	8	13
Total	55	34	11	100

Source: Data Folha Survey, 1995.
Note: Numbers in rows and columns may not add to total figures because of rounding.

then the proportion white would be only 49 percent and nonwhites would constitute 51 percent. Thus, table 4.2 suggests that, depending on the method of classification used, the proportion of the population that is white could vary from 49 to 61 percent. The 1991 census figure of 55 percent suggests that the official count represents a midpoint between the two equally acceptable methods for counting whites.

Table 4.3 shows how the same sample is distributed from another perspective. Specifically, it shows the distribution of self-classified whites, browns, and blacks according to how interviewers classified them. Whites were more likely to be consistently classified than browns or blacks. Eighty-nine percent of respondents who self-identified as white were similarly classified by interviewers. Thus, there is nearly a 90-percent consistency rate for the white-nonwhite divide. This compares to only 71 percent of self-identified browns and 59 percent of blacks. Thus, interviewers and respondents are more able to agree on who is white than who is brown or black, which demonstrates that the white-nonwhite distinction is the most conceptually clear racial divide in the minds of Brazilians. These results support collapsing the brown and black categories into a single category since the brown-black distinction is clearly more ambiguous than the white-nonwhite divide.[26]

Tables 4.2 and 4.3 also demonstrate the tendency to whiten among the Brazilian population. For example, in the case of inconsistently classified browns, respondents and interviewers preferred white over black. In particular, table 4.3 shows that interviewers classified more than twice as many self-classified browns as white (20 percent) compared to black (9 percent). Also, the fact that there was a high level of agreement about classification as white, while only 58 percent agreed about who is black, further confirms the existence of whitening.[27]

TABLE 4.3
Percent distribution of persons who self-classified as white, brown, and black by interviewer classification: Adult population in urban Brazil, 1995

	Interviewer classification			
Self-classification	White	Brown	Black	Total
White	89	11	0	100
Brown	20	71	9	100
Black	2	40	58	100

Source: Data Folha Survey, 1995.

GENETIC ROULETTE?

Twine (1998) argued that African origins are commonly denied when one self-classifies in Brazil, whereas the one-drop rule in the United States generally prevents African-origin persons from denying classification as black. While mixed-race persons with a generous amount of European appearance can sometimes deny being black, this is considered deception or "passing" in the United States, while the same person may be legitimately classified as white in the Brazilian system. Thus, in terms of racial classification, miscegenation tends to whiten the population in Brazil, while in the United States the same process blackens the population. Indeed, Brazilians who call themselves white may have nonwhite ancestry. Brazilians understand this possibility, but North Americans often assume that white is a "racially pure" category.

Harris (1963) found cases of full-blooded siblings in Brazil who were classified into different racial categories, including white. While that study demonstrated that ancestry did not exclusively determine race, current data allow us to probe much deeper. In this section, I interrogate three data sources: a genetic study of ancestry among Brazilians by race; a 2000 survey asking respondents if they had black, indigenous, or European ancestors; and the 1991 census, which examines the racial classification of children by parents. Using these data, one can ask: To what extent are racial classification and ancestry correlated? Is the relation between ancestry and race more important at one or the other end of the color continuum? Does European or African ancestry have stronger effects in predicting classification toward lighter or darker categories? To what extent is racial classification random with respect to ancestry or genetic background?

Genetics researchers at the Federal University of Minas Gerais, in a study of Y chromosomes among a regionally representative sample of two hundred unrelated Brazilian males who self-identified as white, found that only 2.5 percent of the sample had lineage in the male line from sub-Saharan Africa, and no one in the sample revealed Amerindian lineage in that line.[28] However, examination of their matrilineage using mitochondrial (mt) DNA, revealed that Amerindians contributed 33 percent and Africans another 28 percent of the total mt DNA pool of white Brazilians, revealing that many Brazilians who identify as white have non-European ancestry. This finding of substantial race mixture along the maternal line is consistent with Brazil's history of miscegenation between Portuguese males and African or indigenous females. The fact that such high levels of mixture were found among whites demonstrates the irrelevance of the racial-purity concept to racial classification in Brazil.

A random survey of the state of Rio de Janeiro in 2000 supports the findings of the genetic study. The survey asked respondents if they had any ancestors who were European, African, or indigenous. The results are summarized in table 4.4. Thirty-eight percent of persons who self-classified as white claimed to have some African ancestry, while another 14 percent had mixed indigenous and European ancestry. Only 48 percent of self-identified whites claimed to have strictly European ancestry.[29] This reveals that for the many Brazilians who identify as white admitting to having nonwhite ancestors is not problematic. Although the whitening ideology may lead them to downplay these ancestors, claiming African ancestry and identifying as white is not inconsistent in the Brazilian system.[30] On the other hand, the stigma associated with being Indian, and especially African, may have prevented others from making similar declarations. Given evidence from the genetics study, the self-declaration does not seem to be far off.

These data also challenge beliefs about who classifies in the brown and black categories. Browns are classified by the black movement and government institutions as negros or Afro-Brazilians, but this may be an inaccurate label. Table 4.4 shows that 14 percent of Rio de Janeiro residents who identify as brown do not have African ancestors. States in the North like Pará and Amazonas that have had a large Indian presence with relatively few African slaves may have substantially larger proportions of browns with no African ancestors. Among those self-identifying as black, only 25 percent claim that they have only black ancestry, and another 9 percent report black and indigenous ancestry only. Therefore, 66 percent of blacks claim to have some European ancestry. This may seem surprising considering that the black census category includes only a small proportion of the population, which analysts have often assumed

TABLE 4.4
Ancestry of self-classified whites, browns, and blacks:
State of Rio de Janeiro, 2000

Breakdown by Ancestry	Self-Classified Color		
	White	Brown	Black
European only	48	6	—
African only	—	12	25
Indigenous only	—	2	—
African and European	23	34	31
Indigenous and European	14	6	—
African and indigenous	—	4	9
African, indigenous, and European	15	36	35
Total	100	100	100
Any African	38	86	100

Source: CEAP—Federal Fluminense University.

to be those with no white blood. Although these persons, like Brazilians in general, may be especially willing to affirm their European ancestry, the fact that these persons choose to classify as black instead of brown suggests that a preference for whitening is not so strong that one drop of white blood automatically makes one nonblack.

The racial classification of children vis-à-vis their parents may shed further light on the extent to which race mixture is accepted and to which whitening occurs. Figure 4.4 shows how parents in each of the three racial categories classify their children according to the 1991 census. Note that in every possible mother-father color combination, children are classified in multiple categories, further demonstrating the relatively low salience of ancestry in the racial classification of Brazilians. In six of the nine categories, most children are classified as brown. As expected, where parents are both black or both white, the vast majority of children are classified as the same color. Where the mother is white and the father is brown, 55 percent of children are classified as white.

Assuming genetic randomness, there is an even chance that the racial classification of children in figure 4.4 is either white or black. That is, if the proportions in the nine bars of figure 4.4 were added up and there

**Percent Distribution by
Color of Children**

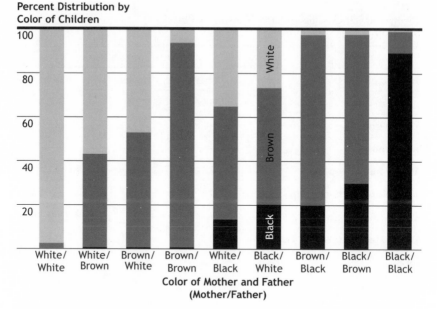

FIGURE 4.4 Color of children by color of mother and father: Brazil, 1991. (1991 Census of Brazil.)

were no bias in reporting, the proportion black and the proportion white should be the same. However, the figure suggests that Brazil's genetic roulette wheel is rigged in favor of the white category. Of course, that is due to the socially desirable process of whitening and not actual genetics.

The sum of the white bars is about 270, while the sum of the black bars is about 175. This means that parents are more than one-and-a-half times as likely to classify their children as white rather than black, although we could have expected, on the basis of biology alone, that the chances would have been equal. An examination of individual bars further illustrates this point. For example, 94 percent of the children of two brown parents are also classified as brown, but of the remaining 6 percent, virtually all are classified as white. In addition, about 10 percent of black-black combinations are classified as brown and 2 percent as white, while only 2 percent of white-white combinations are classified as brown and none as black. Thus, the clear tendency for whitening the racial classification of children would, by itself, eventually lead to the elimination of blacks after several generations. Figure 4.4 also suggests that the desire to whiten is stronger for women than for men. The greater tendency to whiten children when the mother is lighter than the father may derive from women's more limited economic-mobility prospects and thus their greater reliance on whitening to enhance the possibilities for their children by presumably giving them a more favorable racial identity.[31]

SOCIAL EFFECTS ON RACIAL CLASSIFICATION

The previous sections revealed a significant level of ambiguity and a tendency toward whitening in Brazilian racial classification. But is ambiguity and whitening merely random, or can we find patterns in the degree to which they occur? In particular, is ambiguity and whitening more likely to be found in some sectors of the Brazilian population than in others? The literature on Brazilian racial classification suggests class or social status may affect the extent to which Brazilians whiten, but it is nearly silent in the case of other variables like region and gender. With the 1995 Data Folha survey, I examined the effects of education, racial composition (a proxy for region), gender, and age on racial classification. There is little or no work on difference by region or racial composition since empirical studies tend to concentrate on a single locale. Also, the effects of gender have been notably absent from the studies and age has only become an important variable in recent studies.

Education. Social scientists studying Brazil have paid particular attention to whether high education or other status variables lead to classification in lighter categories. Anthropological fieldwork in Brazil in the 1950s and 1960s found a tendency for race-color identity to shift toward white among wealthier and better-educated nonwhite individuals. For example, Hutchinson (1957, 46) found that relatively wealthy and well-educated persons in one town "who clearly show traces of *Negro* blood are called and treated as white with no constraint or embarrassment." However, the methods for examining the relation between class and racial classification were unclear. Persons with some black blood may normally be classified as white in Brazil, regardless of class or status. It is also possible that their observations may have been influenced by North American understandings of race. Indeed, Wagley (1952a) commented in the introduction to his edited book on racial classification that his observations and those of his colleagues were naked-eye judgments, necessarily affected by their social and cultural experiences. In an exceptionally systematic analysis, Harris (1970) showed discrepancy in racial classification among observers and comparisons of self-classification to etic or "objective" criteria. However, his analysis of status effects was less rigorous.

Other anthropological studies, though, have cast doubt on the extent to which status differences influence race. Wagley (1952a) concluded that if money actually whitened one's racial classification, its effect, if any, was mostly on the degree of nonwhite social acceptance. Based on his study of Colombia, which he contends is very similar to Brazil in terms of the dynamics of racial identity, Wade (1993) generally agreed with Wagley but more pointedly argued that whitening one's racial classification may be open to a person of mixed blood or appearance in some regions or contexts, but that a typically black person is classified as black no matter how wealthy he or she is.

If one is to test the notion that money whitens, then one has to choose a reference. Whitening in relation to what? Analysts may give empirical status to that idea, but what they really mean by it is not always clear or sensible. Certainly, the reference cannot be to U.S. conceptions of whiteness. Also, since there is no objective way to classify race, then one cannot whiten in relation to what one's race "is." In my mind, this leaves three possible interpretations that make any real sense. First, money whitens an individual's identification or classification by others as they become more socially mobile; second, a person is classified in lighter categories in situations or contexts when he or she appears wealthier; and finally, money whitens a person in relation to how one identifies oneself or vice versa. All of these seem valid but there is little empirical evidence that money whitens, using any of these methods.

Mostly for reasons of data availability, I chose the third method. In particular, I used the 1995 survey with interviewer- and self-classification variables to show how a status variable like education affects the probability of being classified in a lighter category than one self-identifies. That method also allowed me to model statistically not only the effect of education but also the simultaneous effects of region, gender, and age. I provided details about the methodology in an earlier article.[32] Specifically, table 4.5 shows the predicted probabilities that white, brown, or black respondents will be consistently classified by interviewees according to education and sex and depending on the racial composition of the urban area in which they reside. I present these probabilities for two urban areas that are approximately 25 percent and 75 percent white, respectively; this roughly represents the respective racial compositions of the states of Bahia and São Paulo.

Table 4.5 shows that ambiguity is lowest for persons with high education and at the light end of the color spectrum. In other words, highly educated persons who self-classify as white tend to be more consistently classified by interviewers and themselves than persons with low levels of education. Among the highly educated, 93 (males) or 94 (females) percent of self-classified whites are consistently classified as such in Bahia; 98 per-

TABLE 4.5
Probability of being similarly classified by interviewers for self-classified whites, browns, and blacks by education and region

| | Self-classification | | | | | |
| | White | | Brown | | Black | |
	Male	Female	Male	Female	Male	Female
Low education						
Bahia[a]	65	69	76	79	52	42
São Paulo[b]	87	88	65	69	60	50
High education						
Bahia	93	94	69	72	62	22
São Paulo	98	98	56	58	70	28

Source: Simulation based on 1995 Data Folha Survey of Brazil, as shown in Telles 2002.
[a]Urban areas that are about 25% white.
[b]Urban areas that are about 75% white.

cent of self-identified white Paulistas with high education, both male and female, are consistently classified as white. By contrast, self-classified white males and females of low education are consistently classified accordingly about 87 and 88 percent of the time in São Paulo and only 65 and 69 percent of the time in Bahia. On the other end of the color continuum, low-educated blacks are more likely than their high educated counterparts to be consistently classified. Specifically, interviewers are especially likely to whiten the racial classification of highly educated persons who identify themselves as black.[33] This is especially true for females.

The overall effects of whitening by education are not as great as previously suggested and are sometimes mixed. The claim that poor whites are black and wealthy blacks are whites is a gross misrepresentation of the effect of status on race. I am sure this is not surprising to most Brazilians, but many North Americans seem to have accepted that idea based on Carl Degler's account. Pelé, for example, is one of Brazil's wealthiest individuals and certainly one of its most prestigious. However, he is often considered black, or perhaps mulatto, but never white. Moreover, although being black was compatible with the fame accorded by his sports superhero status, Pelé's blackness is not always overlooked by Brazilians. For example, when he became the minister of sports in 1995,[34] I heard several racist jokes by Brazilians, attesting to the fact that they saw a high political position as being inappropriate for a black person, even

TABLE 4.6
Relative chances of self-identifying as moreno or negro compared to census categories and moreno compared to negro by education, gender, and age: Adult population in urban Brazil, 1995

| | Compared to census categories | | |
Characteristics compared	Moreno	Negro	Negro vs. moreno
Education			
Medium vs. low	0.65	2.04	3.29
High vs. low	0.40	2.90	8.26
High vs. medium	0.62	1.45	2.51
Female vs. male	1.06	1.44	1.37
Age			
20 vs. 40 year olds	1.06	1.41	1.31
40 vs. 60 year olds	1.13	1.99	1.72

Source: Simulation based on 1995 Data Folha Survey of Brazil. Bailey and Telles, unpublished.

one as prestigious as Pelé. A similar reaction occurred when he dated blonde superstar Xuxa in 1983. Although money may whiten in some cases, its effects are limited to persons with phenotypes in an ambiguous zone that separates persons who are clearly white from those that are clearly nonwhite.

The choice of moreno for persons on the dark end of the racial continuum may be a form of whitening. The ambiguity with the term moreno allows persons who might not have the option of calling themselves white to escape the more stigmatized nonwhite categories. This may be especially true for more highly educated persons, if we are to believe the money whitening idea. On the other hand, the term negro, which activists prescribe, seems to resonate particularly well with middle-class blacks.[35]

Based on the open-ended question about color in the 1995 Data Folha survey, table 4.6 presents the relative propensities of classifying as moreno compared to negro for select characteristics. These results assume that the value of all other variables are held constant and are based on a statistical simulation, which I presented in a paper with Stan Bailey.[36] The first column of table 4.6 shows that Brazilians with a high level of education are 40 percent as likely as those with a low level of education to describe themselves as moreno. Conversely, persons with a low education are about two-and-a-half times more likely than those with a high level of education to choose moreno. Regarding the choice of negro, the second column shows that respondents with high levels of education are almost three times (2.90) as likely as those with low levels of education; and those with medium levels of education are about twice (2.04) as likely as a person with a low level of education to choose negro over a census racial term. Finally, the last column shows that highly educated persons are more than eight times (8.26) as likely as persons with low levels of education to choose negro rather than moreno. In sum, the term moreno is especially likely to be chosen by less-educated persons; while negro is more likely to be chosen by the highly educated. In this case, money darkens.

Gender. The nature of racial classification in Brazil appears to be influenced by gender, especially regarding the use of the black category. Given the especially negative connotation of the black category and greater cordiality afforded to women, Brazilians may seek to avoid offending dark-skinned women of high status by labeling them as black. To refer to another person as preto, the term for black in the census, is considered offensive, but to refer to a woman as preta is especially demeaning and nearly inconceivable in the case of a high-status woman. The findings from table 4.5 bear this out. Women and men are more or less equal in terms of the consistency with which they are classified as white and brown but are less consistently classified in the black category. Interviewers are less likely than respondents to classify women in the black category; this is especially true for highly educated women. For example, highly educated women who self-classify as black in São Paulo are similarly classified by interviewers only 28 percent of the time and only 22 percent of the time in Bahia; the comparable figures are, respectively, 70 and 62 percent for their male counterparts. This suggests a high level of avoidance of the black (preto) category for interviewers and respondents in terms of classifying women. The gender differences for choosing moreno or negro, on the other hand, are relatively slight, as table 4.6 shows.

Region. Studies of racial classification in Brazil have been almost exclusively based on small samples of towns in the predominately nonwhite North and Northeast, but my experience has been that the nature of race varies across the Brazilian subcontinent. In particular, the North and Northeast may be particularly subject to ambiguity in racial classification because of relatively extensive miscegenation over several centuries. In contrast, places that now have large proportions of whites tend to have been the destinations of massive European immigration from 1880 to 1930. The incipient ethnic communities that emerged in these places have made ethnicity an important division in these regions, where immigrants of various nationalities settled and whites mixed less with nonwhites because of their demographic predominance. I expect that in such a context, the African-origin population would be more likely to be delimited as a group and thus have more salient racial identities than in traditional Brazilian locales where they are a numerical majority. Therefore, it seems reasonable to hypothesize that residents of mostly nonwhite places, compared to their compatriots in mostly white areas, would be more likely to have physical characteristics nearer to the ambiguous boundaries separating racial categories, thus leading to greater racial ambiguity in places with more nonwhites.

The anthropological literature also claims that race is relational, and thus we might expect the racial composition of local communities to affect classification. Wade (1993) notes that in Colombia, where black communities "appear to be more common than in Brazil," whitening refers to the acceptance of blacks in nonblack society, which may occur through distancing oneself from black communities, culture, and networks, including migrating out of predominately black regions and into primarily white ones. According to Wade, such individuals may downplay their blackness rather than racially reclassify, while ambiguous-looking persons might actually reclassify. According to this argument, race might be particularly inconsistent in predominately white communities.

Table 4.5 reveals that racial classification is more consistent for the white and black categories in mostly white places like São Paulo compared to mostly nonwhite places like Bahia. For example, among males with low levels of education, respondents and interviewers agree on who is white 87 percent of the time in São Paulo but only 65 percent of the time in Bahia. On the other hand, classification as brown is more consistent in places like Bahia, as would be expected since brown is the catch-all category for persons who do not fit into the white or black category. Thus, the classic studies of racial classification in Brazil seem to have overstated ambiguity and the effects of status, largely because they were based on studies of predominately nonwhite locales. By contrast, studies of racial classification in the southern half of Brazil were rare, perhaps because classification was considered less problematic there.[37]

Age. Although I do not show the results, I also found differences by age.[38] Younger cohorts are especially likely to identify in black and white categories and disregard the brown category, although interviewers often categorized them as brown. Additionally, I found that the term negro is more likely to be used by younger persons, while age differences in classifying as moreno are insignificant. The odds of a twenty-year-old respondent choosing negro compared to the census categories are twice (1.99) as large as the odds that a sixty-year-old will do so. This supports previous findings that the term is especially popular among young persons.[39] Similarly, twenty-year-olds are 72 percent more likely (1.72) than sixty-year-olds to classify as negro rather than moreno. Thus, it seems that young persons are socialized to identify increasingly in black and white categories, upholding 2000 census evidence that the popular Brazilian racial classification system is becoming increasingly bipolar. These results may reflect the effects of the black movement and cultural globalization, where the growing influence of African diasporic music and movie industries are dominated by societies where racial classification is less ambiguous.[40]

RACIAL CLASSIFICATION AND CULTURE

Scholarly debate questions whether ethnicity (or race) is defined mostly by the "cultural stuff" that defines each group or by the boundaries that groups draw to delimit themselves from others.[41] In societies where racist ideologies are present, race sets people apart through categorization based mostly on physical appearance or ancestry, but the U.S. experience suggests that racial distinctions also align with cultural differences, such as language, cuisine, religion, and dress. I have heard similar assumptions made about Brazil. Specifically, they assume that there is an Afro-Brazilian culture and therefore black people must practice it while white people do not.

Van den Berge (1977) argued that Brazilian ties to African culture have remained stronger than in the United States because (1) slaves in Brazil were more likely to have been African natives shortly before abolition; (2) regional or tribal identities could be better maintained in Brazil because slaves of the same or similar language were less likely to be split up; and (3) Brazilians, and the Portuguese colonists before them, had far greater trade and cultural ties to Africa than the English or the North Americans. Mattory (1999) shows continuing diasporic exchanges between Afro-Brazilians and the Yoruba of West Africa throughout the nineteenth century. Also, as discussed in chapter 2, African culture in Brazil has also been maintained in much of the twentieth century because of state actions. Relatedly, African culture has been appropriated and acknowledged as a central element in national Brazilian culture. Whites practice it as well. By contrast, African cultural influences in the U.S. are generally ignored or marginalized to the African American community.[42]

One of the strongest legacies of Africa in Brazil is African-based religions. Even though most Brazilians of all colors are Catholic, many also participate in Afro-Brazilian religion. It would seem that the existence of such religions would be a strong indicator of black identity in Brazil. However, Prandi (1995) noted that whites often outnumber blacks and mulattos in *umbanda* rituals in the mostly white states of São Paulo and those to its south, although there is disagreement about whether umbanda is primarily "African." Although Bastide (1965) referred to umbanda, *candomblé,* and other religions as African, Renato Ortiz (1978), found that umbanda, in contrast to candomblé, is a truly "Brazilian national religion." Specifically, he argued that it is the product of the incorporation of African elements into the tenants of a white-dominated religion. Brown (1994) noted that the Africanness of umbanda is diluted because the majority of its leaders are mulattos and middle-class whites, and all the offensive (to whites) black personages found in traditional African religions are eliminated. Candomblé is considered more African and close to its West African Yoruba origins. However, as João Reis (2002) noted, practitioners of candomblé have long recruited whites and mixed-race persons as their protectors against the constant repression by Bahian authorities.

Table 4.7 shows the extent to which whites, browns, and blacks participate in African-based religions. The top panel provides national participation rates but divides these religions by umbanda and candomblé. The bottom panel shows participation rates in both umbanda and candomblé for major metropolitan areas since regional differences may be large. Note that these figures are likely to have underestimated the proportion of persons who actually participate in these religions, because respondents to the census could only identify one religion. Given the stigma attached to these religions and their questionable status as religions for some, respondents of all colors may have been likely to choose Catholic or Protestant instead of an Afro-Brazilian religion. However, the relative proportion by race reveals some important differences, and I cannot see any reason why there would be racial differences in the propensity to declare an Afro-Brazilian religion.

The top panel shows that, nationally, white and brown participation in umbanda and candomblé is similar. The primary cleavage is between blacks and nonblacks. Blacks are twice as likely as nonblacks to participate in umbanda and three to four times as likely to participate in candomblé. The bottom panel demonstrates that brown and white participation rates are also similar across metropolitan areas except in Rio de Janeiro and Porto Alegre, where browns are intermediate to whites and blacks and where participation by all groups is greatest. The bottom row shows that, nationally, whites participate more than browns in Afro-Brazilian religion, but this appears to reflect the regional concentration of whites in the southern half of Brazil, where rates of practicing Afro-Brazilian religions are greater than in the northern half.

Besides religion, other cultural practices are often associated with Afro-Brazilians and presumably differentiate Brazilian cultural practices

TABLE 4.7
Participation in African-based religions of Brazilians by color

	Whites	Browns	Blacks
Nationally by religion[1]			
Umbanda	0.8	0.8	1.7
Candomblé	0.3	0.4	1.3
By metropolitan area[2]			
São Paulo	0.7	0.8	1.7
Rio de Janeiro	2.7	3.4	4.8
Belo Horizonte	0.4	0.5	0.9
Salvador	0.2	0.2	0.4
Recife	0.4	0.5	1.0
Fortaleza	0.2	0.2	0.4
Porto Alegre	1.8	5.4	8.1
Curitiba	0.3	0.5	1.0
Belem	0.3	0.3	0.8
Brasilia	0.9	0.9	2.1
National	0.6	0.4	1.6

[1]Source: Reginaldo Prandi. 1995, "Raça e religião," Novos Estudos 42 (July).
[2]Source: 1980 Census.

by color. Table 4.8 presents the results of questions from the 2000 survey of the state of Rio de Janeiro about the extent to which different cultural forms are important in the lives of whites, browns, and blacks. Although there were questions about nearly thirty cultural practices, I only present the results for those practices where there appeared to be variation by race.[43]

As I found for Afro-Brazilian religions, the findings in the first three columns of table 4.8 show that the most salient racial distinctions based on self-classification are between blacks and nonblacks. Self-identified blacks are significantly more likely than whites and browns to view *capoeira* (a form of martial arts practiced by slaves), funk, rap, samba (popular music associated with Carnaval), a belief in *orixás* (Yoruban deities), and wearing white clothes on Friday as important in their lives. Browns are generally intermediate to whites and blacks but are generally more like whites.

TABLE 4.8
Percent of persons identifying following cultural forms as important:
State of Rio de Janeiro, 2000

Cultural forms	Self-identified			Interviewer-classified		
	Whites	Browns	Blacks	Whites	Browns	Blacks
Capoeira	33	37	45	34	41	38
Funk	9	9	16	7	13	13
Rap	12	12	23	11	15	20
Samba	54	56	64	53	59	63
Throw offerings into sea for *Iemanjá*	15	17	24	16	16	26
Consult *búzios*	8	12	16	8	11	20
Belief in *orixás*	16	20	25	15	17	29
Wear white clothes on Friday	8	11	14	8	9	17
N	504	364	172	519	462	180

Source: CEAP/UFF survey, 2000.

I am concerned that such cultural attributes may help determine how one racially classifies rather than vice-versa. The last three columns thus show results when color is based on interviewer categorization. The finding that the proportion of self-identified blacks who identify with *capoeira* and rap is greater than for interviewer-identified blacks suggests that black culture may affect black self-classification, but these findings are not consistent. Findings for *orixás, búzios* (a medium for communicating with the *orixás*), and white clothes on Friday (worn to pay homage to the *orixás*) run in the opposite direction, which would reject this hypothesis. Based on this preliminary analysis, then, a separate black ethnicity in Brazil, to the extent that such indicators define ethnicity, is therefore limited to the darkest proportion of the population. In this sense, blacks and browns appear to be quite different.

Conclusions

In the case of racial classification, there is no clear "color line" in Brazil but a large grey or brown area. Racial-classification laws never existed in Brazil, so there are not rigid rules for classification as in the United States and South Africa. In Brazil, race is ambiguous because there are several classification systems, there are several categories along the white-black continuum, and they are affected by class and gender. The racial labeling of others also depends on the social situation, the relation of the classified to others and regional and historic specificities. Also, individuals in Brazil generally have a relatively weak sense of belonging to a racial group, compared to their gender and class identities and the racial identities of North Americans. Although Brazilian racial categories and labeling by others are often ambiguous and racial identity is often weak, the racial categories themselves are differentially valued. For some Brazilians, this implies the ability to escape into more positively valued categories, although for most Brazilians, their racial classification is unambiguous.

Miscegenation has been central to Brazilian concepts of race. First of all, Brazilian miscegenation has affected the large majority of the Brazilian population. Even much of the white population has African or Indian blood, while miscegenation has been limited to the roughly 12 percent of the U.S. population that is called "black." Concepts of racial purity for whites, like those in the United States, are virtually absent in Brazil. Also, unlike the United States, where segregation separated the population into black and white, Brazil has celebrated middle categories and avoided legislating rules for racial classification. An ideology of racial democracy and cordiality uses ambiguity and middle categories to avoid the placement of others in particularly stigmatized categories. The term moreno is particularly exemplary.

However, Brazil's traditional system of classification is being challenged as the black social movement gains greater legitimacy and calls for a system that excludes the middle categories increase, forcing the vast majority of Brazilians (Asians and Indians excepted) to identify as either black or white. Despite their absence from the census, the terms moreno and negro are central to the racial terminology and racial perspectives of Brazilians. These two terms increasingly capture a tension between a traditional Brazil of racial ambiguity with its presumed inclusion of nonwhites and a modern Brazil characterized by widely recognized racial exclusion and growing racial affirmation and resistance. The term moreno is emblematic of the fluidity of the traditional Brazilian system, while negro seeks to rescue pride in a black identity, which has long been stigmatized.

Despite the closer ties to African culture found in Brazil as compared to the United States, there is a greater sense of a separate racial identity from whites for black North Americans than for Afro-Brazilians. Religion is an indicator of this. While religion in Brazil can be more directly linked to Africa, religious practice is largely separate by race in the United States, unlike in Brazil. In the United States, unlike in Brazil, black identity and black-white boundaries are based largely on cultural distinctives, such as language and segregated Christian churches. This suggests that the Brazilian nation was especially successful at imposing cultural uniformity across racial categories. However, little cultural separation, weaker racial consciousness, or ambiguous racial identities do not mean that racial boundaries are unimportant. Frederick Barth and his followers have argued that it is the social construction of boundaries that is more important than any cultural content that may define them. This chapter has shown that Brazilians clearly make racial or color distinctions that are not delimited by the cultural content of those in particular racial categories. The following chapters will show that these racial distinctions are used to create social hierarchies, further strengthening the racial boundaries.

Chapter Five

RACIAL INEQUALITY
AND DEVELOPMENT

SCHOLARS have clearly established the existence of racial inequality in Brazil, but systematic and comparative evidence is scattered. In this chapter, I compare Brazil's racial inequality to that in the United States and South Africa, focusing on their income structures and the distribution of whites and nonwhites by income. I then establish a base line of reliable indicators of racial inequality along several socioeconomic-status variables. Inasmuch as I can, I also explore racial inequalities between browns and blacks, as well as by gender. Finally, I examine the relation of Brazil's racial inequalities to its recent development using two strategies. First, I investigate changing levels of racial inequality from 1960 to 1999; and then, I examine the relation between occupational inequality and industrialization across the seventy-three largest urban areas in Brazil.

INCOME INEQUALITY: A COMPARATIVE PERSPECTIVE

Brazil is renowned for being the world champion in overall income inequality. The World Bank's 2000 report shows Brazil as having the third-highest Gini index of income inequality among 150 countries, preceded only by the small countries of Swaziland and Sierra Leone. South Africa is also near the top, in fourth place. In Brazil, the average income of the highest-earning 10 percent is twenty-eight times the average income of the bottom 40 percent.[1] For many analysts and for its elite, Brazil's severe inequalities are at the root of nearly all of Brazil's major social problems, including its poverty, poor health and education systems, high rates of crime, and the lack of social and political integration of the majority of the population.[2]

As long as whites, browns, and blacks are unevenly distributed along the income structure, racial inequality exists. However, both the shape of that structure and the relative position of the population by race along it determine overall levels of racial inequality. In other words, the fact that black and brown men earn 40 to 50 percent of white men in Brazil, while black men earn 75 percent of white men in the United States, could

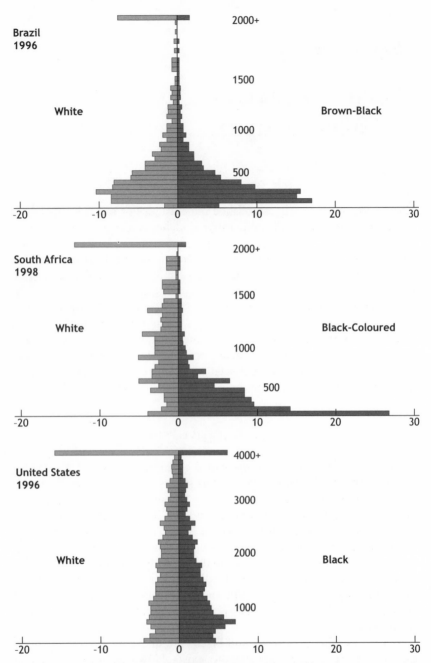

FIGURE 5.1 Percent distribution of the population by monthly income (in U.S. dollars) and race for Brazil, South Africa, and the United States. (Brazil, 1996 figure: 1996 Brazilian National Household Survey [PNAD]; South Africa, 1998 figure: 1998 Survey of Socioeconomic Opportunity and Achievement; United States, 1996 figure: 1996 Current Population Survey.)

simply reflect Brazil's far greater income inequality. In comparative terms, the top 10 percent of Brazilians earn incomes worth 52 percent of the total income of all Brazilians, while South Africa has the second most unequal structure among large countries, in which the top 10 percent of South African earners control 47 percent of the country's total income. The country with the greatest inequality among the so-called industrialized nations is the United States, with a comparable figure of 25 percent of total income for the top 10 percent of earners.

Figure 5.1 portrays the dual effect of income structure and the distribution of whites and nonwhites along that structure for Brazil, South Africa, and the United States. It portrays the shape of these three nations' income pyramids, using data from recent censuses or surveys for all persons with income.[3] For Brazil and South Africa, the steps on the pyramids are calculated in categories of approximately $50 (U.S.) each, and for the United States, in increments of roughly $100, due to the greater incomes generally found in that country. As a rough guide, the income or socioeconomic shape of a society with a large middle class should be larger in the middle rungs, while a society with large income inequalities or a large proportion of poor people tend to look like a wide-based pyramid. The wide base of the income structures of Brazil and South Africa illustrate the existence of many poor persons. This high rate of poverty, coupled with a sizable number of persons in the top rung, reflects their status as the two most unequal large countries in the world. A more rectangular shape for the United States shows that income is more evenly distributed there than in Brazil and South Africa.

The right half of the pyramids, with darker bars, represents the distribution of nonwhites in the three countries while the left side represents the income distribution for whites. The pyramids are not symmetrical because whites and nonwhites are not evenly distributed by income. Thus, the extent of the asymmetry reveals the extent to which there is racial inequality. In all three countries, whites tend to be concentrated near the top and blacks near the bottom, although the differences in racial distribution along the pyramids vary. The figure reveals that South Africa is clearly the most racially unequal of the three societies. Blacks and coloreds are concentrated in the bottom income rungs, where there are few whites. For example, about 27 percent of nonwhite South Africans are in the lowest income bracket compared to only 4 percent of their white co-nationals. Seventy-six percent of black and colored South Africans earn under $300 per month, roughly the poverty rate, compared to 15 percent of white South Africans. This is not surprising given that country's recent emergence from apartheid, which legally mandated a racial hierarchy.

According to figure 5.1, Brazil's racial inequality appears to be intermediate to the United States and South Africa. Browns and blacks are concentrated in the lowest rungs, as they are in South Africa, but many more whites are also at the lowest income levels in Brazil. Persons earning less than $200 (those in the bottom four rungs) represent the lowest-earning 40 percent of Brazilians with at least some income. This group includes 52 percent of nonwhites but only 29 percent of whites. Unlike South Africa, where the poor are almost exclusively nonwhite, a significant proportion of the Brazilian poor is white, as it is among the North American poor.

The difference between Brazil and the United States tends to be at the top end. Racial inequality in Brazil derives mostly from the near absence of nonwhites in the middle class and above, rather than from the absence of whites among the poor. For example, the highest income bracket shown for Brazil ($2,000 or more) consists of 7.5 percent of the national white population but only 1.5 percent of nonwhites. Thus, whites are about five times as likely as nonwhites to be in the top income bracket in Brazil. By comparison, whites in the United States are only twice as likely as blacks to be in the top end of the income structure. On the other hand, white South Africans are about ten times as likely as blacks and coloreds to be in the highest income bracket.

The highest income bracket in figure 5.1 also includes persons making much more than $2,000. The numbers of income categories could have been extended higher, but I closed this interval because the numbers in each bracket would become nearly imperceptible in the figure, especially for nonwhites. The very top of the income distribution—which includes Brazil's business and media executives, judges, doctors, and other high-level professionals—is almost all white. For example, according to the 1996 PNAD, whites outnumbered nonwhites as judges by more than ten to one. Johnson (1996) estimated that 29 "black" representatives served in the federal Congress between 1988 and 1995, out of a total of more than 2,000 representatives. Johnson probably included those that were very obviously mulatto or black or that had declared themselves as such. Currently, at an even more prestigious level, approximately 2 of roughly 1,060 diplomats,[4] 1 of over 100 generals,[5] and 8 of 600 members of the Federal Public Prosecution[6] are black or brown. Until Lula became president on January 1, 2003, all of Brazil's presidents and ministers in recent memory, except Pelé, were white. A 2003 survey of the 500 largest businesses in Brazil found that only 1.8 percent of managers are negro.[7] Although the nature of Brazilian classification makes it impossible to get uncontested precision about the number of nonwhites in such elite positions, there is no doubt that the proportions are very small.

RACIAL INEQUALITY AND DEVELOPMENT   111

HUMAN DEVELOPMENT

In recent years, analysts have placed increasing emphasis on social conditions as an indicator of development as opposed to the traditional reliance on a country's productivity, as the gross domestic product (GDP) measures. To this end, the United Nations and multinational banks have created the index of human development, which measures average national achievements on three basic dimensions: a long and healthy life, knowledge, and a decent standard of living. The specific data inputs include life expectancy, infant mortality, adult literacy, and school enrollment, which are then differentially weighted for calculating an index for all countries. In 1999, Brazil ranked 69th out of 174 countries in human development, which put it between Saudi Arabia and the Philippines.[8] The most developed countries using that index are Norway, Australia, Canada, Sweden, Belgium, and the United States.

The index of human development can also be calculated for subsectors of national populations provided the data are available. For example, I mapped Brazilian states indicating level of human development in chapter 1. I showed that regional differences in racial composition correlated with human development. More directly, Santa Anna and Paixão (1997) calculated the human development index for whites and nonwhites separately at the national level. Their results, presented in table 5.1, revealed that the black and brown Brazilian population by itself would score 0.663, placing it between Guatemala and Honduras at 108th on the world scale. The white population, if it constituted a separate country, would score 0.784 and rank 43rd, alongside Costa Rica, the Bahamas, and Kuwait. The components used to compute the human development index are also shown in table 5.1 for all of Brazil and for whites and

TABLE 5.1
Index of human development (IHD) and select components by race:
Brazil, 1996/1997

	Human development index	Life expectancy at birth (1997)	Infant mortality/ 1000 (1996)	Adult literacy rate (1997)	School enrollment ratio (1997)
Brazil	0.773	67	48	85	78
Whites	0.784	70	37	92	82
Nonwhite	0.663	64	62	72	73

Source: Santa Anna 2001.

nonwhites separately. Life expectancy for whites is six years greater than for nonwhites, and infant mortality is 40 percent less. Adult literacy for whites is 28 percent greater than nonwhites, and the school enrollment ratio is about 12 percent greater.

POVERTY

While inequality refers to the overall distribution of incomes, poverty refers to the bottom of the income structure—specifically, the point under which basic human needs cannot be satisfactorily met. By drawing a line at some reasonable point along the income hierarchy, one can roughly figure the number of blacks, whites, or browns living in poverty or belonging to the middle class. However, this method is only approximate and skeptical readers might claim that this overestimates the actual amount of racial inequality, since nonwhites are especially likely to live in places where the cost of living is lower. This is an especially important issue in a country as large and regionally diverse as Brazil, where costs of living vary widely depending on supply and demand, consumption habits, levels of development, size of urban areas, and other factors.[9] These adjustments not only affect calculations of the poverty rate but have implications for the measurement of racial inequality.

By considering local costs of living and consumption habits of the poor, as well as household size and income, Lopes (1989) calculated the number of urban Brazilians that were living in poverty or indigent in 1989. He defined the poverty line as the minimum income needed to satisfy all of the basic needs of an individual, including food, access to schools, health services, water, and sanitation, and the indigency line as the minimum amount needed to satisfy only basic individual dietary needs. Lopes found that 18 percent of households with black or brown heads were indigent compared to only 6 percent of white households. Another 32 percent of black or brown households—compared to 16 percent of white households—were poor but not indigent. Based on this careful analysis, we can conclude that 50 percent of black and brown households in Brazil were poor in 1989 compared to only 22 percent of white households. Thus, urban browns and blacks were just as likely to be poor as to not be poor (50:50) in 1989. White chances were 78:22 or about three-and-a-half times as likely to be nonpoor than poor. In sum, according to the standard for calculating relative odds, that makes nonwhites three-and-a-half times as likely as whites to be poor.

UNEMPLOYMENT

Differences in unemployment are a leading indicator of racial inequality in the United States and are often considered a particularly good indicator of discrimination. Like unemployment figures for the United States, the official IBGE statistics capture only open unemployment, which refers to those people that were not employed at all in the previous week and were seeking work in the past thirty days. However, this method greatly underestimates the degree to which persons remain unproductive. Alternative unemployment figures are produced by the Brazilian Labor Unions' Department for Statistics and Socio-Economic Studies (DIESSE), based on their monthly surveys of six large metropolitan areas. These figures tend to be higher than those of the IBGE because, in addition to open unemployment, they also count hidden unemployment due to unstable work or discouragement from the job search.[10] The DIESSE statistics for unemployment and weeks unemployed are presented by INSPIR (Instituto Sindical Interamericano pela Igualdade Racial) (1999), which publishes them for negros (browns and blacks) and non-negros (whites and Asians). Thus, the negro category is the same as our nonwhite category, and the non-negro category is, for all intents and purposes, the same as white in all six metropolitan areas. In São Paulo, the Asian population is particularly large, compared to other urban areas, but the white population is roughly twenty times larger.

Table 5.2 shows that the black and brown population in all six metropolitan areas had higher levels of unemployment than whites. For example, in the São Paulo metropolitan area, 16 percent of the combined

TABLE 5.2
Race differences in unemployment for six metropolitan areas, 1998

Metropolitan area	Unemployment rate	
	Negro	Non-Negro
São Paulo	22.7	16.1
Salvador	25.7	17.7
Recife	23.0	19.1
Brasilia	20.5	17.5
Belo Horizonte	17.8	13.8
Porto Alegre	20.6	15.2

Source: Instituto Sindical Interamericano pela Igualdade Racial, 1999.

white and Asian population was unemployed compared to 23 percent of the nonwhite population. Comparable figures include 18 percent for whites and 26 percent for nonwhites in Salvador and 14 and 18 percent for Belo Horizonte. Based on DIESSE's publication, these differences held up even when gender, age, family position, and educational level were kept constant. The published data was available only for negros and thus it did not allow an analysis of brown-black distinctions, although the authors of the study told me that browns were generally intermediate to whites and blacks on unemployment and average levels of income. White-nonwhite differences in unemployment, which the INSPIR data effectively capture, are always smaller than the 2:1 ratio that has historically characterized black-white unemployment in the United States. However, it may be that the white-black (preto) distinctions in Brazil may be more similar to those for the United States.

BLACK-BROWN DIFFERENCES

Thus far we have considered racial inequality between whites and nonwhites, the latter encompassing blacks and browns or mulattos. Carl Degler's *Neither Black Nor White* claims that the main difference between Brazil and the United States is that mulattos have a privileged status in Brazil, unlike light-skinned U.S. blacks. Degler seems to assume that because mulattos in the United States are categorized as black, they are treated like blacks. He contrasts this to Brazil where the status of the mulatto reflects a national belief in whitening, where whiteness is desirable and blackness is stigmatized and to be escaped from. Degler's theory has been challenged by Nelson do Valle Silva (1978; 1985), who uses econometric models to conclude that blacks and browns in Brazil experience similar levels of racial discrimination. In addition, lighter skin tone is also correlated with greater opportunity in the United States. Although white/black distinctiveness in the United States is based on rules about ancestry, in which anyone with "a drop of black blood" is defined as black, light-skinned "blacks" in the United States generally do better than their dark-skinned counterparts, and on a standard of physical beauty, are seen as more attractive.[11] Indeed, Skidmore (1993, 380) notes that Degler seems to overlook the contradiction in his claims that "mulattos have been forced back into the nonwhite category and so feel keenly their deprivation because they are better educated and more socially mobile." Skidmore then asks "but why were they better educated and more socially mobile?"

Figure 5.2 shows the overall income status of Brazilians according to the three color categories used in the census. The figure reveals that the

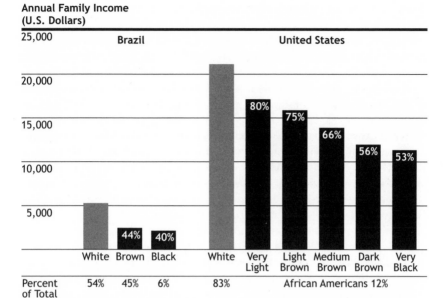

FIGURE 5.2 Mean annual family income in Brazil and the U.S. for whites and by skin color among African-origin population: 1980. (Data for Brazil are from 25-percent microdata sample of the 1980 Brazilian census; data for the U.S. are from the 1979–1980 National Survey of Black Americans as reported by Keith and Herring 1991.)

average incomes of black and brown families is about 40 and 44 percent, respectively, of those of white families. Black and brown Brazilians have much lower incomes than whites, but black family income is close to (90 percent of) brown family income. Thus, there is a huge white-nonwhite gap and a relatively small gap between blacks and browns. In terms of actual income, then, the primary racial boundary in Brazil is clearly between whites and nonwhites.[12]

Similar findings might be expected in the United States. Light-skinned African Americans might earn more than darker-skinned African Americans, but according to Degler's claim, the differences are slight when compared to the much higher earnings of whites. However, data from the National Survey of Black Americans, which is also presented in figure 5.2, demonstrate that family incomes of African Americans range from 53 percent of mean white incomes for the darkest subgroup to 80 percent of white income for the lightest. These results demonstrate greater differences between dark- and light-skinned Africans in the United States than in Brazil,[13] and the gap between white and brown is much greater in

Brazil than in the United States. Ironically, a color continuum thus better characterizes racial income differences in the United States than in Brazil, although subjective notions of race are based on a dichotomy in the United States, but on a continuum in Brazil.

WEALTH

Recently, researchers in the United States have begun to focus on wealth because of the growing availability of data and a stubbornly large wealth gap between blacks and whites. Wealth is what people own and can be drawn on beyond income sources to give their bearers or their children access to expensive items like housing and children's private schooling. Wealth is especially important for racial inequality because it is often transmitted intergenerationally and posthumously, thus reproducing historical inequalities. For the United States, Oliver and Shapiro (1995) find large differences in wealth between whites and blacks of the same occupation or income group. For example, whereas black professional incomes are 75 percent of those of their white counterparts, their net worth is only 18 percent of that of whites.[14] Thus, racial inequalities in private wealth in the United States reveal large inequalities that are not apparent by looking at income, education, or occupation.

Oliver and Shapiro attribute the large racial difference in assets in the United States to institutional and policy discrimination, particularly housing discrimination. For most North Americans, home ownership is their only major financial asset, which they call the sine qua non of the American Dream. However, the chances of owning a home are lower for blacks because they were barred from access to the housing and mortgage markets that continue to give whites vast privileges in securing housing. When blacks own homes, their market values do not increase at a similar rate as the homes of whites, because they are almost invariably located in segregated neighborhoods, where home values remain low. Furthermore, the historical and current restriction of blacks to ghettos and isolated communities, deny African Americans access to jobs and high-quality schools, which itself contributes to income attainment and wealth accumulation.

In Brazil, wealth assets also permit an improved quality of life, over what income by itself allows. For the Brazilian middle class, wealth may allow one to afford private school for kids and provide a cushion against occasional economic downturns. Discrimination against blacks at an earlier time, when racism may have been more severe, may create racial differences in wealth accumulation currently.

Unfortunately, full wealth data for Brazil is unavailable. The only wealth indicator I was able to find was from the PPV (Pesquisa Sobre Padrões de Vida [Survey of Life Patterns]), which provides information on the value of the home that respondents own and reside in. The survey also asked if respondents had bought an automobile, land, telephone, boat, etc. in the past year, but only collected the value of those items that were recently purchased. The value of the home in which one resides is likely to be the greatest financial asset for most Brazilians, but for the elite, it may represent only a minor portion of all financial assets.

I compare home-ownership values among whites, browns, and blacks across the same occupational groups in table 5.3. Specifically, column 4 shows the mean monthly market value of homes for the six occupational groups by color[15] with data from the PPV, which was collected in 1996 and 1997 for the Northeast and Southeast regions of Brazil, which represent most of the Brazilian population. The results demonstrate that racial differences in wealth are greater than those for income, which are shown in columns 2 and 3. For example, among the lowest status category, the value of one's home for whites (83) is more than twice as great as for browns (41) and three times as great as for blacks (27). By comparison, white incomes at that level are less than twice as high as those for browns or blacks. This order of difference is generally repeated at all six occupational levels. If all other assets could be added, racial inequality in wealth would most likely be higher still, especially for the highest occupational bracket. Such large racial differences reveal the added disadvantages beyond income of being brown, and especially black, in Brazil.

DEVELOPMENT AND RACIAL INEQUALITY

The following two sections examine changing income and educational racial inequality in Brazil since 1960. These trends reveal stability or change in racial inequality in the past four decades and thus provide a historical context for understanding current levels and prospects for the future. In exploring these trends, I am particularly interested in the relation between development and racial inequality, a relation that has commanded the attention of sociologists for decades. Development itself has arguably been the most important area of research in Brazilian sociology. The effect of development on racial inequality was a central focus of research on race in Brazil and the United States from the 1950s to the 1980s. Prior to the analysis, I first examine two competing sociological theories that conceptualize how development may affect racial inequality.

TABLE 5.3

Occupational distribution, income and home-ownership value for whites, browns, and blacks: southeast and northeast regions of Brazil, 1996–1997

Occupation[a]	Percent in each occupational category by color (PPV) (1)	Monthly income from primary job[b] (2)	Total monthly income[c] (3)	Market value of owned homes per month (4)
White				
High-level professional	4.5	2870	3434	743
Mid-level professional	9.5	1914	2170	569
Low-level professional	16.4	888	1108	358
Semi-/skilled urban manual	16.7	587	687	223
Unskilled urban manual	38.3	386	435	232
Unskilled rural manual	14.7	120	165	83
Brown				
High-level professional	1.5	2142	3179	441
Mid-level professional	3.3	1288	2034	269
Low-level professional	10.7	490	579	184
Semi-/skilled urban manual	15.5	444	541	140

Unskilled urban manual	38.8	245	281	131
Unskilled rural manual	30.2	70	102	41
Black				
High-level professional[d]	0.3	—	—	—
Mid-level professional	2.2	1196	1312	283
Low-level professional	8.9	534	634	153
Semi-/skilled urban manual	20.5	510	566	129
Unskilled urban manual	41.3	291	313	127
Unskilled rural manual	26.8	63	85	27

Source: Pesquisa Sobre Padrões de Vida (PPV) 1996–1997

$N = 3,785$

[a]High-level professional includes university-educated professionals and large-property owners; mid-level professional includes mid-level professionals and midsize property owners; low-level professional includes nonmanual laborers, low-level professionals, and small-property owners; and semi-/skilled refers to skilled and semiskilled urban workers.

[b]Includes gross monthly salary of primary job (first job or business income) and the value of benefits received in the last 30 days from bonuses or vacation, transportation, food, housing supplements, and any other job-related benefits.

[c]Includes gross monthly salary of primary job (first job or business income), secondary job (benefits included), additional jobs and the value of benefits received in the last 30 days from bonuses or vacation, transportation, food, housing supplements, any other job-related benefits, retirement, social security, permanence, life insurance, alimony, dividends, workers' compensation, lottery or inheritance, money from sale of items, unemployment, value of gifts, and all other sources of income.

[d]$N = 3$

The traditional liberal theory. This perspective argues that industrial development reduces or eliminates racial inequality. Industrialization can be expected to undermine traditional social orders in preindustrial societies, where, after slavery, patriarchal social systems continued to keep blacks and mulattos in low-level, racially defined positions. Theoretically, the new industrialized economic system dislodges persons from their old social positions, which forces new relationships between persons of different races as active competition replaces the structured domination of the old paternalistic system. Job opportunities expand for all, and heightened competitiveness requires industrial employers to evaluate workers on the basis of productivity rather than ascription. Moreover, sentimentality is replaced by rationality and status, and contractual and impersonal relations replace personal ones. This perspective draws largely from Durkheim's belief that modern societies rationally allocate labor on the basis of workers' achieved rather than ascribed characteristics. According to this conventional view, greater universalism also means lower racial inequality in education.

In addition to transforming social relationships and values, industrialization brings about specific organizational changes that support this conventional view. Industrialization tends to concentrate workers in factories so that hiring, firing, and promotion are more impersonal and often decided by several supervisors. Absentee company owners interested in maximum returns on their capital may be solely concerned with productivity and thus focus only on the human capital that workers bring to their jobs. In an increasingly competitive environment, even the most racist owners are forced to hire the most productive workers available. A high level of capital investment puts similar pressure on owners. Greater industrial specialization and complexity also ensures greater mobility of workers, thus leading to greater opportunity for underrepresented groups. The same phenomenon may be obtained in modernized service sectors, which also become increasingly competitive and often ancillary to manufacturing.

Industrialization has been central to academic research on race relations in Brazil, especially during the 1960s when such work focused on the integration of blacks into the newly industrializing Brazilian economy. Although not a traditional liberal thinker but rather a Marxist, Florestan Fernandes agreed that development and particularly the rise of capitalism would erode racial antipathies. Fernandes (1965) claimed that racism was a legacy of slavery, but that capitalism and industrial development would transform Brazil into a modern society based on class identification, which would eventually displace racial ascription. He argued that white hostility and the "social deficiencies," inherited from the dehumanizing system of slavery, had kept Afro-Brazilians from competing with whites; but such effects, he maintained, were beginning to disappear.

The persistence of race theory. The liberal view was first challenged by Blumer (1965) and later by Hasenbalg (1979) with regard to industrialization in Brazil. Blumer, while recognizing the great transformative influence of industrialization, proposed that it might actually reinforce the traditional racial order. Where subordinate groups are highly differentiated and marginalized, industrial organizations may find material advantages in maintaining the racial order, such as avoiding labor conflicts where dominant group workers benefit from the elimination of subordinate group members as potential competitors for jobs. Thus, industrialization would reinforce the prevailing racial ideology, ensuring the continuation of racial inequality. Industrialization's effect would be neutral, although the meaning and function of race may have changed. For the Brazilian case, the denial of racism may have reinforced the perception that there was no problem to fix, entrenching the old racial order.

Wilson (1978) claimed that racial norms from preindustrial times had generally maintained preindustrial inequalities after industrialization, and the continuation of such inequalities in turn reinforced the norms. He noted that in the United States it was only the state, acting in response to political pressures, that had been powerful enough to change racial norms, and thus racial inequality. Most notably, the United States instituted Jim Crow legislation, and more recently, affirmative-action policies. Likewise, in countries like the United States and Brazil, the state implements most educational reform, often independently of industrialization. Redistributive investments in education can compensate disadvantaged populations.

Brazilian development.   Brazil experienced tremendous industrialization from the 1930s—especially after World War II—until about 1980. Growth during the period was mostly modeled on an import-substitution plan. Its objective was to modernize the economy and increase economic growth by diminishing dependence on foreign-manufactured goods. While it had relied on the exportation of a few agricultural products throughout most of its history, by the 1950s, industrialization had become the engine and hope of Brazil's drive to modernization and development. Industrial growth was high throughout most of the postwar period, and by the early 1970s, the value of manufactured goods surpassed coffee among Brazil's exports. Economic growth was particularly intense during the "Brazilian economic miracle" between 1968 and 1974, when it averaged 11.3 percent per year. By 1980, Brazil had become the seventh-largest economy in the capitalist world.

However, this growth disproportionately benefited the middle class. Between 1960 and 1970, the share of the national income for the lowest 40 percent of earners had declined from 11.2 percent to 9.0 percent, while the top 5 percent increased their share from 27.4 to 36.3 percent. Industrialization was concentrated in São Paulo and to a lesser extent in other states of the Southeast and South, while the North and Northeast benefited little from industrialization. In 1981, Brazil experienced its first year of negative growth in decades, which brought with it high unemployment rates, a decline in real wages, shrinkage of the government sector, and the growth of informal and service-sector jobs. Economic growth resumed in 1983, sputtered again from 1987 to 1992, and then resumed again, albeit at a slower pace. By the mid-1990s, it became clear that import substitution had run its course, and Brazil embraced neoliberal economic policies, based on relatively open markets and global trade.[16]

In my investigation of historical trends in patterns of income and educational inequality, I use seven time points from 1960 to 1999. Because of data restrictions, the longitudinal analysis can only begin in 1960, well after industrialization had begun. The time points are 1960, 1976, 1982, 1986, 1991, 1996, and 1999. Unfortunately, national-level data on race are not available for the sixteen years between 1960 and 1976, but subsequently, the data points are about five years apart. As a rough guide, 1960 to 1976 saw tremendous growth; growth continued from 1976 to 1982, although not as fast; and declined in 1981 and 1982. Growth reemerged from 1982 to 1986, but 1986 to 1991 was mostly a period of decline. The two periods since then have experienced slow but continuous growth.

INCOME

A common way to figure out whether nonwhites are narrowing the gap that separates them from whites is to ask if the income of the typical nonwhite is becoming more like that of the typical white. Thus, in figure 5.3, I report trends from 1960 to 1999 in the mean monthly incomes of white women, brown men and women, and black men and women, expressed as a percentage of the income of white men. The figure reveals that the racial gap in income for men has increased since 1960. The mean income of black men was 60 percent of white men in 1960, decreased to 38 percent by 1976, but partially recovered to about 45 percent by 1999. Similarly, brown men earned about 57 percent of white men in 1960, decreased to 44 percent in 1976, and then only slightly increased to 46 percent by 1999. Contrary to the prediction of the liberal theory of industrialization, the racial gap for men increased mostly during the period of Brazil's so-called economic miracle from 1968 to 1974. This is consistent with the fact that, despite economic growth and urbanization, income became more concentrated among the highest earners, the large majority of whom were white.

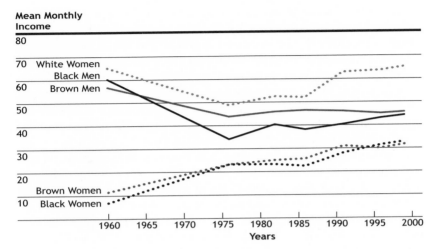

FIGURE 5.3 Mean monthly income of selected color-sex groups as a percentage of white men's income (white men = 100 percent): 1960–1999. (1960 and 1991 censuses; 1976, 1982, 1986, 1996, and 1999 National Household Surveys.)

Similarly, the wages of black males in the United States were only about 40 percent of those of white men in 1940 and had risen to just over 50 percent by 1960. By 1975, though, black men made dramatic gains, as their wages increased to nearly 80 percent of white male earnings. Since then, the relative wages of black men have stagnated or slightly declined. By 1990, they became about 75 percent of those of white men.[17]

Black men in Brazil reported slightly higher incomes than brown men in the 1960 census, but the latter had higher incomes in all subsequent years. The turnaround may be partly due to the fact that browns have been historically concentrated in rural areas and the Northeast but migrated heavily to cities and wealthier regions from the 1950s to the 1970s. However, the small differences between brown and black men may also be due to changes in racial classification over time between the two categories, in which a large proportion of persons that identified as black in the 1950s and 1960s were reclassified as brown in the 1980 census.[18]

For black and brown women, the huge income gap with white men narrowed in each subsequent year for which data are available. In 1960, the mean income of black women was about 8 percent of that for white men, rose steadily to 24 percent by 1976, remained flat until 1986, and then rose to about 32 percent by 1996. The mean income of brown women in 1960 was 12 percent of white male income and subsequently remained very similar to the income of black women, as both slowly but steadily increased throughout the period. These steady increases for the incomes of nonwhite women, unlike men, may be due to increasing enforcement of minimum-wage laws for occupations at the bottom of the income pyramid, especially domestic workers. The income gap between nonwhite men and women narrowed as men's income position worsened, especially from 1960 to 1976, and that of women's improved. While there were roughly 50 percentage points separating nonwhite men from women in 1960, by 1999 the two groups were only about 10 percentage points apart, accounting for greater convergence of the incomes of nonwhite men and women.

For nonwhite women, the more appropriate comparison group may be white women, which would allow us to understand whether trends were similar for women. The mean income of white women relative to white men's was similar in 1960 and in 1999, although it had dropped from 1960 to 1976 but rose steadily after that. Because white women's income dropped vis-à-vis white men, and black and brown women's income increased, racial differences in income among women decreased sharply from 1960 to 1976. Whereas white women earned about 5 times as much as brown women and 8.5 times as much as black women in 1960, by 1976 they earned about twice as much as both brown and black women, and the size of this gap roughly prevailed until 1999. Like Brazil, the greatest gains for blacks in the United States during the period were for women, where mean income steadily rose from a low of 36 percent in comparison to white men in 1962, to about 55 percent by 1975. However, unlike Brazil, the gap between white and black women was nearly eliminated in 1975, although it would increase in the following years.[19]

EDUCATION

Brazil's vast income inequality mirrors similarly great inequality in education. The government disproportionately subsidizes the wealthiest students—most of whom attended private schools until college—to attend high-quality public universities. On the other hand, poorer students attend the poorly resourced primary and secondary public school system, but they often do not qualify for admission to public universities. As a result, they are forced to pay to attend often poor-quality private universities. The wealthiest 7 percent of the population accounts for 27 percent of all college students, while the poorest 40 percent contributes only 5 percent to higher education. The Brazilian government spends three-and-a-half times its income per capita on each public university student, or 6.5 billion dollars each year on public higher education, for only 5 percent of the college-age cohort, which is roughly twenty times its expenditures for each elementary or secondary student. Moreover, Brazil has the lowest professor–college student ratio (9:1) in the world. Based on his comparative study, C. Castro (2001) calls Brazil "the world champion in social injustice in higher education," complementing its title in income inequality.

The Brazilian state has neglected public education at the primary and secondary levels throughout the twentieth century. According to Skidmore (1999, 87), schooling was clearly related to elites' perceptions of the largely nonwhite labor force.

> Employers typically harbored racist attitudes and doubted their workers could ever rise above menial tasks. Conspicuously missing was an appropriate recognition of skilled labor, not only for industry but also for the multiple tasks of a modern economy. While the industrialized countries (and Argentina) were pouring money into public education at the turn of the century, Brazil continued to neglect this basic form of resource development.

Coming to realize in the 1940s, in part, that its high rates of illiteracy retarded Brazil's modernization and democratization, the Brazilian government set out to expand its public school system. Burns (1970, 452) notes that in 1940 there were 3¼ million students enrolled at all levels, and by 1965 the total had reached 11¼ million; but since the number of children had approximately doubled during that period, only 13 of every 1,000 students reached secondary school in 1965. In the 1970s, the public university system grew but the number of students it could serve continued to be small. Regional differences were especially large. For example, the state of São Paulo spent as much on education as all other states combined, and in 1965, 80 percent of its adult population was literate compared to 30 percent of the population in the Northeast.

Racial inequality in education is clearly dependent on one's geographic location, as the case of São Paulo demonstrates. Even primary schools have often not been available in many of the poorer areas of Brazil, a factor which disproportionately affects nonwhites. In addition to whether schools are available, education depends on whether individuals take advantage of them. Whether or not to take advantage of schooling depends on government requirements, usually a minimum number of years of schooling, and individual and family needs and resources. In response to poverty, families often depend on children to leave school and seek ways to earn income at an early age. For nonwhites, they are particularly likely to drop out early because they tend to have less resources than whites and perceive less chance of school success.

Income depends largely on education because workers are rewarded for their knowledge and skills, so higher education means greater income. This is especially true in Brazil. In a comparison of Brazil, South Africa, and the United States, Lam (2000) demonstrates that the mag-

TABLE 5.4
Distribution of years of schooling completed by race and sex, 25–64 years of age: Brazil, 1999

Years of Schooling	White		Brown		Black	
	Male	Female	Male	Female	Male	Female
0	8.4	8.8	22.2	21.6	20.6	22.0
1–3	12.6	12.9	20.3	19.4	19.5	19.4
4–7	31.5	30.7	30.3	30.1	32.3	31.0
8–10	15.0	14.0	12.1	11.5	13.3	12.3
11–14	21.1	22.8	12.7	14.6	11.7	12.5
15+	11.4	10.8	2.4	2.8	2.6	2.8
Total	100.0	100.0	100.0	100.0	100.0	100.0

Source: Pesquisa Nacional de Amostra por Domicilios, 1999.

nitude of this relation is especially great for Brazil, where returns for income are about 15 to 20 percent greater with each additional year of schooling starting around the seventh grade. For example, at the extremes, an average nonwhite man with a college education in Brazil earns 11.3 times as much as his counterpart with no schooling. This situation is worsening in Brazil as returns to education have increased sharply for the university-educated but have decreased for those with primary and secondary education. Lam demonstrates that racial differences in education are smaller in South Africa compared to Brazil.[20] For example, among twenty- to twenty-four-year-olds, whites in South Africa completed an average of 11.8 years of education and similarly aged blacks completed 9.3 years, whereas nonwhite Brazilians of that age averaged 5.7 years of schooling while whites averaged 7.5. Thus, black South Africans have higher average schooling even than white Brazilians, especially for recent cohorts. However, despite smaller racial differences in education, racial differences by income are greater in South Africa than Brazil. This reflects a significantly weaker correlation between education and income in South Africa. In the United States, the correlation between education and income is intermediate to Brazil and South Africa, although the payoffs for additional years of education are the lowest, because of the United States' lower level of overall income inequality. In sum, the payoffs to years of education in Brazil are relatively straightforward and especially large.

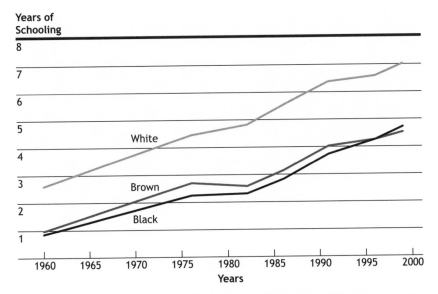

Years of
Schooling

FIGURE 5.4 Mean years of schooling for population ages 25 to 64 by color: 1960–1999. (1960 and 1991 censuses; 1976, 1982, 1986, 1996, and 1999 National Household Surveys.)

Table 5.4 shows the distribution of years of schooling for the Brazilian population aged 25 to 64 in 1999, by race and sex. Between 8 and 9 percent of whites (8.4 percent of males and 8.8 percent of females) have not completed a single year of school, compared to more than 20 percent of black and brown men and women. At the other extreme, 11.4 percent of white men and 10.8 percent of white women completed at least 15 years of school. By contrast, only between 2 and 3 percent of black and brown men and women completed the same level of education, with women doing marginally better. The findings from this table support Hasenbalg and Silva's (1991) research showing that nonwhites drop out at higher rates than whites at each point in the educational pipeline.

Figure 5.4 shows that whites, browns, and blacks aged 25 to 64 consistently increased their schooling during the 1960 to 1999 period.[21] This age range includes many persons who completed their schooling decades prior to the year being investigated, but nevertheless this is an important indicator of racial inequality for Brazil's adult population. Since there is little gender difference in schooling by race, I combine males and females in the figure. Mean years of schooling in Brazil increased from about 2 to 6 years from 1960 to 1999 according to that figure. The means for both

Years of
Schooling

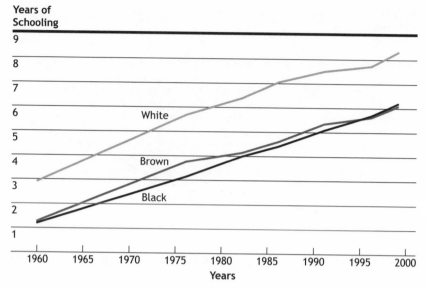

FIGURE 5.5 Mean years of schooling for population ages 20 to 29 by color: 1960–1999. (1960 and 1991 censuses; 1976, 1982, 1986, 1996, and 1999 National Household Surveys.)

blacks and browns went from 1.0 to 4.6 years, while that for whites went from 2.6 to 7.0 years. Although schooling increased for all categories, the white-nonwhite gap increased from 1.6 to 2.4 years.

To better understand more current conditions of education, I also calculate the mean years of schooling from 1960 to 1999 for the population aged 20 to 29. Although a lower age limit of 25 is preferable because it is likely to include persons that are still in school, I use a cutoff at age 20 because it captures the most recent educational completion.[22] Figure 5.5 shows those results. Young whites steadily increased their schooling from 2.9 years in 1960 to 8.3 in 1999, while nonwhites went from 1.3 to 6.1 years of schooling during the same period, much like that for the population aged 25 to 64.[23] Both figures thus demonstrate that the absolute gap between whites and nonwhites increased, although the relative gap narrowed. Despite tremendous growth during the first half of this period and uneven growth thereafter, racial inequality in average education was, thus, mostly unaffected.

Average years of education may hide inequalities at particular points in the educational hierarchy, but especially at the extremes. For example, although the racial gap in education may have remained the same, the gap

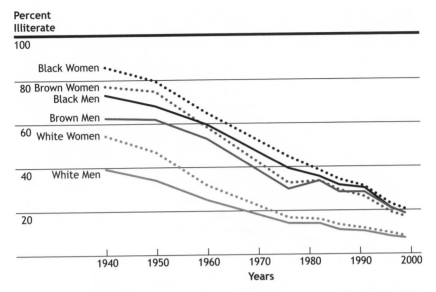

Figure 5.6 Percent illiterate by color and sex: 1940–1999. (1940, 1950, 1960, and 1991 censuses; 1976, 1982, 1986, 1996, and 1999 National Household Surveys. Note: 1940 and 1950 data are for persons 20 years and older, while other years refer to population over age 10.)

may have narrowed at one end but expanded at the other. Figures 5.6 on illiteracy and 5.7 on college completion show that this is exactly what occurred in Brazil.

Illiteracy has historically been a key indicator of citizenship in Brazil since illiterates could not vote until 1988. Unlike the other indicators of socioeconomic status, data for illiteracy by color is available from the 1940 and 1950 censuses.[24] Figure 5.6 shows the proportion of the population that is illiterate by color and sex from 1940 to 1999, and it demonstrates consistent declines for all color-sex groups. White men consistently had the lowest illiteracy rates and black women the highest throughout the fifty-nine-year period. While 39.2 percent of white men were illiterate in 1940, by 1999 only 7.4 percent were.[25] Most black and brown men and women were illiterate until 1960 and thus could not vote until 1988. The electoral reforms of the 1988 Brazilian Constitution meant that the more than 35 percent of the brown and black population that was illiterate was allowed to vote for the first time. Black women's illiteracy declined from 85.5 percent to 20.5 percent from 1940 to 1999. By 1999, sex differences had become small, whereas the most distinctive gap that remained by 1999 was between whites

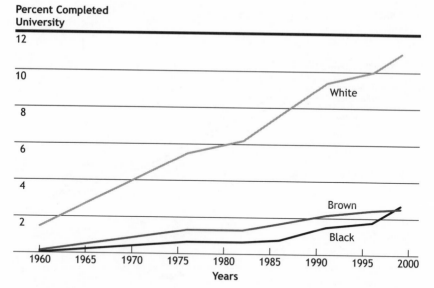

FIGURE 5.7 Percent of population ages 25 to 64 that completed university by color: 1960–1999. (1960 and 1991 censuses; 1976, 1982, 1986, 1996, and 1999 National Household Surveys.)

and nonwhites. White men's and women's illiteracy converged at about 7.5 percent in 1999, while the illiteracy of black and brown men and black and brown women came together at between 17 and 21 percent.

At the other educational extreme, Figure 5.7 shows trends in university completion for persons 25 to 64 by color from the 1960 to 1999 period. At this level, the racial gap has consistently grown from 1.3 percentage points in 1960 to 8.3 in 1999. Although the percentage of blacks and browns finishing college has gradually increased, the numbers for whites increased at a much faster rate. While only about 1.4 percent of whites had completed college in 1960, about 11.0 percent completed college by 1999. By contrast, almost no nonwhites had completed college in 1960, and by 1999 only 2.6 percent of that population had. Thus, while gains from Brazil's tremendous industrial and economic growth have been largely reinvested in expanding its higher education system, these benefits have gone disproportionately to whites.

By contrast, educational differences between blacks and whites in the United States have certainly narrowed in roughly the same period.[26] By 1982, when the average years of schooling had reached 12 years, the white-black gap was nearly erased. Although racial differences in college enrollment increased in the 1960s, they decreased dramatically in the

1970s as the proportion of black men and women attending college rose from under 8 percent in 1965 to 19 percent in 1982. This compares to white men, whose enrollment rates were about 30 percent in both 1965 and 1982, although they dropped in several intervening years.[27] White women's college enrollment in the United States went from about 2 percent in 1960 to 27 percent in 1982, suggesting that they may have been the greatest beneficiaries of affirmative action in the university.

OCCUPATION

For sociologists, occupation is often believed to represent the best single indicator of status in a society. Like income and education, occupation represents one's position in the social hierarchy, but it has the advantage of being similar over time and across space. Racial inequality using occupation may thus be conceptualized as the occupational advantage or disadvantage of one group over another along a scale of ranked occupational groups.

Table 5.3, which I previously used to examine wealth, shows the distribution of whites, browns, and blacks in six major occupational groups (column 1), the monthly income from an individual's primary job (column 2), and the monthly income from all sources (column 3). Column 1 results reveal that 4.5 percent of whites are in the highest occupational group compared to 1.5 percent of browns and 0.3 percent of blacks. Based on the evidence from chapter 4 about whitening by Brazilians of high socioeconomic status, these data may have overestimated the percentage of browns and underestimated the percentage of blacks in the highest occupational category. However, because the differences are so large, I expect that substantial differences by color remain even if the whitening effect could be controlled. At the bottom of the occupational structure, only 14.7 percent of whites are in the unskilled rural category compared to 30.2 percent of browns and 26.8 percent of blacks. Nonwhites, and especially browns, are the most represented in this category, reflecting their greater predominance in rural areas.

Columns 2 and 3 reveal that whites earn more than browns and blacks in nearly every occupational group. For example, white rural workers earn a total of $120 monthly from their primary job compared to $70 for browns and $65 for blacks. From all sources, whites earn $165 compared to $102 for browns and $82 for blacks. Given the heterogeneity of these occupational groups, the differences in income might reflect racial stratification in specific occupations for each group, although it may also result partly from nonwhite concentration in the poor Northeast.

As the comparative income structures suggested, Brazilian nonwhites are more underrepresented in high- and mid-level professional occupations than in the United States. However, whites in Brazil are more likely than U.S. whites to share unskilled blue-collar occupations with nonwhites. Whites are more than three times as likely as nonwhites to be in high-level professional occupations in Brazil, according to comparable figures by Farley and Allen (1987, 264). Whites in the United States are about 1.8 times as likely as blacks to be in that occupational group. At the other extreme, about half as many whites as nonwhites were in the lowest category of urban occupational groups in both countries. Because the occupational structure, like the income structure, in Brazil is clearly smaller at the top and has a much wider base at the bottom, persons in high-level professional occupations thus constitute a more elite group in Brazil than in the United States. In Brazil, that occupational category is smaller, and average incomes are much higher than incomes for intermediate occupations, as the table shows. This reflects the fact that Brazil's high income inequality is largely the result of the top 5 or 10 percent earning much more than the rest. By contrast, there is a much smaller difference in income between the comparable top two occupational groups in the United States.[28]

INDUSTRIALIZATION AND OCCUPATIONAL INEQUALITY

Returning to the issue of development, I now examine the relation between occupational inequality and levels of industrialization across urban areas. Unlike the previous sections that examined income and educational inequality over time, I take a different methodological tack for examining occupational inequality. Specifically, I analyze the relationship between racial occupational inequality and level of industrialization for the seventy-three largest urban areas in 1980, which is the last year of continuous economic growth in Brazil since before World War II.[29] A multivariate statistical analysis of these urban areas allows me to make conclusions about the industrialization-racial inequality relation with a much greater degree of confidence than the longitudinal analysis did. While the cross-sectional approach cannot necessarily be generalized historically, it has the advantage of allowing for the careful control of variables, besides industrialization, that might affect inequality. For example, multivariate analysis allows me to isolate the effect of industrialization from education, since both are thought to affect inequality. Also, the seventy-three urban areas available for 1980 provide the large sample size needed for the analysis. This compares to only fifteen or so time points that would be available for a multivariate longitudinal analysis.[30]

To measure racial occupational inequality, I used the index of net difference (ND) using three hierarchically ranked occupational groups.[31] Intuitively, net difference can be interpreted as the probability that individuals from one or the other racial group will be in higher-ranked occupational groups when individuals in the two racial groups are randomly paired. While ND measures overall occupational inequality, I use an odds ratio index to capture racial differences in managerial and professional occupations, since I expect the middle-class boundary is particularly rigid in Brazil.[32] For industrialization, I used the percent of the total labor force that is employed in manufacturing industries in each urban area.

Such a comparison is important in Brazil because local levels of industrialization vary widely across Brazil for historical reasons. Prior to the 1930s, agricultural production for export was greatest in the Northeast, but the shift from agricultural to industrial production moved the center of the economy to the Southeast. Brazil's import-substitution policies accelerated industrialization, especially in places like São Paulo, thus accentuating unequal regional growth and development.[33] Also, high fertility and rural-to-urban migration caused rapid population growth, which affected the capacity of various regions to absorb increasing numbers into the modern job sector.[34] Modern, highly industrialized areas in the Southeast fared far better than those in the Northeast, which had bloated informal economies and almost no industrialization. Also, the Brazilian government made quality higher education much more available in industrialized regions. According to a major study in 1982, not one of the top-20 universities was to be found in the Northeast.[35]

According to students of Brazilian race relations, changes from a traditional order have thus been especially great in the southeastern and southern regions, where "the dynamics of industrialization, rapid urbanization and massive European immigration have profoundly transformed race relations."[36] In these regions, according to Van den Berghe (1967), race relations have clearly moved toward a competitive mode and away from the paternalistic mode extant in other regions, where labor is divided along racial lines, and thus racial inequality is high. While analysts acknowledge that racial composition, urbanization, and immigration patterns all influence regional differences, they often point to industrialization as the key factor underlying regional variation in racial outcomes. However, such conclusions for Brazil are generally based on the comparison of two or three regions, and thus the independent effect of industrialization cannot be discerned.

Before proceeding to the multivariate analysis, I illustrate the bivariate relationship between industrialization and racial inequality among the seventy-three urban areas in figures 5.8 and 5.9. Figure 5.8 demonstrates the net-difference scores of racial inequality in all urban areas, which

Racial Occupational
Inequality (Net Difference)

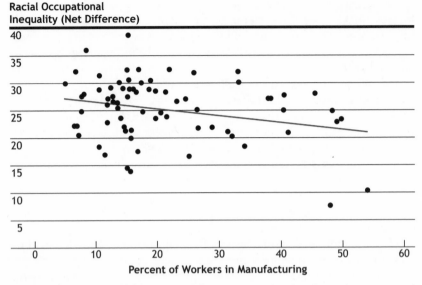

Percent of Workers in Manufacturing

FIGURE 5.8 Relationship between industrialization level and racial occupational inequality in the 73 largest metropolitan areas of Brazil: 1980. (1980 census.)

range from 7.6 to 38.7. That is, whites are 7.6 to 38.7 percent more likely to hold higher-status occupations than nonwhites. Moreover, figure 5.8 shows that overall racial inequality is slightly correlated with industrialization at the bivariate level, with more industrialized places tending to have lower levels of racial inequality.[37] Similarly, figure 5.9 shows that whites are two to twelve times as likely as nonwhites to hold professional and managerial jobs, with such inequality varying slightly with industrialization. Racial inequality at the top of the occupational structure is greater in more industrialized places. A comparison of figures 5.8 and 5.9 thus reveals that more industrialized areas have lower levels of overall racial inequality but greater racial inequality at the top of the occupational structure.

However, the bivariate correlation of industrialization to racial inequality, using either of the two measures, is not strong, but this may be due to the confounding effects of other variables. To capture whether industrialization truly has an effect requires that we control for variables such as education, which may help explain the variations in the local levels of inequality. With the introduction of these variables, the relationships shown in figures 5.8 and 5.9 may be sharpened, may go away, or even be reversed. Table 5.5 presents the results, using four models to capture the effects of multiple variables on the two indicators of racial in-

Racial Inequality at
Professional/Managerial Level

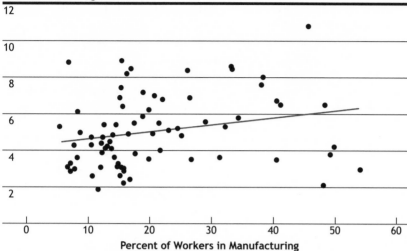

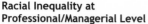

FIGURE 5.9 Relationship between industrialization level and the relative likelihood that whites and nonwhites are in professional or managerial occupations in the 73 largest metropolitan areas of Brazil: 1980. (1980 census.)

equality. The first model regresses net difference on industrialization and two variables that control differences in migration and the effects of industrial domination by São Paulo.[38] The second model for net difference includes the educational inequality variables, which allow testing the extent to which variation in racial inequality among urban areas may also or only be due to educational differences, as some authors suggest.[39] Finally, model 3 is similar to model 1, and model 4 is similar to model 2 except that the dependent variable is for the odds-ratio index measuring racial inequality in professional/managerial occupations instead of overall occupational inequality. In sum, models 1 and 2 of table 5.5 refer to overall racial occupational inequality as did figure 5.8, and models 3 and 4 refer to racial inequality at the top of the occupational structures as in figure 5.9.

In multivariate analysis, a value or regression coefficient reveals the direction and strength of the relation between percent in manufacturing and racial inequality. The regression coefficients for industrialization are negative and statistically significant from models 1 and 2, which means that greater industrialization is related to lower overall racial inequality, thus supporting and apparently tightening the loose relation between industrialization and racial inequality shown in figure 5.8. Indeed, the

TABLE 5.5
Regressions of occupational net difference and odds ratio of being in professional/
administrative occupations on industrialization and educational inequality: 73 largest
urban areas in Brazil, 1980

Independent Variables	White: nonwhite occupational inequality (net difference)		White: nonwhite inequality for (odds ratio) being in professional/managerial occupations	
	(1)	(2)	(3)	(4)
Industrialization	–.135*	–.120**	.055*	.022
	(.059)	(.028)	(.025)	(.017)
Racial inequality (odds ratio) at 4+ years of schooling	—	8.036** (1.01)	—	—
Racial inequality (odds ratio) at 12+ years of schooling	—	.877** (.159)	—	.722** (.082)
Mean years of schooling	—	4.355** (.703)	—	1.037** (.441)
Intercept	25.323	–24.450	5.799	–7.376
R^2	.163	.862	.306	.745

Note: Numbers in parentheses are standard deviations in the first column and standard errors in the second and third columns. Control variables in all models not presented are whether in São Paulo State and the white: nonwhite odds ratio of being a migrant.
*$p < .05$ **$p < .01$

relationship between industrialization and inequality sharpens with the introduction of education controls, as indicated by the halving of standard errors for model 1 to model 2. Thus, these findings support the conventional theory that industrial development leads to lower racial inequality. However, the size of the coefficients (.135 and .120) indicate that the net difference between a highly industrialized area with about 35 percent of its labor force in manufacturing and a poorly industrialized area with about 10 percent employed in manufacturing, would be about 3 points or a little more, which means, at best, a 20-percent difference in racial inequality. Thus, while Brazilian industrialization seems to have reduced overall racial inequality in those places which mostly benefited from it, there was a long way to go before eliminating this inequality.

The effects of industrialization on the top of the occupational structure, though, are different. Unlike its effect on overall racial inequality, model 3 suggests that industrialization produces greater white-nonwhite inequality in access to professional and managerial occupations, although model 4 shows that these effects are washed out with the introduction of the education variables. A comparison of models 3 and 4 thus suggests that the effect of greater industrialization on racial inequality at that level is indirect. Specifically, development leads to local expansion of higher education, precisely where racial inequality is increasing. As I have shown, whites have disproportionately benefited from university expansion in Brazil.

Relatedly, table 5.5 shows that education-related variables explain much more of the variation in occupational racial inequality than levels of industrialization. R^2s at the bottom represent the proportion of the variation in inequality that is explained by the variables in the model. The huge improvements in R^2 with the introduction of the education control variables in models 2 and 4 over models 1 and 3, respectively, demonstrate that about half of the variation in inequality across metropolitan areas can be attributed to variations in educational inequality.

Conclusions

The findings in this chapter show that the Brazilian socioeconomic structure is largely divided along racial lines. On virtually all summary indicators of social conditions in Brazil, nonwhites score well below whites. Nonwhites, on average, have persistently earned less than half the incomes of white Brazilians since the 1970s. Comparatively, Brazil's racial gap is far greater than that for the United States, because Brazil's nonwhite population is less likely to be in the middle class and because of its greater income inequality in general. Despite Brazil's slightly higher levels of overall income inequality, racial inequality is lower than in South Africa because persons in poverty there, unlike Brazil, are almost entirely black.

This chapter has also shown considerable male-female and brown-black differences among the nonwhite population. Gender inequalities among the nonwhite population continue to decrease, like they do for the white population, although they remain significant. By contrast, racial inequality persists despite development, and in the case of the middle class, it continues to increase. Also, much of the national data I have presented in this chapter show that browns tend to be slightly better off than blacks, although brown-black differences in income and wealth become clearer when occupational differences are considered. Overall, though, white-nonwhite differences are generally greater than those between blacks and nonblacks, making it the primary racial divide in Brazil. Indeed, the position of the mulatto population in the United States, although defined as "black," is better relative to dark blacks in the United States than in Brazil.

Since 1950, Brazil has experienced tremendous economic growth, making it one of the largest industrial economies in the world. During these years and after, illiteracy plummeted, Brazil went from predominately rural to urban, and its higher education system greatly expanded. Despite these advances, racial disparities have increased at the top of the social structure. The expansion of higher education during the period led to the sizable growth of a professional middle class, but by disproportionately benefiting whites, it produced a growing racial gap in access to a university education. Thus, the Brazilian case demonstrates that industrial development may actually *increase* racial inequality in the top part of the class structure, contrary to the traditional liberal or the more modern perspectives, which argue that industrialization either reduces or does not affect racial inequality. Increasingly sophisticated technology, organizational complexity, and pressures on increasing production required by growing competition in world capitalist markets require an increasingly educated labor force. In this scenario, the Brazilian state decided to invest heavily in higher education, while nearly ignoring education at the primary or secondary level, and effectively, education for nonwhites. Consequently, Brazilian development has brought with it stunted social development, including greater racial inequalities.

Chapter Six

RACIAL DISCRIMINATION

> We don't have a racial problem. In Brazil,
> blacks know their place.
> —*Popular saying*

W E OFTEN assume that racial inequality is due to discrimination, but there is really no automatic link. In Brazil, racial inequality is sometimes thought to be simply the result of historical inequalities such as those created by slavery, so that its disappearance simply requires the passage of time. Thus, the nondiscriminatory mechanism of class rather than racial discrimination reproduces racial inequality, according to this perspective. Racial inequality has also been explained as being due to the lower human capital and disadvantaged geographical characteristics of browns and blacks, which may or may not be related to discrimination. For example, some argue that nonwhites have lower incomes than whites largely because they are more likely to reside in the poorly resourced Northeast or simply because they have lower levels of education, which is presumably unrelated to discrimination. Another explanation is that because "money whitens," then racial inequality is overestimated.

Light and Gold (1999) note that, in comparison to whites and many other ethnic groups, blacks in the United States are disadvantaged because of both discrimination, particularly in the labor market, and resource disadvantage. Resource disadvantage may refer to factors as diverse as historical conditions, education, wealth, access to networks, social capital, and self-esteem. Given the interrelationship between resource disadvantage and discrimination, how do we isolate discrimination? This is no easy task. Discrimination is often diffuse, difficult to measure, and has multiple manifestations. Therefore, multiple forms of evidence are required to make a compelling case. In the following sections, I present three statistical tests that isolate racial discrimination from resource-disadvantage variables including region, education, occupation, and even interfamily and neighborhood differences. Furthermore, these tests seek to control for potential status-whitening effects on racial classification—a concern that has been absent in previous statistical studies of discrimination. Specifically, I examine racial differences in social mobility in São Paulo, income attainment using alternative racial classifications, and schooling among multiracial siblings. In the second part of this chapter, I describe the mechanisms through which discrimination is propagated and maintained.

SOCIAL MOBILITY

Unlike measures of racial inequality, which capture a snapshot of inequality at a single point in time, measures of social mobility can capture the extent to which national populations or national subgroups differentially shift from one socioeconomic status to another over a generation. For comparing national populations, these studies often seek to capture the extent of fluidity or rigidity in their social systems. For subgroups, scholars are often interested in understanding discrimination and the extent of equality of opportunity. To what extent do children inherit the occupational status of their fathers or move up or down the occupational ladder? More specifically, do whites and nonwhites experience different rates of intergenerational mobility? Until the late 1970s, most scholars argued that racial inequality in Brazil persisted because there is little social mobility overall in that country. Since there had been only three or four generations since slavery, they argued that nonwhites have therefore not had enough time to catch up. Even progressive sociologists like Florestan Fernandes (1965) argued that the racial differences of his time were largely due to the recent emergence of Afro-Brazilians from slavery[1] and that they would eventually disappear, as nonwhites gradually acquired the necessary human and cultural capital to compete with whites.

By asking respondents in a survey about their current occupations, their occupations at younger ages, and their fathers' occupations, analysts can determine the amount and direction of mobility over respondents' lifetimes and from fathers to children. Using the 1973 National Household Survey (PNAD), Pastore (1982) showed that there has been a significant amount of mobility in Brazilian society, enough to have erased or greatly attenuated racial inequalities since slavery, if opportunities were equally distributed. In the 1950s and 1960s, the years which Pastore's study mostly covered, greater mobility could be achieved, because the relative number of higher status occupations increased, while low status occupations, particularly those in agriculture, decreased. Also using the 1976 data, Hasenbalg (1979) showed differential rates of mobility for whites and blacks, concluding that mobility opportunities were differentiated by race.

Pastore and Silva (2000) reanalyzed Brazilian mobility more than twenty years later, using the 1996 National Household Survey.[2] They reaffirmed Pastore's earlier findings of substantial social mobility in Brazilian society and Hasenbalg's findings about large racial differences, although they found that by 1996 most mobility had become circular. In other words, it depended more upon population shifts between occupations as opposed to changes in the occupational structure itself; a slower economy produced fewer new jobs. Pastore and Silva also examined racial differences and found that, among Brazilian men whose fathers held the same occupation, white sons are 12 percent more likely to be in higher-status occupations than nonwhites. Based on further analysis, they concluded that 81 percent of this disparity can be attributed to racial differences in the level of schooling completed, while the remainder is due to racial inequality in securing occupations despite similar levels of schooling.

Several other of Pastore and Silva's findings are worth noting. First, most of the sample had fathers who were employed in the lowest occupational category (mostly unskilled agricultural occupations), including 66 percent of browns, 57 percent of blacks, and 49 percent of whites. Among respondents whose fathers were in these occupations, 30 percent of white sons remained at the lowest socioeconomic level with rural jobs compared to 42 percent of nonwhites. This finding suggests that the rates of rural to urban migration among whites, blacks, and browns differ substantially, which would seem to account for differences in mobility and, specifically, differences in the ability to improve educational status since urban areas clearly offer greater chances for schooling. The findings from these studies are important because they establish that social mobility in Brazil is greater than is often expected. In addition, they show that on a national level, whites are clearly more likely than blacks and browns to be upwardly mobile.

However, there are two major problems with understanding racial differences in mobility using a national sample. First, mobility, or the lack thereof, may have occurred in very distinct places. Greater white mobility may be due to the fact that whites are more likely to reside in more economically vibrant regions like the southern half of Brazil, where upward mobility opportunities are greater. Relatedly, nonwhites are more likely to have migrated to these regions from the Northeast, but their migrant status, and not their race, may account for lower mobility. Second, evidence presented in chapter 4 demonstrates that mobility itself may whiten one's racial classification.

To minimize these problems, I examine intergenerational mobility in the São Paulo metropolitan area for those born in the state of São Paulo.[3] By limiting the sample to natives in one metropolitan area, I can examine differences among those persons who were educated in and spent their working careers in the same labor market. Whites, browns, and blacks in the same metropolitan area compete for the same jobs; however, they may be sorted into different jobs by race throughout their lives. Also, the effect of status on turning browns into blacks is small in São Paulo, as I described in chapter 4.[4] Finally, São Paulo has the advantage of being sufficiently large that the National Household Survey (PNAD) provides enough cases to draw statistically significant conclusions.

Table 6.1 presents the mobility rates for males and females differentiated by race. Although I had expected that racial differences in mobility might be reduced by examining a single metropolitan area, a comparison with Pastore and Silva (2000) shows that racial differences are actually greater than those found for the national sample. The top half of the table shows that among white male respondents whose fathers worked in unskilled agricultural occupations, 9 percent moved to the highest occupational level and 10 percent to the second highest. By contrast, 4 percent of nonwhite males rose to the highest occupational group and another 4 percent to the second highest. For those whose fathers were in unskilled urban occupations, 23 percent of white sons remained in these occupations compared to 43 percent of the nonwhite sons. Regarding upward mobility for these same occupational groups, twice as many whites (20 percent) as nonwhites (10 percent) attained the second-highest level, and 13 percent of whites reached the highest level while no (0 percent) nonwhites did.

Results from the bottom half of table 6.1 demonstrate that racial differences in mobility are even greater for women. The large majority of daughters of unskilled rural workers in São Paulo themselves became unskilled urban workers, regardless of their color. However, the figure was 86 percent for nonwhite daughters and 72 percent for white daughters. Racial differences are larger among the daughters of manual workers. Seventy percent of the nonwhite daughters of unskilled urban workers remained at the same occupational level as their fathers compared to 40 percent of white daughters. Sixty-seven percent of nonwhite daughters of skilled and semiskilled manual workers fell to the unskilled urban manual category compared to 44 percent of white daughters from similar origins. These data reveal that mobility in Brazil has been overstated because it tends to focus on males, at least in São Paulo. Rather, female mobility is more influenced by class origins, although like those of men, women's occupational prospects are also strongly shaped by race.

Based on the results in table 6.1, table 6.2 calculates absolute and relative differences between white and nonwhite males and females. The largest and most consistent difference is in the likelihood of males to be-

TABLE 6.1

Occupational mobility from father to respondent by sex and race:
São Paulo metropolitan area

Father's occupation	Respondent's occupation						
	Unskilled urban manual	Semi-/ skilled urban manual	Low-level profes- sional	Mid-level profes- sional	High-level profes- sional	Total	N
White males							
Unskilled rural	29	37	15	10	9	100	112
Unskilled urban	23	26	18	20	13	100	238
Semi-/skilled urban	23	31	19	18	9	100	250
Low level	20	13	31	20	16	100	168
Mid level	8	10	23	36	23	100	93
High level	6	6	11	32	45	100	76
Nonwhite males							
Unskilled rural	24	52	16	4	4	100	25
Unskilled urban	43	30	17	10	0	100	40
Semi-/skilled urban	22	56	15	6	1	100	73
Low level	27	31	23	19	0	100	26
Mid level*	20	9	20	40	20	100	5*
High level*	0	29	28	43	0	100	7*
White females							
Unskilled rural	72	3	16	8	1	100	71
Unskilled urban	40	9	32	15	4	100	137
Semi-/skilled urban	44	9	26	14	7	100	179
Low level	25	11	38	20	6	100	121
Mid level	32	11	27	19	11	100	73
High level	13	7	35	21	24	100	46
Nonwhite females							
Unskilled rural	86	0	9	5	0	100	22
Unskilled urban	70	3	17	7	3	100	30
Semi-/skilled urban	67	8	15	6	4	100	52
Low level*	6	6	19	6	0	100	16*
Mid level*	33	17	50	0	0	100	6*
High level*	0	33	67	0	0	100	3*

Source: 1996 Brazilian National Household Survey (PNAD).
Note: Limited to 20–59-year-old respondents in urban occupations, residing in São Paulo metropolitan area and born in the state of São Paulo.
*Sample size at these levels are so small that results are statistically insignificant.

TABLE 6.2
Absolute and relative differences in white and nonwhite mobility by sex:
São Paulo metropolitan area

	Respondent's occupation				
Father's occupation	Unskilled urban manual	Semi-/skilled urban manual	Low-level non-manual	Mid-level non-manual	High-level non-manual
Males: Absolute differences					
Unskilled rural	5	−12	−1	6	5
Unskilled urban	−20	−4	1	10	13
Semi-/skilled urban	1	−15	4	12	9
Low level	−7	−18	8	1	16
Mid level	(−12)	(10)	(3)	(−4)	(3)
High level	(6)	(−23)	(−17)	(−11)	(45)
Males: Relative differences					
Unskilled rural	1.2	0.7	0.9	2.5	2.3
Unskilled urban	0.5	0.9	1.1	2.0	13+
Semi-/skilled urban	1.0	0.6	1.3	3.0	9
Low level	0.7	0.4	1.3	1.1	16+
Mid level	(0.4)	(10+)	(1.1)	(0.9)	(1.1)
High level	(6+)	(0.2)	(0.4)	(0.7)	(45+)
Females: Absolute differences					
Unskilled rural	−14	3	7	3	1
Unskilled urban	−30	6	15	8	1
Semi-/skilled urban	−23	1	11	8	3
Low level	(19)	(5)	(19)	(14)	(6)
Mid level	(−1)	(−6)	(−23)	(19)	(11)
High level	(13)	(−26)	(−32)	(21)	(24)
Females: Relative differences					
Unskilled rural	0.8	3+	1.8	1.6	1+
Unskilled urban	0.6	3.0	1.9	2.1	1.3
Semi-/skilled urban	0.7	1.3	1.7	2.7	1.7
Low level	(4.2)	(1.8)	(2.0)	(3.3)	(6+)
Mid level	(1.0)	(0.6)	(0.5)	(19+)	(11+)
High level	(13+)	(0.2)	(0.5)	(21+)	(24+)

Source: 1996 Brazilian National Household Survey (PNAD).

Note: Limited to 20–59-year-old respondents in urban occupations, residing in São Paulo metropolitan area and born in the state of São Paulo. Number in parentheses based on very small samples.

come mid- and high-level professionals. The second panel shows that white males are two to three times more likely than their nonwhite counterparts of the same lower-class origins to become mid-level professionals. The relative chances of whites becoming high-level professionals are even greater. For nonwhite females, a ceiling effect occurs between unskilled and semiskilled or skilled jobs. Since nonwhite women are concentrated in those occupations, the results suggest that the glass ceiling for females is only one story high. The large majority of women who are professionals, come from families where their fathers are also professionals. Thus, class effects, along with a significant race effect, prevent black and brown women from becoming professionals. In sum, while nonwhite males encounter a glass ceiling that prevents them from entering middle-level professional jobs and above, nonwhite women seem to be stuck in boots that are glued to the floor of the occupational structure.

These findings make it startlingly clear that race, independent of class, region, and a money-whitening effect, is a powerful force for determining one's life chances. Moreover, an often forgotten fact is that the reproduction of racial differences in social mobility from one generation to the next contributes to increasing racial inequality over time and not merely to maintaining it. In the unlikely event that racial differences in mobility were to suddenly end, given the extent of Brazil's current racial inequality, it would still take several generations for Brazil to reach racial equality.

Controlling Human Capital and Racial Classification

A further test of whether structural factors alone can explain racial inequality uses a human-capital model to control such effects. If racial differences remain after controlling for human capital, this is further evidence that racial discrimination occurs. Because discrimination cannot be directly measured, the unexplained part of the income difference, after controlling for racial differences in human-capital and labor-market characteristics, is often attributed to racial discrimination in hiring and promotions. Human-capital studies of race in Brazil, particularly Nelson do Valle Silva's (1978, 1985) pioneering work, did much to demystify racial democracy and the belief that income differences had nothing to do with discrimination. Based on national-census and household-survey data, these studies showed that as much as one-third of the differences in income between whites and nonwhites cannot be explained by racial differences in variables like education, work experience, social origins, and region. This portion of the difference has traditionally been believed to approximate the extent of labor-market discrimination.

Given the strong evidence from several human-capital studies showing the persistence of unexplained white-nonwhite income differences, the scholarly discussion has turned mostly to the extent of black-brown differences. N. Silva (1978, 1985) found that the unexplained income difference between browns and whites was similar to that between blacks and whites and thus he concluded that the extent of discrimination against browns and blacks was similar. Degler's (1986) well-known "mulatto escape hatch" theory claimed that mulattos in Brazil enjoy a favored status vis-à-vis blacks. Silva's conclusion became widely accepted and for many researchers it served to legitimize the collapsing of browns and blacks into a single negro or nonwhite category. Moreover, black-movement leaders used it as "proof" that browns and blacks received similar levels of discrimination and therefore should unite as negros. However, empirical studies by other analysts since then have found that browns generally earn more than blacks and that blacks are more discriminated against than browns.[5] For some reason these studies have received less attention.

Since money whitens one's racial classification, Wade (1993) believes that data based on self-classification overestimates discrimination against browns since it deflates brown income. He finds that blacks often identify as brown when they migrate to nonblack communities or otherwise leave the social networks of black communities. Based on fieldwork in Colombia, Wade concludes that in many South American countries, including Brazil, the primary racial cleavage is between blacks and nonblacks, because discrimination against blacks is much harsher than against browns. He thus supports Degler's argument about the "mulatto escape hatch," arguing that Degler's detractors erroneously relied on estimates that are based on self-classification and are thus flawed. While Degler is vague about the relative position that browns occupy between whites and blacks, Wade expects brown income to be much greater than black income and closer to white income, especially after controlling for human-capital and labor-market variables.

In a research article that I published with Nelson Lim in *Demography*, I used data from the 1995 Data Folha Survey to investigate the strength of Wade's claim that browns earn incomes that are more similar to white than black income, when race is assessed by others. I treat the complex methodological issues in that article but present a summary of the results in figure 6.1.[6] After controlling for a range of human-capital (sex, education, age) and labor-market characteristics (region, size of urban area), the figure shows that whites earn 26 percent more than browns when race is based on interviewer classification, while income for persons classified as black are 12 percent lower than for browns. Using similar methodologies, several researchers have found that U.S. black men suf-

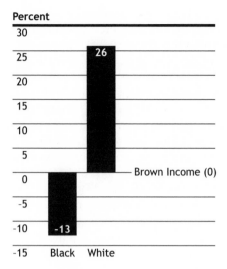

FIGURE 6.1 Income gap between whites and browns and blacks and browns using interviewer-based racial classification while controlling for education, age, sex, region and urban area size: Urban Brazil, 1995. (Telles and Lim 1998.)

fered a 13 to 15 percent loss in earnings due to labor-market discrimination.[7] The loss for brown and especially black men in Brazil is thus greater than it is in the United States.

Our results also showed that white-brown (and thus white-nonwhite) inequality is greater using interviewer classification, suggesting that studies using official data, which presumably rely on self-classification, underestimate the extent of discrimination in Brazilian society. This is the opposite of what Wade had expected. We also demonstrated that interviewer-classified race explains racial differences in income much better than self-classified race.[8] This is consistent with the sociological notion that perceptions of another's race weigh more heavily than self-identification in terms of determining labor-market outcomes.

These findings also refute N. Silva's well-known challenge to Degler wherein he argues that there are no brown-black differences, as well as Wade's claim that the primary racial cleavage in countries like Brazil is between blacks and nonblacks. The income disadvantage of browns relative to whites, based on interviewer classification, is roughly two-thirds as large as that for blacks. Thus, the primary racial cleavage is between white and nonwhite, even though blacks tend to be more discriminated against than browns. Given the especially high income concentration among the top 10 percent of the population and the highly skewed returns

TABLE 6.3
Percentage difference in monthly income by color, according to self-classification and interviewer classification, compared with consistently classified browns

Self-classification	Interviewer classification		
	White	Brown	Black
White	25	4	−40
Brown	26	—	−12
Black	16	0	−13

Source: Telles and Lim 1998.

on education found in Brazil, especially large white-nonwhite differences in *actual* income are not surprising. Also, the greater regional disadvantages of browns compared to blacks offsets what would otherwise be larger black-brown differences in actual income.

The findings of greater inequality due to interviewer classification are mainly a result of persons who self-classified as brown but were classified as white by interviewers. Table 6.3 shows that such persons had 26 percent more income than persons classified as brown by both interviewer and respondents. Persons who self-classified as white but were classified as brown by interviewers had only 4 percent more income than consistently classified browns. These findings therefore indicate that official statistics, to the extent they are based on self-classification, tend to inflate brown income or, conversely, deflate white income. This is directly contrary to what Wade had expected.

Although human-capital models may present the best available estimates of labor-market discrimination, these are not perfect. In such models, discrimination is based on the unexplained income differences between the two racial groups after all human-capital variables are accounted for. Since variables such as family wealth, family structure, social networks, migration, and the quality of education are not captured by the model, critics argue that the residual cannot be interpreted as solely due to labor-market discrimination. In the next section, I therefore present yet another model, which I believe controls for many of these problems.

THE ULTIMATE TEST: MULTIRACIAL SIBLINGS

As I demonstrated in chapter 4, it is not uncommon for brothers and sisters in Brazil to be distinctly classified by race. With a data set as large as the 1991 census, the existence of a large sample of sibling pairs that were distinctly classified by race permits a natural experiment that can isolate the effects of racial discrimination from neighborhood location, various class effects, age and gender. Since these siblings are all residents of the same household, it seems racial differences in their current schooling success can be directly attributed to racial or color discrimination, including differences in treatment by parents and school personnel. Treatment by parents may include the decision of enrolling the child in the same school. The accumulation of racially biased actions, including gestures and comments, by teachers, school personnel, and other members of society may result in unequal educational outcomes by race, even among siblings. In this section, I examine the extent to which white, brown, or black siblings remain in the age-appropriate grade, as opposed to dropping out or repeating grades. Grade repetition is especially important in Brazil where many adolescents remain in school but are not passed to higher grades and thus fall behind the normative grade for their age.[9]

Figures 6.2 and 6.3 show differences in educational progress among age-proximate siblings of the same sex but of different colors from ages 9 to 16.[10] Figure 6.2 samples all pairs of brothers, who are separated by two or fewer years of age, where one is white and the other is brown or black. I then plot the percentage of brothers who are in the age-appropriate grade by race and age. Those not in the age-appropriate grade have either begun school late, have fallen behind because of grade repetition, or have dropped out of school entirely. I then present comparable information for female siblings in figure 6.3.[11]

Figure 6.2 shows that white brothers are more likely than their non-white siblings to be in the age-appropriate grade. The advantages accruing for white brothers persist throughout ages 9 to 16; although the differences are particularly great from 9 to 11 and narrow thereafter, when less than 30 percent of these children remain in the age-appropriate grade. At age 10, 47 percent of the whites in the sample are in the age-appropriate grade compared to 37 percent of their nonwhite brothers. The drop is greatest for browns and blacks from ages 9 to 10, while the sharpest fall for the white brothers is between ages 10 and 11. Differences by race among siblings are not as great for females, as figure 6.3 shows. Nevertheless, white sisters tend to do better than their non-white siblings.

I believe the educational differences shown in figures 6.2 and 6.3 for multiracial siblings are a rigorous test of racial discrimination for two reasons. First, they seem to control well for social effects on color classification. Color is likely to be as fluid among sibling pairs as it is among the general population. However, I suspect that the designation of children by parents as white, brown, or black best reflects the relational nature of racial classification in Brazil, since race in these cases is being

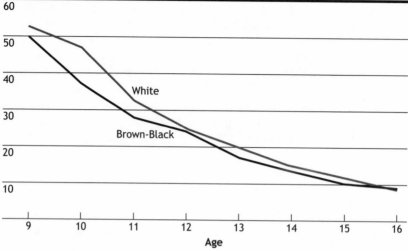

FIGURE 6.2 Percent of white males ages 9–16 and their brown-black brothers with age differences of two years or less in age-appropriate grade: Brazil, 1991. (1991 census.)

designated by the same person (the census respondent of that household, which is usually a parent), who I presume is intimately knowledgeable about the comparative color of each household member. Second, even though the differences may appear small, they provide strong evidence that race makes a difference, independently of class, family, neighborhood, and a host of other social- and cultural-capital factors. Of course, these findings greatly underestimate overall racial inequality, because such siblings represent a small numerical minority of the Brazilian population, and racial differences in schooling across families are likely to be much greater than those within families.[12]

How Discrimination Works

In the past few pages, I believe I have presented incontrovertible evidence demonstrating the existence of racial discrimination in Brazil. The remainder of this chapter then goes the next step by showing the particular mechanisms of racial discrimination in Brazilian society, which ultimately lead to persistent racial inequality. The large majority of acts of

**Percent in Age-
Appropriate Grade**

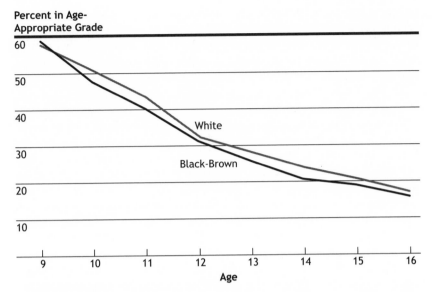

FIGURE 6.3 Percent of white females ages 9–16 and their brown-black sisters with age differences of two years or less in age-appropriate grade: Brazil, 1991. (1991 Census.)

discrimination are subtle and thus generally not recognized as discriminatory. These include a series of informal institutional mechanisms—which create barriers for nonwhites and privileges for whites—and a web of individual causes—including slights, aggressions, and numerous other informal practices—both of which originate from a culture that naturalizes the racial hierarchy. Commenting in the late 1960s about the new post–Jim Crow system in the United States, Baron (1969, 144) noted, "the web of urban racism entraps black people much as the spider web holds flies—they can wiggle but they cannot move very far." For Hanchard (1992, 155), Brazil presents a classic case of "racial hegemony," which "denies the existence of racial inequalities, while simultaneously producing them." Thus, despite the absence of formally racist systems, these analysts believe that contemporary racism and racial discrimination are firmly established through informal means in Brazil, as they now are for the United States.

Consciously egregious and direct racism directed at particular individuals, especially in the forms of racial insults, are the practices most recognized as constituting racism in Brazil.[13] These incidents are commonly written up in the press and are the targets of Brazil's antiracism laws.[14] A high-profile example occurred recently in Rio de Janeiro when the state governorship changed hands from Benedita da Silva to Rosinha Matheus, who is the wife of former governor and then presidential candidate Anthony Garotinho.[15] As the family of Anthony Garotinho was getting ready to retake possession of the state governor's office, he announced that he needed to "disinfect" the governor's residence (Palacio de Guanabara) before moving in, in an apparently racist reference to outgoing black governor Benedita da Silva.

When such an explicit statement is made, it is often dismissed as an exception to the Brazilian character and is associated with a more virulent U.S.-style racism. However, the fact that an important politician made it suggests that such sentiments are not so alien to Brazilian society. On the other hand, such practices may be less important to the maintenance of racial inequality than more subtle individual and institutional practices. These practices, which in Brazil derive from a way of thinking that naturalizes the racial hierarchy rather than from a willful intent to be racist, reveal the hidden or silent nature of Brazilian racism, as black activists have long pointed out. But this type of racism is becoming increasingly common throughout the world, as legal and explicit racism are on the decline. Winant (2001) maintains that modern racism worldwide exists as a "common sense," which has become part of culture where perpetrators are increasingly unimportant. In Brazil, this common sense is often articulated through the belief that blacks know their place.

Institutions often discriminate, regardless of the beliefs held by those who work in them. Institutional pressures to maintain a racial hierarchy often structure individual choices. Attorney Hedio Silva, the director of an NGO that promotes antiracist causes in employment and labor unions, provides an example of how individuals may act in discriminatory ways even though not of a racist mind themselves. He describes the example of a white personnel director who does not hold antiblack sentiments, who feels comfortable around blacks, socializes with them, and perhaps is married to a black woman, but is under institutional pressure to hire white workers. While he understands how discrimination has unjustly kept black workers, including members of his own family, from formal employment, he also knows that if he hires black workers, he puts his own job in jeopardy. Although the firm has not explicitly told him to admit only white workers, he knows that he will be evaluated on his ability to hire workers who maintain or improve the institutional profile of his company. Given a nationally shared ideal of what constitutes a desirable profile, he correctly surmises that white workers are preferable. The general culture disseminates and accepts the idea of a racial hierarchy, which Brazilians in turn perceive as natural; this provides them with a logic for understanding and legitimizing the racial order.

Stereotypes

Discrimination begins with societal images of nonwhites known as racial stereotypes. Prejudice is based on stereotypes involving a judgment or mental image that people make of others based on attributes like race and gender. Stereotypical judgments are a common human response in human interactions where there is little or no information available about the other. However, they also may persist after supplemental information about the individual is known. Allport (1954) noted that this "inflexivity" is what distinguishes prejudices from simple prejudgments. Despite contrary evidence, gained through knowledge of others, people often do not discard or correct adverse images of certain groups. At best, individuals who defy stereotypes are simply known as "exceptions to the rule."

Stereotypes of browns and blacks in Brazil are usually negative. Racial stereotypes in Brazil include the idea that "negros are only good in music and sports," to which 43 percent of Brazilians agreed in the 1995 national survey. A more racist stereotype is "negros who don't do it on entering, do it on leaving" ("it" is popularly understood as "screwing up"), with which 23 percent agreed in the same survey.[16] Incidentally, similar numbers of whites, browns, and blacks agreed with both of these statements. Thus, blacks and browns, like whites, hold similar stereotypes of negros. Bailey (2002), using the 1995 and 2000 surveys, also finds little difference by color in a wide array of attitudinal responses. He attributes this to a lack of racial group sentiment in Brazil. On the other hand, 85 percent of Brazilians, with no difference by race, believed that "if blacks were well fed and had schooling then they would be as successful as whites," suggesting that Brazilians commonly believe that nonwhites could overcome their putative limitations.

Available evidence suggests that some stereotypes of blacks in Brazil may not be as harsh as those in the United States. Although it is difficult to find comparable U.S.-Brazil questions on racial attitudes, I did find one. The question was, who is smarter? Eighty-three percent of Brazilians claimed that there is no difference regarding level of intelligence between whites and blacks, 8 percent believed whites are smarter, and 6 percent believed blacks are smarter. Similar percentages are found for whites, browns, and blacks.[17] The United States stands in stark contrast: only 42 percent of U.S. whites believed there is no difference and 57 percent thought whites are smarter. However, 66 percent of U.S. blacks believed there is no difference, 18 percent believed whites are smarter, and 16 percent that blacks are smarter.[18] This example further demonstrates a greater racial divide in popular racial beliefs in the United States compared to Brazil, where racist and antiracist feelings are shared equally by white, brown, and blacks. On the other hand, this example may illustrate that a societally desirable response of racial democracy, rather than real inner beliefs, is being expressed.

HUMOR AND THE SUBTLENESS OF RACISM

Humor is an important part of Brazilian culture. Joking, for example, is common in the workplace and in most places that Brazilians interact. Racial humor and racist jokes are part of this culture and are generally taken in stride with other types of humor. Racial humor is based on common stereotypes and naturalizes popular images held of blacks by downplaying their seriousness. However, such humor popularizes and reproduces negative stereotypes about blacks, potentially impairing black self-esteem. As with humor in general, persons who negatively react to humorous insults are told they "can't take a joke." A sense of political correctness, which often acts informally to censor such jokes in the United States, is relatively absent in Brazil.

Racist humor against blacks is exemplified by a song performed in 1996 by a popular clown and children's entertainer. The song, "Look at her Hair," was performed by Tíririca but was later censored by the courts. The song's lyrics are:

> Hello folks, this is Tíririca
> I am also into Axé Music
> I want to see my friends dancing
> [Refrain] Look, look, look at her hair.
> It looks like brillo to scrub a pan
> When she passes by, she gets my attention
> But her hair, it's hopeless
> Her stink almost made me faint
> You know, I can't stand her smell
> [Refrain 3 times].
> It looks like brillo to scrub a pan
> I already sent her to take a bath
> The stubborn girl won't listen
> That black woman [nega] stinks, can't stand the way she stinks
> Smelly animal [bicha] smells worse than a skunk.[19]

The fact that this song was written and performed for children, and by a widely popular clown, may have led many to believe the song was harmless. Moreover, the song was explicitly performed in a lively Afro-Brazilian musical rhythmic form known as Axé, which may have further led people to believe the song was performed by blacks. But, more importantly, the song reflects the naturalness with which black people are derided to the point that explicit racism is so openly, but perhaps innocently, broadcast to children. Indeed, the presumed innocence of Tíririca's song underlies a common belief that such humor is only fun. It is inoffensive and does not have significant negative consequences.

THE MEDIA

Relatedly, racial stereotypes about blacks are common in the media. Despite national pride in being multiracial, Brazilian television, perhaps the most important purveyor of national culture, features actors that are predominately white and, strikingly, often blonde. Black activist Helio Santos frequently notes that Brazilian television without volume could be mistaken for Swedish television. Despite their overwhelming presence in Brazilian society, nonwhites on television are often invisible or relegated to menial roles, although there are beginning to be small changes. When blacks are represented, Brazilian television often reinforces stereotypes about them and cues the viewing audience to associate them with particular forms of behavior. By contrast, white persons and white families are cast as the symbols of beauty, happiness, and middle-class success.

Television has had a huge influence on popular Brazilian culture, mostly through the discourse of the popular *telenovelas* (roughly, soap operas), which seek to portray Brazilian lives and often Brazil's history.[20] In his careful archival analysis of telenovelas over a span of fifty years, Araújo (2000) found that Brazilian television writers and producers have portrayed Brazilians as European, reinforcing the value of white skin and eliminating many popular aspects of Brazilian culture. For example, despite its centrality in national culture, Afro-Brazilian religion is almost never presented in the Brazilian media. Araújo also found that the popular celebration of miscegenation—despite being the dominant theme in the novels of Jorge Amado and others, and being raised to a high place in national culture and identity—has been rarely defended throughout the fifty years of Brazilian telenovelas. However, Araújo notes that in the 1990s blacks finally began to perform in important roles, suggesting that writers and producers are beginning to deal with Brazil's struggle to cope with racial diversity. Still, nonwhites continue to be poorly represented in television.

D'Adesky (2001) found that of the twenty-five telenovelas that aired from 1993 to 1997 on media giant TV Globo, only 7.9 percent of the 830 actors who appeared were black or brown. Similarly, he reports that newspapers and magazines, which attract middle-class readership, tend to portray European images in advertising, although there are some signs that black representation may be slowly improving. Among a total of 1,204 models appearing in advertisements in the leading weekly magazine *Veja* between 1994 and 1995, only 6.5 percent were black or brown. In the leading magazine targeted toward a female audience, *Cosmopolitan/Nova,* only 4 percent of the models used during the same two-year period were nonwhite. All this in a country whose population is nearly half brown or black.

DISCRIMINATION IN EDUCATION

Analysts have long agreed that Brazilians will often voice their racial stereotypes or prejudices, but at one time they disagreed about whether these translated into acts of discrimination.[21] Harris (1952) and Wagley (1952) claimed that the behavior of Brazilians was in no way discriminatory, even though they would express racist sentiments. Fernandes (1965) and Ianni (1987) responded that it was impossible to have racial prejudices but not manifest them in some way or another. At the very least, stereotypes are conveyed in powerful ways through humor and the media, strengthening conceptions about societally acceptable views of nonwhites. However, it now seems clear that racist beliefs lead to discriminatory behavior in Brazil, which I seek to show in the remainder of this chapter.

In the previous chapter, I showed that education accounts for most of the variation in racial occupational inequality among Brazil's largest urban areas. Similarly, N. Silva (1999) found that the amount of schooling that Brazilians attain also accounts for most of the racial gap in white-nonwhite mobility.[22] Thus, schools may be the most important sites for examining how racial inequalities are produced. Undoubtedly, class inequalities are reproduced through education in a variety of ways, which reproduce racial inequalities. This is most apparent by providing better schools to persons with greater financial resources. At the other extreme, poor persons, aside from having to rely on the worst schools, also have diminished learning capacities due to malnutrition and sleeplessness.

As I showed in the examination of multiracial siblings in elementary and secondary school, there is also increasing evidence of racial discrimination in schools that is independent of class. Some racial discrimination in schools may be blatant but discrimination is more likely to take the form of a self-fulfilling prophecy whereby teachers invest more in white students. This leads to the relatively poorer performance of nonwhite students. This combines with a poor image of negros as presented in school textbooks, leading to further negative stereotyping of nonwhites. All this reinforces a greater sense of self-confidence, privilege, and even superiority by whites, and harms the self-esteem of nonwhites.[23] Such racial discrimination is manifested in the entire educational cycle, from preschool to graduate school.

A study based on participant observation in a private preschool in São Paulo revealed that teachers are more affectionate with and overlook discriminatory acts among white students, denying at the same time that racism exists in their school. Cavalleiro (2000; 2001) found that black and brown preschoolers experienced and recognized racial discrimination by being excluded from games and friendships and even receiving explicit racial taunts from other children, which their teachers may have observed but never reacted to. Black and brown children tolerated such racism usually by remaining silent, but occasionally they reacted violently, which resulted in their being punished by teachers. Other types of racial discrimination observed in the preschool were more subtle but nevertheless harmful. Teachers maintained more physical distance from negro children, while they more often embraced, kissed, and made eye contact with white children. For example, based on her observations of parents picking up their children after school, the author notes that teachers would kiss almost all of the white preschoolers good-bye but only a minority of the nonwhite kids. Teachers also made comments such as "cute little one, do you want to be my daughter and come live in my house"[24] to the white children but rarely to the negro and brown children. Teachers also presented white preschoolers with greater challenges and signalled to them that relationships with negro children should be avoided.

While the racially distinct treatment of preschool children is alarming, racial discrimination occurs against children from even before their birth. Comments indicating preferences for lighter-skinned children are common before and after the births of children. Such children are generally considered more attractive and well behaved. This preference is also apparent in the case of adoption, where potential parents sometimes state color preferences on the application form. A newspaper recently reported that of 122 official requests in Rio de Janeiro from families seeking to adopt children, 44 of these indicated that they only would accept white children, while an additional 25 would also accept brown children, and 4 noted that they would even accept black girls. None of the adoptive families indicated a willingness to accept black boys, although several did not indicate any color preference.[25]

The lack of appropriate role models and stereotypes may also contribute to low self-esteem among negro schoolchildren. Black role models are virtually absent in Brazilian textbooks, and African history is rarely taught in school. When they exist, they tend to be in sports and in popular music. Their absence leads to a response of lowered expectations for nonwhite youth by themselves and by society in general. The popularity of the apparently humorous but racist children's song about black women sends the message that it is widely accepted that black people, especially black women, are inferior and it is acceptable to joke about them. Textbooks depicting blacks as lazy, uncivilized, and violent have been common in Brazilian schools, although in recent years, the Ministries of Justice and Education have attempted to recall and outlaw all schoolbooks with racist material, but this program has had mixed success.[26] For example, Monteiro Lobato, who is perhaps the most well-known author of children's books in Brazil, portrayed blacks in derisively negative roles and these books continue to be widely used in Brazilian schools. The derogatory references in his books have been censored although many schools have yet to receive the edited versions.

In Brazil, low opinions of negros result in a self-fulfilling prophecy as teachers invest more in children who are farthest away chromatically, socially, and culturally from belonging to the black group. As one teacher in Southern Brazil referred to a group of her light-brown students, "those girls are more disciplined and study harder. Their mothers are mulattas and their fathers look white. They are always very clean and they don't mix much." And of the black students, "they can't learn, they are lazy, and they give up right away. They only want to know about samba and soccer. It's in their blood."[27] The same teacher also expressed that mixed-race students should whiten themselves and distance themselves from blacks. It is not clear how many teachers hold this view; this particular teacher may have been unusual in that she expressed her views so openly. In any case, many teachers, consciously or not, invest in lighter children because they believe that those children are more likely to succeed, and thus a good education will be more beneficial to them.

Studies have found a strong rejection and negation of blackness among older black and brown schoolchildren due to the strength of the whitening ideology. Such youth have internalized the idea of black inferiority and seek their salvation by somehow "becoming whiter" by, for example, socializing with light-skinned children.[28] Oliveira (1999) finds that mixed-race middle-class couples often avoid discussions of race because the darker partner may see the benefit and possibility for becoming white; the children of those couples tend to avoid or deny their African origins. Alternatively, she also finds that children of mixed-race parents who learn about racial discrimination at home tend to perceive societal rejection of nonwhites and find that it is possible to take pride in their African ancestry and reject whitening.

There is also a spatial-discrimination argument that helps explain educational inequality by race. In her study of São Paulo, Rosemberg (1991) found that black and brown children were more likely than white children to attend public rather than private schools and to take night courses. Among those attending public schools, nonwhites were particularly likely to attend the poorly resourced schools of the urban periphery. Public schools in São Paulo vary widely in quality, and suburban schools lack modern technical and pedagogical resources, qualified teachers and counselors. For children in São Paulo suburban schools, classroom time is reduced because of a constant absence of teachers. Rosemberg found that even at the same socioeconomic levels, nonwhites were more likely to attend schools of poorer quality in both night and day shifts and in both private and public systems. She concluded that spatial segregation by race independent of class was the most probable explanation.

Additionally, teachers at schools with predominately white student bodies favor white students and discriminate against nonwhites, and better and more experienced teachers may also seek out such schools. School officials may have established client relations with particular schools, which have disproportionately large numbers of white students. All these factors reinforce one another as whiter schools come to be thought of as being better schools so that school quality and race correlate even more, independently of class. However, given the moderate levels of residential segregation in Brazil, the kind of school segregation that is found in the United States, where whites and blacks of the same class often attend highly segregated schools, is less common.

Success in college is the primary determinant of professional class status, and the few nonwhite students that complete secondary school in Brazil continue to suffer disadvantages as they make the transition to college. The previous chapter showed that the racial gap in college attendance has increased consistently over the past forty years. Since a university education is widely considered to be the key to middle-class status, the *vestibular* (the college entrance exams), thus becomes the greatest determinant of middle-class status. Admission to the university depends entirely on the *vestibular*, which determines the careers students will pursue. As I discussed in the previous chapter, because of their superior private pre-college education, the wealthiest students get into the best universities, which are generally public. Wealthy students are also admitted disproportionately into the more prestigious and financially rewarding disciplines such as medicine, engineering, and law. When they are admitted to prestigious universities, poorer and nonwhite students are more likely to be sorted into low-prestige fields, such as education and the humanities. When they are not, poorer students often must pay for their education in an inferior private college.

LABOR-MARKET DISCRIMINATION

Attitude surveys in 1995 and 2000 indicate that adult Brazilians believe racial discrimination is greatest in the labor market. In the 2000 survey, 54 percent of the total population of the state of Rio de Janeiro identified work as the place of greatest racial tension in Brazilian society, followed by the neighborhood (16 percent), school (13 percent), and religion (7 percent). In the 1995 national survey, blacks were more than twice as likely than browns to identify discrimination for persons of their color in hiring and in promotions.[29] While research evidence suggests that most racial inequality is produced through formal education, these opinion surveys, of adult respondents who have generally completed their schooling, point to a strong perception of labor market discrimination in Brazil. Nevertheless, much of it is also produced in the labor market as the human capital model earlier in this chapter strongly suggested. In this section, I present further evidence of labor-market discrimination and show the diverse ways this discrimination is manifested, from the job search to hiring to promotion.

Before the mid-1940s, specific racial terms were commonly used in employment advertising to exclude nonwhites; these were gradually supplanted by the term *boa aparência* (good appearance) by 1950. Damasceno (2000) documents that this term was used until well into the 1980s and was popularly known to mean "whites only." Other terms such as "good health," "good teeth," or "presentable" were also used in employment advertising as code words to exclude blacks and browns. According to Damasceno, the shift from explicit racial discrimination to "aesthetic discrimination" was consistent with the emerging ideology of racial democracy. It was not until the 1980s that *boa aparência* and similar terms were declared illegal because, in a climate of an emerging consciousness about racism, they were finally recognized as purposefully discouraging nonwhite applicants.

In her extensive research of contemporary São Paulo labor markets, Bento (2000) found that personnel departments of large companies continue to hire, promote, and fire based on racial and gender stereotypes. Although the companies Bento studied tended to be in highly competitive markets and employed modern administrative methods, their actual policies and procedures for decision making were often ambiguous, secretive, and ultimately discriminatory because they relied on individual decisions. She found that once basic criteria like schooling and experience were met, personnel workers would rely on racial and other stereotypes to infer about vague and subjective qualifications deemed necessary to fill particular jobs. Such racial profiling is especially problematic in Brazil, where the number of qualified persons tends to greatly exceed job availability, allowing employers to choose among many well-qualified candidates.

Bento (2000) also found that, once they were hired and had been promoted, nonwhite workers, especially black women, faced further difficulties. This was especially true when they occupied supervisory positions, because this reverted the logic of the Brazilian racial hierarchy. In the rare cases where negros were supervisors, white colleagues felt uncomfortable, and discrimination became more intense and visible. Black and mulatto supervisors reported that subordinates created "traps" or strategies that led their supervisors to make errors, consequently reinforcing the stereotype of black inferiority. They also reported that clients and subordinates were inconsiderate and did not grant them the same prestige and recognition as their white status equals. Additionally, professional colleagues of nonwhite supervisors were constantly distrustful of them.

Such discrimination is a reflection of everyday racism, which blacks of all social classes constantly face. Aside from education and the labor market, blacks find that police, shopkeepers, doormen, and neighbors are often distrustful of them. Even friendly relations often have elements of racism. I found that even the small proportion of middle-class negros in Brazil often face inconveniences and slights that their white friends do not. For example, I found it common for middle-class negros, who are often with white status equals, to be introduced by name along with their occupation or some other status symbol, while the whites are presented by name only. Such disparate treatment may seem subtle but is likely to be consequential when combined with other everyday incidents.

SOCIAL NETWORKS AND PATRONAGE

Perhaps the most clear and convincing evidence of labor-market discrimination can be seen when paired testers portraying black and white job applicants with similar qualifications are sent out for job interviews and their treatment and rate of acceptance is examined.[30] Such experiments are often used in the United States to demonstrate in court that blacks, despite having similar qualifications as whites, suffer from greater chances of being denied employment. Although there have been attempts to use such a strategy by Brazilian journalists,[31] these studies did not use the strict controls needed to meet the high standards of evidence required by U.S. courts.

Given the potential benefit for establishing compelling evidence of the pervasiveness of discrimination to apparently skeptical Brazilian courts (see chapter 10), through the Ford Foundation, I funded researchers at the University of São Paulo in 1998 to replicate the paired-tester methodology. Unfortunately, they were unable to carry out this test because its methodology depended on employment advertising, which was far less common in the Brazilian job market compared to the United States where it was developed. These researchers discovered that the vast majority of hiring was done by word-of-mouth for the receptionists and "office boy" occupations that they sought to investigate. They chose these occupations because they were predominately held by whites, although many negros were qualified to compete for them. While they never got to the point of directly testing discrimination, the planning stages of their research revealed the great importance of social networks and clientelism in hiring.

Most recruiting and hiring for these jobs used networks and patronage systems. Such informal methods favor whites, so that employers often do not directly deny jobs to nonwhites. Rather, blacks and browns seem to be discriminated against by being denied access to these networks or they are less likely to know job sponsors. When they do have access, job sponsors and networks are likely to screen out nonwhites, and especially blacks, themselves. Job sponsors may mostly recommend other whites because they themselves prefer whites or assume employers prefer whites.[32] Similarly, persons in networks with information about jobs, including those that currently hold such jobs, are also likely to recommend whites, especially because it may enhance their own status in the eyes of their employers.

While social networks depend on numerous ties and relations among social equals as well as with status superiors, patronage often depends on a single person of superior status who monopolizes local economic resources. According to E. Costa (1985), Brazil's system of patronage since the colonial period made poor whites and freed brown and black workers dependent on the white elite. In that system, social mobility was not acquired through market competition but through decisions by the white elite based on their patron relations. This patron-client relation was part of a naturalized social hierarchy, which emphasized reciprocal relationships rather than personal freedom and personal rights, which are valued by the North American system. Although this system is likely to have favored whites, it also permitted some blacks and especially mulattos to move up the social ladder and into white middle-class society.[33] As a result, mulattos occasionally rose in the social ranks, especially those who were the godsons and illegitimate sons of influential white men or their clients.

Despite its historical roots, patronage extends to modern Brazil and may have even increased with industrial development. Hagopian (1996) showed that during the 1960s traditional elites were able to maintain their power in modern areas through control over greater resources resulting from Brazil's industrialization and economic growth. With technological advances in agriculture and changing employment relations in the countryside, industrialization pushed rural migrants into cities, increasing the client base for traditional elites. Moreover, as industrialization increased government resources and public-sector jobs, which increased more than those in private industry, these jobs could be offered to friends and allies.

Political patronage may be especially important today in small cities and rural areas, where traditional elites are able to control state resources and to exchange them for favors from friends. In such places, favors from patronage are more likely to go to whites than nonwhites, because of the tendency for racially homogenous relations and friendships, and because white clients may start out with more social and economic capital to exchange. There are currently 6,000 municipalities in Brazil, each of which has resources, including employment, that can be allocated to clients. Patrons are especially important in poor small towns and rural areas, especially in the Northeast where the population relies on patrons for just about everything, including basic medical care in exchange for political support.[34] Demographer André Caetano (2001) provides one example of the importance of these relations: he finds that 70 percent of female sterilizations in the Northeast, where 44 percent of all women of childbearing age are sterilized, were arranged by politicians in exchange for votes or other clientelistic favors.

Recent research in economic sociology shows that hiring, even in the modern employment sector in the United States, continues to be governed by social-network ties. Given the historic and continuing importance of personalism and patronage in the Brazilian social system, social networks are likely to be especially important to job seekers in that country. Rather than being fully open and discontinuous from personal life, as it is often conceptualized for the United States, Da Matta (1991) suggests that the workplace in Brazil is more often an extension of the web of familial and personal relationships. For example, he notes the continuing importance of "the mediator" for socializing young people of the upper and middle classes into familiarity with the rules and mysteries of entering the labor market. The continuing significance of networks and patronage reinforces racial inequality and is thus contrary to the predictions of Florestan Fernandes and others that such ties would eventually be displaced by impersonal and productivity-based criteria.

FAMILY STRUCTURE

Along with schools, the family is the other great socializing institution of contemporary society. In the United States, racial differences in family structures are thought to be a major determinant of black disadvantage. In families, parents provide children with different levels of material, social, and emotional support, which determines the well-being of their children and prepares them for their adult lives. The ability of parents to provide support depends on their own well-being and status, which is shaped by race and family structure, among other things. In traditional two-parent families, incomes tend to be higher and household tasks can be divided among the adults. Children of two-parent families also benefit from having both male and female role models, which has been shown to be important for children's own self-confidence.

High rates of poverty and lower rates of educational achievement among Afro-North Americans are sometimes attributed to disproportionate numbers of single-mother households. These numbers increased rapidly in the 1970s as the economic base of black workers changed dramatically.[35] Currently, most black children in the United States are born to single mothers.[36] In 1998, 58 percent of all black households were headed by one parent as compared to 23 percent of white households. These figures are up from 33 and 9 percent in 1970.[37]

However, such differences are not nearly as stark in Brazil. Although a pattern of single motherhood is thought to derive from slavery, Slenes (1999) has shown that slaves often had family lives despite barriers imposed by their masters. In a separate analysis of the 2000 census, 11.7 percent of white families, 13.1 percent of brown families, and 13.9 percent of black families reported being of the single-mother type. Goldani (1989) reported similar figures for 1984, although these were up from about half those levels in 1960.[38] Thus, single motherhood is less likely to explain Brazil's racial gap in socioeconomic status, as racial differences are small compared to the large differences in the United States.

THE BRAZILIAN STATE AND THE SHAPING OF RACIAL INEQUALITY

While the United States and South Africa legislated explicitly racist policies, the postabolition Brazilian state has not, except perhaps for its immigration policy. However, other state policies have had the consequence of shaping Brazil's current racial hierarchy. We have already noted the important effects of education, although there is no direct evidence that this was willful discrimination at the state level, except to the degree that the state has ignored education for the poor. The two areas in which we know the state has purposefully sought to maintain a racial hierarchy on a large scale have been slavery and, more recently, immigration policy.

The Brazilian economy and its Portuguese predecessor relied on the institution of slavery, which depended entirely on a system of racial domination. Through regulation by and support of the state, Africans were enslaved and forcefully moved to the Americas. State agents ensured their servitude through highly repressive means, including torture. Thus, the Brazilian state formalized extreme racial inequality, until 1888. Since abolition, mobility rates have been high enough that nonwhite disadvantage could theoretically have been largely overcome by now. Instead, Brazil's transition from slavery to free work did almost nothing to change the relations between blacks and whites, and between workers and owners. Above all, the legacy of Brazilian slavery created a pattern of social practices that has differentiated the treatment of black and white workers since then.

Brazilian immigration policies continued to ensure racial inequality for at least two decades after abolition. In an effort to "whiten" and civilize the Brazilian population, employers, in collusion with the federal and state governments, sought European immigrants to replace slaves, barring African, Asian, and black North Americans from coming to Brazil.[39] Many of the 1.5 million European immigrants came to Brazil with ship fares and lodging subsidized by the state of São Paulo. Upon their arrival, these immigrants were favored for employment, granted better jobs, and in some cases, given land or sold land at better terms than for natives. In the south of Brazil, the governments established small farms for immigrants under government tutelage, and in 1892, the state of São Paulo established the Office of Land Colonialization and Immigration, which granted provisional titles to immigrants on formerly public lands.[40]

At the same time, blacks and mulattos, many recently freed from slavery, were left to their own devices and were virtually excluded from the formal economy. Their former owners often kicked out freed slaves so that they were no longer assured of the subsistence they previously received.[41] Formerly freed blacks and mulattos even lost their few legal rights, including the right of the elderly to remain on plantations and the guaranteed support for children of slaves that were automatically manumitted in 1872. After abolition, black and brown men got precarious jobs and women often became domestic workers in cities, leaving them with the responsibility of raising children. In some cases, planters restored former slave rights only as a form of paternalism, not out of legal obligation. It was only with the end of massive immigration, which engendered a growing demand for labor in the late 1920s, that blacks and mulattos were able to compete for skilled blue-collar jobs in São Paulo's industrializing economy.[42] A similar story might be told for other industrializing areas. However, much of Brazil was untouched by industrialization or immigration, especially where blacks and browns were in the majority. Little or no industrialization in such places meant little mobility. The few available opportunities in such places were largely reserved for the small white and light-mulatto population.

Although not racially explicit, the implementation of repressive laws often disproportionately affected black persons, well after abolition. Two examples stand out. First, the *Lei da Vadiagem,* a policy which criminalized loafing or hanging around, was generally applied to unemployed black men.[43] Also, the African religious practice of *candomblé,* the Yoruba-based religious ritual, was highly regulated and repressed by police in Bahia until 1976. The performance of *candomblé* rituals required permission from authorities, and *terreiros* (places for *candomblé* rites) had to be registered with the local police.

Regional policies of the federal government have also directly led to greater racial inequality although the extent to which government actions intended to create inequality of any kind is not clear. Beginning in the 1930s, Brazil's development policies favored the Southeast, and especially São Paulo, by subsidizing industrialists in that region, while failing to provide necessary subsidies for export-oriented agriculture and incipient industry in the Northeast.[44] These policies had a huge impact on racial inequality since they favored the white population, which has been disproportionately concentrated in the South and Southeast.

POLICE ABUSE AND RACE

Finally, the historically powerful Brazilian justice system continues to wield its influence in discriminatory ways. Despite democratization, police violence increased in the 1990s. While official respect for political rights has expanded, torture continues to be widely employed in Brazil as a method of investigation, particularly in the extraction of confessions.[45] In the State of São Paulo, where the best statistics on police actions are collected, the state's military police have killed hundreds of civilians each year since they began keeping records in 1981, as Caldeira (2000) describes. In one year, 1992, police killed 1,470 civilians.[46] Comparatively, New York City police kill about 20 civilians each year. In 1987, the most brutal year of the apartheid regime, police in all of South Africa killed 172 people.

Piovesan and her colleagues (2001) estimate that roughly 50 percent of all police killings can be classified as summary, arbitrary, or extrajudicial executions. The ratio of killed to wounded civilians, also known as the lethality index by criminologists, has been on the order of two or three to one in Brazil, which suggests large numbers of summary executions. Also, an investigation by the São Paulo State Ombudsman in 1999 found that 52.6 percent of police killings involved shots in the back, 23 percent of the victims received five or more bullet wounds, and 36 percent suffered shots to the head. The victims of these police killings are disproportionately black or brown. The National Movement for Human Rights NGO created a database on homicides with information collected from daily newspapers in the twenty-seven states of Brazil. For the 16 percent of cases in 1999 that had information on the color of the victim, 85 percent of the victims of police and death squads were nonwhite.[47] Specifically, 61 percent were listed as negro, 18 percent as moreno, 6 percent as pardo, and 15 percent as white.[48]

Using various documents from jury-trial courts[49] in the City of São Paulo, W. Cano (2002) found that 33.0 percent of civilians intentionally killed by the police were brown and another 13.3 percent were black, while the general population was 24 percent brown and 4 percent black. Cano's study paid careful attention to potential racial-classification problems. In the documents he used, racial-classification is based on the initial police incident report using census categories and it is generally maintained throughout the judicial process.[50] Also, because there is relatively little ambiguity about racial classifications in São Paulo, Cano's findings are especially strong evidence that the police target nonwhites for execution, especially those at the dark end of the color continuum.

Based on civil police incident reports, Cano also examined police killings in the state of Rio de Janeiro and found that in the period 1993 to 1996, police killed 2.7 times more white civilians than they wounded. By contrast, the lethality index was 5.1 for browns and 4.3 for blacks. Skeptical that most of these differences by race were due to the disproportionate residence of nonwhites in favelas, where police are more likely to use their weapons, Cano broke down the lethality index by race for favelas and for the rest of the city. Outside the *favelas*, he found that police killed 1.9 times as many whites as they wounded, 3.2 times as many browns, and 2.6 times as many blacks. In the favelas, the lethality index was 4.6 for whites, 9.0 for browns, and 8.2 for blacks, thus removing Cano's initial doubt that racial bias occurred beyond class.

According to these statistics, browns are more likely than blacks to be killed by police once shot, but blacks are much more likely to be shot by police in the first place. While they make up only 8.4 percent of the state population, blacks comprise 29.8 percent of those killed and 26.8 percent of those wounded by police. Browns comprise 31.6 percent of the population but are 40.4 and 30.6 percent of the killed and wounded, respectively. Although these figures are not precise given the especially great ambiguity of distinctions between browns and blacks, they demonstrate a general pattern of greatest victimization for blacks, followed by browns and then whites, and these differences persist despite whether they occur in middle-class or poor neighborhoods.

The contention that race is solely a class issue is also rejected by the common experiences of middle-class blacks, who are disproportionately confronted by police. Even prominent black figures—such as the former São Paulo secretary of justice, Lidvaldo Britto—report often being pulled over and questioned by the police. In another case, an African American friend of mine was looking for an apartment in an upscale Rio de Janeiro neighborhood when he was accosted at gunpoint by the state military police. The officer withdrew his gun only when his real-estate agent came running to the car, yelling "Don't shoot him! He's an American!"

A study by Mitchell and Wood (1998) further support these observations. Based on victimization self-reports from the 1988 national household survey (PNAD), they found that independent of the effects of region, urban-rural residence, income, education, and age, black men are more likely than white men to have been the target of physical assault and are especially likely to have been victims of police aggression. Brown men were intermediate to white and black men. Blacks were 2.4 times as likely as whites to be assaulted by the police, even after controlling for the locational, social class, and age differences. For these reasons, it is easy to understand why blacks are more likely to fear and distrust the police than whites.

Racial profiling is also common among the Brazilian police. Blacks are disproportionately pulled over and questioned at police checkpoints (blitzes) in major urban areas. I systematically observed one such blitz in Rio de Janeiro when, out of approximately 200 cars that passed in a fifteen-minute period, nearly all of the approximately 20 black and mulatto male motorists who passed were pulled over, while no white motorists were stopped. This seems to be the general conception among Brazilians. In the 2000 Rio de Janeiro state survey, 95 percent of the population agreed that negros are frequently pulled over during these blitzes. One analyst of the police claims that they have historically treated negros as "born suspects." He describes how officers in São Paulo teach cadets that police do not stop blacks because of their race but because they act in suspicious ways. A commonly utilized situation for training police to deal with crime is specifically referred to as the case of "four crioulos in a car."[51]

Data differentiated by race for the prison population, like those for police, are difficult to come by in Brazil and vary in quality. The best available data seem to be for São Paulo. Kahn (2002) reveals that 16.0 percent of the São Paulo state's prison population is black compared to 3.6 percent of the general population, while 26.0 percent of those in prison are brown compared to 21.7 percent of civilians. Thus, if we are to compare prison and civilian population statistics, blacks are overrepresented 4.4 times in prisons, while browns are overrepresented by a factor of 1.2. By contrast, whites are underrepresented in prisons since they comprise 72.4 percent of the state's population but only 57.0 percent of the prison population. Thus, blacks are 5.6 times as likely as whites to be in prison, while browns are 1.5 times as likely as whites. Based on what we know about racial classification in São Paulo, my sense is that these figures overestimate white-black differences and underestimate white-brown differences. Persons on the darker end of the brown category may be especially likely to be classified as black when they are suspected criminals and when they are in the penal system.

These data compare to the United States where blacks were 7 to 8 times as likely as whites to be in prison in the 1990s.[52] Thus, racial differences in incarceration are not as large in Brazil as in the United States today, although it is not clear why. While blacks constitute only 12 percent of the U.S. population, they are 50 percent of state and federal prisoners. This compares to the 1950s, when African Americans were one-third of the incarcerated population.[53] The U.S. experience shows that huge racial differences in incarceration grew mostly because of drug-related crimes, in which blacks were far more likely to be arrested and convicted, despite similar levels of illicit drug use by blacks and whites. Wacquant (2000) theorizes that this shift represents a changing form by which the United States state controls blacks—from former Jim Crow segregation in the South and ghettoization in the North to today's imprisonment accompanied by hyperghettoization in the cities.

It is important also to note the large cross-national differences in the scale of incarceration. There are about eleven times as many prisoners in the United States as in Brazil. The total Brazilian prison population is about 150,000, which includes many pretrial detainees, while the U.S. prison population is more than 1.7 million.[54] Thus, the United States had about eleven times as many prisoners as Brazil even though its population is only about 50 percent larger. Comparing racial difference in incarceration in the United States and Brazil therefore requires further analysis to control for the huge differences in the size of the prison population and the distinct structure of crimes for which North Americans and Brazilians get imprisoned.

THE BRAZILIAN SOCIAL STRUCTURE AND RACIAL COMPOSITION

And last but not least, we might wonder if Brazil's great income inequality has something to do with race itself. After all, whites are almost exclusively at the top and nonwhites are concentrated at the bottom. So far, this chapter has sought to show the most probable causes of racial inequality, especially to the extent that they can be documented or observed. But could there be something more? Could the very class structure of Brazilian society be affected by race? Figure 6.4 suggests that there may be something to this. Income inequality across Brazilian urban areas tends to decrease with the proportion of the respective population that is white. Thus, the very structure of inequality seems to be related to race, although the relationship is not necessarily causal. Differences in historical development explained largely by industrialization help to explain this relationship because industrialization is more developed in places with higher proportions of whites. But is this merely historical coincidence? Did industrial development policies favor places with more whites? The answer is probably yes but perhaps for reasons that were not explicitly motivated by race. Although coffee generated the capital for industrialization in São Paulo, was it the only factor? The Brazilian state's

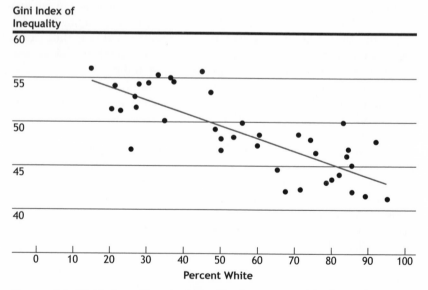

FIGURE 6.4 Gini index of income inequality by percent white for 40 largest urban areas: Brazil, 1980.

preference for European workers was clearly inspired by beliefs in white superiority, and thus it is quite possible that race may have motivated policy makers to continue promoting industrialization in places where European immigrants settled.

At a cross-national level, we might also ask similar questions. Why is it that Brazil has a more disparate income distribution than almost any other major country at similar levels of development, comparable only to South Africa? Why do more racially homogenous countries tend to have lower levels of inequality? One might point to their needs for a highly exploitable labor force, where racial difference is used as the primary characteristic for exploitation. Such an explanation might also account for regional differences in Brazil. Thus, one could argue that racism drives inequality. I cannot satisfactorily point to cause and effect but nevertheless raise these issues because they are troublesome.

CONCLUSIONS

This chapter has provided compelling proof of the existence of racial discrimination beyond inequalities based on class or region or as an artifact of race data itself. It has also shown the mechanisms through which discrimination differentially affects the life chances of Brazilians by race. Although manifestations and causes of racial discrimination are often different from the United States, racial discrimination in Brazil is undeniable. The previous chapter showed that Brazil's hyperinequality contributes to high levels of racial inequality. This chapter showed that racial discrimination differentially sorts whites, browns, and blacks into that hierarchical system largely through informal but widely shared rules about the appropriate place for members of each racial category. In particular, it showed further evidence of a glass ceiling that disproportionately keeps nonwhites from mobility into the middle class. Although browns are preferred over blacks in the Brazilian system, the primary racial boundary is between whites and nonwhites, as mobility into the middle class is nearly blocked for both browns and blacks.

This and other forms of discrimination are sustained by a culture that sets standards about the value of persons by race. A racist culture is reinforced, naturalized, and legitimized through such mediums as humor, popular sayings, television, and advertising. That culture is acted out through direct discrimination in education and employment, as well as through the exclusion of nonwhites from the important social networks in Brazilian society. The state is also complicit in perpetuating this culture and shaping racial inequality. I have emphasized the role of immigration policies that created racial inequalities in the past and continue to structure them today, and state agents, like educators and the police, who continue to act in racially biased ways.

Brazil's ideologies about miscegenation have served to disguise Brazilian racism in many ways. The mechanisms of racial discrimination are sometimes similar to the United States but are often different. Discrimination has been historically subtler than in the United States, although subtle racism is becoming increasingly common in the United States. Racism has been more hidden and indirect in Brazil for many reasons, including the greater importance of class-based mechanisms for reproducing racial inequality, the apparent absence of either formal or de facto extreme segregation in schools, and the greater role of social networks rather than direct exclusion in employment. However, Brazil's class discrimination and high levels of inequality have racial components, including race as a criteria for mobility into the upper reaches of that system and greater inequalities where the nonwhite population is larger. On the other hand, other aspects of the Brazilian racial system are not so subtle. The dissemination of racial stereotypes, as manifested in humor, and the greater invisibility of black representation in the media, appears to be more blatant in Brazil than in the United States today.

Chapter Seven

INTERMARRIAGE

> The friction here was smoothed by the lubricating oil
> of a deep-going miscegenation, whether in the form of a
> free union damned by the clergy or that of the regular
> Christian marriage with the blessing of the padres
> and at the instigation of Church and State.
> —*Gilberto Freyre*, The Masters and the Slaves *(1933)*

BRAZIL'S POPULAR IDEOLOGY holds that intermarriage, like race mixture more generally, is especially prevalent in Brazil. Throughout the period of racial democracy, and to some extent today, Brazilians have proudly held this belief up as evidence that race makes little difference to life outcomes. Similarly, intermarriage is commonly used by sociologists to gauge the extent of intolerance among groups of people in which high rates of intermarriage indicate little social distance between these groups. Milton Gordon's (1964) well-known theory of assimilation regards intermarriage as the ultimate indicator of structural assimilation. He reasoned that high rates of intermarriage were a clear sign that subordinate group members had been generally accepted at the familial level, thus breaking down the major barriers to their full acceptance by the dominant society. He noted how the descendants of European immigrants eventually intermarried with native whites in the United States, but the descendants of black migrants from the South to the North of the United States did not, and thus they continued to face strong barriers to social acceptance. Gordon's thinking is widely accepted by sociologists today who see low white-black marriage rates in the United States, indicating a persistent and nearly impermeable boundary between those two groups that is much greater than that involving whites and U.S.-born Asians or Latinos. If intermarriage rates for Brazil are much higher, as sometimes believed, then Gordon's theory would similarly imply that its racial boundaries are much more fluid or nonexistent.

However, several leading scholars of Brazilian race relations claim that these presumed high levels of intermarriage are exaggerated products of Brazil's nationalist ideology that is rooted in extensive miscegenation during slavery. Slavery created vast power differentials between whites and blacks in both the United States and Brazil, but miscegenation is likely to have been much higher in Brazil during that time because Portuguese migration to Brazil was primarily male, while migration to the United States was largely by families. White males were thus especially likely to exploit their power relations with female slaves. Although harder to prove, Gilberto Freyre believed that cultural factors, along with the imbalanced sex ratio, led to greater Brazilian miscegenation. He believed that the Portuguese had greater tolerance for nonwhites because they had lived alongside the dark-skinned Moors for centuries. Indeed, they were largely products of miscegenation with Moors themselves.

The extent to which Freyre's use of miscegenation referred to stable unions as opposed to sexual liaisons is not always clear. Given his classic referral to sixteenth- and seventeenth-century Brazil, many of these unions were likely mere liaisons involving extremely unequal power relations. With a sleight of hand, Freyre suggests that race relations were more fluid in Brazil because of sexual unions. However, while intermarriage, including concubinage and formal marriage, may be an indicator of more fluid race relations, interracial sexual liaisons are probably not. The historical evidence on the extent of unions by type is scant, but the demographic context and evidence for Cuba suggest that formal interracial unions were not uncommon. Many mulattos, often the progeny of mixed-race relationships, as well as some blacks, were freed during the time of slavery, thus making interracial unions viable. Also, given the scarcity of white women, many white males had extremely low chances of finding a white spouse. As a result, they are likely to have sought unions, often in the form of concubinage. To the extent that nineteenth-century Cuba might parallel Brazilian trends, white males may have also petitioned for marriage in particular circumstances. Martinez-Alier's (1989) work on nineteenth-century Cuba shows that formal marriages were more common among the nobility, and the concept of a good marriage was closely related to ideas of racial purity. However, in her analysis of marriage petitions, she found that low status white men sometimes formally married nonwhite women in gratitude for their generous assistance during difficult times, to prevent their dying in sin from their illicit unions or because they were simply oblivious to social norms.

Goldstein (1999) claims that today racial mixture in Brazil occurs mostly through sexual relations, not actual intermarriage. Marx (1998) and Skidmore (1993), although they recognize greater miscegenation in Brazil during slavery, claim the amount of Brazil's miscegenation in the contemporary period is exaggerated, while miscegenation in the United States is greatly understated. Similarly, several Brazilian demographers examine intermarriage through official statistics and conclude that, contrary to popular beliefs, Brazilians prefer to marry persons of their own color.[1] They thus imply that the much-touted idea of extensive Brazilian race mixture is groundless, although they do not provide any cross-national data that allows for comparative analysis. These views are consistent with sociological theories that would expect high levels of discrimination, as I described in the previous chapter, to lead to low intermarriage rates. Either Brazil has low rates of intermarriage or there is something wrong with the theory. Therefore, I first set out to investigate the extent to which the ideology about miscegenation is grounded in the empirical reality of intermarriage.

INTERMARRIAGE IN THE UNITED STATES VS. BRAZIL

In the United States, the existence of antimiscegenation laws until 1967 ensured the presence of rigid racial boundaries. There was rarely any black-white intermarriage before then. Since then, there has been some increase, but the numbers continue to be small. Table 7.1 shows that in 1960, when bans against marriage were still in effect in several southern states, less than 1 percent of black men and women were married to whites. By 1992, the number had grown to 4.4 percent for black men and 2.3 percent for black women. Because of a much larger white population, the effect of these marriages on white rates is smaller. Although it may have doubled or even more, the proportion of whites married to blacks was only 0.2 or 0.3 percent, for white men or women by 1992. That such low levels of black-white intermarriage persisted for twenty-five years after the Supreme Court invalidated all antimiscegenation laws suggests that social taboos against such unions remains very strong. In South

TABLE 7.1
Black-white marriage rates in the United States, 1960 and 1992

	1960		1992	
	Color of spouse		Color of spouse	
	White (%)	Black (%)	White (%)	Black (%)
White men	99.9	0.1	99.8	0.2
White women	99.9	0.1	99.7	0.3
Black men	0.8	99.2	4.4	95.6
Black women	0.9	99.1	2.3	97.7

Source: U.S. Bureau of the Census, Internet Release Date: 06/10/98. Tables 1 and 2.
Note: This table excludes marriages involving spouses from other racial categories.

TABLE 7.2
Interracial Marriage Rates: Brazil, 1991

A. Distribution of all couples by race

		Husband			
		White (%)	Brown (%)	Black (%)	Others (%)
Wife	White (%)	45.4	10.3	1.0	0.3
	Brown (%)	7.7	28.2	1.7	0.01
	Black (%)	0.7	1.1	2.6	0.1
	Others (%)	0.2	0.14	0.02	0.7

B. Racial distribution of the husbands of white, brown, black, and other wives

		Husband				Total (%)
		White (%)	Brown (%)	Black (%)	Others (%)	
Wife	White (%)	79.7	18.0	1.8	0.5	100.0
	Brown (%)	20.4	74.8	4.4	0.4	100.0
	Black (%)	15.9	23.9	59.9	0.3	100.0
	Others (%)	19.9	13.5	2.3	64.3	100.0

C. Racial distribution of the wives of white, brown, black, and other husbands

		Wife				Total (%)
		White (%)	Brown (%)	Black (%)	Others (%)	
Husband	White (%)	84.1	14.2	1.3	0.4	100.0
	Brown (%)	26.0	71.1	2.6	0.3	100.0
	Black (%)	19.1	31.6	48.9	0.4	100.0
	Others (%)	24.8	11.6	1.4	62.2	100.0

Source: 1991 Census of Brazil

Africa, similar laws lasted until 1992, resulting in virtually no intermarriage in the contemporary period. Using the 1996 South Africa census, Jacobson and his collaborators (2001) calculated that 99.2 percent of white men and 99.6 percent of white women were married to white spouses (data not shown).

Intermarriage rates for Brazil have been far higher than the United States or South Africa, as tables 7.2 and 7.3 show. By adding the diagonal cells in the table, which indicate endogamy or in-marriage, panel A of table 7.2 reveals that 77 percent of all married Brazilians in 1991 were in endogamous marriages. The remaining 23 percent of marriages were

TABLE 7.3
Interracial Marriage Rates: Brazil, 1960

A. Distribution of all couples
by race

		Husband			
		White (%)	Brown (%)	Black (%)	Others (%)
Wife	White (%)	59.1	4.7	0.7	0.04
	Brown (%)	4.0	21.5	1.6	0.01
	Black (%)	0.5	0.9	6.2	0.00
	Others (%)	0.2	0.1	0.00	0.6

B. Racial distribution of the husbands of
white, brown, black, and other wives

		Husband				
		White (%)	Brown (%)	Black (%)	Others (%)	Total (%)
Wife	White (%)	91.5	7.3	1.1	0.1	100.0
	Brown (%)	14.7	79.5	5.8	0.0	100.0
	Black (%)	6.6	12.0	81.4	0.0	100.0
	Others (%)	2.2	1.1	0.5	96.2	100.0

C. Racial distribution of the wives of white, brown, black, and other husbands

		Wife				
		White (%)	Brown (%)	Black (%)	Others (%)	Total (%)
Husband	White (%)	92.9	6.3	0.8	0.0	100.0
	Brown (%)	17.4	79.2	3.4	0.0	100.0
	Black (%)	8.6	18.5	72.9	0.0	100.0
	Others (%)	5.9	1.1	0.3	92.7	100.0

Source: IBGE, Censo Demográfico

therefore among persons of different color, with the large majority of
these involving persons of proximate color. Racial boundaries thus appear to have been more easily traversed in Brazil as nearly a quarter of
marriages there are interracial. Certainly, these rates may also reflect the
ambiguity of Brazilian racial classification, but the differences are so
large that greater negro-white intermarriage in Brazil cannot be denied,
regardless of fuzziness in classification. In fact, if one accounts for
whitening, then marriage to a lighter-colored partner may whiten that
person, making the Brazil-U.S. differences larger still. Any suggestion
that Brazilian and U.S. rates are converging is greatly premeditated.

A common observation about Brazilian intermarriage is that it is asymmetrical by sex. Intermarriage, where it occurs, is often believed to be predominantly between nonwhite men and white women.[2] Panel B shows how the husbands of white, brown, black, and other women are distributed by race, while panel C shows the racial distribution of wives for men of different colors. Indeed, as in the United States, rates of intermarriage are different for men and women in Brazil. A comparison of panels B and C of table 7.2 demonstrates that white women are more likely to outmarry than white men. For example, the percentages in the left-hand column and top row of panel B indicate that 79.7 percent of white women were endogamously married, while panel C reveals that 84.1 percent of white men were. By contrast, about 16 percent of black women were married to whites as were 19 percent of black men.

Among those outmarrying, white men and women chose brown over black partners by an order of roughly ten times. Approximately 18 percent of married white women had brown husbands in 1991 compared to only 2 percent that had black husbands, and 14 percent of married white men had brown wives compared to 1 percent that were married to black wives. Similarly, brown men were ten times likely to marry white women (26.0 percent) as black women (2.6 percent), while brown women were almost five times as likely to marry white men (20.4 percent) as black men (4.4 percent). These results provide evidence of a strong tendency toward whitening, although, as I will show later, the relatively low rate of white and brown marriage to blacks is *partly* attributable to the relatively small size of the black population.

Intermarriage rates in 1960 were substantial in Brazil but were clearly less than in 1991, as table 7.3 shows. The sum of the diagonals in panel A of the table shows that endogamous marriages accounted for 87 percent of all marriages in 1960. Thus intermarriages increased from 13 percent to 23 percent of all Brazilian unions in the thirty-one-year period, according to the censuses. Panels B and C of table 7.3 demonstrate that about 92 percent of white women and 93 percent of white men had white spouses in 1960. Roughly, the same pattern of intermarriage found in 1960 emerged again in 1991, although outmarriage increased for all race and sex groups. The greater gain was in the rate of white-brown marriage, suggesting a substantial breakdown in the white-brown boundary during the period. Outmarriage was only slightly greater for white women than for white men in 1960 but by 1991, white women were significantly more likely to outmarry. Only 7 percent of white women were married to brown men in 1960, but by 1991 this number had more than doubled to 18 percent. Black endogamy fell from approximately 81 to 60 percent for women (panel B) and from 73 to 49 percent for men (panel C), which is particularly high considering that a large segment of blacks reclassified as brown during the period, as described in chapter 4.

The national differences in intermarriage suggest that racial barriers are much stronger in the United States and South Africa than in Brazil. Recent antimiscegenation laws in the first two countries may account for lower intermarriage in the United States and South Africa compared to Brazil, but more than thirty years after the end of these laws, black-white intermarriage continues to be rare in the United States. However, a true comparison of intermarriage, especially when used as an indicator of tolerance, must account for differences in racial compositions, and in Brazil, racial composition varies widely across regions.

GEOGRAPHIC DIFFERENCES

In the 1940s, Afro-American sociologist E. Franklin Frazier (1942) noted that regional differences in Brazilian levels of racial tolerance declined from north to south. He felt racism in the Brazilian South to be particularly intense and thus most like the United States. Similarly, Thales de Azevedo (1996) claimed that residents of Salvador, Bahia, were especially tolerant of race differences, as evidenced by an apparently higher rate of intermarriage.[3] Based on his review of race-relations studies, Carl Degler also concluded that as one moves south resistance to intermarriage strengthens, but that intermarriage between races is considered undesirable by whites in all areas of Brazil. Moreover, Degler (1986, 187) noted that there was less objection to marriage with mulattos than with blacks. Degler's observations were largely based on evidence showing that as many as 65 percent of marriages in Bahia involved persons of different color, while only 25 percent of mulatto and 11 percent of black men married white women in the city of São Paulo, and only 4 percent of marriages were interracial in a town in the state of São Paulo.

Yet the attitude surveys that Degler also cited revealed a different pattern. The percentages of white college students who would accept blacks and mulattos marrying into their family in the northeastern city of Recife were 14 and 24 percent, respectively, and 10 and 14 percent in São Paulo. One study found that in Rio de Janeiro, 37 percent and 43 percent of white secondary students would similarly accept blacks and mulattos marrying into their families, while the figures for Florianópolis in the South in a sample of middle-class whites of various ages were 23 and 28 percent. Although evidence of actual intermarriages demonstrated that they are more frequent in the Northeast, the attitude surveys did not provide strong evidence of greater resistance to intermarriage as one travels south. In fact, they ran contrary to Degler's conclusions in that whites in the Northeast held slightly more negative attitudes against intermarriage from the Brazilian population in other regions. This apparent incongruity was not questioned by Degler, who overlooked the important issue of racial composition, focusing instead on attitudes and the theorized but unmeasured effects of economic development and immigration for explaining regional differences.

A careful analysis of intermarriage requires controls for racial composition. Sociological research demonstrates that although intermarriage may be the best indicator of social distance, intermarriage indicators are strongly affected by local compositional factors. Characteristics of local marriage markets determine the likelihood of chance encounters between any two groups. Specifically, the relative size of the outgroup is fundamental to ascertaining the degree of outmarriage. Where the size of the potential outmarriage group is larger, the chances of marriage to its members also increases. Propinquity, the chance of encountering a particular other person, is obviously a prerequisite for intermarriage, although it does not necessarily imply greater rates of interracial marriage. For example, Salvador has greater white outmarriage rates than Rio de Janeiro, which in turn has greater white outmarriage than São Paulo. Whereas Frazier and Degler interpreted this as an indicator of relative levels of tolerance, it may simply be due to the size of the nonwhite population. Racial composition could also account for Brazil-U.S. differences, since the proportion of the population that is black or mulatto in the United States is much smaller than in Brazil. I examine these hypotheses in the following paragraphs.

Fortunately, the relation between intermarriage and local racial composition can easily be displayed graphically. In figure 7.1, I show how intermarriage and racial composition are related, using 1980 census data for the seventy-three urban areas with populations over 100,000. Urban areas approximate local marriage markets because they represent the places where members of various racial groups are most likely to come into contact with each other. Because an analysis of intermarriage by urban areas should limit the analysis to those unions that are likely to have begun in the same area, I tried to include only couples that recently married and whose marriage occurred in the same metropolitan area. Since the 1980 Brazilian census did not ask respondents how long or where they had been married, I restricted couples in the sample to currently married couples that resided in the same urban area five years before and in which the wife was younger than twenty-five years old.[4]

Figure 7.1 plots white outmarriage to nonwhites in the seventy-three urban areas by the percent of the local population that is brown or black. The data reveal a tight correlation between outmarriage by whites and

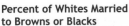

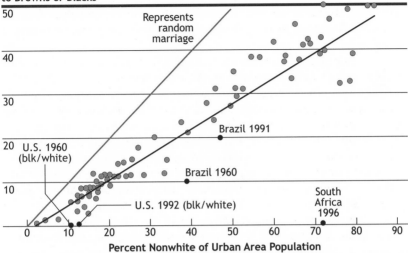

FIGURE 7.1 Percent of Whites Married to Nonwhites (Browns or Blacks) by the Percent of Nonwhites in the Population. (1960, 1980, 1991 censuses of Brazil; 1996 South African census; 1960 U.S. census; 1992 U.S. Current Population Survey.)

the size of the nonwhite population, demonstrating that local differences are mostly due to the fact that the likelihood of encountering nonwhites varies widely. These figures are statistically very robust given the strength of the correlation, the huge sample size for each urban area, and the representativeness of urban areas.[5] Because the white/nonwhite composition is related to geography, where the percent white increases roughly as one goes from north to south, white outmarriage is greater as one travels north in Brazil, but for reasons of racial composition more than anything else. This suggests that regional differences in the degree of white tolerance of nonwhites, as demonstrated by intermarriage, are false or, at best, highly exaggerated.

Furthermore, national endogamy rates vary widely across urban areas and thus are not generalizable, as figure 7.1 demonstrates. As many as half of recently married whites in 1980 had nonwhite spouses in places where a larger majority of the total population is nonwhite. By contrast, there is little intermarriage where nonwhites are less than 10 percent of the population. On average, about 28 percent of whites are married to nonwhites in urban areas; about 72 percent marry other whites where nonwhites and whites each constitute 50 percent of the population. A composition of 50 percent white or nonwhite is important, because at that point, if there were complete randomness, half of whites would marry whites and half would marry nonwhites. Therefore, we can surmise that whites are 2.6 (72/28) times as likely to marry whites as nonwhites, if they reside in an urban area with equal numbers of whites and nonwhites.

White marriage to nonwhites increased at the national level from 1960 to 1991, net of racial composition. Growing intermarriage in the thirty-one-year period was largely attributable to the increasing proportions of nonwhites, but the shrinking distance between the national rates and the line that indicates randomness in marriage suggests other factors as well. This change may be due to a growing geographic proximity between whites and nonwhites or to a growing tolerance of nonwhites.

The ease at which intermarriage occurs between whites and nonwhites in Brazil is striking when compared to the United States and South Africa. Figure 7.1 also plots national white-black intermarriage rates for the United States and white-nonwhite rates in South Africa. Rates for both the United States (in 1960 and 1992) and South Africa (African and coloured in 1996) lie close to the x axis, reflecting the near-absence of intermarriage, demonstrating that interracial marriage is far greater in Brazil.

Differences in composition account for some of the national differences in intermarriage, but they continue to be large when compositional differences are adjusted. Brazil's nonwhite portion of the population is nearly four times the size of that for U.S. blacks, so if the United States had Brazil's racial composition, the 1992 white marriage rate to blacks would increase from approximately 0.3 percent to 1.2 percent. Alternatively, if Brazil had the U.S.'s composition, its rate would decrease from about 23 percent to just under 6 percent. Therefore, after adjusting for racial composition, the extent of intermarriage in Brazil is still nearly twenty times as high as that for the United States. As I showed earlier, where whites and nonwhites comprise equal portions of the population, Brazilian whites are 2.6 times as likely to marry other whites (endogamously) compared to blacks or browns whereas U.S. whites in a similar urban area would be more than fifty times as likely to marry endogamously compared to marrying with blacks.[6]

The focus on white outmarriage so far reflects my intent to understand the degree of white tolerance for blacks and browns. Since intermarriage rates between two groups (e.g., whites and nonwhites) are complementary, nonwhite outmarriage rates are inversely related with the percent white. That is, outmarriage from the perspective of nonwhites would be lowest in the Northeast and highest in the South. Thus, if Azevedo and Degler had applied their assumption from the perspective of nonwhites, they would have observed that nonwhite tolerance for whites is greatest in the South and lowest in the Northeast. Or would they? Perhaps if they had taken the nonwhite perspective, they would have discovered the folly of using intermarriage rates to indicate regional differences in tolerance.

INTERMARRIAGE ACROSS SOCIAL CLASSES

The Brazilian narrative of race mixture is often treated as uniformly affecting all sectors of the Brazilian population. While the elite themselves may be products of earlier miscegenation, my own sense about Brazil has been that there is relatively little interracial marriage among the middle class. By contrast, it is common to see poor Brazilians of all colors associate among themselves without apparent regard to race. I suppose part of this may be due to the relative lack of middle-class blacks or browns. Because whites are more likely to be in various tiers of Brazilian society, while the large majority of nonwhites are in the lower status levels, the extent to which they are likely to come into contact with each other differs by class, which in turn may affect intermarriage. As in explaining regional differences, theories about propinquity or the size of the outgroup may thus be relevant.

Therefore, I examine intermarriage across educational strata using the 1991 national census. Figure 7.2 presents a histogram illustrating rates of white outmarriage by years of schooling for men and women in marital unions. Although women outmarry more than men at all educational levels, marriage to nonwhites is consistently lower as levels of schooling increase for both men and women. More than one-quarter (25.9 percent) of white males and 29.0 percent of white females in the least-educated category (less than one year of schooling), are married to browns or blacks. This compares to only 5.4 percent of white males and 8.0 percent of white females in the most-educated strata. While there is substantial intermarriage at the lower socioeconomic tiers of Brazilian society, intermarriage at the high end is uncommon.

Differences by level of schooling, like regional differences, might be explained by racial composition. To examine this possibility, the rightmost bar for each educational level in figure 7.2 indicates the percent nonwhite with the respective years of schooling. These bars show that 62 percent of Brazilians with less than one year of education are brown or black, while 15 percent of those with fifteen or more years of schooling are nonwhite. Thus, it appears that just as intermarriage is affected by local racial composition across urban areas, intermarriage by education is also correlated with racial composition. Whites are more likely to outmarry at those educational levels where there are more nonwhites. While this

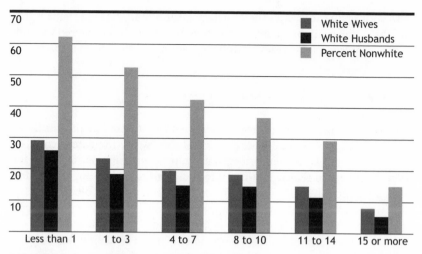

FIGURE 7.2 Percent of white males and females married to browns or blacks by years of schooling: Brazil, 1991. (1991 census of Brazil.)

suggests that differences in intermarriage by class may be more related to demography than to the extent of tolerance, it also shows that whites experience large differences across classes in having nonwhite family members as spouses, parents, cousins, in-laws, aunts, uncles, etc. A similar argument may be made for nonwhites, although the pattern is inverted. The few blacks and mulattos with higher education will be more likely to marry whites, simply because their peers are especially likely to be white.

WHITE ATTITUDES ABOUT INTERMARRIAGE IN BRAZIL

The attitudinal studies that Degler cited were limited to highly select samples, such as college students in Recife, high school students in Rio de Janeiro, and a group of middle-class persons in Florianópolis. Thus he provided us with no generalizable knowledge of Brazilian racial attitudes. To compensate for this, I examine prevailing racial attitudes of Brazilian whites about intermarriage and the principle of miscegenation using random samples. Unlike the attitudinal studies that Degler used with their dubious generalizability, a 2000 representative survey based on random sampling of the Rio de Janeiro state population asked respondents a series of four questions about their behavior and attitudes regarding intermarriage and race mixture. I examine the response of self-identified white respondents to these questions in table 7.4, and I also disaggregate whites to those who claim some black ancestry and those who do not. Specifically, the columns refer to the proportion of whites that: are married to someone of a different color (column 1); have ever dated someone of a different color (column 2); answered that they would marry a black (negro) person (column 3); and agreed with the statement "It would be better for Brazil if there were more racial mixture" (column 4). Twenty-four percent of all self-identified whites reported being married to someone of a different color, while 44 percent claim to have dated someone of a different color. Eighty percent of self-identified whites said they would marry a black (negro) person, and 81 percent agreed that more race mixture would be better for Brazil. The second and third rows differentiate between whites who claim to have African ancestry and those that did not, because I suspect that there may be a continuum among the white population in which those who claim African ancestry might practice and sympathize more with miscegenation. This hypothesis was upheld as revealed in the table, but the differences were small yet consistent. Whites claiming to have some African ancestry were only slightly more likely than those without to have married or dated a black person, expressed a willingness to do so, or agreed that racial mixture was good for Brazil.

TABLE 7.4
Responses by self-identified white persons to questions on intermarriage and miscegenation: State of Rio de Janeiro, 2000

	Are you or were you ever married to someone of a different color?	Have you ever dated anyone of a different color from yours?	Would you marry a black (negro) person?	It would be better for Brazil if there were more racial mixture.	N
	(1) Yes (%)	(2) Yes (%)	(3) Yes (%)	(4) Agree (%)	
All whites	24	44	80	81	477
Whites claiming some African ancestry	28	46	83	87	174
Whites claiming no African ancestry	22	43	78	75	271

Source: CEAP/Data UFF Survey.

WHITE OUTMARRIAGE TO BROWNS VS. BLACKS

Degler's (1986) principal conclusion was that the main difference between Brazil and the United States was that mulattos in Brazil had a status somewhere between whites and blacks, whereas in the United States,
mulattos were similar to blacks. In short, Degler believed that racism was
especially intense against blacks in Brazil, making the better treatment
given to mulattos the crucial difference in race relations between Brazil
and the U.S. He relied largely on available attitude studies of intermarriage and evidence showing mobility for mulattos in the nineteenth century to support his claim. In this section, I examine this hypothesis for
marriage by replicating figure 7.3, except that I separate white-brown
from white-black marriages.

As before, I adjust the rates by the racial composition of the urban areas.
As for local and national differences, lower rates of white marriage to blacks
compared to browns as shown in tables 7.2 and 7.3 might be explained by
the fact that the black population is much smaller than the brown population. Figure 7.3 thus plots the relationship between white outmarriage
to browns and the relative size of the brown population, as well as white
outmarriage to blacks and the relative size of the black population.[7]

Figure 7.3 shows that whites are more likely to marry browns compared to blacks, even when the size of the brown and black population is
similar. Although white outmarriage to browns and blacks increases consistently in proportion to the size of the brown and black populations,
the rate of increase or the slope of white outmarriage to browns is distinctly greater than for white outmarriage to blacks, suggesting markedly
greater white tolerance of browns compared to blacks. For example, an
urban area that is 15 percent black would usually have less than a 3-percent
white-black marriage rate, while a 15-percent brown area would have
nearly a 10-percent white-brown marriage rate.

The figure also shows that the six urban areas with the smallest brown
populations have white outmarriage rates to browns that are comparable
to those for blacks. These happened to be five of the six urban areas (Blumenau, Joinville, Florianópolis, Pelotas-Rio Grande, and Caxias do Sul)
of the two southernmost states: Santa Catarina and Rio Grande do Sul.
Unlike the rest of the country, these results suggest that there is less fluidity across the white-brown divide there compared to the remaining
twenty-four states to the north, consistent with the findings for racial
classification in chapter 3. Thus, Frazier's observation in 1942 that race
relations in the extreme South were more like the United States, seems to
have been accurate in this regard. While marrying a mulatto in Brazil is
apparently much less stigmatized than marrying a black person in most

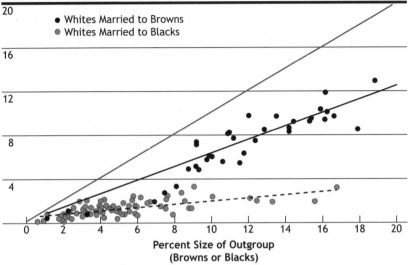

Percent of Whites Married to Browns or Blacks

- Whites Married to Browns
- Whites Married to Blacks

Percent Size of Outgroup (Browns or Blacks)

FIGURE 7.3 Relationship between white outmarriage to browns or blacks and size of nonwhite outgroup (close-up of figure 7.1 from 0 to 20 percent).

of Brazil, such distinctions are relatively unimportant in the extreme South, where whites apparently treat browns and blacks similarly.

I would normally downplay brown-black differences when using the census data because of the high level of fluidity between the two categories, especially when such differences are small. However, figure 7.1 shows that, besides being large, such differences hold up across urban areas and they are highly predictable based on population composition. Thus, I believe the results convincingly show a racial continuum in which mulattos are clearly favored over blacks by whites in marriage. They point to substantial fluidity in marriage among persons of similar color, especially between whites and browns. Although there is relatively little white marriage to blacks as opposed to browns in Brazil, it is nevertheless greater than in the United States.

EFFECTS OF INDUSTRIALIZATION AND IMMIGRATION

The potential effects of two other variables on intermarriage rates are worth mentioning: immigration and industrialization. As I explained in chapter 5, the UNESCO researchers representing the so-called São Paulo school of race relations stressed the influence of economic development or industrialization on race relations, but their predictions about intermarriage were sometimes opposite those they expected for the labor market.

Two contrasting views forecast how capitalist development would affect interpersonal or horizontal race relations. Fernandes (1965) predicted that the declining salience of race in the labor market would be reproduced at the level of interpersonal relations. Racial intermarriage would thus be expected to increase with economic development. However, Cardoso and Ianni (1960) and Van den Berghe (1967) argued that because racial competition increases, whites would seek other ways of maintaining racial separation, such as placing greater emphasis on proscriptions against outmarriage to blacks and mulattos.

The massive immigration of Europeans between 1885 and 1935 to selected destinations is sometimes believed to have influenced the particular character of Brazilian regions and thus the local extent of intermarriage. For example, some researchers have attributed apparently greater levels of racial discrimination in São Paulo and the South to the influence of immigrants, concluding that immigrants heightened racial prejudice by bringing racist ideologies with them[8] and because they entered the Brazilian labor force in low-level jobs and had to compete directly with blacks and mulattos.[9] Fernandes (1965) contended, however, that foreigners in the state of São Paulo learned racism from the native Brazilians, pointing to cities like Campinas, which had relatively few immigrants but a high level of racial prejudice. Unlike the native Luso-Brazilians, Italian immigrants in particular had substantial interaction with Afro-Brazilians because they shared a similar class status. Reaching similar conclusions as Fernandes, Staley (1959), in a unique study with a small cross-regional sample, found that opposition to intermarriage was similar across regions and between foreign and native grandparents.

In a related study with the 1980 urban data that I presented earlier, I examined the effects of industrialization and immigration. I found that more industrially developed places have slightly higher intermarriage rates, but these effects were small compared to racial composition. Also, the effects of industrialization were slight compared to its effects on occupational inequality. On the other hand, the extent of immigrant influence, measured by the extent to which the population over sixty was foreign born, had no effect on intermarriage rates, after controlling for racial composition and industrialization.[10] Thus, my data suggest that industrial development acts to increase intermarriage slightly, while immigration has no effect.

Status Exchange in Brazilian Intermarriage

A theory known as "status exchange in interracial marriage" posits that members of racially subordinate groups can marry members of the racially dominant group in exchange for bringing other valued status characteristics to the marriage, such as education or social class. Davis (1941) and Merton (1941) both outlined this theory, focusing on an exchange they believed to occur between upwardly mobile black males and poor white females in the United States. Specifically, Davis and Merton believed that black men exchanged their higher class but lower racial status for the higher racial but lower class status of white women. Davis believed that race was exchanged in the United States similarly to the more explicit exchange of caste status as found in India. Thales de Azevedo (1966) made a similar argument for Brazil.

A common explanation for Brazilian intermarriage is the popular belief in whitening. With a convoluted eugenics logic that the combination of black and white genes would eventually produce a white, or at least a progressively lighter, population, this belief in whitening became the way out of a racially determined future of inferiority. Although whitening is no longer state policy, it has become an individual strategy for mobility among many nonwhite Brazilians. For individuals, marriage to a lighter partner came to represent a "cleansing of the womb" that would result in a better future for lighter children. In turn, this way of thinking ensured the persistence of race mixing.[11] The popular whitening ideology strategy has apparently thus become the engine for the persistence of actual Brazilian miscegenation.

However, the flaw in the whitening theory is that it works only for the partner with darker skin. Why then would the lighter person marry a darker person, especially in the context of a whitening ideology, where darkness and especially blackness is stigmatized? John Burdick's (1998) *Blessed Anastacia*, an ethnography of various neighborhoods in Rio de Janeiro, is particularly useful for understanding this paradox. Burdick finds a status-exchange system in which white men may be attracted to nonwhite women who use limited resources, including their beauty or a high level of devotion, to offset their blackness. He finds a parallel process at work for white women. For many young black and brown men, having white women (preferably a blonde) is a symbol of success, honor, and power, which is consistent with the whitening ideology. White women are attracted to dark men because of their eroticized sexuality, and because they also claim to receive greater devotion from them compared to what they receive from white men. At a social event, Burdick (1998, 29) witnessed the following interaction:

A black man married to a white women excused himself to return home. His drinking buddies started to harass him, "Ah, man you should have married a black woman! Then you wouldn't have to go running off like a slave!" . . . A dark black female friend [commented], "That is the truth. They treat their darker wives like dirt."

Burdick also found that white men have their pick of darker women but avoid the darkest. They prefer mulattas or morenas, who are considered to be the embodiment of Brazilian sexuality and pleasure, as popularized in the novels of Jorge Amado and by Brazilian songs and films.[12] Burdick thus demonstrates how dark-skinned persons also possess valued attributes that they use to exchange for whiteness, although the simple fact of having light skin brings a power advantage to lighter-skinned persons in marriage and dating. Although intermarriage may represent less rigid racial boundaries, Burdick finds that it also represents greater privilege for persons of lighter skin color.

Thus, an interracial marriage exchange system may occur in Brazil although not with the same assets that Davis and Merton envisioned. Although these ethnographic findings are important because they direct our attention to an important process, they cannot be generalized. Do such exchanges only occur in select populations, or could they be generalized through findings that use large, representative data sets? Unfortunately, variables like beauty and devotion are not easily found in such data, but one variable, years of schooling, is available and is an important indicator of status. Under the status-exchange theory, we would expect that intermarried spouses of lower racial status might also tend to have higher levels of schooling. Table 7.5 tests such a hypothesis for Brazil. Specifically, it examines the extent to which various types of intermarried Brazilian couples have the same education (column 2), or whether the wives (column 1) or the husbands (column 3) have higher education. The final column shows the extent to which darker spouses have an educational advantage, so that a positive number would support Davis and Merton's theory for the Brazilian case. I use years of schooling in the table because it is the only ordered status variable that is available for all men and women in the Brazilian Census.

The final column shows that in five of the six cases, darker spouses tend to have more schooling than their lighter mates, which is an especially significant finding since schooling tends to be lower for persons with darker skin color. Therefore, these findings generally support an exchange of race for status. However, these findings are significant only in the case of marriage between blacks and nonblacks. Black men and women are more likely to have higher education than their brown or white spouses, while there is virtually no cost involved in marriages between

Table 7.5
Educational homogamy among Brazilian marriages for intermarried couples:
Brazil, 1991

| | | Education of spouse | | |
| | | | | Educational advantage of darker spouse [a] (years) |
Couple by color	Male higher	Equal	Female higher (%)	
White husband/brown wife	27.6%	44.5%	27.9%	+0.3
White wife/brown husband	26.5%	44.7%	28.8%	−2.3
White husband/black wife	27.1%	44.0%	28.9%	+1.8
White wife/black husband	29.4%	44.9%	25.7%	+3.7
Brown husband/black wife	24.1%	47.8%	28.1%	+4.0
Brown wife/black husband	26.8%	48.4%	24.8%	+3.7

Source: Demographic Census, 1991.
[a]Indicates educational disadvantage.

browns and whites. For white husbands and brown wives, there is almost no (0.3) educational difference, and brown husbands have significantly lower (-2.3) levels of education than their white wives. These findings demonstrate that blacks, unlike browns, have especially low status in the Brazilian marriage market and therefore pay an especially high cost to "marry up" to lighter partners.

Black Women in Marriage and Dating

While black, brown, and white men compete for white women and mulattas, black women are disproportionately passed up in romance and marriage by white, brown, and black men. This seems to account for their greater likelihood of being single throughout their lives or of having late marriages.[13] According to Goldani (1989), white women spend 65 percent of their adult lives in marital relationships compared to 59 percent of brown and only 50 percent of black women. Because sex differences in mortality mean that there are more women than men in adult ages, there is a greater likelihood that women will remain single. The burden of this male deficit in marriage is transferred to black women through Brazil's racial pecking order. Specifically, white and brown women overcome the shortage of available white and brown men by marrying darker men, which ultimately creates a shortage of black men available to black women. The tendency for men to marry lighter women, whereby over half (51 percent) of black men marry out compared to only 40 percent of black women, means that black women are often abandoned in the marriage market. Based on his interview, Burdick (1998) shows how young black girls experience these statistics:

> At dances, black girls (*pretas*) tend to cluster away from morenas, mulatas, and white girls (*brancas*). One of them states "The black *funkeiras* are always by themselves" said Carlinha, a teenage *preta*, "dancing alone and with each other. . . . It is hard to stand next to *uma menina mais clara* [a lighter girl] at a party. A guy passes by, he looks not at you, he looks at her, he says something to her."(39)

CONCLUSIONS

The idea of miscegenation as presented by racial-democracy ideology has sought to encapsulate a Brazilian self-image of sociability and to represent the antithesis of segregation, which describes societies like the United States and South Africa that continue to be deeply divided by race. This chapter has shown that Brazil's ideology of race mixture is not limited to history or to the realm of sex and pleasure. Despite widespread and persistent racial discrimination in Brazilian society, intermarriage is far higher in Brazil than in the United States or South Africa. While Brazilians prefer endogamy, more than one-fifth of whites marry nonwhites, whereas white marriage to blacks in the United States and South Africa is rare. Although race continues be a significant variable in determining partner choice, the very real possibility of such marriages in Brazil suggests that, in comparative terms, Brazil's miscegenation is real and indicates relatively widespread interracial sociability.

There are several clarifications that should be made for understanding the greater tendency for Brazilians to intermarry. First of all, Brazil's pattern of intermarriage is still far from random, revealing only the partial integration of nonwhites. Also, intermarriage by whites is mostly with mulattos. Thus, despite the fact that browns are objectively more like blacks in status, a greater social acceptance of the mulatto seems to help account for Brazil's greater intermarriage. However, rates of white marriage with blacks are nonetheless greater than in the United States or South Africa.

One reason for greater intermarriage in Brazil is the greater propinquity or exposure of whites to nonwhites. This also explains wide differences in intermarriage across geography and class. Intermarriage occurs mostly in the Northeast, where whites are most likely to interact with browns and blacks. While regional differences in intermarriage have been interpreted as the result of a more tolerant system of race relations in the Northeast, this really has little or nothing to do with differences in tolerance. Rather, propinquity or the extent of interracial interaction determines nearly all of the regional variation. Similarly, intermarriage is most prevalent among poor whites, who are especially likely to be exposed to nonwhites. For similar reasons, it is uncommon among dominant middle-class whites. On the other hand, propinquity cannot explain most of the U.S.-Brazil difference. When whites and nonwhites comprise similar proportions of the population, whites are 2.6 times as likely to marry whites rather than blacks or browns in Brazil, while the comparable ratio is over 50 for the United States. Clearly, intermarriage is not nearly as stigmatized in Brazil as it is between whites and blacks in the United States for cultural reasons rooted in distinct histories. In Brazil, the predominance of men throughout most of the period of slavery led to much miscegenation and occasional interracial unions that were later promoted by the miscegenation-based ideologies of whitening and racial democracy. On the other hand, North Americans have historically practiced segregation, largely in an effort to keep black men from white women.

However, when intermarriage occurs, love does not always trump racism. Far from it. Freyre's representation of Brazil's miscegenation ignored the tremendous costs to nonwhite people, and especially black women. In the marriage market, whiter skin is preferred and persons with the darkest skin, especially women, are largely rejected. Even when barriers to intermarriage are overcome, the burden of dark color persists in the constant negotiating involved in the business of marriage. Also, intermarriage brings spouses and in-laws of diverse colors into the same household or family, where marriages are frequently not accepted and become the subject of gossip and intrigue. Conversely lighter-skinned persons often trade heavily on their whiteness in exchange for status and other advantages that they receive from darker-skinned partners. Although many interracial marriages are surely loving and enduring, the significance of race for those marriages is unlikely ever to fully disappear.

Chapter Eight

RESIDENTIAL SEGREGATION

> The mass of poorly educated and unskilled blacks would
> be thrust out to the periphery more rigorously than ever
> with an intensified drive of forced removals and tougher
> enforcement of anti-squatter laws in the cities. It was
> sometimes called the "Brazilian option," which, by
> deracializing the insider group, would give the impression
> that apartheid had been dismantled. But the key to it
> was that the Afrikaner *volk* was to remain in overall
> control and South Africa was to remain its nation-state.
> —*Alister Sparks, referring to how some*
> *government officials expressed South Africa's*
> *plans for postapartheid reform (1990)*

AT THE LEVEL of simple observation, North Americans will often point
to racial segregation in Brazilian cities, transposing an image of U.S. urban ghettos to Brazil. Favelas, they note, are primarily black, like ghet-
toes in the United States. When I first resided in Brazil in the late 1980s,
this analogy seemed like an appropriate representation of Brazil's urban
reality. However, when I discussed the relation between race and the city
with a Brazilian sociologist, he told me that there is no racial segregation,
but merely class segregation, and that racial residential differences existed only to the extent that they were coterminous with class. One's ability to pay for housing in often highly stratified real-estate markets is the
only limit to where one could live. Otherwise, Brazilians of different colors were randomly distributed across urban neighborhoods. If poor
neighborhoods are mostly black and brown while middle-class neighborhoods are almost entirely white, it is because nonwhites predominate in
the lower class, while whites comprise most of the middle classes. Furthermore, he claimed that unlike the United States there are no laws stat-
ing where blacks must live, presumably believing that segregation in the
United States continued to be sanctioned by law. Finally, he explained
that Brazilian conceptions of race are continuous and not categorical like
those of the northern European tradition, precluding the possibility of
racial segregation. At the time, this represented a typical understanding

of residential distribution by race in Brazil, which was in accordance with the belief in racial democracy and extensive miscegenation.

A few years later, an incident in Rio de Janeiro clearly dispelled that colorblind version of Brazilian cities, at least in my mind. On October 18, 1992, scores of young people from poor communities in Rio de Janeiro's "North Zone" arrived in busloads and walked in large groups (known as *arrastões*) along the prestigious beaches in Rio's "South Zone," startling beachgoers into running away. The reactions to this event by South Zone residents revealed their prejudices and insecurities about the poor residents of the North Zone and from the spatially near but socially distant favelas (shantytowns) of nearby hillsides. Furthermore, the fact that the youth from the North Zone appeared to be almost entirely nonwhite while the South Zone residents were virtually all white and quite conscious of, even haunted by, the color differences, made this a racial as well as a class issue. This was seen in the reactions of the middle-class residents, which ranged from declarations of fear about the "bands of poor dark people" to the preparation of martial-arts clubs in the South Zone to defend against another "invasion."[1]

Although they had occurred in the past, these particular sweeps were important because they were highly publicized in the media. Occurring just before the municipal elections, many believed that the importance given them by the media represented a conspiracy to scare local citizens about the real possibility that Benedita da Silva, a black favela resident, would become mayor of Rio de Janeiro. TV Globo, Brazil's media giant, filmed these *arrastões* live, raising conspiratorial questions about how the media was able to arrive on time and set up their cameras at exactly the right place for the short-lived raids. These events brought to light the tenuous relation between the predominantly black poor and the white middle class in Rio, a problem that had been conveniently neglected in the past because of the physical distance generally separating the two groups. Thus, this example not only revealed the class tensions of Rio de Janeiro but racial tensions as well. Even though both race and class were implicated in the public mind by the *arrastões*, many analysts and policy makers continued to believe that the variable of race could simply be reduced to class; that event began to raise some doubts. Rather, it seemed that much of the white middle class had decided to make blacks into public enemies, both socially and politically.

The Sociological Importance of Residential Segregation

Residential segregation occupies a central role in North American sociological debates about race relations and racial inequality. Massey and Denton (1994) refer to black-white segregation in the United States as

American apartheid, in which persistent and rigid housing discrimination against black North Americans can account for much of black disadvantage, including lingering racial stereotypes, oppositional black identities, and the formation of an underclass. Persistently high levels of segregation affect access to schools, jobs, and health care; has damaging effects on child development; concentrates poverty; and therefore brings crime. Urban racial segregation is often considered the linchpin of racial inequality, presumably in the belief that if residential segregation could be eliminated, then the entire edifice of racial inequality would come tumbling down.[2] A perusal of this literature might lead some to believe that this is the case anywhere black and white people live in the same cities, but such conclusions are based solely upon the case of the United States. However, ideas about Brazil are often exaggerated in one direction or the other, ranging from U.S.- or South Africa-style segregation[3] to a prominent view deriving from the idea of Freyre's rural patriarchical family, where everyone lives together in harmony.

There are various reasons we should examine the Brazilian case, not least of which is the fact that there may be more racial segregation in Brazil than many Brazilians would like to acknowledge. On the other hand, hard statistics about residential segregation would also provide a fairly objective indication of comparative Brazil-U.S. segregation. Given the widely varying speculations about the nature of Brazilian residential segregation compared to the United States, this chapter seeks to establish the degree of segregation in Brazil and draw out the overall implications for race relations. My main contention is that racial segregation in Brazil is not self-apparent and requires systematic measurement. Also, interpretations of segregation indexes need to be understood as reflecting a history that neither imposes assumptions from systems of legalized black-white segregation like the United States and South Africa, nor embraces the racial democracy ideology, which obscures a true understanding of how race and class operate in Brazil.

In this chapter, I first examine regional differences in racial composition from 1872 to 1999, as background for understanding the racial composition of Brazilian cities and to understand that racial segregation in Brazil has long been at the regional level. I then examine the nature and extent of racial segregation in Brazilian urban areas using the 1991 and 1980 censuses. I map segregation in São Paulo and Rio de Janeiro at the level of large districts using the 1991 public-use sample and employ the 1980 data to compute summary segregation indexes for several large urban areas based on census tracts. Districts represent very large spatial areas, often with populations in the hundreds of thousands, while census tracts roughly represent neighborhoods, each with an average of 200 to 250 households; however, information at the census tract level is not publicly available. Through special permission from the IBGE, I was able to compute segregation indexes from 1980 census tract data for the forty largest urban areas in Brazil.

REGION, URBANIZATION, AND RACIAL COMPOSITION

As I showed in chapter 1, whites are a majority in the relatively well-developed South and Southeast, where 57 percent of Brazil's 170 million people live; but they are a numerical minority in the less developed regions. The 2000 census reports that 73 percent of whites, 54 percent of blacks, and only 37 percent of browns live in these two regions. Figure 8.1 shows the history of concentration among racial categories in the South and Southeast since 1872. White immigrants settled primarily in these two regions since mass immigration began in the mid to late nineteenth century, while nonwhites slightly decreased their relative numbers in those regions from 1890 until 1950. From 1872 to 1890, there was a significant increase in the proportion of blacks in those areas, perhaps related to the prospect of work for freed slaves in coffee production in Rio and São Paulo.

Despite the economic boom of the Southeast throughout much of the twentieth century, there have been surprisingly small movements of the nonwhite population southward. The largest movement to that region has been since the 1950s, when large-scale migration from the Northeast began. The black proportion in the two southern regions increased from 54 to 60 percent, and the brown population went from 33 to 37 percent between 1960 and 1980. Brazilian industrial growth thus led to some shifts in the population by race, but these hardly affected the historic regional concentration of whites, browns and blacks.

By contrast, industrialization in the United States produced much greater racially differentiated shifts. Farley and Allen (1987) showed that, while 89 percent of the black population resided in the U.S. South in 1910, by 1970 less than 40 percent of the population lived there. Much of the difference may be accounted for by the fact that slavery was limited to the South region in the United States while it was national in Brazil. Also, industrialization was not as massive in Brazil as it was in the United States, although it seemed to produce better conditions than were available in other Brazilian regions. Finally, the threat of racism to one's personal safety was a constant concern in the U.S. South, unlike Brazil. Blacks faced racial violence in the South, often in the form of lynching, which may have led them to migrate irrespective of the economic opportunities they could find in the North.

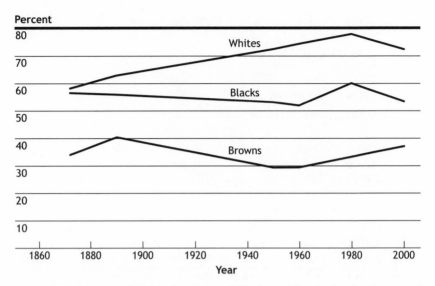

Percent

FIGURE 8.1 Percent of whites, browns and blacks residing in the Southeast and South: 1872–2000. *Sources:* 1872, 1890, 1950, 1960, 1980, and 2000 censuses of Brazil.

From 1980 to 2000, as Brazil's industrial economy began to sour, blacks and whites began to move out of the South and Southeast, while the numbers of browns increased slightly. The proportion of whites in the two southern regions decreased by 5 percentage points for whites and 6 percentage points for blacks. Nevertheless, the Brazilian population continues to be spatially uneven by race, as it has been for the past century. Unlike regional differences in racial composition, there has been a greater convergence of urbanization levels by color. Based on the 1999 National Household Survey and 1960 census, 84 percent of whites, 80 percent of blacks, and 74 percent of browns now live in urban areas, compared to 1960 when 51 percent of whites, 43 percent of blacks, and only 37 percent of browns lived in urban areas. Residence in urban areas, though, continues to be differentiated by region. Nonwhites are especially likely to live in the poorest regions and in the rural areas of these regions, making them the poorest of the poor by virtue of location.

MACROSEGREGATION IN BRAZIL'S TWO GIANT CITIES

Maps 8.1 and 8.2 illustrate the 1990–1991 racial composition of districts for the metropolitan areas of São Paulo and Rio de Janeiro. These two metropolitan areas are by far the largest in Brazil and rank among the

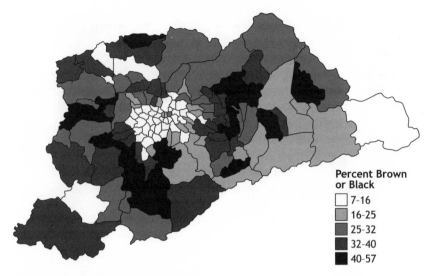

Percent Brown or Black

☐ 7-16
16-25
25-32
32-40
■ 40-57

MAP 8.1   São Paulo metropolitan area

largest in the world. São Paulo, with a population of 18.6 million, has 128 districts with an average population of about 145,000 in each district. Rio de Janeiro has 11.3 million persons with 45 districts, on average 257,000 persons per district. Thus, the descriptions of segregation presented in these maps illustrate spatial differences based on very large areas.

District Level.   Map 8.1 shows that the districts in the São Paulo city center, characterized by their middle-class status and high density, are predominately white. Almost all of those districts have populations that are less than 16 percent nonwhite. With the exception of five districts, the districts in the remaining rings around the city center are all more than 16 percent nonwhite, with a maximum of 57 percent nonwhite. The largest concentrations of nonwhites are in the first ring of the south-southwest periphery, in several districts east of the city center, and in the outer ring of the distant north-northwest periphery. Interestingly, the five peripheral districts in which whites are a large majority are located in different parts of the metropolitan area, often amidst largely nonwhite districts.

In the case of the Rio de Janeiro metropolitan area, map 8.2 shows that the greatest concentration of whites is in the two geographically small, but very dense South Zone districts. A large proportion of their nonwhite population lives in favelas scattered throughout the area. A ring around the geographically tiny and predominantly white center has larger concentrations of nonwhites (15 to 45 percent) but is still mostly white,

Percent Brown
or Black
☐ 0-15
▨ 15-30
▨ 30-45
▨ 45-60
■ 60-75

MAP 8.2 Rio de Janeiro metropolitan area

especially near the beach. Majority-nonwhite districts are found in the second and third rings, which are the poor Rio suburbs, generally referred to as the Baixada Fluminense. Although the favelas near Rio's center are well known, most of Rio's poor population lives in its suburbs. The largest concentrations of nonwhites are located in the northern and eastern parts of the outer periphery. Note that a model of centralization by race can generally be found in both Rio de Janeiro and São Paulo, although a pattern of increasing nonwhite concentration outward from the city center is more apparent in Rio.

Neighborhood Level. Although centralization of the middle class and peripheralization of the poor have roughly characterized the structure of Latin American cities,[4] such a simple description is insufficient and increasingly inappropriate for understanding levels of residential segregation in the complex and often multinucleated urban areas of Latin America. The proliferation of favelas on both the less-valued real estate of the periphery and the contested areas of middle- and high-income central cities makes understanding residential segregation at the neighborhood level a necessity. In the past, most research about Latin American patterns of segregation has focused on the extent of centralization to describe segregation, largely because centralization describes an urban form derived from colonial (and even precolonial) times that is relatively easy to observe and, if measurable, requires data for only two areas: the central city and the periphery. Centralization thus refers to the population living in the periphery compared to the central area, as maps 8.1 and 8.2 illustrate to varying degrees for São Paulo and Rio de Janeiro. However, centralization is an urban form that is overly simplistic and often inappropriate for describing Brazil's spatially complex metropolitan areas.

Particular urban forms typical of pre-twentieth-century cities, such as the centralization model, evolved from environmental and technological constraints, including the availability of cars or multistory office construction. In recent years, security technology has become important for permitting suburbanization of the São Paulo middle class.[5] Although Rio de Janeiro follows more of a centralization pattern than São Paulo, the extent of segregation is underestimated at the district level because neighborhoods within large districts are often segregated. Favelas, which are largely nonwhite,[6] and middle-class neighborhoods often exist side by side, as is commonly portrayed for Rio de Janeiro.

Also, favelas themselves may be racially segregated, which would be captured by the indexes based on census tract data. For example, Cantagallo, a favela in Rio de Janeiro which overlooks the predominately white south-zone district of Ipanema on one side and Copacabana on the other, is divided into two sectors: Pavão-Pavãozinho and Cantagallo. I have been told by a resident there that Pavão-Pavãozinho, which is reached via Copacabana, is inhabited largely by *nordestinos* (migrants from Brazil's Northeast), who mostly straddle the white and brown color categories. On the other hand, Cantagallo, above Ipanema, primarily houses native Carioca residents, who are mostly dark brown and black in color. Although Pavão-Pavãozinho and Cantagallo are commonly considered a single favela by outsiders, the division becomes increasingly apparent as the drug trade occasionally restricts access between the two communities.[7] The point is that the color differences between the two poor neighborhoods show that class alone may not explain spatial segregation.

To examine segregation at the neighborhood level, I employ two measures that have been widely used in the United States: the dissimilarity and exposure (or isolation) indexes. Table 8.1 shows the dissimilarity index, the index of white exposure to nonwhites, the nonwhite isolation index, and the racial composition for the largest metropolitan areas of Brazil and the United States. The dissimilarity index is the standard measure of segregation; it measures *evenness* in the distribution of racial and household-income groups across the census tracts of metropolitan areas, or the extent to which social groups are differentially distributed across neighborhoods in an urban area. The concept of evenness is particularly suitable for capturing the amount of segregation found among the mosaics of households and neighborhoods that characterize the landscapes of Brazilian metropolitan areas. Specifically, the dissimilarity index (D) measures the percent of group A that would have to move out of their current census tract in order to have the same evenness of distribution as group *B*. The value of *D* varies from 0, where groups *A* and *B* are evenly distributed throughout the urban area, to 100, where *A* and *B* do not share any census tracts, i.e., complete segregation.

In the first column of table 8.1, I present the dissimilarity indexes between whites and nonwhites in the ten largest metropolitan areas of Brazil[8] and in the eight largest metropolitan areas in the United States. For the United States, I use dissimilarity indexes for 1980 based on block-level data, where blocks are approximately of the same size as those in the Brazilian census tracts. There were an average of 930 persons per U.S. block and between 840 and 1,020 persons per Brazilian census tract.[9] In the case of exposure indexes for the United States, I was able to find only those based on the larger census tracts, which, when compared to block-level data, tend to provide higher estimates of the extent of white exposure to blacks than exposure indexes based on blocks.

The table shows that, compared to the extreme levels of racial segregation found in the United States, racial residential segregation using the traditional dissimilarity index is moderate in Brazilian metropolitan areas. The highest index of white versus nonwhite dissimilarity is 48 for Salvador, indicating that 48 percent of the nonwhites and 48 percent of whites would have to move out of their neighborhoods so that they would be evenly distributed across neighborhoods. The other nine metropolitan areas have dissimilarity indexes in the fairly small range of 37 to 41.

Dissimilarity is much higher in U.S. urban areas, with values ranging from 75 in New York to 92 in Chicago. Although dissimilarity indexes have gradually decreased on average during the past two decades in the U.S. metropolitan areas, they are still far greater than those in Brazil where the indexes are not likely to have changed greatly since 1980.[10] Black-white segregation continues to be extreme in the United States, while it is only moderate in Brazil, roughly comparable to that between whites and Asians in the United States.

The dissimilarity index does not capture the extent to which individuals are exposed to or isolated from members of other groups. Therefore, I also calculated exposure indexes that measure the extent to which members of a certain social group are exposed to those of another group by virtue of living in the same neighborhood. Unlike the dissimilarity index of segregation, this measure is largely driven by the racial composition of an area. For example, whites are more likely to be exposed to blacks in places where the latter are a larger portion of the population, but dissimilarity is not necessarily affected. Specifically, the index of white exposure to nonwhites measures the proportion of nonwhite neighbors residing in the census tract in which the average white person lives. Like the dissimilarity index, the exposure index also varies between

TABLE 8.1
Segregation indexes and racial composition of the 10 largest Brazilian and 8 largest U.S. metropolitan areas, 1980

Metropolitan area	Dissimilarity	White exposure to nonwhites/ blacks	Nonwhite/black isolation	Percent nonwhite/ black
Brazil:[a]				
São Paulo	37	21	37	25
Rio de Janeiro	37	32	50	40
Belo Horizonte	41	35	58	45
Recife	38	50	70	73
Porto Alegre	37	12	23	15
Salvador	48	56	82	77
Fortaleza	40	54	75	69
Curitiba	39	13	26	16
Brasília	39	37	57	46
Belém	37	59	77	72
United States[b]				
New York	75	6	63	21
Los Angeles	81	4	60	13
Chicago	92	4	83	20
Detroit	73	5	77	20
Washington	79	12	68	28
Philadelphia	88	6	70	19
Houston	79	8	59	18
Baltimore	81	9	72	26

Source: Indexes for Brazil are calculated from 1980 census of Brazil at the census tract level; interaction indexes at the census tract level for the United States are taken from Massey and Denton 1987; U.S. dissimilarity indexes are based on block level data from Farley and Allen 1994, table 5.6.

[a]Nonwhite/black refers to blacks and browns in Brazil.
[b]Nonwhite/black refers to blacks in the United States.

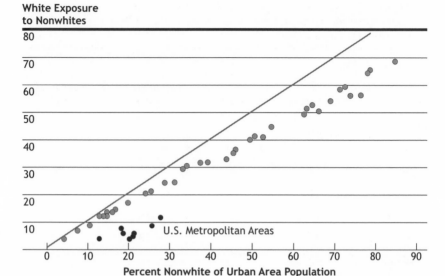

FIGURE 8.2 White residential exposure to nonwhites in relation to percent non-white in 40 largest Brazilian and 8 largest U.S. metropolitan areas. Note: Non-white refers to blacks and browns in Brazil and to blacks in the United States.

0 and 100, where a score of 0 would mean that the average white person has no black or brown neighbors, and 100 would indicate that all of the neighbors of the average white person are non-white.[11]

The second column of the table shows exposure indexes of whites to nonwhites ranging from 12 to 59 in the ten largest Brazilian metropolitan areas compared to 4 to 12 in the eight U.S. areas. Whites in the southern cities of Porto Alegre and Curitiba, on average, are the most segregated on the exposure dimension; these whites live in neighborhoods that are about one-eighth nonwhite (scores of 12 and 13, respectively). This is about the same as for Washington, D.C., which has the least segregation on this dimension among U.S. urban areas. However, in general there are very large cross-national differences. Most strikingly, whites are much more likely to live next to nonwhites in Brazilian metropolitan areas that have racial compositions similar to those found in many U.S. cities. For example, Los Angeles, which is similar in racial composition to Curitiba and Porto Alegre, has an exposure index of 4. For the mostly nonwhite Brazilian urban areas, white exposure to nonwhites is much greater than in the urban United States. In three cases—Salvador, Fortaleza, and Belem—the average white person tends to have mostly nonwhite neighbors.

To illustrate the U.S.-Brazil difference, figure 8.2 plots the relation between the residential exposure of whites to nonwhites by the percent white for the forty largest Brazilian metropolitan areas and the eight largest U.S. metropolitan areas; this is similar to figure 7.1 for intermarriage indexes. It shows that white residential exposure to nonwhites in Brazil is clearly greater than in U.S. cities of comparable racial composition, mirroring the findings for intermarriage. The difference would be even larger if we consider that the U.S. exposure indexes are based on census tract rather than block data.

Returning to table 8.1, column 3 shows the isolation index for nonwhites, which represents the extent to which the average nonwhite in an urban area has nonwhite neighbors. The four Brazilian metropolitan areas with majority nonwhite populations (Recife, Salvador, Fortaleza, and Belem) have exposure indexes that fall within the U.S. range. In other words, the exposure of nonwhites to whites in those cities is about as limited as it is in the United States. Salvador, which has a score of 82, presents the greatest spatial isolation of nonwhites in Brazil, and the likelihood that nonwhites in Salvador live near other nonwhites is similar to that for black isolation in Chicago (83), the most segregated of major U.S. metropolitan areas. However, while limited residential interracial contact is driven mostly by housing discrimination in the United States, comparable levels, where they exist in Brazil, are mostly due to the large numbers of nonwhites in these urban areas.[12]

EXPLANATIONS FOR RACIAL SEGREGATION

There is a small yet rich literature on residential segregation in Brazil which suggests that economics, racism in housing markets, and ethnicity may together account for racial segregation. Pierson (1942) investigated residential segregation in his seminal study of Salvador. Based on his impressions of various parts of the city, he observed that the skin color of residents varied according to the quality of the neighborhood: the poorest and most overcrowded areas of the city were inhabited by blacks, dark-skinned mulattos, and a limited number of light-skinned mulattos, while whites and, occasionally, light-skinned mulattos lived in the middle-class sectors of town. Thus, he described a landscape of considerable residential segregation by color although he concluded that it existed only to the extent that color and class were coterminous. During the 1950s and early 1960s, research sponsored by UNESCO reported substantial residential segregation in Rio de Janeiro[13] and in Florianópolis,[14] but these studies also concluded that in both cases segregation was highly conditioned by social class. Interestingly, the UNESCO-supported research revealed widespread racism and racial prejudice in Brazil, which contradicted the earlier literature, but did not extend such conclusions to spatial segregation.

On the other hand, there is evidence that discrimination in housing markets may account for some segregation. Surveys of racial attitudes conducted by the UNESCO-supported researchers found that a consistent 30 to 40 percent of whites claimed that they would not be willing to accept blacks or mulattos as neighbors.[15] These findings support the existence of racism that might lead to residential segregation, although they do not provide direct evidence of housing discrimination. However, the results of the 1995 national survey by Turra and Venturi (1995: 156) found little resistance by whites to having blacks as neighbors, suggesting that perhaps attitudes may be changing. Ninety-three percent of whites and 94 percent of browns reported that they would not care if several black (negro) families moved into their neighborhood. I am a bit skeptical about using such attitudinal data to gauge the level of racism in Brazil today, since responses about one's own racism (not societal) may be conditioned by a societal belief in racial tolerance.

There are plenty of examples of incidents in Brazil that suggest discrimination in housing, such as Brazil's well-known "elevator apartheid." Apartment buildings in Brazil generally have two elevators: the "service" elevator, which servants and workers are required to use, and the "social" elevator, which residents and their guests use. Middle-class blacks often complain that doormen often require that they use the service elevator when visiting middle-class friends. To my knowledge, there are no existing studies of how racism and racial discrimination might affect Brazilian housing markets, aside from the 1995 survey. Perhaps the instability of housing markets and the rapid growth of the poor population in metropolitan areas have not allowed for the consolidation of racially separate housing markets. Since so much housing in Brazilian cities is makeshift and exists in the gray area between legal and illegal, systematic housing discrimination is less likely to be found in most neighborhoods. However, even in stable Brazilian middle-class housing, there does not seem to be the strong association between property values and the racial composition of neighborhoods produced through blockbusting, redlining, or any other method similar to those that led to the high levels of segregation found in the United States.

In the United States, residential racial segregation largely originated in Jim Crow segregation in southern cities, while it was mostly the product of outright housing discrimination and a hardening color line in the North. Residential segregation grew in the early twentieth century in northern cities, especially through violence against blacks, restrictive covenants, and blockbusting by realtors.[16] These forms of housing segregation have been absent in Brazil. More importantly, the institutional agents that largely produce extreme segregation in the United States, such as real estate agents, managers, lending banks, and insurers, are not involved in most of Brazil's urban housing markets due to its largely makeshift and informal status. On the other hand, other practices that continue to fuel racial residential segregation in U.S. cities, such as white avoidance of black neighbors, outright discrimination, and, perhaps, some steering by agents and discriminatory bank lending practices against wealthier non-whites seeking to purchase formal housing, may also exist in Brazil. Another possible explanation for segregation among persons of similar income, besides discrimination and culture, may be racial disparity in the extent of accumulated wealth, which may be independent of income, as I showed in chapter 5.

There may also be some self-segregation by nonwhites. This may be partly because of residents' desires to minimize their contacts with whites so as to avoid potential racial discrimination. Although driven by general societal racism, nonwhites may find it easier to obtain housing in neighborhoods that already have significant numbers of nonwhites. In addition, self-segregation by whites, browns, and blacks may represent cultural attachments through proximity to institutions and like-minded persons. Rolnick (1989) finds that the African-origin population in São Paulo and Rio de Janeiro tends to be concentrated in certain poor neighborhoods, near other "co-ethnics" and generally near Afro-Brazilian cultural and religious institutions like *samba* schools and *terreiros de candomblé*. These neighborhoods often emerged around the cores of former slave neighborhoods. Racially distinct neighborhoods may also emerge from the coincidence of regional identities with the racial composition of these regions. Specifically, network-based migration flows seem to channel migrants from particular states, with widely distinct racial compositions, into separate neighborhoods. In the case of São Paulo, for example, migrants from the predominately white state of Paraná are concentrated in one part of the city, whereas migrants from predominately black and brown Bahia are concentrated in another.

To explore whether Brazil's moderate segregation is an effect of class, I present dissimilarity indexes in table 8.2 between whites and nonwhites for six income groups in the five metropolitan areas where whites, browns, and blacks are represented across most income levels. I examine the extent to which racial groups are segregated across households with the same family income to test whether economics can explain the extent of racial segregation. I determine which racial category to place the household into by the color of the household head. This is somewhat problematic since many households are multiracial, which itself may help explain lower levels of segregation in Brazil. Nevertheless, a large majority of households probably do not include both white and nonwhite members.

Table 8.2 is also different from table 8.1 in that it examines dissimilarity between whites and browns, and between whites and blacks. Among the forty largest urban areas, I examine five because only these provided the necessary minimum of three black or brown households per tract at middle or high income levels. This lower limit permits a fairly robust analysis of segregation at higher income levels avoiding random departures from evenness that might otherwise occur using very small populations. Only Salvador had enough nonwhites earning more than $1500 per month, while the other four met the minimum criteria for nonwhites for the $750–1499-per-month category. Aside from the methodological considerations, this problem also demonstrates that the residential isolation of whites is virtually assured by the absence of a significant nonwhite middle class.

Table 8.2 demonstrates that residential segregation among whites, browns, and blacks cannot be accounted for only by socioeconomic status; moderate racial residential segregation occurs among persons of similar income in the five metropolitan areas. Thus, economics itself cannot explain racial segregation in Brazil. Either self-segregation, racism, or both contribute to residential segregation in addition to class.

The table also shows that in nearly all cases segregation increases with income, demonstrating the greater importance of race in housing for the middle class than for the lower class.[17] For example, whites seem to noticeably increase their spatial distance from blacks in the highest income bracket, presumably where blacks have overcome the segregation assured by class. In Belo Horizonte, white-black segregation in the highest income bracket (375–749) is 11 points over the next highest income group (225–374), while Rio de Janeiro registered a 9-point difference and Salvador a 7-point increase among comparable groups. Rather than simply suggesting different levels of racial tolerance by income, greater segregation at higher income levels may reflect that middle-class whites have greater control in selecting residences by color through the formal housing market than those who must obtain homes through poor informal markets. The low levels of racial segregation among the poor (except in the very lowest income group) may reflect the precarious housing situation of the poorest sectors of the Brazilian population, where they have little control or concern over the color of their neighbors.

According to Rolnick (1999), three times as many urban Brazilians reside in self-constructed and unregulated housing as those living in regulated housing produced by private entrepreneurs. Given the nature of such housing, decisions for the poor about where to live are especially likely to be based on criteria like walking distance to work (because bus fares are often not affordable) or where members of one's social network (e.g., friends, kin) live who can assist with tasks such as child care or

TABLE 8.2
Indexes of dissimilarity among whites, browns, and blacks by family income group: Five metropolitan areas in Brazil, 1980

Metropolitan area and income group in Brazilian reais	Dissimilarity between:	
	White vs. black	White vs. brown
Salvador		
75–149	52	50
150–224	55	52
225–374	55	51
375–749	62	50
750–1499	—	51
1500 and over	—	51
Feira de Santana		
75–149	51	47
150–224	57	46
225–374	59	48
375–749	62	47
750–1499	—	52
Rio de Janeiro		
75–149	42	38
150–224	46	39
225–374	45	39
375–749	54	42
750–1499	—	55
Belo Horizonte		
75–149	44	41
150–224	45	42
225–374	46	42
375–749	57	45
750–1499	—	55
Barra Mansa-Volta Redonda		
75–149	36	39
150–224	36	36
225–374	38	36
375–749	42	36
750–1499	—	55

Source: 1980 census of Brazil. Also found in Telles 1992.

housing construction. In the context of extreme poverty where survival is paramount and social pressures and preferences to live in racially separate neighborhoods are not overwhelming, the possibility of extreme segregation seems unlikely. Also, since households and families are more racially integrated among the poorest sectors of the population, as the previous chapter showed, extreme residential segregation as in the United States is especially unworkable among the poor.

Also, results in table 8.2 demonstrate that white-black segregation is almost always greater than white-brown segregation. This strongly suggests a color continuum in the treatment of browns and blacks, especially at higher income levels. When income is controlled, segregation of blacks from whites is almost invariably greater than white-brown segregation; however, the differences are not as great as those for intermarriage. That is, while whites are almost as likely to live in the same neighborhoods with blacks as with browns, they are considerably less likely to maintain close or intimate social relations with blacks.

As incomes increase, the residential fortunes of browns and blacks diverge. White-black segregation increases with income at a greater rate than does white-brown segregation. White-brown segregation in the lowest income category is always less than black-white segregation, but these differences are small compared to higher income categories. In Salvador, Rio de Janeiro, and Belo Horizonte, whites are slightly more segregated from browns than blacks at a difference of 2 to 4 percentage points; but, at the $375–749 income level, there is a 12-percentage-point difference in white-brown and white-black segregation. Salvador, the only metropolitan area with a significant nonwhite group in the top income bracket, is atypical in that white-brown segregation is fairly stable at all income levels.

On the other hand, white-black segregation in Salvador for the poorest group is higher than in any of the other four urban areas but it is especially great at the $375–749 income level. Specifically, white-black segregation increases 10 points between the lowest (52) and the highest category (62). Such a difference or more in black-white segregation between these two income categories also occurs in Feira de Santana, Rio de Janeiro and Belo Horizonte. In Belo Horizonte, black-white segregation increases 13 points between the lowest (44) and highest (57) income groups.

CONSEQUENCES OF RACIAL SEGREGATION

Racial segregation has important consequences for the development of the Afro-Brazilian community and for its participation in Brazilian society. Segregation generally translates into inequalities in access to labor

TABLE 8.3
Residential dissimilarity of income groups by race from population earning over
$1500 per month; Rio de Janeiro metropolitan area, 1980

Dollars	Whites	Browns	Blacks
0–74	83	91	99
75–149	67	72	88
150–224	50	53	62
225–374	40	43	51
375–749	36	39	48
750–1499	34	36	(46)

Source: 1980 census of Brazil.
Note: Parentheses indicate small sample size subject to sizeable error.

and consumer markets that tend to be located in or near white and middle-class neighborhoods, as well as access to schools, hospitals, and police and fire protection. Psychologically, segregation limits exposure to middle-class role models, thereby further inhibiting mobility as opportunities for interracial and interclass interactions are constrained. The U.S. case points to better social-mobility outcomes for poor children, regardless of race, who grew up in neighborhoods where there was relatively little poverty concentration and where there was greater access to a middle class. Since blacks are much more likely than whites to grow up amidst concentrated poverty in the United States, such neighborhood differences account for much of the racial differences in adult socioeconomic outcomes.

Table 8.3 demonstrates that nonwhites, and especially blacks, are more spatially distant from the middle class in Brazil, and thus, as in the United States, blacks are more likely than whites of the same income level to live in concentrated poverty. Specifically, the table examines the extent of dissimilarity in Rio de Janeiro between whites, browns, and blacks of various income levels compared with the highest earning population category (over $1500 per month), which is nearly all white. As expected, the table's findings demonstrate that physical distance from the middle class decreases as income increases for all color groups. For whites, for example, the lowest-earning group has a dissimilarity score of 83 with the richest group, while the second highest income group has a score of 34. However, the degree of segregation from the middle class is greater for browns and greatest for blacks. In the case of the poorest blacks, they are nearly perfectly segregated (99) from the middle class. These findings thus point to a factor that has generally been neglected by scholars of race in Brazil: greater spatial distance of blacks to middle-class persons compared to whites of similar socioeconomic status implies less access to resources such as professional role models, better job networks, and superior urban infrastructure, all of which builds social capital and improves quality of life. Nonwhites and especially blacks are likely to have lower life chances simply because they are most likely to be physically distant from the middle class and live in concentrations of poverty.

On the positive side, greater racial segregation, no matter what the cause, often means the existence of dynamic ethnic neighborhoods, where ethnic affinities create a greater valuation of shared residential space, promoting cultural life and helping to empower ethnic groups toward greater participation by uniting common interests and controlling political spaces. The case of black (negro) districts like Liberdade in Salvador—where Afro-Brazilian music and culture are produced—Brasilândia in São Paulo, and Madureira in Rio de Janeiro are prime examples.

Moderate segregation has widespread implications for other features of Brazilian race relations, especially when compared to other countries with large populations of persons of African and European descent. Clearly, Brazil's lower levels of segregation have allowed relatively high levels of interracial interaction, including interracial friendship and intermarriage, at least among the poor. On the other hand, the absence of parallel institutions resulting from extreme segregation has ironically created barriers to social and political mobilization of Afro-Brazilians. In the United States, black churches, banks, and universities formed out of segregation and provided black North American communities with the capital to develop leaders, to form a significant middle class, and to mobilize human resources toward political ends. Additionally, residential segregation restricted the networks of blacks to other blacks, which facilitated heightened group identity and racial consciousness. Black churches in particular provided a space exclusively for blacks to discuss issues facing their communities and to develop strategies for combating racism and discrimination.

SALVADOR, BAHIA, AS AN EXCEPTION

The spatial insularity of Afro-Salvadorians is likely to have contributed to the development of a strong Afro-Brazilian culture and identity that has emerged in that city. The work of ethnographers at the Federal University of Bahia demonstrate that for many years there has been a clear sense of African Brazilian ethnic identity among a large part of the African-origin population in Salvador; this is less common in other Brazilian metropolitan areas.[18] For example, *blocos afros* (all-black groups of dancers in the Carnaval parades) are unique to Salvador. There, greater residential segregation is probably both result and cause of a relatively strong sense of ethnic identification among nonwhite Salvadorans. The large tourist industry engendered by this Afro-Brazilian culture in Salvador is well known to many foreigners. Indeed, I have heard the city's mayor proclaim that Salvador is an African city (and he is not referring to Johannesburg!). He seems to mean "African" in a cultural sense, where blacks are granted nearly free run of the cultural realm, and where the culture of Africa is celebrated, apparently in exchange for relinquishing claims to economic and political power so that it can continue to be monopolized by a small white elite. The African sense of Salvador is illustrated by its *terreiros, orixá* statues, and *moqueca* restaurants that have become an established part of the urban landscape, while hiding the deep poverty of the Afro-Salvadoran periphery. African culture and identity are thus negotiated with and regulated by a clientelistic and powerful elite that recognizes, lives with, defends, and even promotes symbols of Africanness, in turn ensuring its own legitimacy and allowing it to maintain its control over sponsorship and favors.

The creation of a distinctive ethnic identity in Bahia is often thought to be a result of the maintenance of cultural elements from Africa. The question still remains as to why these elements have been maintained to date, fully 115 years since the end of slavery. I believe that the racial isolation of the African Brazilian population of Salvador has been the major determinant for the maintenance and construction of this identity. Distinct cultural elements, whether "African" or African Brazilian, are reinforced in an environment which residentially isolates the worlds of many African Brazilians in Salvador from whites. Additionally, such isolation produces other conditions that fuel ethnic identification on the basis of race. These include the generation of African Brazilian institutions and the existence of a significant mulatto middle class, unique to Brazil, which provides service functions to residents and can take advantage of ethnic markets which provide opportunities for entrepreneurship, especially in the culture industry. A separate African Brazilian community in Bahia favors the formation and maintenance of an African Brazilian culture and the construction of a separate identity, which is reinforced through daily ingroup interaction. However, this seems to be quite unlike most of the rest of Brazil.

Conclusions

Like intermarriage, Brazil's limited miscegenation is manifested on the urban spatial level. Brazilian segregation is moderate when compared to the extreme black-white segregation still found in major U.S. cities, where segregation is sometimes considered the linchpin of racial inequality.

Whites often live side by side with blacks and mulattos in poor Brazilian neighborhoods. These arrangements are a much rarer phenomenon in the United States.

The regional and class concentration of persons by race, though, leads to a wide range of interracial exposure experiences across Brazilian urban areas. Although actual interaction between whites and nonwhites in Brazilian urban areas may often be limited, the spatial proximity of many Brazilians across race means that they are more likely to have a shared culture and develop interracial friendships. This is probably carried over for many years and over multiple generations so that residential proximity is both a cause and a consequence of interracial sociability. Residence reinforces interracial sociability within the same class in Brazil to a far greater degree than it does in the United States. This is a positive side of Brazilian race relations; like intermarriage, Brazilian residential segregation patterns reflect greater interracial fluidity and lower salience of racial boundaries than we observe in the United States, at least on the horizontal dimension of sociability.

Like intermarriage, such interaction is largely limited to poor Brazilian neighborhoods in most though not all regions, and occurs primarily between the poor minority of whites with the poor majority of blacks and browns. Middle-class whites in Brazil have few black or brown neighbors, except perhaps as servants, largely because the latter have been kept out of the middle class. Thus, segregation exists between whites and the nonwhite population, and this in itself—whether or not it can be explained by class—has important implications. Also, the disadvantage of nonwhites seems to be explained partly by their greater spatial isolation from the middle class. While Brazil's moderate segregation has allowed for levels of cross-racial interaction and fluidity which are far greater than those in the United States, it has also dimmed the prospects for resistance by the victims of racism because of its effect on racial consciousness and nonwhite middle-class formation. As a result, the nature of black movement organizing has quite distinct structural foundations in the two countries.

Chapter Nine

RETHINKING BRAZILIAN
RACE RELATIONS

THE BASIC contributions of this book have been to develop a more informed and complete understanding about race relations in Brazil through a systematic analysis of empirical data and to interpret those findings in the context of evolving Brazilian ideologies and understandings of race. At the most general level, while nineteenth-century scientific theories of white supremacy have since become discredited, such ideas remain deeply embedded in social thinking in Brazil. Race continues to carry meanings about one's worth and proper role in Brazilian society. Guided by ideas of racial hierarchy, Brazilians, like North Americans, impose racial categories on their fellow humans and treat them accordingly. As a result, nonwhites in Brazil are more than three times as likely as whites to be poor or illiterate, and white men, on average, earn more than twice as much as black and brown men; such differences have persisted for at least the past forty years.

Although this is a familiar story for observers of U.S. race relations, actual Brazil-U.S. differences are much more complicated. Product of a particular set of demographic, cultural, economic, and political forces, Brazilian race relations must be understood in their own context, rather than as a variant or a stage of U.S. race relations, which have nearly become a universal model for *the* sociology of race relations. The Brazilian case emerged from a nation building project which stressed integration through race mixture, rather than segregation. Relatedly, many other aspects of race in Brazil stand apart from the North American case although the persistent social practice of racial discrimination is similar. The dynamics of race in Brazil differ sharply from the models and theories that social scientists have assumed.

A DIALOGUE WITH EARLIER STUDIES

Social scientists have been interested in understanding race in Brazil for decades. I began in chapter 1 and showed, throughout subsequent chapters, that the social science literature is marked by two generations of research that produced nearly contradictory findings about the extent of racism. The first generation, from the 1930s to 1960s, showcased the wonders of Brazil's miscegenation, while ignoring or downplaying inequality and racism. The first generation consisted mostly of North Americans who examined racism in the North and Northeast, although they were inspired by the master scholar and shaper of Brazilian national identity, Gilberto Freyre. The first generation could find stark contrasts between Brazil and the formally racist Jim Crow system of the United States at the time. They observed much more fluidity in racial classification and marriage and friendships among persons of different colors in Brazil and concluded that there was little racism and certainly no color line in Brazilian society. They concluded that Brazil, unlike the United States, was well on its way to integrating the descendants of African slaves.

By contrast, the second generation, beginning in the 1950s, focused on Brazil's racism and racial inequality while refuting or ignoring Brazil's miscegenation. They disagreed with the first generation and concluded that racism was widespread and profound, rivaling systems of racial domination throughout the world. They discovered pervasive prejudice and discrimination, relatively rigid white-nonwhite distinctions and limited white relations with blacks and browns. The second generation was exclusively Brazilian at first, knew less about the United States than the first generation, and focused on the South and Southeast. Some of the difference in their conclusions can therefore be accounted for by their comparative knowledge and regional focus. Although they were aware of the dismantling of the ongoing formal segregation in the United States, they seemed to be less concerned with explicit comparisons to the United States. Throughout the 1980s and 1990s, though, both Brazilian and U.S. researchers further supported the second-generation findings, often through statistical analysis of racial inequality using national-level data sets. As a result, an emerging binational consensus accepted second-generation findings, and by default, many discredited the findings of the first generation.

Despite such contrasting conclusions, I find support for many of the findings of both generations. By dividing race relations into two dimensions, I show that the second generation's conclusions about racial discrimination and inequality—the vertical dimension—coexist with many of the first generation's findings of fluidity and interracial sociability—the horizontal dimension. Thus, I believe that the major difference in the distinct conclusions for the two generations of race relations scholars was their respective analytic emphasis on either horizontal or vertical race relations. By concentrating on one or the other dimension or one or another region, I believe that their explanations were consequently incomplete in explaining Brazilian race relations in the broad sense.

By limiting their analysis to the horizontal dimension of sociability, the earlier generation concluded that race relations were much better in Brazil than in the United States. Like the dominant North American sociological theories, they believed that relatively high levels of intermarriage and low levels of residential segregation were key determinants of the extent to which nonwhites would assimilate or be accepted by whites. They were optimistic that racial inequalities were temporary, as Brazilian society had avoided the egregious racism and profound racial distance of the United States. For the first generation, differences in social status by race were believed merely to reflect the recency of slavery, but the horizontal integration they perceived suggested to them that Brazilian society would soon change, as racial inequality would diminish with successive future generations. The Brazil they described thus offered liberal North Americans a hope that race differences could be transcended.

On the other hand, the second generation presented a Brazil that was marred by racism. They emphasized the vertical dimension of inequality as they perceived much mobility in the industrializing South and saw recent European immigrants leapfrog over blacks and mulattos in the labor market. By overlooking horizontal relations, they suggested that race relations in Brazil were as bad as those of the United States. In this book, I have largely sought to reevaluate these studies, which covered racial classification and vertical and horizontal relations.

I began in chapter 1 by calling the possible coexistence of such phenomenon "the enigma of Brazilian race relations." In this chapter, I seek to reconcile the findings of those two literatures and integrate them with other features of the Brazilian system. I first summarize some of my main findings regarding racial classification and vertical and horizontal relations. I then attempt to show how the horizontal and vertical components fit together in the Brazilian system. Finally, I discuss their implications for culture, politics, and a black social movement. As throughout the book, I emphasize comparison with blacks and whites in the United States.

RACIAL CLASSIFICATION

Race relations of both the horizontal and vertical kind first depend on how persons get classified into particular categories. Although social meanings based on race are omnipresent, memberships in particular categories are often not fixed. This is particularly true for the Brazilian case where racial classification is especially ambiguous or fluid. The way persons classify each other and identify themselves are sometimes contradictory and also vary depending on the social situation. Furthermore, racial terms are numerous and are often inconsistently applied. That fluidity also reflects considerable cultural integration of Brazilians of all colors. By contrast, race in the United States has historically been defined by hypo-descent rules, where anyone with a small amount of black ancestry is considered black. Such rigid or essentialistic definitions in the United States are slowly changing in the direction of greater ambiguity, but they are far from being as fluid as in Brazil. Relatedly, racial self-identity is not a core component of identity for many Brazilians as it is in the United States, and there is little sense of solidarity with or *belonging* to a racial group.

Brazilians often prefer the notion of color rather than race because it captures such fluidity. Nevertheless, the Brazilian notion of color is equivalent to race because it is associated with a racial ideology that ranks persons of different colors. Whether one uses color or race, persons are typically racialized, and their perceived status depends on their racial or color categorization. External definitions of race are especially important because they often impart power and privilege in social interactions to lighter-skinned persons. According to the general Brazilian societal norm, bodily appearance—influenced somewhat by gender, status, and the social situation—determines who is black, mulatto, or white. The Brazilian system of whitening has long allowed escape from the stigmatized black category, in which many persons with African ancestry identify or are classified in intermediate as well as white categories. On the other hand, while some persons may be able to escape being black or nonwhite, others cannot. Some remain black or brown no matter how wealthy or educated they become. An apparently more recent phenomenon is that of darkening, reflecting a growing racial consciousness.

In Brazil, the existence of a mulatto category is both cause and consequence of an ideology of miscegenation and not an automatic result of the actual biological process of race mixture. Miscegenation does not create mixed-race persons, as the U.S. case shows. There, mixed-race persons are simply "black." In the Brazilian ideology, mulattos are valued as the quintessential Brazilians in national beliefs, although they are often marginalized in reality and are much more similar to blacks than to whites in the Brazilian class structure. Racialization occurs on a color gradient where the meanings attached to different skin colors account for different levels of discrimination. Blacks (pretos or negros) in popular conceptions of the term are those at the darkest end of the color continuum, but in an increasingly used sense of the term (negro), it includes mulattos or browns as well. Traditionally, black refers to a small proportion of the national population but in the newer rendition, it may refer to roughly half of the population. The Brazilian system therefore does not have clear rules for defining who is black, and avoidance is often attainable, at least in name. Ambiguity thus allows many Brazilians to switch

TABLE 9.1
Postabolition racial classification in Brazil and the United States

Social dimension	Brazil		United States
	Mulattos	Blacks	Blacks (inc. mulattos)
Distinction from whites	Ambiguous	Clear[a]	Clear
Black consciousness	Low	Moderate	High

[a]But very ambiguous distinction from browns.

identities instead of being confined to discrete categories. On the other hand, one's appearance constrains millions of Brazilians to being black, defined in either its more or less restricted form.

Table 9.1 summarizes many of the classificatory distinctions between Brazil and the United States. I highlight two points in the table that are important for understanding cross-national differences in racial classification. First, while classificatory distinctions from whites are often ambiguous for millions of Brazilians who straddle the white-mulatto categories, millions of others do not have the possibility of ever being classified as or treated as white. There is virtually no ambiguity when making distinctions between white and black (preto), or in many but far from most cases, between white and brown. In the U.S. case, as I previously mentioned, mulattos are clearly distinguishable from whites on the basis of hypodescent rules, as they are classified as black. On the other hand, they constituted a separate category from blacks earlier in U.S. history and continue to receive better social treatment than dark blacks. Also, the extent of black consciousness varies widely in Brazil and the United States. Roughly speaking, there is little sense of a black consciousness for mulattos in Brazil and a moderate sense for blacks (pretos) in Brazil. We know this, for example, by the proportion of self-described browns and blacks that accept the term negro for themselves. Racial identity is not usually salient, although racial categorization by others is. By contrast, racial consciousness is much stronger for blacks (including mulattos) in the United States, where race is a core component of identity.

VERTICAL RELATIONS

Brazil's major problem today is social, more than political or economic. Democratization has become consolidated as there has been a smooth transition to the election of a leftist president, and the economy, despite hyperinflation and negative growth in the 1980s, has resumed a path of steady (but slow) growth. However, the distribution of societal wealth is arguably the most unequal in the world. Moreover, nonwhites are at the bottom of Brazil's grossly distorted economic pyramid. As a result, the vertical exclusion of mulattos and, especially, blacks is greater than vertical exclusion for blacks in the United States. Although their importance was denied in the past, the profound racial inequalities of Brazil are now well known.

I have identified three factors that are primarily responsible for Brazil's profound racial inequalities: *hyperinequality,* a *discriminatory glass ceiling,* and a *racist culture.* Brazil's hyperinequality underlies many of Brazil's social problems and has led to a huge gulf in the average incomes of whites and nonwhites, creating substantial differences in material wealth, social status, and access to social capital. That inequality is not merely material but also encompasses inequality in power relations, justice, subjective sense of worth, and ability to participate in social life, including work, education, health, and housing. A highly unequal Brazilian educational system is most responsible for Brazil's world-class inequality, and inequality is greater in places where there are more nonwhites.

Brazil is a middle-income country by world standards, but its hyperinequality has forced at least one-third of its population into poverty. This includes about half of blacks and browns. On most indicators, Brazil now has the highest income inequality of any major country in the world, with South Africa as the only major country that occasionally competes with it on that score. Brazilians in the top 10 percent of the income structure currently earn, on average, twenty-eight times more than average persons in the bottom 40 percent. The greater racial income inequality of Brazil compared to the United States is thus largely, but not exclusively, due to the more unequal income structure of Brazil. On the other hand, Brazil is no South Africa, where the poor are almost entirely black. Many poor Brazilians are white, although poverty is disproportionately nonwhite.

The primary social cleavage in Brazilian society is between a small middle class, which is almost entirely white, and the poor and working-class majority, which is multiracial but disproportionately nonwhite. Although the white middle class is able to maintain separation from darker persons through a socioeconomic hierarchy that has long been among the most unequal in the world, this is not solely a class boundary. Race is fundamental to determining who gets into the middle class. An informal but highly effective discriminatory glass ceiling prevents lower-class blacks and browns from entering the middle class much more so than their white lower-class counterparts. Thus, the socioeconomic position of nonwhites in Brazilian society is due to both class and race.

Alarmingly, the glass ceiling is hardening with Brazil's development. In recent decades, Brazil's university system has greatly expanded, and the skill and educational levels required for middle-class jobs has grown. At the same time, inequality between whites and nonwhites in access to the middle class has grown, largely because of a growing racial gap in college attainment. Higher education in Brazil has expanded significantly throughout the past four decades, and whites have mostly been its beneficiaries, leading to the widening racial gap. Because education is so tightly correlated with income in Brazil, higher education for blacks and browns is fundamental if they are to enter the middle class in significant numbers.

An almost entirely white middle class uses race and class to reduce competition for middle-class status. This system provides the privileges of access to and deference from a large, inexpensive, and mostly nonwhite servant class. The low cost of labor for the middle class also allows them to pay for private education for their children and ignore the public educational system. By greatly reducing the competition from the masses of Brazilians that attend the poor public schools, private schooling greatly enhances their chances for entering the public university, Brazil's most important passport to middle-class status. At the same time, this educational cleavage greatly impairs the ability of the mostly nonwhite lower classes ever to become middle class. White privilege is thus advanced through a defense of class interests, which the predominately white middle class uses to secure and maintain control over societal wealth and resources and to reduce competition for their social positions.

Blacks and browns are nearly absent from the middle class, although the experiences of the few have demonstrated that racism persists independently of class. The few middle-class blacks and browns continue to suffer from discrimination in ordinary everyday interactions, and in some cases, they are not able to benefit from their class privilege, as they must face constant skepticism and doubt about their position. At the other end of the class structure, poor whites, by contrast, can more often pass beyond the barriers that eliminate competition for societal wealth and resources than can poor browns and blacks. Although racial distinctions are more ambiguous than the United States, the white-brown distinction is fairly rigid for the middle class, especially where the proportion of the population that is white is greater. Thus, as one ascends into the middle class, racial boundaries harden.

Many whites in Brazil continue to be poor or working class, and thus there is a large supply of white persons who compete with browns and blacks to enter the middle class. This may include phenotypically light-brown persons who may sometimes be accepted as white or nearly white, especially in regions where whites are a numerical minority. Poor whites who are often neighbors, friends, and even relatives (including siblings) of blacks and especially browns, are more likely than nonwhites to squeeze through social barriers to high-status positions. Poor whites tend to be preferred to poor browns and especially blacks in schooling and in the market for middle-class jobs, especially when middle-class whites are not available. Aside from being granted greater social prestige on the basis of their appearance, poor whites also have greater access than nonwhites of similar social standing to the networks and patronage that are important in the Brazilian labor market.

Race is an easy marker for class exclusion, creating a class structure in which blacks and browns are kept in the lower ranks. Race and class thus both become important signifiers of status in a status conscious society. Racial and class hierarchies are encoded in informal rules about social interaction and are considered natural, in which one's status or position in the hierarchy is assumed to give one greater rights or privileges. Either factor clearly limits mobility or social acceptance. Race and class together severely impair it.

Although hidden behind the façade of miscegenation, a racist culture is ubiquitous in all social interactions among whites, browns, and blacks in virtually all social situations. It is based on a web of beliefs that subordinate positions are the proper place for browns and blacks and that social spaces that involve control and access to resources should be occupied by whites. From vertical relations like hiring and promotions to horizontal ones like hanging out with friends or enduring the dating market, slights against blacks and browns accrue to the many other slights that preceded them, often harming the self-esteem of brown and especially black persons. Such treatment intensifies with each successively darker shade of skin color.

This racist culture is reinforced, naturalized, and legitimated by the media and popular culture through humor and common dictums, such as "everyone knows their place" or, more crudely, "each monkey on its branch." These sayings provide the possibility of a widely recognized racial hierarchy that is perceived as natural. As long as society's members internalize that system, Brazilian racial domination persists with a minimum of conflict and without the need for segregation. Although most white Brazilians deny they are racist, there is a widely held sense that the favored position of whites in Brazilian society is a natural fact. Despite the positive value given to racial democracy and miscegenation, the holders of these values do not perceive an inconsistency between the cordiality among different racial-group members and their ideas of the proper place of nonwhites in the hierarchy. Cordiality and the claim of racial democracy can smoothly coexist with the racial hierarchy as long as nonwhites accept their place in the system.

Finally, it is important to note that mulattos are less discriminated against than blacks, as the human-capital models have strongly suggested. Mulattos are also socially closer to whites, as indicated by evidence for marriage and residence. Thus, they are more likely to benefit from the material and symbolic benefits of social proximity to whites, including greater access to patrimony and social networks. Their racial status is more flexible than blacks since their ability to become white sometimes increases with social mobility, especially in places where there are relatively few whites. However, most mulattos have similar class positions as blacks, but their advantages—as conferred by a system of whitening—help explain why mulattos are often unwilling to identify as negro or with the black movement.

HORIZONTAL RACE RELATIONS

Despite Brazil's profound racial inequality, this study has also shown that there is substantial intermarriage and residential proximity between whites and nonwhites. Thus miscegenation in Brazil is not mere ideology. Race mixture occurs in the intimate and residential realms of Brazilian life much more than in the United States, where the worlds of blacks and whites are clearly segmented. In this sense, Brazil is very different from the United States. Although U.S. society is changing—as white attitudes towards blacks soften—behavioral indicators like intermarriage and residential segregation show the persistence of a wide racial gap in that country. As many have noted, black-white interactions in Brazil do not have the tension, hostility, and suspicion often found in such relations in the United States. While the social systems of both countries successfully integrated descendents of European immigrants, the Brazilian melting pot has been more successful at integrating the African-origin population at the horizontal level. These social facts are positive signs that Brazilian race relations are comparatively mild. Much higher rates of intermarriage and lower rates of residential segregation than the United States today suggest weaker racial boundaries in Brazil. This is especially true among the poor and among persons of proximate color in Brazil.

The miscegenation ideology therefore reflects reality to a significant degree and should not be dismissed as merely ideology. Rather, it needs to be accepted as a key explanatory variable for understanding other dimensions of Brazilian (and perhaps other Latin American) systems of race relations. The Brazilian nation as imagined by its elite in an earlier period reflected Brazilian experience which in turn has had great implications for the way the country has evolved. But greater race mixture and fluid race relations are not of much consolation to the majority of Brazil's

TABLE 9.2

Postabolition race relations in Brazil and the United States on vertical and horizontal dimensions

| Social Dimension | Brazil | | United States |
	Mulattos	Blacks	Blacks (inc. mulattos)
Relative degree of current racial exclusion			
Vertical	Moderate-high	High	Moderate
Horizontal	Low	Moderate	High
Historical excl./incl. in state intervention			
Vertical	Exclusion (whitening)		Exclusion (Jim Crow)
	Neutral (racial democracy)		Inclusion (affirmative action)
	Inclusion (affirmative action)		Neutral (color-blindness)
Horizontal	Inclusion		Exclusion (Jim Crow)
			Neutral

nonwhites who are poor or nearly so. Racism and racial inequality, along with a highly unequal class structure, persist in excluding black and mixed-race persons from enjoying the opportunities afforded by Brazil's economic development and its emerging citizenship rights. Thus, the Brazilian case shows that fairly high rates of intermarriage and low levels of residential segregation do not necessarily imply greater acceptance of outgroups, contrary to the assumptions of sociological theory. Such theory is limited by its strict adherence to a U.S. model, whose racial logic cannot be generalized.

I summarize the relative degree of racial exclusion on the vertical and horizontal dimensions between the United States and Brazil in table 9.2. Vertically, mulattos and especially blacks are highly excluded from the Brazilian middle class. In contrast, while a large number of blacks occupy the lowest strata of U.S. society, there is also a fairly large middle class, especially in recent years. Whites are four to five times as likely to hold middle-class positions in Brazil, while they are between one and two times as likely to be in the middle class in the United States. As data for intermarriage show, horizontally, Brazilian mulattos have close social relations with whites, especially those of their social class, when compared to Afro-North Americans. By contrast, U.S. blacks continue to experience high levels of residential segregation from whites and rarely intermarry. Brazilian blacks are intermediate in terms of intermarriage, although their residential segregation from whites is clearly in the moderate range, closer to Brazilian mulattos than to U.S. blacks. Ultimately, the U.S.- Brazil difference is an issue of racial boundaries, which vary on the horizontal and vertical planes. On the horizontal plane, racial boundaries in Brazil are much more easily traversed than in the United States. However, on the vertical dimension, racial barriers are more insurmountable than in the United States.

EXPLAINING CROSS-NATIONAL RACE-RELATIONS DIFFERENCES

Before analyzing how vertical and horizontal relations coexist, I explain why such distinct characteristics evolved in the United States and Brazil. Why are there such large cross-national differences on both the horizontal and vertical dimensions? These are not the outgrowth of natural processes, but I believe they are largely the result of respective state actions. States have been particularly powerful actors in shaping social boundaries, including those by race. The U.S. and South Africa experiences certainly suggest that states themselves are powerful enough to create major changes in race relations. Even major structural forces, like industrialization, have relatively little influence on race relations, compared to state imposition of segregation or, in a positive sense, affirmative action, or the more subtle shaping of ideology by the state. The evidence in this book similarly suggests that state interventions have helped shape distinct configurations of race relations in the two countries, although they were also constrained and influenced by other variables such as demography, earlier ideologies, and personal identities.

State actions in Brazil and the United States have varied over time, but their effects in each time period have had a lasting influence in shaping the current system of race relations. I summarize these in the bottom half of table 9.2. Beginning with the then accepted scientific proof of the 19th century that whites were biologically superior to nonwhites, Brazil and the United States both responded by actively seeking ways to diminish the influence of nonwhites. North Americans created a system that sought total racial segregation for its white majority from nonwhites. The United States instituted formal racial segregation, especially through racial classification, antimiscegenation laws, and discriminatory housing practices, separating the lives of blacks and whites in the United States until the mid-1960s. Segregation left a persistent and wide racial divide at the horizontal level. Segregation also led to the creation of parallel institutions by blacks themselves and to strong and separate racial identities. Officially, formal segregation in the United States lasted from 1896 (*Plessy vs. Ferguson*) to at least 1954 (*Brown vs. the Board of Education*), although segregation laws persisted until the mid-1960s. Since then, a series of federally instituted policies not only ended formal segregation, but through affirmative action and the voting rights act, they sought to promote the nonwhite population on the vertical dimension. This led to a very large increase in the size of the black middle class and racial inequality that is currently much less severe than Brazil's. However, the U.S. state hardly promoted improvements in the fluidity of horizontal relations. Despite the civil-rights reforms of the 1960s, taboos against intermarriage and residential mixing, as well as the one-drop rule, strongly persisted with the legacy of segregation. Even antisegregatory housing laws since the 1960s are poorly enforced, and consequently, extreme residential segregation between blacks and whites persists.[1]

By contrast, the Brazilian state eschewed segregation but rather promoted intermarriage through both its whitening and racial-democracy ideologies. Before that, race mixture was greater in Brazil than the United States throughout the colonial period because of the much greater predominance of males over females among the European colonizers. This demographic fact set the stage for what would happen to race in the early Brazilian republic and thereafter. In response to nineteenth-century scientific racism, the Brazilian elite decided to promote further miscegenation, but with the massive infusion of white blood drawn from millions of European immigrants. They sought to design a white nation through European immigration and its optimistic prediction that white genetic traits would predominate in race mixture, eventually whitening the black element out of its mostly nonwhite population. As scientific theories about race began to be discredited, the Brazilian state began to promote a self-image of a racial democracy that was based on miscegenation, a large dose of African culture, and an aversion to racism. These factors would become central to Brazilian national identity. Brazil stressed racial integration, although in the more abstract sense of peoplehood, nation, and culture, rather than inclusion in the polity or in the sense of equal opportunity. At the same time, the Brazilian state failed to redress racial inequality until very recently. As a result of such comparative actions, Brazil now has greater racial inequality than the United States but it is more horizontally integrated.

The greater vertical inequality of Brazil may also be explained by economics, coupled with state decisions. In the labor market, employers in places like Brazil with large amounts of "surplus labor," often have a wide choice among potential workers. In those areas, elimination of workers on the basis of race may not affect competitiveness if several potential employees are perceived to be equally qualified. Similarly, Brazilian elites have generally disregarded basic education, instead pouring valuable resources into higher education for the middle classes. They have had little concern if a large segment of the population receives little schooling, because they regarded quality education for only a small segment of the population as necessary for development. As a result, racial inequality is further enhanced. For the majority attending public schools, the few available resources go to white students for regional, economic, and directly discriminatory reasons. Thus, to the extent that labor and educational markets remain poorly developed in the context of racist social behavior, this vicious cycle becomes a machine for perpetuating racial inequality.

Rather than examining the nineteenth-century causes of either adopting segregation or miscegenation, this book has instead focused on the contemporary consequences of the respective systems. However, given some debate about what led multiracial countries to implement legal segregation or not, it is worth adding my opinion to the fray. I believe that the reasons for the divergent routes taken by state elites in the United States and Brazil were affected by a mix of factors, including politics and labor-supply concerns, but mostly racial identities and sensibilities. The role of politics takes center stage in a well-known account that compares Brazil with the United States and South Africa,[2] but the author of that study discards the other equally plausible reasons. In the first place, Brazil was able to attract an alternative labor supply from Europe, whereas the U.S. South, where the large majority of blacks resided, could not. To keep wages down and therefore remain competitive, southern employers may thus have encouraged state repression of black labor for its expanding cotton industry.

The sensibilities of the Brazilian elite seem to have been especially important. The barriers to implementing segregation in Brazil, despite political or economic reasons, would have been greater than in the United States or South Africa, because Brazil had no tradition of a sharp classificatory color line that was necessary for segregation, and a large part of the white population, including many members of the elite, were themselves products of miscegenation. Many nonwhites had become well integrated into national culture and in horizontal social relations. A system of segregation would thus seem unworkable if there were no clear place to divide the population by race and undesirable because it violated cultural norms or excluded many members of the elite.

DEVELOPMENT AND RACE RELATIONS

Traditional sociology often looked to economic development as the primary engine that would bring major societal change. Classical sociology believed that, with development, ascriptive characteristics like race would become less important, and modern societies would come to depend on universalism and rationalization in their valuation of others. Van den Berghe (1967) made a particularly ambitious effort to predict the nature of race and racism as societies went from paternalism to competitive race relations. His model theorized that racial inequality would decline as societies shifted from ascription to achievement, and consequently, greater labor-market competition between whites and nonwhites would lead to greater racial antagonism and to whites limiting their personal contacts with nonwhites. Although he did not have strong evidence to support his claims, Van den Berghe's theory was particularly elegant and, despite its inaccuracy, ventured to make unambiguous claims about changing race relations on the horizontal and vertical planes. Challengers to this conventional view never stated their theories so clearly but generally seemed to expect no change, believing that race would continue to be functional to capitalist and industrial development.

Using a framework similar to Van den Berghe's, I investigated the effect of development on horizontal and vertical race relations in recent Brazilian history and presented some comparative data for the United States. Figure 9.1 plots my conclusions and those by Van den Berghe, who used Brazil and the United States as well as South Africa and Mexico as his exemplary cases. By drawing a two-dimensional graph with the degree of horizontal exclusion on the x axis and vertical exclusion on the y axis, I illustrate the simultaneous effect of development on the two race-relations dimensions. Van den Berghe expected exclusion on the horizontal plane to grow with development. The lighter line plots this prediction for Brazil and the United States. The darker lines plot actual changes based on evidence from this book. In Brazil, exclusionary horizontal relations hardly changed at all from their previous moderate range. In the United States, there were slight declines in horizontal exclusion, but interracial sociability between blacks and whites there remains extremely limited. Whereas Van den Berghe expected that high levels of racial inequality would be reduced with development in both countries, racial inequality hardly changed in Brazil (on most indicators) while it dropped significantly in the United States. Thus, it seems that economic development had little to do with this, but rather the comparative differences seem to be explained by U.S. government intervention designed to reduce racial inequality in the form of affirmative action compared to the lack of similar action in Brazil.

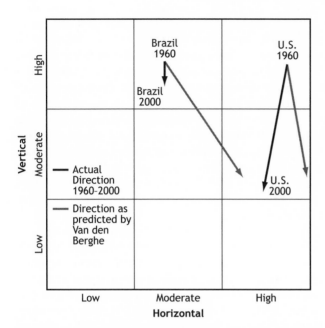

FIGURE 9.1 Black-white social distance in the United States and Brazil on vertical and horizontal dimensions: 1960–2000.

RECONCILING VERTICAL AND HORIZONTAL RELATIONS IN BRAZIL

I have shown in this book how integration or assimilation at the horizontal level coexists with a high level of racism and racial inequality in Brazil. But how can they? If there is so much intermarriage, how can there be discrimination? Based on the U.S. model with which I began chapter 1, sociologists have theorized that such inclusive horizontal relations would indicate low levels of racism and racial inequality. This is the logic of assimilation theory. However, racial inequality in Brazil continues to be high for the more than one hundred years since the end of slavery and, despite economic development and miscegenation, is growing in important respects. Thus, the Brazilian case presents an apparent paradox for understanding race relations. Miscegenation does not undermine the racial hierarchy. If racism is so intense as to keep blacks and mulattos in the lower rungs of the labor market, even more so than in the United States, how is it that sociability across racial lines is so much greater than in the United States? How do these coexist in practice? When persons are racist, can they be selectively racist, that is, more racist in vertical than in horizontal relations?

More intermarriage and less residential segregation do not necessarily mean that Brazilians are less racist than North Americans overall but it seems that they are to the extent that racial systems can be limited to horizontal relations. Racial differences in social interactions seem to have distinct meanings for Brazilians compared to North Americans. Racial intermarriages are stigmatized today as they were in the past in both countries, but the policing of the intermarriage taboo through social sanctions is much greater in the United States. Racial intermarriage is highly taboo in the United States, but the greater permissiveness of intermarriage in Brazil does not negate the maintenance of the racial hierarchy. The fact is that whiteness in Brazil continues to confer advantages, even in the close relation of intermarriage. A racial hierarchy is maintained in Brazil in several ways.

Interracial sociability has little effect on dominant-group whites, so that it does not threaten their status position. The status of the white middle and upper classes and their social distance from nonwhites, unlike poor whites, is maintained through Brazil's hyperinequality. Brazil's highly unequal class hierarchy thus reinforces the racial hierarchy, limiting middle-class-white interaction with nonwhites. Most intermarriage is among the poor, which also has lower residential segregation and experiences less rigid racial distinctions. By contrast, interracial sociability exists mostly as ideology for the middle class, except in hierarchical relations, which characterizes the interactions that the vast majority of middle-class whites have with blacks and browns. Middle-class whites treat nonwhites in a cordial manner at the same time as they keep them from becoming class equals.

Also, interracial sociability varies by region and whites are concentrated in the mostly white southern half of Brazil, further limiting their interaction with nonwhites. Also, the white-nonwhite line is especially rigid and exclusive there, especially for the middle class. Thus, for the roughly 75 percent of whites that lives in the more developed South or Southeast, white contact with nonwhites is limited by the small size of the nonwhite population and especially sharp racial boundaries. On the other hand, for dominant-group whites in predominately nonwhite regions, racial distance is maintained by a steeper class hierarchy, characterized by more paternalistic social relations and greater racial inequality than in the South or Southeast.

However, cross-national differences remain for even the white middle class in predominately white regions. In Brazil, they are more likely to marry nonwhites than similarly positioned North Americans. This suggests greater tolerance for blacks and especially mulattos in Brazil, even among dominant-group members, not to mention the large number of poor and working-class whites. While such levels of intermarriage may signify healthier race relations for Brazilian society on the horizontal level, racism does not vanish for those individuals involved. Rather, a system of status exchange often operates in relations between interracial couples and in the dating market prior to marriage. In those contexts, whiteness is a valued property that can be traded for greater diligence, devotion, class status, or other benefits provided by the darker spouse. The very belief that whitening through marriage is desirable for dark-skinned persons is based on the racist assumption that it will improve darker persons, both biologically and socially, but status exchange ensures that this system also works for light-skinned persons. Finally, the racial hierarchy within these marriages themselves often endures. Although explicit racism is often submerged in such relations, it is able to raise its ugly head at any time.

The Brazilian case also shows that racial discrimination and inequality persist despite the absence of extreme residential segregation, as in the United States. Residential segregation, then, is not a linchpin of racial inequality, as some analysts have suggested it is for the United States. Extreme segregation, as in the United States, is simply not necessary to maintain high levels of racial inequality, as the Brazilian case shows. Blacks and whites may live next door to each other and even intermarry, but racial ideologies continue to be a highly salient feature embedded in social practices, which in turn, act to maintain racial inequality. For middle-class whites, though, residential exposure to nonwhites is limited, especially for those who live in predominately white regions. It is important to note that such whites comprise the bulk of the Brazilian elite today.

Although race is important in both systems, the boundaries that keep blacks and mulattos in subordinate vertical positions are more class-related in Brazil than they are in the United States. A system of gaping economic inequality in Brazil serves to keep nonwhites from competing with middle-class whites and generally limits interracial contacts to those where there are large status differences. Class boundaries are considered legitimate and are policed socially and by the state, whereas explicit racial boundaries are not. Most notably, the public education system is one of the most unequal in the world and the justice system ardently defends middle-class interests. However, race is an unspoken feature of this boundary making by class. The justice system, for example, represses the poor and is especially likely to target blacks. In the United States, racial boundaries have historically been explicit and largely accepted. Policing of racial boundaries, by either the population or the state, has historically been considered legitimate in the United States. Despite these differences, though, the racial hierarchy is ultimately reproduced in both countries.

Horizontal racial boundaries have been much more permeable in Brazil. Unambiguous racial boundaries keep whites and blacks in the United

States from marrying or living next to each other and these boundaries are largely maintained through social conventions and taboos. Moreover, U.S. segregation directly created rigid black-white boundaries through classification rules and established separateness in social relations. Since then, racial boundaries have become self-reinforcing through high rates of endogamy, extreme spatial segregation, racially coded friendship networks, a sense of groupness by race and, to a larger extent than in Brazil, shared cultural symbols by race. While such forces in the United States may have created greater racial polarization, they also have facilitated organized resistance to racism by the formation of highly salient identities based on race. In Brazil, greater sociability of persons across racial lines, especially for persons of the same social class, often led to residential, friendship, and familial ties among persons of different colors. Also, the lack of classificatory rules and the celebration of a mixed-race type also led to the blurring of racial divisions in Brazil. While such relations represent a positive feature of Brazil's human relations, they also weakened the possibility of group solidarity, therefore undermining a potential foundation for mobilizing to combat racism.

POLITICAL IMPLICATIONS

Brazil's racism and racial inequality are peacefully reproduced, for the most part, largely because of miscegenation. Thus, it is important to understand horizontal and vertical relations as parts of a system of racial domination, rather than simply as separate entities. While Brazil's fluid horizontal relations may be interpreted as signs of a less racist system, they also facilitate vertical racial domination. This system is efficient largely because it is powered by miscegenation rather than the more primitive motor of segregation. Indeed, the Brazilian system has been able to use miscegenation or fluid horizontal race relations to allow racial injustices and inequalities to persevere without state intervention, for a relatively long period of time. Brazilians have been able to point to their miscegenation as proof that there is little or no racism in their country, therefore diverting scrutiny away from racism as the source of Brazil's racial inequality. Good horizontal relations, in a sense, have been used to cover up bad vertical race relations.

Until very recently, the Brazilian state has also been able to avoid interventions that redress racial inequality, because it has used the nature of its racial system to diffuse black resistance. Specifically, the ideology and fact of race mixture have impeded the ability of Brazil's black movement to fight against racism and become strong enough to influence state decisions for developing antiracist social policy. Elites have resisted black-movement demands with rationales based on miscegenation contending that: race mixture is proof that there is no racism; state actions on behalf of racial groups are not possible because race mixture has blurred racial distinctions; and race-specific interventions would only harden or polarize racial boundaries that were smoothed over by centuries of race mixture. Although Brazil's system grew mostly out of historical constraints rather than elite designs, it nevertheless resulted in a more effective system for maintaining racial domination.

In response, the black movement asserts that miscegenation devalues and even seeks to destroy blackness and prevents the formation of black identities needed to sustain an effective antiracist movement in pursuit of a true racial democracy. The belief in whitening divides a potentially unified black movement into blacks and a larger number of dark-skinned persons that can escape the black category. At the same time, racial democracy in the past paralyzed the black movement by denying the existence of racism. In the past, elites labeled black-movement resistance as racist itself and even seditious because it sought to create racial divisions in a society that was presumably free of racism. Relatedly, Brazilians have trumpeted the historical existence of nonwhites among the elite, a far more common occurrence in the past, as blanket proof that blacks are not discriminated.

Ironically, antiracist resistance in Brazil has also been impaired by the absence of extreme segregation, as in the United States. North American segregation sharply delineated black-white differences and thus facilitated antiracist organizing by creating racially bounded social networks; parallel institutions such as churches, banks, and universities; unambiguous rules for racial classification; and distinct cultural forms, including language and religion. Afro–North Americans could easily recognize a shared sense of racial exclusion, and parallel institutions allowed for the formation of a black leadership class. In Brazil, political organizing on the basis of class has been the historical trend, in which class identities have been stronger than racial-group identities. The relatively proximate residential and familial social relations among persons of different colors but of the same class have facilitated interracial class organizing, but arguably, at the expense of a popular black movement.

CULTURAL IMPLICATIONS

Brazil's history of race relations has cultural consequences that are also quite distinct from those in the United States. In its nationalist modernizing project since the 1930s, Brazilian elites promoted racial democracy and African culture as part of the national culture. Brazilian elites

TABLE 9.3
Postabolition cultural dimensions of race relations in Brazil and the United States

	Brazil		United States
Social dimension	Mulattos	Blacks	Blacks (inc. mulattos)
Cultural distinctions from whites	Low	Low-Moderate	Moderate
Continuity with Africa	Moderate	High	Low
State intervention in promoting African culture	Moderate	Moderate	None

commoditized and commercialized African culture, taking advantage of the fact that a significant number of African-born Brazilians survived into the twentieth century as did close contacts with West Africa. Although blacks and mulattos were often its purveyors, Afro-Brazilian culture was shared across society with little regard to racial distinctions. Although a stronger sense of African-based culture is passed down among some black (preto) families, especially in places with predominately black populations like Salvador and in *quilombo* communities, there have not been institutional mechanisms like segregation to reproduce it as a racially separate realm. Blacks participate more in so-called Afro-Brazilian culture than whites or mixed-race persons, although nonblacks are also involved to a considerable degree. The primary racial divide is thus between blacks and nonblacks in culture, even though it is between whites and nonwhites socioeconomically. But the cultural divide by race is relatively small compared to that in the United States. In sum, cultural integration of whites, browns and blacks is clearly greater in Brazil.

U.S. blacks (and whites for that matter) seem to have less direct cultural continuity with Africa,[3] but segregation has had the unintended consequence of shaping racially differentiated cultural forms and attitudes. As a result, U.S. blacks are often distinguished from whites not only by color or ancestry but on the basis of language, religion, spirituality, family life, and political and racial attitudes. This is much less the case in Brazil. Although aspects of Afro-North American culture can certainly be traced to Africa, black culture was mostly made in America, and particularly, in segregated black communities. North American society provided a weak structural basis for ethnic preservation of African culture, but extreme segregation permitted an evolution of distinctive subcultures by race built upon a few remaining vestiges of the original culture.[4] Thus, despite closer ties to Africa, the Brazil case demonstrates how racial distinctions do not necessarily evolve into cultural differences, leading a prominent analyst of Brazil to call the Brazilian system "blackness without ethnicity."[5] These comparative cultural features of race relations are summarized in table 9.3.

The Black Movement and the End of Racial Democracy

Despite the absence of a mass-based mobilization, Brazil's small black movement has recently been able to influence state actions, by scoring four major victories. It has (1) debunked the racial-democracy ideology among the general population, (2) changed elite thinking on race along the white-negro lines, (3) engaged the Brazilian government in discussing public policies that redress racism, and (4) has begun to secure public policies designed to make real impacts on racial discrimination and inequality. The recent successes of the black movement are particularly significant because, unlike other social movements, their precepts challenge the very essence of Brazilian nationhood. The black movement has long been considered "un-Brazilian," as Gilberto Freyre once stated. Whereas the idea of a Brazilian nation is built on the concept of a united and racially tolerant people forged through miscegenation, the black movement poses a countervision based on racialized identities to oppose racism and racial inequality. Despite these gains, the black movement has not yet been able to achieve at least two other challenges it has laid out for itself: creating a mass movement and, relatedly, constructing a popular negro identity. These are often presented as interrelated phenomena.

Leaders of the black movement sometimes argue that their inability to produce a mass movement is fundamentally due to their inability to transform individuals who are disparaged for their color into negros, who will affirm their blackness and confront the forces that subordinate them. Thus, they insist on constructing essentialized black-white identities among Brazilians and shun popular forms of racial classification. Their negative categorization and social treatment by others notwithstanding, why should many dark-skinned Brazilians identify as negro if a whitening ideology allows them a more positive identity in either a more acceptable color category or as part of a unified national category? Similarly, why accept a political racial identity if they can partake of Brazilian culture at least as much as members of the dominant white category and even socialize to a great extent with whites, thus allowing many of them a sense of inclusion?

Thus, a paradox for Brazilian democratization is: How does it ensure appropriate citizen rights for millions of persons that are victims of racism but that, for a series of reasons, will not mobilize against it? How then does the small black movement create a broad constituency to defend appropriate inclusionary mechanisms? Race relations depend on how persons are categorized, a process in which more powerful persons ascribe and impose categories on others. However, the extent to which these forces can be changed may depend on the capacity of those categorized as subordinates to recognize such categories as part of their own identities. Who else, besides the victims of racism, are likely to organize and demand effective measures to combat racism? The Brazilian classification system presents special challenges in this sense. For the black movement, how do they organize persons under a category that is both highly stigmatized and can be escaped from? In Brazil, blacks can become mulattos and many mulattos can become white, or at least moreno, a uniquely deracialized category.

The U.S. civil-rights movement created a model for a mass black movement and a leadership based on identity politics, but this was largely because of segregation. In the United States, segregation made "black" a permanent status, and so the only possibility was to remain black. Segregation had created institutions for the forming of a strong leadership class as well as a fairly self-contained black population. Moreover, it had become apparent to virtually all blacks that legal segregation was blatantly offensive and defied their democratic rights. By contrast, conditions for Brazil's black movement are far different. Structural conditions in Brazil, while they promoted miscegenation, impaired the formation of a mass black movement to effectively demand significant social change. Also, mass social movements in the style of the Afro-American civil-rights movement have not developed at all in recent Brazilian history, except perhaps among rural landless workers. Nevertheless, a small but growing number of the victims of racism has been able to affirm their blackness and lead social demands to redress racism. At least in the current context of democratization and the coincidence of favorable forces, a mass movement has not been necessary for creating the recent antiracist victories. Black-movement gains in recent years have depended on its ability to use the media and make foreign and domestic human-rights alliances, as well as the relative openness and interest on issues pertaining to race and racism by President Cardoso himself. However, the black movement's manipulation of Brazilian government sensitivities in international politics may be the most important factor.

RACE AND INTERNATIONAL POLITICS

In the past, the idea of racial democracy in Brazil represented an antithesis to segregation that was able to deny racism, noting how miscegenation and Luso-Brazilian culture had uniquely softened the racial antagonisms found in other societies. Racial democracy could be sold in a world where large and often powerful multiracial nations had egregiously racist systems throughout the twentieth century. At home, the contradiction between the ideology of racial democracy and the practice of racism was managed by elites, both wittingly and unwittingly, by constantly reminding the population of how racially democratic Brazilian society was compared to the polarized and egregious U.S. and South African systems. By affirming its antiracism, racial democracy served the expressive purpose of integration for Brazilian nationalism, but it mostly failed as an instrument for attenuating or ending racism. In social interactions, whiteness would continue to be valued and blackness devalued, although Afro-Brazilian culture and the racial democracy ideology became widely cherished symbols of Brazilian nationalism for at least half a century.

A reputation for racial tolerance continues to be important for the Brazilian government, which strives to continue setting itself apart from the United States (and other countries) on race issues, especially as it seeks to become an international leader and ally itself with nonwhite countries. Its reputation for racial tolerance has long been parlayed as social capital for fostering such ties. However, the presence of black-movement leaders in high-level international forums since the late 1990s, has devalued that capital. Together with an international human-rights and antiracist movement, the black movement has been able to trade on the antiracist reputation that the Brazilian government greatly values, especially in the context of its democratic opening and their government's growing commitment to international human-rights norms and laws. Racial democracy had long been accepted in the international community as describing Brazil's unique system of racial tolerance, but it has been unmasked largely through the black movement's activism in international forums.

Brazil must now make special efforts to maintain any reputation for racial tolerance. Brazil's international reputation for racial tolerance reached a saturation point by the 1990s, as the United States and South Africa had both terminated their unabashedly racist systems and adopted antiracist ideologies. As a result of this and the unmasking of its racial democracy, Brazil's reputation for racial tolerance thus lost currency in international circles. Like all other multiracial countries, except perhaps the hegemonically powerful United States, which generally dismisses world opinion, Brazil would be called to implement international conventions for combating racism. To be at least as tolerant as other multiracial countries these days, it is not enough to simply have an antiracist ideology or to have no explicitly racist laws, as even the United States and South Africa now meet these conditions. It requires, at minimum, active state intervention for combating Brazil's informal racism and severe racial inequality which has by now become common knowledge in diplomatic circles. Otherwise, Brazil risks becoming the new international pariah of racial inequality. To maintain some reputation of racial tolerance in the arena of foreign diplomacy, even if less than in the past, Brazil has had to choose to either admit to a history of racial intolerance and institute policies to redress racism or maintain its historical denial of racism. The latter would seem unsustainable for very long.

THE FUTURE

Brazil's future in diminishing racial discrimination and inequality will largely depend on the black movement's ability to exert pressure on the new government. Using international mechanisms will surely be an important part of this strategy. Nation-states increasingly need the support of their populations to further their foreign-policy agendas, especially as domestic NGOs have gained a limited but growing role in foreign policy circles. On the other hand, states can also decide to shut themselves off from the international community, although this is increasingly risky and unlikely for Brazil. Thus, it is important that the black movement continues its attempts to mobilize the victims of racism. There are signs that the black movement is being successful in slowly increasing its ranks, although there seem to be limits to reaching their presumed constituency, particularly the large mixed-race population. Although many ordinary dark-skinned Brazilians continue to avoid classification as black, they seem to increasingly recognize the burdens of being black, which itself is important for mobilization to redress racial discrimination.

Today, Brazil's racism is widely recognized, the black movement has become acknowledged as legitimate defenders of human rights, and research on race relations has become an important part of Brazilian academeme. These represent a historical turnaround for Brazil. At the same time, race mixture and long-standing anti-racism continue to be valued as a unique and positive feature of Brazilian culture. Nonetheless, racial discrimination persists. For nonwhites, whitening through race mixture and even self-classification continues to offer the possibility of individual improvement, and whites continue to enjoy the privilege of racial status. Thus, the terrain on which race is understood in Brazil has shifted away from the racial-democracy era in many fundamental ways, although it is still informed by its values. However, discriminatory social practices continue to be largely informed by the even earlier white-supremacy phase of Brazilian race thinking. Brazil's new era of affirmative action will hopefully bring further positive change.

Chapter Ten

DESIGNING APPROPRIATE POLICIES

THROUGHOUT this book, I have demonstrated how racism, racial discrimination, and racial inequality have persisted in Brazil more than one hundred years after the end of slavery. In the past twenty years, Brazil has sought to democratize and seeks to create equal opportunities for the disadvantaged, but its legal commitments began well before that. A series of legal prohibitions against various kinds of discrimination have existed since 1940, and these were consolidated in a 1989 criminal law. Since then, hundreds of antiracism laws have been passed in many Brazilian states and municipalities. Affirmative-action policies began on a large scale only in 2001, although Brazil adopted an international convention that required national policies to assure equal opportunity in the labor market as early as 1968.[1]

Antiracist or antidiscrimination law seeks mostly to combat discrimination through remedies to which victims can appeal after they have suffered discrimination, mostly by punishing offenders. Affirmative-action policies include a broader set of mechanisms designed to create equal opportunities and reduce overall racism, sometimes by promoting victims of discrimination.[2] Of course, the two sets of policies overlap, since affirmative action can become antidiscriminatory law. In this chapter, I seek to show that both kinds of policies are important in Brazil and discuss possibilities for improving those that exist. I also show how ideological and other arguments are used to dilute the effectiveness of antiracist law and to challenge affirmative action. I draw on the extensive discussion and debate of recent years and particularly address arguments against race-conscious policies. I also make comparisons with the U.S. experience where appropriate and I introduce regional variations.

ANTIRACIST LAW

A democratic society requires laws that can effectively uphold the citizen rights of all society, especially its most disadvantaged members. As throughout the rest of Latin America, though, justice-system reform in Brazil may be the main barrier to democracy and to extending such rights to all. As Caldeira (2000) notes, there is a continuing disjuncture between formal democratization and application of the law. Despite the best intentions of progressive laws and policies, which have slowly made their way into Brazil's legal codes and are commonly defended by leading justice system officials, such policies are often poorly applied. Laws are often ignored in Brazil, especially when they defend the interests of the powerless. In Brazil, it is widely believed that "there are laws that stick and those that don't stick," and laws against racism invariably fall in the second category. In contrast, laws were historically used to maintain social order and protect private property through the repression of blacks. Such laws tend to stick. It is about these, which persist to date, that criminal justice system personnel often refer to, claiming that "the law is preferentially directed to the three Ps: *pobres, pretos e prostitutas* [poor people, blacks and prostitutes]."

By virtue of their low social standing and poverty, most Brazilians are excluded from enjoying the most basic of rights. Many are illiterate and often do not have even birth documents or official identification. Also, while political and civil rights have been formally extended to most Brazilians, access of disadvantaged populations to justice, abuse by the police, impunity of elites, and the precariousness of the penal system continue to escape significant reform. As Brazilian sociologist Bernardo Sorj (2000) states:

> the legal framework values equality, respect for individual and collective rights and limits to public power. Brazil is in reality, a country of inequality and injustice, violating its legal precepts and the most basic principles of civility. (1)

In practice, the law is made even more inefficient because of the way it is implemented. Brazil's judicial establishment, which continues to have great influence on the Brazilian legal system, has typically represented conservative sectors and thus has had an individualist bias. The law guarantees individual rights and duties, while at the same time its concepts and commands are often violated by those with power. For example, a common saying states, "to my friends, anything they want and to my enemies, the law," demonstrating the flexible use of laws by powerful people in Brazil, including state authorities.

The abuses described above all disproportionately affect blacks and mulattos. However, the Brazilian legal system, like much of the rest of society, also sees issues of racism as unimportant.[3] Laws specifically designed to combat racism and racial inequality are almost never implemented. In the following paragraphs, I present two cases which characterize justice-system reasoning in cases against racism.

Two Cases

The Tíririca Case.   As described in chapter 6, popular children's performer Tíririca released a song with Sony Records that demeaned black
women. In response to the legal interventions of the Center for the Coordination of Marginalized Populations (CEAP), a Rio de Janeiro–based
black-movement NGO, a judge ordered Sony Records to cease further
production and sales and collect all records held in store inventories; but
this intervention occurred only after the record had sold 320,000 copies.
Despite the censorship, black-movement attorneys filed lawsuits in civil
and criminal courts in various states against Tíririca and Sony for violating Brazil's antiracism laws. Sony attorneys called various witnesses to
the stand, including well-known black performers, who claimed that the
lyrics were merely "innocent bantering" and that Sony was not a racist
company.[4] A criminal court in the state of Rio de Janeiro rendered the
first decision, denying relief, holding that neither performer nor producer
had a racist intent; that such songs in Brazil had long been produced[5]
without anyone ever complaining; and that Tíririca, as a nonwhite performer, could not be considered racist under the law. Under that decision,
Tíririca and Sony Music were then legally free to produce the song, although they would await decisions from the other courts.
    The personal history of Francisco Everardo Oliveira, Tíririca's real name,
weighed heavily in his defense and the final verdict. Oliveira was a poor and
barely literate migrant from the underdeveloped northeastern region of
Brazil, who became successful as a clown and singer. Oliveira's mother is
black, and Oliveira himself is described as having "brown skin, kinky black
hair and a thick voice," although he wears a blonde wig for performances.
Oliviera describes himself as a religious person devoted to Our Lady of
Aparecida, who is Brazil's patron saint and, as he emphasizes, a black
woman. He claims that his black wife, who refused to bathe for several days,
inspired him to write "Look at Her Hair." Tíririca supporters claimed that
the black movement and others were jealous of his success.
    The Tíririca incident continued to be fought in several other Brazilian
courts, and black-movement leaders intended to make it into an exemplary case for building antidiscriminatory jurisprudence. Supreme Court
Justice Nelson Jobim, who began to support black-movement legal initiatives, claimed that the black movement would have little chance of
success in the Tíririca case, because he believed there would be little sym-
pathy in favor of the black movement's argument. However, the 2000
survey for the state of Rio de Janeiro found that, upon reading Tíricica's
lyrics, 67 percent of the population judged them to be racist or in bad

taste. Despite this, the popular press had claimed that the public sentiment did not believe the song to be racist, apparently based on the presence of a handful of avid Tíririca fans at his court hearings. However, the
prosecution was able to frame the case as obviously not racist with ideas
about race that reflect popular commonsense beliefs.

The Leda Francisco Case.   A 1997 case involved a black woman named
Leda Francisco. In this case, Ms. Francisco and a merchant had agreed to
reimbursement for the payment of a product that had been delivered late.
According to court records, the merchant had suggested Ms. Francisco
suspend her check, which she did after politely requesting reimbursement
for the bank charge. To this, the merchant responded "I don't like doing
business with blacks; blacks shit when they enter and when they leave,"
and said to Ms. Francisco's white friend, "I am surprised that you associate with her." Unable to sleep and seeking an apology, Ms. Francisco returned the next day and was again insulted about her blackness (called
"neguinha safada"), as witnessed by police who arrived on the scene.[6]
She was able to have her case tried under the racism laws. Ms. Francisco
was eventually denied relief. In her decision, the judge stated:

> There was no reason for imprisoning the merchant. There was no failure to
> serve or deny access to the accused's store as required in article 5 of Law 7716/
> 89. On the other hand, the racial question and racism should be ignored in
> favor of peaceful relations among the races. In a tolerant country like ours, it
> is important to erase such things so that society goes on harmoniously. No one
> wants racism. Our guide is the law.

ANALYSIS

These two cases involving racism revealed several problems with gaining
justice under Brazilian law. Both cases showed that ideology plays an extraordinary role. In the case of Leda Francisco, the judge defended a
strong version of the racial-democracy idea as she boldly opined that
racism should be ignored in favor of racial harmony. The judge in the
Tíririca case viewed the song as clearly acceptable in Brazilian culture,
which the black movement set out to defy to gain attention for themselves. Personal ideologies, shaped partly by a tradition of authoritarian-
ism and contradictory beliefs about the status of blacks, continue to be
important guides for individual justice-system officials and the general
legal culture. For a judge to claim that Tíririca's lyrics merely constitute
inoffensive banter misconstrued as racism suggests that racism is deeply
ingrained in Brazilian culture. In both cases, black-movement arguments
that these were examples of the constant devalorization of black people,

which perpetuates Brazil's racial hierarchy by harming the self-concept of the black population, seemed to be ignored.

In a systematic analysis of several racial discrimination cases, Seth Rascussen (2000) finds that a judge's ideology of race and understanding of racial discrimination best explain the variation in the logic behind inquiry and judicial findings. Since racial discrimination according to Brazilian law is construed as an act of prejudice, the law requires judges to evaluate prejudicial attitudes of the defendants, which in turn is mediated by the judge's own ideology of race. This belief seems to be incorporated at all levels of the justice system, including judges, police, and prosecutors.

The Tíririca case also revealed the situational and ambiguous nature of Brazilian race classification and the ideology that Brazilians, who are largely of mixed race, cannot be racist since their ancestry and culture is largely black. Tíririca himself was called a mulatto in several press reports and court records but was also referred to as black or negro. He would call himself a mulatto, but in the context of making a case against the black movement, the court and press could conveniently refer to him as black. Tíririca does not proclaim himself as black but claims his wife and mother are and that he worships a black saint. Although Tíririca does not identify as black, he claims that his black ancestry and reverence for a black saint demonstrate that he cannot be racist. Rascussen (2000) calls this the "mulatto defense."

A related problem is that local tribunals display an overall lack of seriousness in terms of their handling of crimes of racism, and judges dislike imposing the harsh criminal sentences mandated by the Constitution for racist infractors. Judges and prosecutors, as members of Brazilian society, view alleged incidents of racism as fairly innocuous and are not willing to put violators of these laws behind bars for the kinds of behaviors that are common in Brazilian society. In the case of Leda Francisco, the judge clearly preferred to ignore racism. Racist comments, as both cases revealed, are considered inoffensive and of little consequence. Even prior to the possible registration of a case, the police also tend to treat cases of racism as unimportant, and complaints, when they are registered, are often not followed up by investigations, and the investigation cases often do not reach court. According to Hedio Silva Jr., of the 250 cases registered in the now extinct Special Racial Crimes Police Precinct of São Paulo, none ever resulted in conviction. Nationally, there have been several convictions since 1951, but no one has ever served a criminal sentence for racism as required by law.[7]

A further problem is that the application of antiracist law has been limited to only the most blatant and egregious types of racism which usually involve racist insults (*injuria*). Although these are the most commonly recognized forms of racism in Brazilian society, they represent only a small part of the many forms of racial discrimination. Similarly, such acts also reflect the justice system's narrow perception of what constitutes racism. More importantly, black-movement activists have been able to use these cases to demonstrate to the Brazilian public that even blatant racism occurs in their society.

Also, Brazilian law requires that relief for victims under Brazil's anti-racism laws requires that racism be intentional. That is a very high standard, which further diminishes the likelihood of conviction. Tíririca claimed, and the court agreed, that he had no racist intent but was merely referring to his unbathed wife. Indeed, they also assured us that Tíririca showed deep respect and love for particular black persons. Brazilian social etiquette, guided by its antiracist ideology, presumably forbids the manifestation of explicit racism, but Brazilian law finds that these lyrics are not enough to prove racist intent. This suggests a strong disjuncture between Brazilian values and legal practice.

Related to racist intent, under the Brazilian legal tradition, an individual perpetrator must be responsible. However, critical-race theorists argue that while racism had perpetrators under white supremacy, it began to be increasingly detached from its perpetrators, as white supremacy was gradually replaced with white hegemony. Although this shift began in the 1960s in the United States, it began at least thirty years earlier in Brazil.[8] In that context, the antidiscrimination laws in Brazil may therefore be especially ineffective. For the vast majority of cases involving subtle racism, perpetrators cannot be identified with much certainty in a culture where racist acts are commonplace and largely unconscious. Some judges seem to doubt that any normal Brazilian can be a perpetrator because of their supposed antiracist values. In addition, this system brings a focus on punishing an individual rather than doing anything for victims.

By the 1970s, Derrick Bell, the field's most influential source, was concerned with the ineffectiveness of the spate of civil-rights laws of the 1960s in the United States. He began to recognize that the limitations of the law derived from three principles: (1) the framers of the Constitution sought to protect property over justice; (2) whites support justice for blacks only when they gain; and (3) they will not support such gains that threaten their own status. Bell became the most influential source of the new field of critical race theory, whose proponents have sought ways to improve the effectiveness of law. These theorists have generally concluded that racism is a normal part of culture and discrimination is often unconscious and unintentional without any attempt to harm. Nonetheless, the effects of such racism are frequently manifested through slights and aggressions, which can lead to misery, alienation, and despair among many of its victims. Antiracist law does not address these forms but only deals with expressed or blatant forms of racism. Progressive jurists in Brazil, especially those associated with the black movement, have also noted such problems in their own country and have thus sought alternatives.

ALTERNATIVE USES OF LAW

Because of the ineffectiveness that the few victories have on achieving a modicum of racial justice, black-movement attorneys have sought alternative strategies for using the law. One avenue that was beginning to be examined by black-movement attorneys in 1999 was the use of civil rather than criminal laws to try cases of racism. This follows a more general trend of seeking to reform a justice system that has been historically preoccupied with criminalization and punishment. Civil cases, they believe, would increase the likelihood of conviction; potentially provide legal, economic, and psychological support for victims; secure income for the legal services of black-movement organizations; and allow for speedier and less expensive trials. Attorneys also sought to introduce civil legislation to invert the burden of proof. Instead of victims being required to prove they were discriminated against, the alleged discriminator would be required to prove that he took measures not to discriminate. Relatedly, companies found guilty of discrimination would temporarily lose access to credit or public financing.[9]

Another avenue for redressing Brazil's racism is through international courts. The Additional Protocol for the American Convention on Economic, Social and Cultural Rights (San Salvador Protocol) and its monitoring agencies, the Interamerican Commission of Human Rights and Interamerican Human Rights Court, will take appeals in cases where domestic remedies have been exhausted. Not surprisingly, these cases represent an affront to the Brazilian justice system. Out of nearly 1,000 cases, as of July 2002, roughly 70 cases are pending in the Interamerican Court against Brazil. This is up from 2 cases in 1994 out of a similar total, reflecting the isolation until recently of the Brazilian human-rights community.[10]

The increasing use of the Interamerican system is largely the result of the efforts of Human Rights Watch-Brazil and CEJIL (Center for Justice and International Law), both international human-rights NGOs, and more recently, the Global Justice Center, a Brazil-based NGO established in 1999, which has been especially responsive to racial-discrimination cases in its defense of human-rights violations. These cases have often involved suits defending entire black communities against the Brazilian government. In one case, for example, the Global Justice Center and the Center for Black Studies (NEN), a black-movement NGO, denounced the Federal Republic of Brazil for the arbitrary and unjustified murder of a young black solider, Wallace de Almeida, and for failing to prosecute the police involved. Extensively citing the study by Ignacio Cano (2002) in their arguments, they noted the unnecessary and lethal force that the Rio de Janeiro police commonly use, especially against black men.[11]

More recently, a collective of Brazilian and U.S. organizations denounced both the Brazilian and U.S. governments before the Interamerican Commission for violating the land rights held by a traditional African-origin (*quilombola*) community, located on the eastern edge of the legally protected Amazon region. The Brazilian government constructed the Alcântara space port there in 1983, which they claim to have done for national security purposes. However, in 2000, the Brazilian government signed a defense-technology agreement with the United States, allowing it to profit from U.S. government and private launchings at this site. These actions, clearly not for national security, would further displace the native population and prohibit them from constructing more homes, accessing their traditional cemeteries, and planting crops in areas of the proposed expansion.[12]

Aside from its courts, the international human-rights system includes the UN and other international organizations, which hold forums for international governments to discuss human rights and pass human-rights conventions. These forums pressure countries to position themselves with respect to human rights, under the auspices of the international community, and declare whether to become signatories and thus commit to international human-rights laws. While powerful countries, particularly the United States, often ignore these treaties, arguing that their rule of law and democratization are well established, peripheral countries are concerned that their positions regarding these treaties affect their international reputations. International human-rights organizations like Amnesty International and Human Rights Watch carefully monitor, document, and publicize human-rights abuses in countries like Brazil. Moreover, foreign aid is sometimes tied to a country's human-rights record, which is especially important in Brazil since it is one of the largest debtor countries in the world. Globalization and the international human-rights system have thus greatly influenced Brazil's human-rights legislation; however, actual practice is another issue.

Another strategy proposed by progressive jurists, including those of the black movement, is to use the laws adopted in the 1988 Constitution for defending collective rights (*direitos difusos*),[13] which are rights for groups that cannot be guaranteed for individuals. Theoretically, whereas the criminal laws currently in the books benefit at most a single victim, these could be used to promote large-scale social change, such as reducing inequality of various types. For example, attorneys have successfully pursued this strategy by requiring the government to subsidize anti-HIV drugs for persons with AIDS.[14] In the case of racial discrimination, attorneys might use statistical evidence showing racial differences in the effects of institutional actions such as government provision of social services, a strategy that has been used in the United States. Since the inability to obtain education is the biggest impediment to black progress and racial equality, such strategies could be used to correct discriminatory patterns and resultant inequality in schools, which affect large numbers of people. Also such changes could set important jurisprudence for similar cases. Collective-rights actions are closely related to affirmative-action policies, except that collective rights would be mandated by the justice system or the Public Prosecution as opposed to being mandated by the executive or legislative branches of government.

According to legal scholar and former member of the Public Prosecution, Joaquim Barbosa Gomes (2001), the Public Prosecution (*Ministerio Publico*) should monitor and propose such actions to redress racial discrimination. The current law makes this possible, although the Public Prosecution faces political obstacles in its mission to defend the population against elite interests. Nevertheless, the potential for the Public Prosecution to successfully defend the public good surfaces occasionally; this was demonstrated in 1999 by a civil public action. As part of a government campaign to educate the public about its intent to prohibit firearms, a billboard advertisement showed a youth with a pistol in his hand, outfitted with a cap and eye patch. The billboard's caption read, "Disarm the bandits and not the good citizens." At the instigation of the state of São Paulo's Public Prosecution, a judge required the advertising company to remove its billboards on the basis of antiracist laws. According to the state prosecutors, "the advertiser's message reinforced racial prejudice by showing a poor black youth as a bandit."[15] An even greater prospect for change is the Public Prosecution's efforts in the states of Minas Gerais and Ceará to require public universities to increase their admissions of public secondary students. Such actions represent real gains in efforts to promote collective rights.

Discrimination is produced largely through institutions, such as the media and school systems, which, except for general principles of guaranteeing equal opportunity, are largely unaffected by antidiscrimination laws. For example, public funding in some municipalities might be diverted or preferentially directed to schools that enroll relatively large proportions of white children, but antiracist law in Brazil as it is practiced currently would be unable to undo this kind of discrimination. Because of this, the potential impact of the law in affecting racial inequality would be minor. Although it may cure some of the minor symptoms of racism (e.g., racist acts), Brazilian law has not been able to address the major symptoms (e.g., racial inequality) or the root causes (e.g., ideology or institutional racism). Thus, large-scale social policies, which include affirmative action, including universalist policies like those that fight poverty, may offer the greatest hope for addressing Brazil's racial inequalities.

AFFIRMATIVE ACTION

The recent implementation of race-conscious affirmative action in late 2001 represents the first time the Brazilian government has used public policy to explicitly promote, rather than subordinate, the black population. In the past, slavery and immigration policies helped create the racial inequality that persists today; but the new racial quotas now seek to reverse this. Although the Brazilian government signed UN Convention 111 in 1968, which mandated the promotion of racial and ethnic minorities in occupations, no one ever expected such policies to be implemented, until the Durban Conference. The Brazilian government unexpectedly created racial quotas despite a near absence of discussion about them, catching policy analysts and public opinion off guard. However, without their sudden imposition, serious discussion about race in Brazilian society and policies to redress racism probably would never have occurred. Regardless of their design or their potential benefits, the implementation of these policies has projected the issue of race and racism to a level never before seen in modern Brazilian history. Brazilians now largely agree that racism exists and that racial inequality is high. Therefore they often argue that something must be done to alleviate these problems. There is less agreement about the appropriate policy solutions.

Proposed solutions involve affirmative-action policies that are both race blind and race conscious. Race-conscious policies are often perceived as a North American solution, appropriate only for a highly segregated and racist system where race is a primary barrier to mobility. Opponents also argue that race-conscious policies are contrary to Brazilian philosophical, cultural, and legal traditions. Instead they propose that universalist or class-based policies for reducing inequality and poverty can effectively redress racial inequalities, without considering race. However, opponents of race-conscious policies are increasingly less likely to deny the existence of racial discrimination.

The U.S. example, although distinct from Brazil in many ways, may offer some important lessons. Opponents of U.S. race-conscious policies often use some of the same arguments as opponents of these policies in Brazil. For example, while affirmative action in the United States began mostly in the 1960s with broad-based support, it has suffered major setbacks in states like California and Texas, including rulings declaring that race cannot be used for university admissions. Under a changing racial ideology that is now called color-blind or laissez-faire racism, public opinion supports the principle of racial equality but largely rejects race-conscious social policies.[16] As a result of changing public opinion and state-level decisions to end such policies, there has been a new surge in affirmative-action literature and a major rethinking of how to maintain racial diversity, especially in higher education. Supporters of U.S. race-conscious policies demonstrate that affirmative action has had positive benefits for minorities but that racism and underrepresentation persists. The recent University of Michigan Law School case decided by the U.S. Supreme Court upheld the use of race as one criteria in admissions decisions. This ruling, as well as the rethinking occasioned by the scaling back of affirmative-action policies, can surely provide valuable lessons for Brazil. Soon after that ruling, one of the lead attorneys defending the University of Michigan traveled to Brazil to help supporters of affirmative action strategize to defend the Rio de Janeiro state laws on racial quotas. The case will soon be similarly tried in the Brazilian Supreme Court for constitutionality.

Before making such comparisons, it is important to note that I intend the U.S. case as merely one example. Other non-U.S. examples may be found, including in other Latin American countries. Needless to say, there are many differences between Brazil and the United States, as I have made clear throughout this book; however, there are some similarities, and the U.S. comparison might help us not to reinvent the wheel at every turn. A prominent example of difference is the case of Brazil's *quilombos* (rural black lands and communities). The beginnings of federal affirmative action through the Ministry of Agrarian Development's acting to recognize and title all *quilombo* lands represents an important break from the U.S. model from the start. This shows that other examples apart from the United States are important for understanding affirmative action internationally. Another example can be found in Colombia's extensive legislation (Ley 70) that recognizes Afro-Colombian communities and seeks to protect their territories and strengthen the rights of their members.[17] Additionally, the case of *quilombos* in Brazil has long been central to black-movement demands, not only because of its material effects on thousands of poor people, but also because of its symbolism for black political struggle. Many of these residents are direct descendants of slaves who held out and resisted Brazilian slave owners on these very lands. In the 1988 Constitution, the recognition of *quilombos* represented one of the first black-movement conquests at the federal level, but implementation of land titles has been mostly stalled.

The goals of affirmative action, whether race conscious or not, should be to improve racial justice, create role models for young blacks, strengthen the sense of self-worth among blacks and promote racial diversity at all class levels. To do so in Brazil requires attacking the three major barriers to achieving a true racial democracy: hyperinequality, the glass ceiling, and racist culture. If the Brazilian government is to make a significant difference in the lives of most black and brown people, Brazil needs to develop a set of policies that combine universalist social-development policies to reduce Brazil's hyperinequality with race-conscious affirmative action that can break the glass ceiling and alleviate racist culture. In the rest of this chapter, I present arguments for such policies. I seek to systematize them and distill the main points of the discussion surrounding public policy and race as well as to suggest new avenues for policy development. Since such policies are fairly new for Brazil and since the Brazilian case is unique in some respects, the potential political and technical problems, as well as the opportunities for designing these policies, will require continuous discussion, experimentation and reevaluation.

REDUCING INEQUALITY THROUGH UNIVERSALIST OR CLASS-BASED POLICIES

Macrolevel policies aimed at economic growth are a central feature of the neoliberal agenda, however, they often do not include mechanisms to effectively redistribute income or reduce poverty and attack Brazil's hyperinequality. Brazil's economic growth has had relatively little effect on poverty and has often increased inequality.[18] Similarly, the liberal argument has also argued that economic development will eventually eliminate or diminish racism and racial inequality. However, the findings from chapter 5 show that this clearly is not the case. Rather, the barriers preventing nonwhites from entering the middle class have strengthened. Creating only universalistic policies may well have the effect of increasing racial inequality, as poor whites will be in the best position to take advantage of new opportunities, further isolating the black and brown poor.

Many economists agree that educational reform is necessary to significantly reduce Brazil's vast inequality and poverty. Improvements in education are perhaps the most economically efficient and politically acceptable means for redistributing income. Ideally, secondary education would be guaranteed and required for all children and at minimum, everyone should be functionally literate. The average educational level in

Brazil is now 4 years for nonwhites and 6 for whites, and the university system currently has the capacity for only 10 percent of the college-aged population. Many Brazilians cannot read, and most who can do not understand what they read. The poor state of Brazilian mass education is revealed by a recent study finding that Brazil was ranked the lowest among thirty-two countries, in terms of literacy.[19]

Wilson (1996) argues for universal policies to help the poor in general. He claims that affirmative action will not remedy the problems of the most disadvantaged in the U.S. case. This argument seems especially applicable to Brazil, given the large number of poor and undereducated persons and the large size of the informal Brazilian economy. For Wilson, most blacks and browns need to escape from poverty and the symptoms it produces, including crime and inadequate housing. Without universalist policies, a large proportion of nonwhites (and many whites) will continue to be poor. He further argues that blacks from the most advantaged families disproportionately benefit from preferential policies in college admissions, and from promotions and hiring in middle-class jobs, leaving the problems of most blacks intact.[20] For this reason, Brazil needs similar universalist programs, including those that can provide a decent minimum salary, ensure unemployment income and a livable old age pension, eliminate child labor, and most importantly, make large improvements in public education and ensure that families have the material conditions for their children to attend school.

Unlike the United States, these are problems that are at the core of Brazil's economic development. A large percentage of the Brazilian population, which includes a disproportionate number of nonwhites, is outside of the formal economy. Blacks and browns are also especially likely to reside in the Northeast and in rural areas, places that are especially underdeveloped. Solutions for these poor populations are thus largely about employment creation and regional development, issues that have occupied the mind of economists and policy makers for years. However, the search for finding solutions for these problems should not preclude the need to find remedies for persistent and growing racial inequality in the middle and upper echelons of Brazilian society.

At the top end of the educational system, some have called for quotas for students from public schools. This may be considered a universalist policy in the sense that it does not use ascribed characteristics like race but merely links up a public secondary-school system to its higher-education counterpart. Since nonwhites are disproportionately represented among public school-secondary students and are rarely in private schools, such a policy is also likely to reduce racial inequality in access to the university. Given that the private/public school divide is the most apparent institutional cleavage determining the quality of Brazilian schools and nonwhites are almost invariably in public schools, this policy could well increase black and brown representation at the university level.[21] However, it could also fall short of its intended effects. White secondary students in public schools would probably be in better positions to take advantage of these quotas, since they tend to be more successful in the schools for reasons outlined in chapter 6, and because predominately white public schools are better resourced than predominately nonwhite schools. Such a policy might further increase racial inequality, leaving nonwhites further isolated at the bottom of the social structure, unless college attendance were to become universal or close to it.

In the United States, similar class-based solutions have been used to replace race-conscious affirmative action in university admissions, most notably through the so-called Texas plan. The Texas plan was implemented as a response to a high court ruling that the University of Texas used unconstitutional race-based quotas for admissions. The University of Texas thus opted for a class-based policy, believing that it could maintain the levels of racial diversity they previously achieved under the quota system. Banking on the fact that schools were highly segregated in Texas, the state congress ruled that all graduates in the top 10 percent of their high school classes would be permitted to attend the state public university of their choice.[22] For the first two years of its existence, racial diversity was roughly maintained for undergraduate admissions in Texas.[23] However, racial diversity precipitously declined at the graduate level, particularly in the law and medical schools, where the 10-percent rule did not apply. Some version of this plan could benefit Brazil but mostly in those cases where nonwhites are a large majority. In most places, though, the results might be less efficient than in Texas, because white-nonwhite segregation in Brazil is lower, and because nonwhites in Brazil disproportionately drop out before completing secondary education.

Kahlenberg (1996) argues in favor of class-based policies and for the end of race-conscious policies in the United States. However, he is also concerned with maintaining racial diversity and thus argues that class must be defined broadly beyond income to include socioeconomic factors that disadvantage racial minorities. Since U.S. blacks experience more concentrated poverty and more family breakdown and because they have lower amounts of accumulated wealth, then institutions should seek to recruit persons having these characteristics, rather than using race directly to select candidates. He also argues for abolishing regional preferences that advantage white students and claims that class-based slots be very generous in order to guarantee that substantial numbers of blacks are admitted. Finally, he believes that antidiscriminatory laws need to be effectively applied to punish discrimination where it is found to occur. Although such class-based affirmative action would almost certainly benefit minorities, it does not overcome other mechanisms of racial discrimination. What about the low self-esteem or anxiety of blacks resulting from a culture that constantly signals their inferiority? In the Brazilian case, what about the few middle-class blacks and mulattos who would be excluded from class-based programs but have barely gained a toehold in the middle classes, where they are often treated as oddities?

Cardoso's minister of education, Paulo Renato Souza, was a key spokesperson for universalist programs, although he rejected race-conscious policies.[24] During the Durban conference in 2001, he declared, "when an effort is made to improve the lives of the poor, one is, in large measure, improving or trying to emphasize issues of the black population."[25] I agree, but I also believe that educational reform and other universalist programs must include mechanisms to ensure that black and brown people benefit at least as much as whites. Without them, even greater racial inequality could result. Indeed, in the past forty years, this is exactly what has occurred at the college level.

Breaking the Glass Ceiling through Race-Conscious Policies

Much of the attention in developing Brazil's affirmative action thus far has focused on admission to the university, which is highly appropriate since unequal access to university education has become the major impediment to racial equality in Brazil. Some kind of race-conscious policy is necessary in order to overcome Brazil's huge racial inequality in access to the middle class. Quotas for university admissions and in the workplace—which have sprung up in several states of Brazil—are perhaps a necessary beginning, because they reveal real action beyond rhetoric and academic debate. Quotas represent an important first step in dealing with racial inequality at the university level, although they often do not go far enough. For example, getting black and brown students into the middle class, as should be the goal of these programs, requires programs that can keep these students in colleges; this would require the implementation of programs such as writing assistance, counseling, and financial aid, and after graduation, mechanisms to help them land jobs appropriate to their education, which would help them overcome their relatively weak social capital. Quotas have also sparked a national policy debate about ending the Brazilian government's historical apathy about redressing racism and racial inequality. Surprisingly, there has been little or no opposition to quotas from anyone denying discrimination, which reveals that the racial-democracy belief has largely disappeared.

This case for affirmative action in the university has been eloquently made by an influential publication reflecting on the past thirty-odd years of affirmative action efforts in U.S. universities. William G. Bowen and Derek Bok (1998), former presidents of Princeton and Harvard Universities, respectively, analyzed data on 80,000 undergraduates using rigorous statistical methodologies in order to argue that, while affirmative-action policies have slowly lessened racial inequalities, large gaps remain. They thus argue that it is far too early to end university affirmative action in the United States. Most notably, they find that the racial gap in precollege preparation is wide and unlikely to be eliminated during their lifetimes because of the long history of racial differences in "resources, environments and inherited intellectual capital." However, they also conclude that black students have made enormous improvements in standardized test scores and graduation rates from all fields and at all levels. Furthermore, affirmative action has created a sizable black middle class. Successful blacks often serve as role models for younger blacks, and many have become committed to serving previously neglected black communities.[26]

While the gap in higher education has been increasing in Brazil, it has narrowed in the United States. The cross-national differences in Brazil and the United States are consequently mirrored in the racial composition of the middle classes. I illustrate this change in figure 10.1 by showing the change from 1960 to 1996 in the likelihood that nonwhites are in professional occupations compared to whites in the United States and Brazil.[27] Specifically, I present relative odds ratios of the likelihood that whites are in professional occupations compared to nonwhites, using the 1960 census for both countries and the respective U.S. and Brazilian 1996 household surveys. The years 1960 and 1996 represent the time just previous to, and thirty years following, the beginning of U.S. affirmative action; all of this was time during which there was no affirmative action in Brazil.

Figure 10.1 dramatically reveals that racial inequality declined in the United States but increased in Brazil during the past forty years. In the United States, white males were 3.1 times more likely than black males, and white females were 2.8 times as likely as black females, to be in professional occupations in 1960. However, by 1996, that inequality had fallen to 1.6 for males and 1.4 for females in the United States, demonstrating how affirmative-action policies have increased the size of the black middle class. By contrast, Brazilian males had about the same level of racial inequality at the professional level as the United States did in 1960, but racial inequality increased from 3.1 to 4.0 in the case of Brazilian males, and 3.4 to 4.8 for Brazilian females. Despite potential methodological quibbles, the trends are undeniable. Affirmative action in the United States has been a major success for getting North American blacks

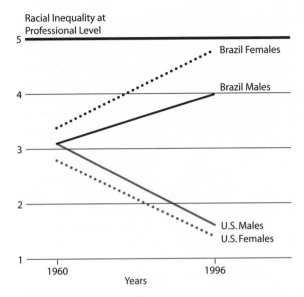

FIGURE 10.1 Relative likelihood that whites are in professional occupations compared to nonwhites (blacks in the United States, blacks and browns in Brazil): Males and females in Brazil and the United States, 1960 and 1996. (1960 U.S. data: Employment and Earnings, Vol. 7, No. 1, July 1960; 1996 U.S. data: Employment and Earnings, U.S. Department of Labor, Bureau of Labor Statistics, January 1997; Public Use Sample of 1960 Brazilian Census; 1996 PNAD.)

into universities and into the professional labor market, even though it hasn't eliminated racial inequality. By contrast, Brazil's racial inequality at this level remains high and continues to grow. Without race-conscious affirmative action in Brazil, this disturbing trend is likely to continue.

Race-conscious affirmative action in the labor market is important as well. Several federal government ministries have instituted quotas for hiring as well as preferences for government subcontractors with large non-white work forces. Local and state governments have instituted similar programs. Preferences for subcontractors with work forces comprising larger proportions of nonwhites are likely to decrease employment discrimination for those companies participating in them. Such policies at higher levels are also likely to ensure that blacks and mulattos who complete college make the transition to work free of racial discrimination. Race-conscious policies are also necessary in blue-collar occupations, since class-based policies will not prevent labor-market discrimination. The problem that remains is what to do with the large number of unemployed persons and with those employed in the informal work force. In that sense, there is no substitute for universalist policies that seek full employment and generally improve the livelihood and life chances of these persons.

Based on a review of published affirmative-action studies, a study by Holtzer and Newhart (2000) concluded that (1) affirmative action promotes distributive justice by increasing employment for women and minorities among the organizations that use it; (2) employers using affirmative action recruit and select more carefully by looking more broadly for employees and evaluating them on more criteria; and (3) employers engaging in affirmative action pay nothing in the job performance of their employees. If anything, minority- and female-employee job performance is better, even in cases where white-male credentials were superior, because of other attributes uncovered by the use of a broader set of hiring criteria. Aside from active promotion through quotas or affirmative action, employers must therefore implement more formal personnel procedures. Leaving decisions to informal decision processes invites abuse, as Bento (2000) shows for São Paulo. This is especially important when workers are not affected by limited affirmative action. A challenge thus remains as to extending programs beyond a handful of government ministries and local governments, and especially to the private sector.

BRAZIL'S UNIVERSALIST MANTRA

I have thus far pointed to the need for both class- and race-based social policies to reduce Brazil's racial inequality. Discussions about the best way to reduce racial inequality often get hung up on either-or solutions. I firmly believe that both are needed: the first to eliminate Brazil's hyper-inequality, and the second to break the glass ceiling that prevents non-whites from entering the middle class. However, while universalist policies are increasingly supported, there has been much more controversy regarding race-conscious policies. In the following sections I discuss the major barriers to implementing race-conscious policies and present counterarguments as well, beginning with Brazil's mantra of universalism.

In contrast to the race-conscious policies, it seems that, at least at the rhetorical level, universal redistribution policies have become widely accepted. Indeed, many sectors of the Brazilian elite seem to vigorously support black-movement demands for reducing racial inequality but have pushed for universalist polices while rejecting race-conscious measures.[28] This obsession with universalism or a class-based approach was demonstrated at a 2001 meeting of the Interamerican Development Bank, which black-movement leaders attended. Brazilian government minister Roberto Brant expressed a widely held sentiment in response to a newspaper interview, noting that, while he mentioned a litany of Brazilian social ills, he didn't mention "race" or "blacks." He declared:

> that was on purpose, our problem is not racism but poverty. We have discrimination and we have laws to stop it . . . we can't bring to our country a discussion which has no basis in our reality.[29]

Brant's statements epitomized the universalism argument by adding that racial discrimination rarely exists in Brazil; although he went against the general public acknowledgment of racism, on the other hand, he may have simply sought to make a strong, although probably ineffective, argument about why there should not be race-conscious policy.

A common argument is that race-conscious policies will make Brazilians newly conscious of group differences and create resentments across racial lines. Although many now dismiss racial democracy as myth, many argue that it embodies Brazilian values of universalism, and the absence of strong racial divisions such as those found in the United States. Brazilians often argue that racial distinctions between blacks and whites in the United States continue to be sharp. They attribute black-white polarization to race-conscious policies, including segregation in the past and affirmative action today. However, it seems to me that if racial distinctions were not divisive in the past, as commonly believed, then race-conscious policies are unlikely to make them so now. In the U.S. case, there has been hostility and polarization between blacks and whites since slavery. If anything, affirmative action, or at least some set of factors during the period since the initiation of these policies, has softened these conflicts and distinctions. For one thing, post-civil-rights reforms have made North Americans aware of racism and have made the practice of explicit racism socially undesirable.[30] The case of women further supports this. As far as I can tell, polarization between males and females does not seem to have grown because of affirmative action for women. Similarly, I cannot foresee this happening for race in Brazil.

The case for universalistic rather than race-conscious policies has also been argued from a legalistic perspective, as the Federation of Private Schools, the plaintiff in the State University of Rio de Janeiro case has done. Resistance to affirmative action includes claims that affirmative action is unconstitutional, violating Brazil's legal universalism (*isonomia*). Opponents claim that the Constitution seeks equality of opportunity and not equality of results; but the 1988 Brazilian Constitution specifically promulgates equality of results in several ways. Article 3 states that the Federal Republic of Brazil "fundamentally" seeks to create a free, just, and undivided (*solidaria*) society, eradicate poverty and marginalization, reduce social and regional inequalities, and provide special incentives to protect women in the labor market; this article even suggests the use of affirmative action for women and for the physically disabled.[31] Thus, the constitutionality of affirmative-action programs in Brazil seems to have a solid legal foundation.

There are also several precedents for affirmative action. A congressional law in 1990 mandated that "up to 20 percent" of positions in public-service exams be reserved for the disabled, and in 1991 that large firms would be required to fill 2 to 5 percent of jobs with physically disabled persons.[32] In 1996, Congress established that at least 20 percent of candidates for elected offices be women, and in 1997 increased this percentage to 30, which has led to a 110-percent increase of women in city councils throughout Brazil. Also, the Brazilian government ratified the CERD and Convention 111 of the International Labor Organization in 1968, which mandated the promotion of social and economic equality for minorities through national policies. Still earlier in Brazilian history, Getulio Vargas supported affirmative action with the so-called two-thirds law, which required that at least two-thirds of all hiring by firms on Brazilian soil must be of native-born Brazilians. This effectively allowed blacks and browns to enter the industrializing labor markets formerly dominated by immigrant workers.[33]

Another argument deriving from a culture that values universalism is that race-conscious policies, and especially racial quotas, stigmatize nonwhites. The argument claims that, for example, a university diploma will be a second-class degree for black (negro) persons, regardless of whether that person was admitted on the basis of quotas or not. I suppose this may occur, but it seems like a small price to pay for a program that is designed to compensate for societal discrimination and is almost certain to reduce racial inequality. Also, there are already a significant number of nonwhites in many universities, so quotas would merely increase their proportion. It seems to me that stigmatization of blacks overall would decline from today's levels, because they are frequently stigmatized on the basis of their concentration in the lower tiers of Brazilian society. For reasons of racial stigma, quota programs should thus be supplemented with campaigns to educate the public about their necessity. Presumably, nonwhite students will take the same courses and have the same expectations placed on their schooling as whites. Because of differences in prior schooling, one cannot expect that the average black student will suddenly do as well as the average white student, but given the opportunity and the proper resources, many may do better.

The strict use of universalist policies has also had very strong support from the left. The traditional Marxist view holds that class is the central problem in terms of exploitation and that attention to race distracts from and divides the working-class struggle. Orthodox Marxists believe that the emancipation of workers—or, in the more moderate version, reduction in poverty and inequality—necessarily leads to an end or a reduction in racism and racial inequality.[34] For many, race consciousness is a type of false consciousness. At best, scholars like Florestan Fernandes and Octavio Ianni granted that racism was a product of capitalist alienation, thus denying its existence prior to or beyond capitalism. For them, societal cleavages had material bases, and ideology was important to the extent that it legitimized and served capitalist interests. They argued that the ideas of race and racism and their effects are never autonomous from capitalism. The major organization representing the left, the Worker's Party (Partido dos Trabalhadores or PT), has also emphasized class, but the new Brazilian president, who represents that party, supports race-conscious actions. The acknowledgment and strong support for race-based policies by the PT leadership may largely reflect the growing political clout of blacks and mulattos qua blacks (negros) within the party ranks.

QUOTAS AND MERITOCRACY

Brazil's recent affirmative-action plans have thus far focused on racial quotas, especially for university admissions but also for government service positions. Quotas are extreme forms of affirmative action, because they fix a set number of slots for a particular population in employment or college admissions. As I observed in 1996, when discussion of such policies was just beginning in Brazil, affirmative action was commonly believed to be equivalent to quotas, a notion reflecting the conception of diversity from the United States that is played up in the media.[35] This is still the case today. Quotas are clearly the most efficient method for guaranteeing greater representation of blacks and browns but they also face the greatest opposition among various types of affirmative action, because they are thought to directly violate principles of meritocracy and fairness. On the other hand, trying to reformulate quotas into U.S.-style goals risks losing race-conscious policies altogether through the political process.

Some individuals have rejected quotas and other race-conscious policies, alleging that they override the principle of meritocracy. The meritocracy argument is common, as the letters sections of Brazilian newspapers and recent legal actions against the State University of Rio de Janeiro have shown. Critics assume that admission to Brazilian universities, which is based entirely on one's score on the college entrance exams (the *vestibular*), is unambiguously rewarded on merit. However, passing the admissions test seems to be more related to one's ability to pay for the generally expensive course that prepares students for these exams (*cursinho*) and to take a year or more off to dedicate oneself to studying for the exams than to one's ability to succeed in college. Also, the superior quality of schools of the white middle class gives students great advantages for passing these tests. A real meritocracy, as the originator of the term describes it, is utopian because it seeks to reward individuals on the basis of intelligence or cognitive abilities.[36] Entrance into the university thus seems to be based more on "testocracy" than meritocracy, where passing grades on this exam is a questionable test of merit, at best.

The U.S. experience shows that conventional measures like test scores correlate well with short-term success, but longer-term success depends more on other factors. As recent quantitative research for the United States has demonstrated, intelligence or merit is only one of several variables that determine one's lot in life. These variables also include class, motivation, and responsibleness.[37] Surprisingly, a study of Harvard freshmen over three decades showed that students with low Scholastic Achievement Test (SAT) scores and blue-collar backgrounds were more successful than their solidly middle-class peers mostly because of their greater initiative or drive.[38] Merit, as Amartya Sen notes, is contingent on the definition imposed by socially dominant groups. Institutions need to define long-term successes, and this is largely a question of values about what is important. Is it performance in school? Performance or effectiveness in a profession? Service and leadership for poor communities? Being a role model for younger persons? Perhaps there is a need to better define the public good, if this is to be a value used to decide who is admitted to the university.

But even if merit could be measured, it doesn't seem that most Brazilians buy the meritocracy argument. Anthropologist Livia Barbosa (1999) argues that Brazilians do not see individual merit or a work ethic as affecting one's destiny, in the way that North Americans do. Rather, they openly believe that one's position in the hierarchy depends on the social system itself. According to Barbosa, Brazilians see others as having roughly equal ability and believe that the social system has determined their position. Society thus determines one's value; networks and connections are believed to be more important than productivity. Under this logic, quotas might not be as unpopular as they are in the United States. Rather, they might be perceived as a substitute for the lack of access that blacks and browns have to necessary social networks.

Popular-opinion polls support this hypothesis, reporting that most Brazilians support racial quotas.[39] Clearly, the greatest Brazilian opposition to quotas is among the white elite, as the same survey shows. Evidence from the 2000 Rio de Janeiro random household survey demonstrates that a slight majority of blacks and browns and just less than half of whites supported the principle of government obligation in promoting blacks and supported quotas for the university and for employment in "good jobs." Opposition to the government-obligation principle was

particularly strong among college-educated whites in Brazil, while support for such programs was particularly strong among the least-educated
sectors of the population of all colors. Among those with four years of
education or less,[40] between 76 and 86 percent of the black and brown
population supported quotas for either university admissions or employment, and between 59 and 78 percent of whites of the same educational
level also supported quotas. For university-educated whites, only 4 to 6
percent supported quotas.

Public-opinion surveys reveal continuing support for the racial-
democracy values of antiracism and race mixture. For the white middle
class, these values are also important, but their class and race privileges
seem stronger still. This seems to explain why they are especially likely to
oppose race-conscious affirmative action. In principle, black social mobility seems important for them but not if it is threatening to their own
status or that of their families. In this context, privilege trumps values.

Given Brazil's political system, perhaps it's only the elite that count.
Public opinion in the rest of the population may have little importance.
Elisa Reis (2002) found that Brazilian elites tend to support only universalistic programs for poverty reduction or income redistribution. While
elites agree that blacks and women are discriminated against, they
strongly concur, independently of political orientation, that racial quotas
themselves are discriminatory and deny equality of opportunity. Thus, it
seems that middle-class whites will not support actions that significantly
threaten their privileges in securing university admissions and middle-
class positions for their children. However, there is support for race-
conscious policy among a few influential persons of various political
backgrounds, and this trend may be growing. Whereas opposition to
race-specific policies or even recognition of racial divisions was nearly
universal among the left and the right for many years, there has long been
support from leading neoliberal advocates such as Rubens Ricupero and
Roberto Campos.[41] From the left and especially from the Worker's Party,
particular congressional representatives have strongly supported race-
specific policies, but such support seemed to be weak at the top of the
party structure; although there are signs of change with the new president
from the Worker's Party.

RACIAL OPPORTUNISM AND THE BENEFITS
OF RACE-CONSCIOUS POLICY

Race is important because of how others are treated in social interactions.
Therefore, it is perfectly reasonable for the Brazilian state to have developed affirmative-action policies, as it is beginning to do, to counteract the

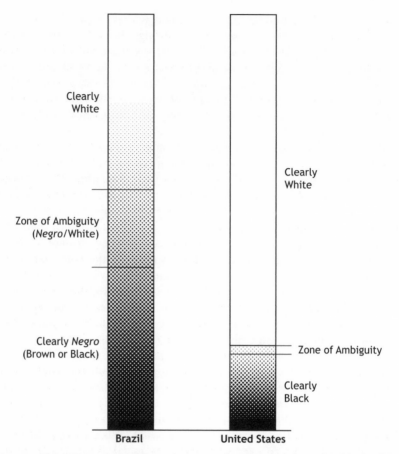

FIGURE 10.2 Primary racial boundaries in classification along the black-white continuum in Brazil and the United States.

problems created by this purely social notion. But this faces especially great problems in Brazil as adverse treatment on the basis of race depends on the situation, the classifier, and other variables. Unlike sex, the lack of discrete racial categories with precise boundaries and the existence of multiple categories make it difficult to define racial boundaries, which is necessary for policy makers deciding who will benefit from affirmative action and especially from quotas. In Brazil, the racial other, although often clear, is sometimes ambiguous. Therefore, race-conscious policies need some cutoff or threshold at which one is deemed "other" or not. In the United States, because segregation required clear classification rules, the old rules of classification became functional to the new correctives designed to restore racial equality. In Brazil, these have not existed.

Figure 10.2 compares racial classification and the white-negro divide in Brazil as used for race-conscious policies in Brazil compared to the black-white divide in the United States. On a scale with varying shades representing the extent of African admixture or appearance among the population, it plots the division between whites and blacks in the United States or negros in Brazil. Nearly everyone having African admixture in the United States is clearly black while persons with small amounts of African blood or appearance are often considered white in Brazil. The reality is even more complicated because many persons have indigenous admixture as well. Most importantly, though, the figure shows that while there is a zone of ambiguity in both countries, a considerably larger proportion of the Brazilian population falls into that zone. Despite the rhetoric of activists claiming that everyone knows who is black, the reality is far different, as I demonstrated in chapter 4.

Browns (pardos) have generally been included as negros in race-conscious policies, even though they do not generally perceive themselves as negros. However, given strong data indicating they suffer socioeconomically because of racial discrimination, that seems justified. But besides browns, do we include or exclude the large proportion of Brazilians that call themselves morenos or whites that claim to have black ancestors? Certainly, in the legal cases against the State University of Rio de Janeiro, such persons have claimed that they should be. As in the case of antiracist law, we might call this a "mulatto defense." Additionally, what about persons that look like soccer star Romario or model Carla Peres, who are generally considered white but have a parent who is clearly mulatto? Although race did not seem to hurt them, could not someone of similar appearance argue that they are disadvantaged because their father was hurt by racism and could not adequately provide for his family? Where do we draw the line between beneficiaries and dominant-group members in the absence of clear rules for making racial distinctions?

The criteria of self-identification, more so than any other criteria, seem to have become well accepted in Brazil and around the world.[42] However, this criterion is problematic, especially because it may not reflect one's classification by typical members of Brazilian society. Its ambiguity is highlighted by President Cardoso's speech reserving slots for blacks in the Foreign Diplomacy School. He announced:

> The criteria of Brazil is a criteria of self-identification. There is no discriminatory criteria: this one is white, this one is moreno, this one is mulatto, this one is yellow, this one is negro. Because that is too difficult. The rainbow is too large. But each one knows their own identity or one they would like to have and they should apply according to their cultural preference, and naturally, based on their life trajectory and some physical characteristic, though not necessarily.[43]

As shown in chapter 4, about 40 percent of self-identified whites in the state of Rio de Janeiro similarly have no problem admitting that they have black ancestors. Darkening one's identification to benefit from affirmative action is a clear possibility for many Brazilians. Since the Brazilian system is based on appearance rather than ancestry, the potential opportunity of having a quality university education for free may lead some former "white persons" to declare themselves as black or brown. For the first time, having black blood may thus offer a strategic advantage. Even Fernando Henrique Cardoso claimed to have "a foot in the kitchen"—meaning he had black ancestors—when he sought black votes for his reelection in 1998. If the president would seek to benefit from such a racial opportunity, why would not many Brazilians who normally consider themselves white?

While I do not think anywhere near the 40 percent of whites in Rio de Janeiro with African ancestors will seek to identify as negro, I do believe that Brazil's ambiguity could present a major challenge to the implementation of racial quotas. In a conversation I had in 1999 with Januário Garcia, the photographer of a program (CIDAN) that has promoted hundreds of black models and actors by putting their photos and resumes on a Web site, he related at least one incident of such ambiguity. Garcia told me that a young man whom he described as clearly white and "surfer-looking" came in asking to be photographed for the Web site. Garcia carefully asked the young man if he knew the purpose of the program and the model responded, "Yeah, I know. My grandmother was a negra, so I guess that makes me a negro." Januário thought, who was I to decide whether he was a negro? So he photographed the model and posted his picture, with résumé, on the CIDAN Web site. However, a perusal of the CIDAN Web site reveals that the vast majority of persons who availed themselves of this free service to promote negros, could easily be classified as brown or black.

Defining black in Brazil may be just as hard as defining who is "high yellow" or "dark black" in the United States, whereas the more general category of "black" in the United States is facilitated because of the one-drop rule; however, a handful of cases demonstrate ambiguity even in the U.S. case. In Massachusetts, a well-known case involves two brothers who were rejected from the Boston Fire Department but reapplied as blacks, claiming that they discovered a great-grandmother who was a light-skinned black; they were later hired. In another case in Washington state, allegations of "racial fraud" led employers to survey employees and request documentation to support the accuracy of self-identification in categories covered by affirmative action.[44] At the conclusion of the survey, 2.5 percent of employees changed their racial status.[45]

Given the extent of racial ambiguity, the magnitude of this problem is likely to be much greater in Brazil, especially in the Northeast and at the working class level. On the other hand, there is relatively little ambiguity among the university educated. Indeed, the consistency of classification between interviewers and university-educated respondents along the white-nonwhite divide in the southern regions was about 98 percent. Where ambiguity is especially likely to be great, though, Brazilians need to find creative solutions. One solution offered before the emerging consensus on self-identification was to include color on one's official identification, which is often based on information from the birth certificate.[46] However, this is problematic because it assumes that racial classifications are rigid and essential. Also, Brazilian parents have long sought to whiten children's color classification on birth registrations, from which all subsequent registrations and racial identification would presumably be drawn. Another proposal, said with some tongue in cheek, by some black activists is to hire doormen or police consultants, because they never seem to err in classifying negros. However, there is likely to be variance and arbitrariness in their decisions as well.

Given that self-identification seems to have been most widely accepted, administrators of these policies have sought further means to assure their viability. Claims that whites would not want to classify as negros because no one wants to be *negro* in Brazilian society, or that the social consequences of classifying as such are too great, may not always hold water. The potential benefits are especially great and besides, who would know other than the admissions officers? Certainly not the police or doormen that apportion negative consequences. A professor at the University of Brasília more reasonably claims that "white" opportunism in using racial quotas may occur, but these problems should not be anticipated. Instead, he recommends evaluating the efficacy of these policies, including the extent of their abuse, after several years.[47]

Another solution is to provide personal-background statements and supply color photographs with job or university applications to help establish legal and administrative mechanisms to adjudicate challenges on a case-by-case basis. Hiring and admissions boards might also include blacks and others sensitive to these issues. Rio de Janeiro's state secretary of science and technology had previously disagreed with the criteria of self-identification and proposed, perhaps flippantly, creating a commission to establish the legal criteria; this commission would consist of geneticists, anthropologists, and black-movement activists. Once the self-identification criteria was established, he threatened to punish anyone found to be lying about their color on university applications under the laws governing fraud.[48] However, another state university representative correctly noted that many persons who would normally be classified as white could never be proven not to be negro.

Still, another possibility is to make quotas or goals generous enough that both whites who become nonwhite as well as persons that are socially considered to be black or brown can be accommodated. The problem is that nonwhites may lose out if there are no mechanisms to assure that they benefit. Similarly, programs for both the poor and negros may be more politically viable in some places, but such programs must be vigilant that poor negros benefit. Finally, the issue of skin color should be somehow considered. Programs for negros are likely to disproportionately benefit lighter-skinned persons, so correctives should be considered, to the extent possible.

The 1990 Americans with Disabilities Act (ADA) may provide lessons for dealing with classificatory ambiguity. This North American law prohibits discrimination on the basis of disability and defines a disabled person as one who has a physical or mental impairment that substantially limits one or more major life activities; has a history or record of such an impairment; or is perceived by others as having such an impairment. The ADA does not specifically name all of the impairments that are covered but deals with challenges regarding qualifying disabilities on a case-by-case basis.[49] Critics of the ADA claim that it is fraught with misuse by persons who demand ADA coverage for being overweight, having "bad backs," or "emotional problems." However, according to the the ADA home page, there have been surprisingly few such cases brought forth more than a decade after its implementation.[50] Deciding who is black in Brazil may not be altogether different. When abuses are reported, further investigation is then appropriate. In a large majority of cases, there is no doubt about who is negro or white in Brazil. The problem lies with those in the grey area between the two categories. In most of those cases, a claim for blackness must be accepted since there is no rule about who is black, except perhaps by resorting to an undesirable blood-quotient rule. Provided the quotas are generous enough to give such persons the benefit of the doubt, these problems might then be minimized.

SPECIAL CONSIDERATIONS
FOR DESIGNING RACE-CONSCIOUS POLICIES

In designing race-conscious policies, whether for college admissions or the labor market, at least three additional factors should be considered: the need for regionalization, the special case of black women, and the legal status of these policies. National and even state policies mandating quotas obviously need to be sensitive to the racial composition of particular places, which varies widely in Brazil. Specific quotas or goals should be appropriate to the local racial composition. For example, the equivalent to a quota for Rio de Janeiro, which is about 45-percent white, should be higher in Bahia, which is about 25-percent white, but lower in Rio Grande do Sul, which is about 80-percent white. Policy makers need to be especially attentive to the number of black students already in the universities, which they often underestimate. For example, in 2002, the State University of Bahia established quotas requiring that 40 percent of newly admitted students be defined as black or brown—the same proportion that had been established for the State University of Rio de Janeiro. However, a census of students there found that more than 40 percent of those already enrolled were black or brown, based on self-classification.[51] This also raises the question of racial classification itself. Could it be that identifying as black or brown is more highly valued in the university setting than in the rest of Brazilian society? If so, such data may overestimate the number of students in Brazilian universities who are socially defined as nonwhite. On the other hand, the State University of Rio discovered it had set its quotas too high in 2001 and lowered them and limited them to negros for 2003. In that case, administrators discovered that applicants that previously identified as white were encouraged to reclassify as brown to improve their chances of gaining admission.

The political and economic costs and opportunities for implementing affirmative action may also vary by region. This is an important consideration that thus far has received little attention. Political support for affirmative action is more likely in places where blacks are a numerical minority like the southern region, since the costs are less, white-nonwhite distinctions are clearer, racial animosity is greater, and one can document a history where whites were explicitly favored through preferential immigration and land distribution. It seems especially difficult to implement affirmative action in the North and Northeast where negros or blacks and browns are a majority, white-nonwhite distinctions are more difficult, and opportunities are fewer. Solutions are thus likely to vary by region.

Mechanisms should be built into policies to insure the inclusion of black women who are at the lowest position on the economic ladder, among all race and gender groups. Dark-skinned women in Brazil are the poorest of the poor. They confront greater health risks, are especially affected by poor reproductive-rights policies, are severely isolated, and are more often subjected to violence. Also, black women are especially likely to be single without husbands, who, for better or for worse, contribute the largest share of income in two-parent families. Therefore, universal policies directed at the poorest will especially help black women, but such policies need to be sensitive to the race-gender issues of black women and must be sure to reach this population. In terms of race-conscious policies, like quotas, it is important that gender bias be monitored. As legal scholar Kimberlé Crenshaw argues, the intersectionality of race and gender simply does not exist in the affirmation-action policies in U.S. law. As far as I know, it does not in Brazil either. There are laws and policies that seek to guarantee rights and protect against discrimination for women, and there are others for blacks, but these often better protect black men and white women than black women.

The legal status of the policies instituted thus far by the federal government are questionable regarding their permanence and enforceability. The affirmative-action policies of the Ministries of Agrarian Development and Justice are administrative decrees, which are very fragile from a legal perspective and can be fairly easily challenged. Ministerial decrees are fourth-level legal acts preceded in ranking by the Constitution, laws voted by Congress, and presidential decrees. Affirmative-action legislation is thus particularly important, as recent gains have come largely through the executive decisions and, although unlikely, could be undone by future administrations.[52] A black-movement organization, the National Office of Black Issues (Escritorio Nacional de Assuntos Negros-Zumbi dos Palmares-ENZP), was established in 1999 to work with and educate members of the national Congress to help establish such laws, but it survived only two years. Their work was patterned on the women's-rights NGO, the Feminist Studies and Assistance Center (CFEMEA), which has worked closely with Brazil's national Congress on women's issues since 1992 and consequently has helped design hundreds of laws, including quotas for women, which together comprise some of the most progressive women's-rights legislation in the world. Getting the national Congress to enact further race-specific social policies may be a taller order, considering the elite's historic ideology about race.

ELIMINATING RACIST CULTURE

Finally, the third major problem in Brazilian race relations is its racist culture. Elimination, or at least reduction, of racist culture and the establishment of genuine universalism thus presents the greatest challenge for the long term. While bold and effective policies might attenuate the effects of the glass ceiling and Brazil's hyperinequality, only massive educational and media interventions, as well as exemplary leadership, could possibly change a racist culture. Media and educational institutions are particularly powerful in the socialization of children and the images they absorb about nonwhite people. The effort to change this image is already underway in schools with the elimination of racist school textbooks, requirements to teach about African history and culture, and teacher training.

Relatedly, media representations must foster Brazil's multiracial character and egalitarian goals, and stop promoting the ideal of whitening. The experiences of the United States would surely make one skeptical of whether this can be done. Negative images of minorities in the media continue to promote racism, although some positive ones may have helped, especially in reducing the most blatant forms of racism. Several Brazilian scholars believe that media efforts would be more successful in Brazil because there is a shared value of racial democracy, which gives that society better raw material for building a system of racial justice. I agree that the attitudes of Brazilian whites place a great value on antiracism, although I am skeptical about whether individual behaviors will change much, given the benefits from racism and the entrenched common sense about the appropriate place of blacks and whites in the racial hierarchy. Will prolonged affirmative action eliminate racism in Brazil? Probably not; but its virulence may decrease. Affirmative action and various forms of antiracist educational campaigns have not eradicated racism in the United States, but the more egregious and explicit forms of racism seem to have decreased.

State collection of racial data is thought to be especially problematic because it reifies the use of race and thus all its negative consequences. Since race has no scientific validity but has been used socially to divide and stratify humankind, ideally we should probably deracialize, starting by no longer collecting race data. This was also an argument made by proponents of California's Racial Privacy Initiative in 2003, which proposed eradicating most data collection on race in that state. Indeed, the liberal French model has long held that France comprises only French citizens and there are no racial distinctions, therefore race data is not collected in France.[53] This may also be part of the rationale for not collecting race data by most Latin American governments. Gilroy (2000) has argued for this approach, the idea being that if we stop talking about race and collecting data about race, then we can get rid of race and racism. But is this really possible, since race is so embedded in the popular consciousness of societies that collect as well as those that do not collect race data? Racism is prevalent in France, throughout Latin America, and in the rest of the world, regardless of whether the concept of race is officially used or race data is collected. Racial profiling by state agents, in everyday interactions and in media images, persists despite the status of data collection. In the absence of data collection and state monitoring, racial injustices may indeed worsen as monitoring mechanisms would consequently be eliminated. Without such data, there is simply no way to know whether or not a society is progressing in the pursuit of racial justice.

Similarly, many analysts believe that we should somehow get rid of the concept of race altogether since it only creates injustices.[54] If we stopped referring to it, the problem would go away. The Brazilian case has shown that this is no solution. The Brazilian state avoided any explicit race-based intervention, against or in favor of blacks, for nearly a century. Nevertheless, racial discrimination and racial inequality have persisted. Race has been consistently used to exclude nonwhites throughout Brazil's history, despite rhetoric about inclusion. States must continue to collect race data and use race-based indicators to monitor inequality and injustice and make the necessary correctives. Societies need to notice race so that their members can learn to live more humanely with others that they consider different. Brazil, like other societies that are multiracial but now seek to combat racism, must walk a tightrope between continuing to use race, which reifies its use, and ending its use, which would allow racial injustice to run amok. As unsavory as race thinking may seem, real gains may require consideration of race for a long time before we can achieve a true racial democracy.

NOTES

CHAPTER ONE
INTRODUCTION

1. This conversation was reported in *Harper's* (June 2002) but otherwise ignored in the U.S. media.
2. Massey and Denton 1994.
3. Pettigrew 1979; Bobo 1989; Massey and Denton 1994.
4. Gore and Figueredo 1997, 11.
5. Hasenbalg 1985; Motta 2000; Guimarães 1999.
6. A notable exception, Sansone's (1996) work defies easy categorization into the two stages. He describes social spaces in which black persons face distinct disadvantages, the labor market, marriage, and relations with the police, or those where race makes little or no difference as in religion, leisure, and friendships.
7. In several published replies, including my own, Bourdieu and Wacquant are vigorously challenged for not understanding the Brazilian realities and the literature (French 2000; Hanchard 2003; Telles 2003).
8. In particular, see Gordon 1964. Also Massey and Denton 1994.
9. The large and growing Latino and Asian populations add another layer of complexity to race in the United States (as do Asians in Brazil), but I focus on black-white relations for the purpose of comparing race relations that evolved from the African slave trade.
10. Perhaps most important in the past twenty years is Carlos Hasenbalg. Although an Argentine national, he resided in Brazil in the years prior to his 1979 classic and has resided there ever since, producing pathbreaking texts on race until the mid-1990s.
11. Degler 1986. On the other hand, Andrews (1991) begins to describe United States–Brazil differences based on available quantitative indicators.
12. Bacha and Taylor 1976.
13. Based on personal interviews with Ivanir dos Santos and Romero Rodriguez.
14. This includes books in English by Lesser (1995, 1999) and Warren (2002).

CHAPTER TWO
FROM WHITE SUPREMACY TO RACIAL DEMOCRACY

1. Schwartz 1993, 11.
2. Curtin 1969.
3. Literally, Dom José, the King of Portugal, proclaimed "let it be known to those who hear my decree that considering its benefits that my subjects residing in America populate themselves and to this end join with the natives through

marriage" (Russell-Wood 1982, 173). Also, Russell-Wood (1982) cites Carlos Barata in which he claims that the Portuguese monarch, unlike the Spanish or Dutch, encouraged intermarriage to protect Portugal's open border with Spanish territories, despite resistance from the Catholic Church.

4. Boxer 1969.

5. In a similar vein, Russell-Wood (1982) found that religious orders of the Catholic Church were closed to mulattos and blacks in the early eighteenth century, although the lack of sufficiently qualified whites led the Church to accept mulattos.

6. Russell-Wood 1982.

7. These data may refer only to the freed population, but this is not clear from the source.

8. Stepan 1991; Wade 1993.

9. Stepan 1991, 1.

10. At least one author (Todorov 1993) has referred to Gobineau as "the most famous racist of them all."

11. Raeders 1976, Skidmore 1974. Goubineau may also have been referrring to the Moorish admixture among the Portuguese.

12. Stepan 1991.

13. Mitchell 1999.

14. Skidmore 1974

15. As described by Skidmore 1974.

16. See Spitzer 1989.

17. Anthony Marx (1998) claims that the reason legal segregation was imposed in the United States and South Africa but not in Brazil is purely political and denies that differences in the nature of miscegenation can account for any difference. For example, Marx denies significant mulatto mobility in the late nineteenth century, despite the historical record showing that much of the Brazilian elite was considered mulatto at the time. According to Gobineau, the large majority of the Brazilian elite was mulatto, but Marx (68) utilizes presentist thinking to establish a historical conclusion. Specifically, he uses statistical findings of a relative lack of mulatto mobility in the 1960s and 1970s as evidence that they did not rise into elite status in the nineteenth century either. The fact that they did, as well as for other reasons related to a culture of extensive miscegenation, reveals how the sentiments and identies of the Brazilian elite differed from the white elite of the United States and South Africa and might help explain why it sought less radical solutions than formal segregation or apartheid.

18. Skidmore 1974.

19. Stepan (1991) notes the greater importance of eugenics in Brazilian social policy because of the need to improve health and sanitary infrastructure for a mostly marginal population, whereas Europe had relatively well-developed social-welfare systems.

20. See Skidmore 1974 and Stepan 1991 for extensive discussions of Brazilian elite thought about race before Gilberto Freyre.

21. Stepan (1991) emphasizes the use of the eugenics theory of constructive miscegenation, while Skidmore (1974) suggests that Brazilian eugenicists mostly ignored mulatto degeneracy.

22. Skidmore 1974; Vainner 1990.

23. Castro 1995; Andrews 1992.

24. Skidmore 1974, 67.

25. According to Viera (1871), *pardo* is defined as "a person with a color intermediate to black and white," and *caboclo* is defined both as "indigenous" and with "a reddish color, close to copper."

26. The 1890 census, like the previous census, used the color categories white, black, and *caboclo*, but the term *mestiço* was substituted for *pardo*. Thus, I combine *mestiço* and *caboclo* to form an equivalent brown category for 1890. In all subsequent years, I similarly put the small number of Indians in the brown category.

27. Although sometimes viewed as a "yellow peril" and nonassimilable, the Japanese were sometimes considered white. Lesser (1999) cites Federal Deputy Acylino de Ledo in a speech before the House who stated, "The Japanese colonists are even whiter than the Portuguese."

28. According to Stepan (1991), Kehl read the German literature closely and openly praised German eugenicists for their "courage" in eugenics matters, especially in encouraging the state to control reproduction. Kehl founded the Central Brazilian Commission of Eugenics in 1931, which he claimed was modeled on the German Society for Race Hygiene. Incidentally, the U.S. eugenics community had also provided the scientific basis for restrictive immigration legislation in 1924 and programs in several states to sterilize "social deviants" as well as the creation and maintenance of segregation and anti-miscegenation laws. See Lombardo 1996.

29. Andrews (1992, 131) demonstrates that a mulatto journalist, Lívio de Castro, had articulated the idea of Brazilian racial democracy as early as 1889.

30. *Folha de São Paulo*, April 11, 1999.

31. Although racial democracy has been attributed to Freyre, its origins remain unclear. In 1945, Freyre published *Brazil: An Interpretation*, in which he first used the term "ethnic democracy." According to Antonio Sergio Guimarães, French sociologist Roger Bastide may have coined the term "racial democracy" in that same year, soon after visiting Freyre. Interestingly, black-movement leader Abdias do Nascimento in 1950 appears to clearly refer to "racial democracy," which he describes as a "doctrine" in 1950. He stated that "We observe that the extensive miscegenation practiced as an imperative in our historical formation . . . is transforming by inspiration and imposition . . . in a well-defined doctrine of racial democracy to become a model for other people" (Nascimento 1950, cf. Guimarães 2002).

32. Even outside observers, such as former slave and abolitionist Frederick Douglass, had made public declarations as early as 1858 proclaiming that "democratic and protestant America would do well in learning the lesson on justice and liberty coming from despotic and Catholic Brazil." Cited from C. Azevedo 1996.

33. Note especially Freyre 1945.

34. He states "of all the problems confronting Brazil there was none that gave me so much anxiety as that of miscegenation. Once, after three straight years of absence from my country, I caught sight of a group of Brazilian seamen—*mulattos* and *cafusos*—crossing the Brooklyn Bridge. I know that they impressed me as being the caricatures of men and there came to me a phrase from a book on Brazil

written by an American traveler: 'the fearfully mongrel aspect of the population' " Freyre 1986, xxvi–xxvii.

35. Bastos 2001.

36. However, this cultural argument has been rejected by those charging that Portuguese colonists in Africa cohabitated infrequently with the natives.

37. Degler 1986.

38. Araujo 1994.

39. Stepan 1991; Araujo 1994.

40. Bacelar 2001.

41. Schwartz (1974, 1992) showed evidence of greater cruelty, torture, and harsh working conditions in Brazilian slavery.

42. Castro 1995; Reis 2002.

43. Stam 1997; Bacelar 2001.

44. Mitchell 1999; Hanchard 1994.

45. Andrews 1992; Butler 1998.

46. Skidmore 1999; Winant 2001.

47. Rascussen 2003.

48. Andrews 1991; Mitchell 2002.

49. Mitchell 2002.

50. The Brazilian government also ratified the Convention on all Forms of Discrimination Against Women (CEDAW) of 1979, which recognized that the eradication of racism is necessary for enjoyment of women's and men's rights. See Banton 1998.

51. IBGE Estudos de Estatística Teória e Aplicada—Vol. 2. Estudos Sôbre a Composição da População do Brasil Segundo a Côr. Rio de Janeiro 1950, 8 (my translation).

52. Conselho Nacional de Estatistica (IBGE) Contribuições para o Estudo da Demografia do Brasil. 1961, 200.

53. I estimated the racial composition of the Brazilian population in the intervening years in figure 2.1 based on immigration levels relative to the national population and assuming that the black population remained at a constant 15 percent, as it was in both 1890 and 1940. The brown population is thus the remainder of the nonwhite and nonblack population.

54. Guimarães 2002.

55. Senator Petronio Portella, cited from Skidmore 1985.

56. Brown 1994.

57. Dzidzenyo 1999; Bacelar 2001. These centers would later become leading centers for race-relations research in Brazil.

58. Skidmore 1999.

59. Goldani 1999.

60. Berkovich 1991.

61. On the other hand, this would overestimate the browning of the black population if the changes from reclassification were particularly great among the cohort being studied, which is possible since it was particularly subject to social mobility and thus a "money whitens" effect. Wood's (1991) figures refer to mature adults in the 1980 census, a time when the majority of the Brazilian popula-

tion was under twenty years old, so the assumptions are especially important. For the assumption to hold, parents would need to reclassify children as brown at the same rate as themselves, which is plausible since children would experience mobility with their parents. Because white-white and black-black marriages are declining as a proportion of all marriages, the number of racially mixed children would have increased anyway. As I will show in chapter 3, from 45 to 95 percent of the children of all other marriages were classified as brown.

CHAPTER THREE
FROM RACIAL DEMOCRACY TO AFFIRMATIVE ACTION

This chapter and chapter 9 are based on observations and diverse types of data, including interviews, which I collected while a program officer of human rights at the Ford Foundation in Rio de Janeiro from February 1997 to August 2000. During this time, I worked closely with eight black-movement organizations that Ford funded, and I participated in meetings with government leaders, several black-movement conferences, and several of the national and international conferences that I mention in this chapter. While I believe it captures many of the important issues and events involved in the formation of public policy regarding black Brazilians, it does not duly consider the important work by the black movement with communities or the work of other organizations that I was familiar with but did not directly follow, such as the work of the labor unions, the Worker's Party, and the Catholic and Protestant Churches.

1. Rodrigues 1999.
2. Mitchell 1985; Hanchard 1994.
3. Mitchell 1985.
4. J. Santos 2000.
5. Andrews 1991, 221.
6. At www.palmares.gov.br. Consulted in August 2001.
7. Hanchard (1994) is largely a criticism of the black movement's historical focus on cultural rather than material interests. As evidence of the cultural predominance, Maggie (1991) found that 500 of the 1,702 Centennial of Abolition events in 1988 were about black culture and 391 were about slavery and abolition compared to 38 on racial inequality and 88 on racial discrimination.
8. Pereira 1998.
9. Silva 1998a.
10. Article 5, paragraph 42 declared "the practice of racism constitutes a crime without the right to bail and without prescription, subject to the punishment of imprisonment." The earlier Arinos law treated racism as a minor offense (*contravenção penal*).
11. Sorj 2000.
12. Johnson 1995.
13. Interview with Ivanir dos Santos, May 2002.
14. From then on, Ford spent generously in support of black-movement activists and goals and research on Brazilian race relations. See Telles 2003 for how

the Ford Foundation has supported these NGOs, in a way not commonly assumed by some critics of the black movement.

15. Dulitzky 2000.

16. During my nearly four years in Brazil from 1997 to 2000, I found only one article that defended racial democracy in any serious newspaper or magazine (Carvalho 1999).

17. Whites in the Northeast were the only group to voice apparently less support for race mixture, although the percentage (76) nevertheless represents a solid majority.

18. The 1976 PNAD was, for most purposes, the first national data set with information about race. Even though it contained information on race, the 1960 data only became available in the mid-1970s, and due to some minor methodological problems, its availability has since been limited. See Silva (1978) for an exception.

19. Oliveira, Porcaro, and Costa 1983.

20. Ministério da Justiça 1997.

21. The proceedings of the conference, including Cardoso's speech, were published in Souza 1996.

22. Interview with Helio Santos, September 2001.

23. Cardoso published his doctoral dissertation on slavery (*Capitalismo e Escravidão no Brasil Meridional: O Negro na Sociedade Escravocrata do Rio Grande do Sul* [São Paulo,1962]) and co-authored a book with Octavio Ianni on contemporary race relations (*Côr e Mobilidade Social em Florianópolis* [São Paulo, 1960]).

24. *Folha de São Paulo,* July 9, 2001.

25. See, for example, Souza 1996; Reis 1996; and Da Matta 1996.

26. Almeida 2003.

27. Maggie 2000.

28. Davis 1999.

29. Moreira 2002.

30. Bento 2000; Instituto Ethos 2000.

31. Instituto Ethos 2000.

32. At www.cidan.com.br.

33. This is the common interpretation although the law itself states that in advertisements "with more than two persons, at least one must be negro" (H. Silva 1998a, 107).

34. According to Almeida (1998) and an interview with Gilberto Leal in September 2001, the 1988 Constitution recognized the legitimacy of the current residents' historic claim to these lands. Although they have been integral to the cultural and material survival of the quilombo descendents, current residents' land rights continue to be ignored and systematically violated. These ancestral lands have been continuously encroached upon by agriculture, logging, and mining interests. Congress had repeatedly failed to pass enabling legislation to regulate quilombo lands and the courts have too often sided with large landowners and big business in legal disputes concerning communal property rights. On economic, cultural, and environmental grounds, rights advocates have thus built a strong case for extending full citizenship to these descendants of former slaves,

and black-movement activists have made the regularization of quilombo lands one of their principal policy demands. Regularization has depended on proving historical rights to the land, using archeological and written evidence that is difficult to obtain. As recommended by the Brazilian Anthropological Association, titles should be given on the basis of self-identity rather than such evidence but the government failed to recognize such claims. Of the more than 500 lands claiming to be quilombos, fewer than 50 had received titles by late 2001. These titles would provide residents with collective ownership of these lands, enabling them to demand schools, health centers, and communications infrastructure that they otherwise are sorely lacking. Without these basic services, many of the remaining descendants of quilombos have been forced to migrate and often must lead marginal lives in urban areas.

35. Ministério da Justiça 1996.

36. Banco Interamericano 1996.

37. Black-movement leaders from Spanish-speaking Latin America had met earlier with the InterAmerican Development Bank. At least one earlier meeting with the IDB also involved an official Brazilian delegation with leading black government representatives, including Senator Benedita da Silva; Dulce Pereira, director of the Palmares Cultural Foundation; and Helio Santos, the coordinator of the Interministerial Workgroup for the Valuation of the Black Population.

38. See Gazeta Mercantil 2001. In 2001, the Inter-American Dialogue created an internship position and partnered with the World Bank, the IDB, and the Ford Foundation to examine race issues in the region. That year the coalition organized a meeting titled "High Level Dialogue on Race, Ethnicity and Inclusion in Latin America and the Caribbean."

39. The Third World Conference against Racism was another of a series of thematic conferences convened by the UN to address social, economic, and environmental problems in a forum designed to debate proposals and achieve political consensus among member states. The World Conference took place in Durban, South Africa, in August–September of 2001. (That country's apartheid system had been the central issue of the two previous world conferences.) The conference sought to review progress in combating racism since the adoption of the Universal Declaration of Human Rights in 1948, which itself was prompted by the racially inspired atrocities committed during World War II. It also aimed to formulate measures for combating racism at the national, regional, and international levels, and to increase awareness of racism. See the World Conference homepage, www.un.org/WCAR.

40. Ivanir dos Santos has observed how little black leaders from other countries know about Brazil. For example, when Nelson Mandela visited Rio de Janeiro in 1990, he proclaimed that one day South Africa would be a racial democracy like Brazil. In another example, Santos reported that he met with the vice chair of the U.S. Congressional Black Caucus in 1997, and the congressman, fully aware that Santos was Brazilian, proclaimed, "Excuse me, but I don't speak Spanish." Interview with Ivanir dos Santos.

41. For most of the past forty years, Nascimento has worked to denounce Brazilian racism outside of Brazil.

42. Statement by H.E. Ambassador Celso L.N. Amorim, permanent represen-

tative of Brazil to the United Nations in Geneva, 56th Session of the United Nations Commission of Human Rights, Geneva, March 24, 2000.

43. Carneiro 2001.

44. Information on government funding provided in an inteview with Ivair Alves dos Santos of the National Secretariat of Human Rights in August 2001.

45. The Brazilian government established the National Committee for the World Conference comprising government and civil-society members, including at least two high-profile black activists. The committee's size and internal composition changed in response to political demands. Also, its legitimacy in the eyes of the black movement was constantly being transformed, and one black-movement representative resigned, accusing the government of lacking genuine interest.

46. Encontro Nacional de Parlamentares Negros, "Carta de Salvador," July 26–28, 2001.

47. Interview August 2001.

48. This included 45 in *O Globo*, 41 in *Correio Brasiliense*, 38 in the *Folha de São Paulo*, 33 in the *Jornal do Brasil*, and 12 in *O Estado de São Paulo*. Cited from Articulação de ONGs de Mulheres Negras Brasileiras rumo a III Conferência Mundial Contra o Racismo, "Cobertura da Imprensa sobre a Conferência Mundial Contra o Racismo," September 1, 2001.

49. Escóssia 2001b.

50. In this ministerial decree and virtually all others, the term "negro" (black) was used, unless it explicitly included browns. Whether or not browns were included under negros was unclear and presumably left to self-identification.

51. *Folha de São Paulo*, October 10, 2001.

52. Supremo Tribunal Federal 2001, 18.

53. *Folha de São Paulo*, December 20, 2001.

54. Instituto Sindical, 2002.

55. Ravazzolli 2002.

56. Gaspari 2002.

57. These are not exclusive and, more often than not, the same person fills both quotas.

58. Historian Eric Foner (2003) provides a similar explanation for U.S. victories against segregation in the early cold-war period. For example, the Eisenhower administration urged Supreme Court justices in *Brown vs. Board of Education* in 1954 to consider that people of other nations "cannot understand how such a practice can exist in a country which professes to be a staunch supporter of freedom, justice and democracy." Also, see Brysk 1995 for how a receptive international human-rights regime helped explain the victories of indigenous peoples in the Americas.

CHAPTER FOUR
RACIAL CLASSIFICATION

1. As reported by Roberto Da Matta 1996.

2. Nogueira 1995 [1955]; Harris and Kottack 1963.

3. Between 1850 and 1920, mulattos, and occasionally even quadroons and octaroons, could be identified through the U.S. census. In the 1930 census, Mexicans were a separate race, and in the 1860 census, the Irish were. Asians were usually a single category, but are now divided into several nationality-based terms. In the 2000 U.S. census, for the first time, multiple race categories could be selected, although only 6 percent of the population chose more than one category. African American leaders now worry that this Brazilianization of race will dilute the power of their numbers and undermine important civil-rights gains like the Voting Rights Act. See Lee 2001.

4. From F. Davis 1991. There were local variations in the timing and importance of the mulatto category. Places like Charleston and New Orleans were conspicuous for their acceptance of the mulatto, even after segregation.

5. Davis 1991; Marx 1998.

6. Sansone 1997; Wade 1993. The Brazilian conception of race is thus similar to the situational or relational conception of ethnicity used by Frederick Barth's (1969) classic *Ethnic Groups and Boundaries*. Anthropologist Charles Wagley used the term "social race" to distinguish the Brazilian concept of race from the idea of race in the US in the 1950s. This may have been appropriate then, when essentialist concepts of race were the norm in the U.S. However, Wagley's distinction may no longer be necessary for social scientists today since they agree that race is always social, although often essentialized in popular beliefs.

7. Skidmore 1974; Omi and Winant 1986; Graham 1990; Jenkins 1998; Nobles 2000.

8. Kottack (1995) reported that when he revisited a town in Bahia in 1980 that he and Marvin Harris studied in the early 1960s, the number of terms used had decreased and racial distinctions were more consistently made.

9. Silva 1987.

10. A list of all these terms may be found in "A Côr do Brasilero," *Folha de São Paulo*, June 25, 1995 (p. 5 of the *Caderno Especial*).

11. Harris 1963; R. Pacheco 1987; Nogueira 1995 [1955]; Sansone 1993; Stephens 1989.

12. These definitions were used by Hutchinson, Wagley, and Levine, and are all described in Stephens 1989.

13. R. Pacheco 1987; Sansone 1993.

14. Telles 1995b.

15. Although never incorporated as an official category, negro has a long history of use by civil-society organizations, since the 1930s with the Frente Negra Brasileira. Also, the Teatro Experimental do Negro was founded in 1944 "to raise black [negro] consciousness"; the first Congresso do Negro Brasileiro was held in 1950; the Associação Cultural do Negro was founded in 1954; and the Movimento Negro Unificado Contra Discriminação Racial (MNUCDR, later shortened to MNU) was organized in 1978.

16. Hanchard 1994.

17. Ministério da Justiça 1996.

18. Despite the recommendations of the Ministry of Justice, census planners, in consultation with various experts and interested parties and after survey testing

various formats of the race question, decided to keep the same categories as used in previous censuses.

19. Usage of the term actually increased as the preferred term for self-identification from 0.5 percent in 1976 to 3 percent of the population in 1995, according to the national household surveys in those years. See Bailey and Telles unpublished.

20. Rosemberg et al 1993; Pinto 1996.

21. Hutchinson 1957; Harris 1963.

22. Goffman 1959.

23. Cohen 1994; Erikson 1968.

24. Sansone 1997.

25. In that survey, conducted by the Data Folha Research Institute, interviewers classified respondents based on the census categories before asking any questions. At the beginning of the questionnaire, respondents were asked to self-identify racially anyway they wanted to and then to identify according to the five census categories.

26. The collapsing of the brown and black categories into a single category in the past has been justified in studies of racial inequality on the basis that much smaller status differences between blacks and browns have been found than between whites and browns.

27. Racial classification collected in a survey may be quite different from one's classification in a job interview because the stakes are distinct. That is, evaluation of another's race may be more trivial for the census interviewer than for the personnel manager. Similarly, census respondents may be less concerned than job applicants about managing or manipulating their racial appearance. But such survey data is critical for sociological research given that the survey interview has become the standard method for collecting race data and the primary data source for studies examining racial differences.

28. Pena et al. 2000; Carvalho-Silva et al. 2001.

29. The survey did not ask respondents how many ancestors of each background they had but merely whether they had any at all. Thus, while many white Brazilians claim to have African or indigenous ancestors, they are likely to have a relatively higher proportion of European ancestry than browns and blacks, confirming that race or color is defined mostly by appearance.

30. In a separate analysis, I found little difference by income in the proportion of whites claiming African ancestry.

31. On the other hand, this finding may also be due to the likelihood that women answer the census questionnaire more than men and that parents may tend to classify children in the same category as themselves. However, census respondents are usually heads of households, which tend to be men.

32. Telles 2002. The analysis is based on a multinominal logit regression model. The age variable is held constant although there were significant differences by age, which I discuss later. Earlier quantitative analysis on the effects of class on whitening were conducted by N. Silva (1987), which I review in Telles 2002.

33. Whitening tends to be by interviewers and not vice versa as I show in Telles 2002.

34. Pelé's nomination represented the first and only time a black person served as a minister in recent decades. Pelé's was not a regular position in the Brazilian Ministry, although his actual title was Extraordinary Minister of Sports.

35. Hanchard 1994; Schwartzman 1999; Turner 1985; Bacelar 2001; Sansone 1996.

36. Bailey and Telles 2002.

37. I do not present results for moreno and negro by region in table 4.6 because I statistically interact them with color, which complicates straightforward description. Suffice it to say that the main findings show that moreno is especially preferred in places that have fewer whites. See Bailey and Telles 2002.

38. Telles 2002.

39. Sansone 1993; Schwartzman 1999.

40. See Sansone 1997 for a further explanation of this hypothesis.

41. Barth 1969; Cornell 1996; Jenkins 1998.

42. See Fry 1977 for the example of *feijoada* vs. soul food

43. Interestingly, there were no significant racial differences in Carnaval. Forty-three percent of whites, 41 percent of browns, and 43 percent of blacks using self-identification and 42, 43, and 43 using interviewer-classification indicated Carnaval is important in their lives. Of course, Carnaval has become an important component of national culture.

CHAPTER FIVE
RACIAL INEQUALITY AND DEVELOPMENT

1. Barros, Henriques, and Mendonça 2001.

2. Sorj 2000; Lopes 1989; E. Reis 2002.

3. Income is measured according to monthly individual income. Also, pyramids were smoothed to avoid heaping at certain income categories.

4. Anani Dzidzenyo (1999) notes that, despite its strong diplomatic presence in Africa, Brazil's Ministry of Foreign Relations has had virtually no black diplomats. I was told that there were two diplomats by a person familiar with Itamaraty staff, but there are no official numbers that I am aware of. I have heard other reports that range from zero to perhaps seven or eight, depending on one's particular way of classifying, but the point is that the number is absurdly miniscule. To further illustrate the absence of blacks in Itamaraty, Raimundo Souza Dantas, as Ambassador to Ghana in 1961, is known as the only black (negro) to have ever served as a Brazilian ambassador. Upon his appointment by President Janio Quadros, Dantas stayed in a hotel in Accra for two months until the Brazilian trade representative was relocated to another posting. He could not accept that Dantas was the ambassador and had refused to give Dantas the keys to the official residence. See H. Costa's (1982) interview with Dantas.

5. Fernando Henrique Cardoso appointed Brazil's only black general in 1996.

6. Estimates from Joaquim Barbosa, a member of the Federal Prosecution familiar with Itamaraty staff.

7. Instituto Ethos de Empresas e Responsabilidade Social. 2003. Perfil Social, Racial e de Gênero das 500 Maiores Empresas do Brasil e Suas Ações Afirmativas. São Paulo.

8. United Nations Development Programme 2001.

9. Rocha 1993.

10. Instituto Sindical Interamericano (1999) defines unemployment to include "persons who, for reasons of survival, persons who were self-employed and in irregular and discontinuous jobs as well as unremunerated work in family enterprises" or persons that did not work or seek work in the past thirty days because they were discouraged or for accidental reasons but in both cases, did seek work in the past twelve months.

11. Keith and Herrring 1991; Allen, Hunter, and Telles 2000.

12. The small brown-black gap may not necessarily reflect a lack of large differences in the extent to which blacks and browns experience discrimination but could also be due to greater discrimination by blacks, compensated by the fact that browns are more likely than blacks to live in rural areas and in the poor northeastern region. I show this to be the case in chapter 6.

13. Dark African Americans (medium brown, dark brown, and very dark) earn about 80 percent of what their brown counterparts (very light and light brown) earn. This compares to a black:brown ratio of 90 percent in Brazil. A large difference in skin tone prevails in human-capital studies that seek to measure discrimination. See Keith and Herring 1991; Allen, Hunter, and Telles 2000.

14. Oliver and Shapiro 1995.

15. For those that do not own the property they reside in, the value for this variable is zero.

16. Baer 1995.

17. Holtzer 2001.

18. Wood 1991.

19. Farley 1984.

20. Lam 2000.

21. Also, a lower limit of 25 years permits the analysis of a population that has for all intents and purposes, completed its education, and the upper limit prevents the distortion in computing averages that occurs by comparing groups where the proportion of the population over age 65 is very different.

22. In a separate calculation, I find that eliminating the 21–25 population has minimal affect on the average because the large majority of persons have completed school by that age.

23. This is also the figure for browns. The comparable black figures are 1.2 and 6.2.

24. IBGE, Conselho Nacional de Estatistíca 1961.

25. Illiteracy data by race is also available for 1890, when 94.2 percent of blacks, 89.1 percent of browns, and 56.2 percent of whites were illiterate.

26. Reynolds Farley 1984. Farley's data cover before 1960 up to 1982, but the trend is for further narrowing in the remainder of the 1980s and the 1990s.

27. Farley 1984.

28. Oliveira, Porcaro, and Costa 1983; Farley and Allen 1987, 272.

29. Baer 1995.

30. I used only seven time points in the previous section.

31. Specifically, ND=100 ($\sum WiCNi - \sum NiCWi$), where Wi and Ni are the proportions of white males and nonwhite males in occupation i, and CWi and CNi are the cumulative proportions of white males and nonwhite males in occupations ranked below occupation i.

32. While ND may be the best single index for capturing overall inequality, it may be overly sensitive to local differences in occupational structure. Odds ratios, which are marginal invariant, specifically measure access to occupations, independent of the occupational structure (although they are limited because they measure differentiation between only two categories). On the other hand, odds ratios are problematic when the meaning of access varies with the margins of the occupational distribution. For example, if a given occupational category represents the top 5 percent of all jobs in one metropolitan area and the top 20 percent of jobs in another, differential access to that occupation usually does not mean the same thing in each of the two areas; in the former it means access to an elite position, whereas in the latter it means access to a more "average" job. Although odds ratios are considered differentiation measures, they become inequality measures when two categories are ranked categories, as they are in this study. Despite debate about the usefulness of a number of inequality and differentiation measures, there is a consensus that both the net-difference and odds-ratio measures are particularly good measures once their limitations are understood. Finally, levels of inequality based on such broad occupational categorizations, as these are in this study, may understate the real racial inequality in Brazil because of large variations in occupational status within these occupational groups, and because nonwhites tend to earn less than whites in the same occupation (Oliveira, Porcaro, and Costa 1983; Lovell 1989). Further methodological details may be found in Telles 1994.

33. Baer 1995; Haller 1982.

34. Merrick and Graham 1979.

35. As measured by overall and per capita faculty publications. See Durham and Schwartzman 1989.

36. Van den Berghe 1967, 70; see also Fernandes 1965; Ianni 1987; Hasenbalg 1979.

37. The negative correlation would be even slighter or nonexistent if we removed two highly industrialized places with especially low levels of inequality. Since these two urban areas (Joinville and Blumenau) have the smallest nonwhite populations and are located in a single state, one might consider this.

38. Because whites and nonwhites in Brazil vary in the extent to which they are natives or migrants, I controlled for the relative odds that whites and nonwhites were natives. This has been shown to be especially important in the Northeast, where white migrants dominate in high-level jobs (Castro and Guimarães 1992); in the Southeast migrants dominate in low-level jobs, but there the migrants tend to be racially heterogeneous. I employ a dummy variable to assess whether or not a metropolitan area is in the state of São Paulo, because that state has some peculiar characteristics (Andrews 1991; Merrick and Graham 1979)

and its metropolitan areas are close together geographically, a situation that might lead to correlated errors.

39. Castro and Guimarães 1992 and N. Silva 1999 both conclude that educational differences are the main reason for racial inequality. To measure educational inequality in this model, I use two odds-ratio measures at the fourth- and the twelfth-grade levels. Mean years of schooling are also included in the second model because levels of education are vital to occupational outcomes.

CHAPTER SIX
RACIAL DISCRIMINATION

1. See also Pierson 1942 and Wagley 1952a.

2. The period covered by the Pastore and Silva's mobility tables by race refer roughly to father's occupation in the 1960s and 1970s and son's occupation in 1996. The authors restrict their analysis of 1996 data to 35- to 49-year-old males who report their current occupation and that of their fathers when both informant and father first entered the labor market, which is usually between the ages of 10 and 14. Thus, father's occupation generally refers to the one held 20 to 40 years ago.

3. Unfortunately, the birthplace question in the National Household Survey (PNAD) for 1996 is for states and thus does not allow restriction to those born in the São Paulo metropolitan area.

4. I did not perform a separate analysis for browns and blacks because of the high level of ambiguity in that distinction and because the sample size of the black population was very small.

5. See Lovell 1989; Paes de Barros, Henriques, and Mendonça 1996; Telles and Lim 1998.

6. Telles and Lim 1998.

7. See Darity and Mason 1998 for a review of these studies.

8. Specifically, we explained more of the statistical variation when we used interviewer classification.

9. Klein and Ribeiro 1991.

10. There were approximately 294,000 male and 268,000 female siblings that fit these characteristics in 1991. With the 10-percent sample of the 1991 census, the estimates of educational progress are thus highly reliable.

11. I begin at age 9 so that younger siblings will be at least age 7, the age when all Brazilian children are legally required to be in school. Also, the white siblings are the reference group. In other words, percentage comparisons of siblings are plotted at the age and grade of the white child, regardless of whether the non-white child is the same age, older, or younger.

12. I assume that most nonwhite children have two nonwhite parents, just as most white children have two white parents. Therefore, most black and brown children suffer the additional burden of their parents' class and race. Nonwhite children of nonwhite parents are more likely to suffer from greater material and social disadvantages than nonwhite children of white-nonwhite parentage. A sim-

ilar argument can be made for white children with two white parents as being advantaged over another white child but with a nonwhite parent. Thus, the findings
of figures 6.2 and 6.3 would even underestimate racial inequality within the same
schools. Also, sibling pairs who are classified as white and nonwhite are more
likely to appear near the white-nonwhite boundary of the color continuum than
average whites and nonwhites (e.g., white or moreno claro compared to pardo
claro), which further understates most racial differences in education.

13. Twine 1998; Guimarães 1999.

14. The frequent newspaper accounts revealing verbal abuses suffered by
blacks and the claims of the black movement about racism in the media are enough
to convince most people of racism. Guimarães (1998) found in the single year of
1988 forty-two articles in the newspapers of three metropolitan areas reporting incidents of racism. The most common cases were of racial discrimination of persons
in residential buildings, nonwhite persons humiliated by police, and racial discrimination in access to work. Often these involved racial slurs or insults, and most
other times, involved clear signaling of racial discrimination by the perpetrator.

15. Benedita da Silva, formerly the elected vice-governor of Rio de Janeiro, became governor when Anthony Garotinho decided to run for president.

16. Turra and Ventura 1995, 129

17. The 1995 Data Folha question was, "Who is smarter, whites or blacks?"
The responses for whites were 84 percent no difference, 9 percent whites, and 4
percent blacks. For browns the respective responses were 82, 8, and 8 percent,
and for blacks, 84, 8, and 6 percent.

18. Taken from Jackman 1994, 237. Ethnographic studies in the 1950s and
1960s revealed that whites generally believed blacks and mulattos were intellec-
tually inferior to whites, so the 1995 results likely reflect greatly changing attitudes about race in Brazil.

19. The song itself in Portuguese:

Alô gente aqui quem tá falando é Tiririca
Eu também estou na onda de Axé Music
Quero ver os meus colegas dançando
Veja, veja, veja os cabellos dela
Parece bombril de ariar panela
Quando ella passa, me chama atenção
Mas seus cabellos, não tem jeito não
A sua catinga quase me desmaiou
Olha eu não aguento do seu grande fedô
Veja, veja, veja os cabellos dela!
Veja, veja, veja os cabellos dela!
Diz a veja, veja, veja os cabellos dela
Parece bombril de ariar panela
Eu já mandei ela se lavar
Mas ela teimou e não quis me escutar
Essa nega fede! Fede de lascar
Bicha fedorenta, fede mais que gambá.

In the last two lines, the words *nega* and *bicha* are double entendres. The word *nega* may be used as an insult to a particular black woman, as I think it was intended in the song, although the word is sometimes used to refer to women generally. *Bicha* may refer to most animals, as I translated it above, but it may also mean worm, leech, or an angry, repulsive, or ugly person. These translations can be found in the *Novo Michaelis Portuguese-English Dictionary*.

20. La Pastina, Patel, and Schiavo 2002.

21. The 1995 survey of racial attitudes asked whether white Brazilians "hold prejudices," not whether they discriminate.

22. Silva (1999) also concludes that unexplained racial differences in mobility are mostly due to differences in the quality of schooling, because the greater income returns to education by whites over nonwhites disappears when one controls for social origin, although this may also be affected by access to social networks.

23. In a rare comparison with the United States, Warren (1997) argues that the poorer performance of black and brown pupils in Brazil cannot be explained by black opposition to educational success because it indicates "acting white," a common explanation for the educational disadvantage of minorities. Typical nonwhite students in Brazil valorize whiteness over blackness, so that their educational disadvantage cannot be blamed on so-called oppositional identities.

24. Cavalleiro 2000, 213.

25. *O Dia* 2002.

26. Despite this ruling, such schoolbooks and classic children's texts with racist content remain on the bookshelves of libraries.

27. Ribeiro and Cardoso 1997.

28. Oliveira 1999; Ribeiro and Cardoso 1997.

29. Twenty percent of black men, 25 percent of black women, 9 percent of brown men, and 10 percent of brown women indicated that there was discrimination for persons of their color where they thought they had a chance of getting a job; slightly lower percentages were found for the four categories in job promotions. Lower percentages were found for the housing markets and in schooling.

30. Fix and Struyck 1997.

31. See for example, *Revista Tudo* 2001.

32. As far as I know, these results have not been written up, but were related to me by the research team which included Antonio Sergio Guimarães and Nadya Castro.

33. Costa notes that North American travelers at the time contrasted this system with the United States where blacks or mulattos were never allowed mobility.

34. See Scheper-Hughes 1992, 110–17.

35. Wilson 1978.

36. In 1998, 69 percent of black children in the United States were born to single mothers, up from 38 percent in 1970 (Cherlin 2002, 148).

37. Bumpass and Sweet 1987, table 9.15. Also, Cherlin 2002, 148.

38. Pacheco 1989.

39. E. Costa 1985; Skidmore 1974; Andrews 1991.

40. Halloway 1980; Andrews 1992.

41. Helena Morley (1948), a slaveowner's daughter, describes the treatment of ex-slaves at the time of abolition.

42. Andrews 1991.

43. Nina Rodrigues had strongly approved of this law.

44. Along with the lack of state subsidies, abundant land and labor led to the further expansion of subsistence agriculture in the Northeast and other areas where modern industry and agriculture were insufficient. See Furtado 1961; W. Cano 2002.

45. Global Justice Center 2000.

46. Caldeira 2000 and Piovesan et al. 2001 show that these numbers hit a low point of 253 in 1997 but increased again in the next two years. In the first six months of 2000, São Paulo police had killed 489 civilians.

47. Piovesan et al. 2001. The same study notes that 82 percent of these were by the police while 17 percent were by death squads.

48. Given the varied newspaper sources and Brazil's multiple classificatory systems in which negro can have various meanings, these designations are most likely not comparable to the census classifications.

49. Translated from Portuguese *Tribunais do Júri*. While criminal proceedings ordinarily are tried before judges who serve as fact finders as well as arbiters on legal issues, trials are held before seven-person juries for intentional crimes against human life (e.g., murder, heat-of-passion manslaughter, and aiding or performing an illegal abortion).

50. The ambiguity of racial classification emerged in 1 percent of the cases in which victims were identified in more than one color category.

51. H. Silva 1998b. *Crioulos* is a term for blacks, which is often used in a derogatory fashion.

52. U.S. Department of Justice, Bureau of Justice Statistics 1997.

53. Smelser, Wilson, and Blumstein 2001.

54. Incarceration escalated rapidly in the United States in the 1990s as result of policies that mandated often lengthy prison sentences for persons committing nonviolent and petty crimes, with black men being the major victims of that change.

CHAPTER SEVEN
INTERMARRIAGE

1. N. Silva 1987; Berquó 1990; Petrucelli 2001.

2. See for example Burdick 1998.

3. He called Bahia "probably the most important Euro-African melting pot in Brazil" (50)

4. This method of approximating recent marriages in the local area was also used by Blau, Blum, and Schwartz (1982) and South and Messner (1986) to analyze intermarriage in the United States. The same authors make strong cases for why racial composition must be accounted for.

5. The total population of the seventy-four areas represented 42 percent of Brazil's total population and 62 percent of its urban population in 1980. Since the sample is a 25-percent sample of the census, the number of couples ranges from 107,992 couples living in São Paulo to 839 couples in Marilia, averaging 10,055 couples per metropolitan area. See Telles 1993 for more details about this methodology.

6. Another possible explanation for such high rates of intermarriage might consider that many marriages in Brazil as recorded by the census are informal rather than state or church sanctioned. A separate analysis of 1991 Brazilian census data showed that endogamous marriages were most likely to be official, but most intermarriages were official as well. The largest racial differences were for white couples, where 19 percent of unofficial marriages with other whites were consensual compared to 33 percent of those with browns and 42 percent of those with blacks. On the other hand, only 28 percent of endogamous brown marriages were informal compared to 33 percent of brown marriages to whites and 45 percent of brown marriages to blacks. Thus, there is some support for this hypothesis.

7. I limit figure 7.3 to urban areas that are less than 20 percent brown or black because the black population of the seventy-four Brazilian urban areas never exceeds 17 percent.

8. Frazier 1942; Willems 1949.

9. Bastide and Van den Berghe 1957; Andrews 1991.

10. Telles 1993.

11. Skidmore 1974; Degler 1986; Burdick 1998.

12. This cult of the mulatta is also found in Freyre (1986, 14):

in our national lyricism there is no tendency more clearly revealed than one toward a glorification of the mulatto woman, the cabocla or Indian woman, the brown-skin or brunette type, celebrated for the beauty of her eyes, the whiteness of her teeth, for wiles and languishments and witching ways, far more than are the "pale virgins" and the "blond damsels."

13. Lazo (2001) shows that by age fifty, 8.5 percent of black women had never been in a union compared to 6.7 percent of whites and 5.5 percent of brown women.

CHAPTER EIGHT
RESIDENTIAL SEGREGATION

1. Veja 1992.

2. Pettigrew 1979; Bobo 1989; Massey and Denton 1994.

3. For a recent example, see Gans 1999.

4. Schnore 1965; Leeds 1974.

5. Caldeira 2000.

6. Ribeiro and Telles (2000) show that 70 percent of the population residing in Rio's favelas in 1991 are brown or black. L. Pinto (1953) showed a similar proportion in Rio with 1950 census data.

7. When I resided in Rio, the head of the drug traffic in Cantagallo was black while his counterpart in Pavão-Pavãozinho was a light colored *nordestino*. This example reveals one way in which poor communities are divided largely (but not strictly) by race. This information based on an interview with José Junior, January 2000.

8. In a separate article (Telles 1992), I calculated segregation indexes for the forty largest urban areas in Brazil.

9. Calculated by an average of 4.2 persons per urban household in 1980 and a range of 200 to 250 households per urban tract.

10. See Telles 1995 for a discussion of how these may have changed.

11. The formulas for computing both of these indexes are found in Massey and Denton 1994.

12. Incidentally, based on a preliminary analysis of the 1993 Survey of Employment and Unemployment in that city, I found several neighborhoods in Salvador, such as those in the Liberdade area, to be over 95 percent black and brown, a number that is unlikely to be found for other large metropolitan areas in Brazil.

13. L. Pinto 1953.

14. Cardoso and Ianni 1960.

15. Cardoso and Ianni 1960; Bastide and Van den Berghe 1957; Fernandes 1965.

16. Massey and Denton 1993.

17. Segregation scores for the lowest earning group (less than 75) are inconsistent with patterns observed for all other groups. This may be due to data errors in which a disproportionate number of respondents may have falsely reported that they had no or almost no income. See Telles 1992.

18. Agier 1992; Sansone 1997, 2003.

CHAPTER NINE
RETHINKING BRAZILIAN RACE RELATIONS

1. Massey and Denton 1994.

2. Marx 1998.

3. On this point, I have no direct evidence but I rely on the findings of others, especially Sansone (1999).

4. Steinberg 1991.

5. Sansone 2003.

CHAPTER TEN
DESIGNING APPROPRIATE POLICIES

1. See H. Silva 1998a for a description of these laws.

2. These definitions are from Resnick 1998.

3. See for example Barbosa 2000; Mitchell 2002; Sorj 2000; Rascussen 2000.

4. *O Dia*, July 22, 1998. Interestingly, this case reveals contrasts in black

political solidarity and the sensitivity of the records market to black consumers in the United States and Brazil. Tíririca's supporters throughout the court case included many black (negro) children and adults, including internationally known black musicians who testified on his behalf. Also, it is not likely that Sony Music, or any other reputable record producer, would have produced a song with such racist lyrics in the United States, and if they did it would certainly not raise such an ardent defense as it did in this case. Such actions would seem suicidal for any company's ability to compete in the U.S. market. The fact that Sony acted this way suggests that similar sanctions do not operate in the Brazilian market, and racial issues are remote to the interests of the huge North American record market, and to U.S. civil-rights groups, despite the rhetoric of Afro-diasporic brotherhood.

5. The well-known songs "O Teu Cabelo Não Nega" (Your Hair Doesn't Negate It) and "Nega de Cabelo Duro" (Hard-Haired Black Girl) were raised by the judge as prominent examples.

6. Estado do Rio de Janeiro, Poder Judiciario, 1a Vara Criminal de Jacarepaguá, Processo 11.257-Inquerito Policial. 1997.

7. *Folha de São Paulo,* July 9, 2001.

8. Winant 2001.

9. *Folha de São Paulo,* July 9, 2001.

10. Based on correspondence from James Cavallaro. Most cases against Brazil make use of an exception to domestic remedies that must be exhausted by claiming that cases against Brazil are generally unduly delayed.

11. "Violação de Direitos: Brasil é processado por violência policial e racismo," *Consultor Juridico,* February 15, 2002.

12. Letter signed by representatives of the affected communities, the Global Justice Center, the Human Rights Society of Maranhão, the Center for Black Rural Quilombo Communities of Maranhão, the Federation of Agricultural Workers in Maranhão, and Global Exchange, to Ambassador Sergio A. Canton, Executive Director of the Interamerican Commission of Human Rights, August 16, 2002.

13. J. Barbosa Gomes 2001.

14. See, for example, Ventura 2000.

15. Oliveira 1999. Incidentally, the advertising company denied being racist, alleging that it represented a reality in which nearly half of the prison population in the state was black. They also claimed that it was not depicting a black person since the photograph was of a Brazilian model whose birth certificate classifies him as white.

16. Schuman et al. 1997.

17. For an explanation of Colombia's experience, see Gutierrez and Ortega 2002.

18. Exceptionally, Brazil's economic stabilization in the mid-1990s significantly reduced poverty rates, but since then, poverty rates have remained at 35 percent of the national population. See Pães de Barros, Henriques, and Mendonça 2001; Baer 1995.

19. Marques 2002.

20. Wilson 1996.

21. Queiroz (2000) shows that 40 percent of browns and 48 percent of blacks in 2000 at the Federal University of Bahia graduated from public secondary schools, compared to 19 percent of whites. See also www.ufba.br/~acordaba.

22. There is also a political dimension built into such plans. By providing greater opportunities to students in poorer schools, it also holds the public system more accountable for providing quality education. If universities find that students from particular schools have particular problems, then the government should look to improve those schools.

23. Much of this diversity was created by the admission of students from schools that had rarely or never sent students to the University of Texas. For a review of this case, see Tienda et al. 2002.

24. Responding to critics of his strict universalist stance, Souza's ministry recently announced a program "to investigate access to higher education for 'afro-descendants and Brazilian Indians.'"

25. *Folha de São Paulo,* August 31, 2001.

26. Bowen and Bok 1998.

27. Figure 10.1 includes all persons declaring occupations and inequality is measured with odds ratios as described in chapter 5. Professional occupations in Brazil refer to the occupations described in chapter 5 and data are from the 1996 PNAD.

28. See E. Reis 2002 for empirical support of this argument.

29. *Gazeta Mercantil,* June 25, 2001.

30. Certainly, an increasing affirmation of blackness in Brazil may have occurred among a few college-educated nonwhites, who are especially aware of racism and the isolation that being black and middle class produces, but this has not necessarily translated into social polarization.

31. Barbosa Gomes 2001.

32. Instituto Sindical Interamericano 2002.

33. Guimarães 1999.

34. This denial of the role of racism by the left was a major factor in the dismantling of the Municipal Secretariat of Black Community Affairs in Belo Horizonte, according to Moreira 2002.

35. Telles 1996.

36. Young 1958.

37. Hauser 2001.

38. Gurnier and Sturm 2001.

39. Telles and Bailey 2002.

40. This represents about half of Brazil's black and brown population.

41. Ricupero 1993, 1998.

42. The ICERD also requires race to be based on self-classification, maintaining that this is an individual's right.

43. Presidential speech, December 20, 2001.

44. Bruce 1998; *Boston Globe* 1999.

45. Another 7.5 percent changed other stated characteristics, particularly veteran status and disability, that would have given them an affirmative-action preference.

46. Escóssia 2001a. Benedita da Silva had proposed a similar solution in the mid-1990s.

47. *Correio Brasiliense* 2002.

48. *O Globo* 2002.

49. The Brazilian law defining who is disabled more clearly defines qualifying disabilities.

50. At www.usdoj.gov/ert/oda/ada.hom1.htm.

51. Figures by Queiroz (2000), also available at www.ufba.br/~acordaba. It is important to note that prior to quotas many students at universities, including those that are fairly elite, are black or brown. However, representation varies widely by the competitiveness of the field of study. For example, 20 percent of undergraduate students in the Federal University of Rio de Janeiro are negros; and 32 percent at the University of Brasilia is negro, but they represent only a handful of medicine and engineering students. However, these numbers, which are surprising to many, raise the issue of whether darkening, for the first time, is desirable and occurring in the university context. Although we do not know for sure, these numbers could therefore be overestimating the number of negros, compared to those that are categorized as such in most other social contexts.

52. There are currently two bills being considered in Congress: one by Senator José Sarney, which proposes that 20 percent of university slots in all Brazilian universities and 20 percent of all civil-service posts go to blacks and browns; and Paulo Paim's Statute of Racial Equality which establishes more ambitious quotas for university, civil service, political parties, films, advertising, and TV programs, as well as reparations of about 102,000 Reais for all "afrodescendants," an obligatory course in the school curriculum on Africans and blacks in Brazil, an ombudsman for race in Congress, and land grants to descendants of *quilombos*.

53. Galap 1991.

54. For an example, see Gilroy 2000.

REFERENCES

Agier, Michael. 1992. "Ethno política: A Dinâmica do Espaço Afro-Bahiano." *Estudos Afro-Asiáticos* 22:99–116.

Allen, Walter, Margaret Hunter, and Edward Telles. 2000. "Skin Color, Income and Education: A Comparison of African Americans and Mexican Americans." *National Journal of Sociology* 12, no. 1 (Winter):129–80.

Allport, Gordon. 1954. *The Nature of Prejudice.* Boston: Beacon Press.

Almeida, Alfredo Wagner Berno de. 1998. "Quilombos: Tema e Problema." In *Jamary dos Pretos: Terra de Mocambeiros.* São Luis: Sociedade Maranhense de Direitos Humanos.

Almeida, Carlos Alberto. 2003. "The Determinants of Lula's Victory." Presentation at UCLA. June 6.

Andrews, George Reid. 1991. *Blacks and Whites in São Paulo, Brazil, 1888–1988.* Madison: University of Wisconsin.

———. 1992. "Racial Inequality in Brazil and the United States: A Statistical Comparison." *Journal of Social History* 26, no. 2:229–63.

Araújo, Ricardo Benzaquen de. 1994. *Guerra e Paz: Casa Grande e Senzala e a Obra de Gilberto Freyre nos Anos 30.* Rio de Janeiro: Editora 34.

Araújo, Zito Joel. 2000. *A Negação do Brasil: O Negro na Telenovela Brasileira.* São Paulo: Editora SENAC.

Azevedo, Thales de. [1966] 1996. *As Elites de Cor numa Cidade Brasileira: Um Estudo de Ascensão Social.* Salvador: Editora da Universidade Federal da Bahia.

Azevedo, Aluizio de. [1881] 1973. *O Mulato.* São Paulo: Livraria Martins Editora.

Azevedo, Célia Maria Marinho de. 1996. "O Abolicionismo Transatlântico e a Memória do Paraíso Racial Brasileiro." *Estudos Afro-Asiáticos* 30 (dezembro):151–62.

Bacelar, Jefferson. 2001. *A Hierarquia das Raças: Negros e Brancos em Salvador.* Rio de Janeiro: Pallas.

Bacha, Edmar L., and Lance Taylor. 1976. "The Unequalizing Spirit: A First Growth Model for Belindia." *Quarterly Journal of Economics* 90:197–218.

Baer, Werner. 1995. *The Brazilian Economy: Growth and Development.* 4th ed. Westport, CT: Praeger.

Bailey, Stanley. 2002. *Racial Boundaries and Racial Attitudes: An Examination of Public Opinion and Ideas about "Race" in Brazil.* Ph.D. dissertation, UCLA.

Bailey, Stanley, and Edward E. Telles. 2002. "Affirmation and Ambiguity in Brazilian Racial Classification." Unpublished manuscript.

Banco Interamericano de Desarrollo. 1996. "Procedimentos del Foro Sobre Alivio a la Pobreza en Comunidades Minoritarias en América Latina: Comunidades de Ancestría African." Washington, D.C. November 13–14.

Banton, Michael. 1998. *Racial Theories.* Cambridge: Cambridge University Press.

Barbosa Gomes, Joaquim B. 2000. "O Uso da Lei no Combate ao Racismo: Direitos Difusos e Ações Publicas." Pp. 389–410 in Antonio Sérgio A. Guimarães and Lynn Huntley (eds.) *Tirando a Máscara: Ensaios sobre o Racismo no Brasil.*
———. 2001. "Ação Afirmativa no Brasil." *Revista do Senado* 150.

Barbosa, Livia. 1999. *Igualdade e Meritocracia: A Etica do Desempenho nas Sociedades Modernas.* Rio de Janeiro: Editora Fundação Getúlio Vargas.

Baron, Harold. 1969. "The Web of Urban Racism." In *Institutional Racism in America,* ed. Louis Knowles, 134–76. Englewood Cliffs, NJ: Prentice Hall.

Barth, Fredrick. 1969. Introduction to *Ethnic Groups and Boundaries,* ed. Frederick Barth. Boston: Little, Brown.

Bastide, Roger, and Pierre Van den Berghe. 1957. "Stereotypes, Norms and Interracial Behavior in São Paulo, Brazil." *American Sociological Review* 22, no. 6:689–94.

Bastos, Elide Ruggai. 2001. "Brasil: Um Outro Ocidente? Gilberto Freyre e a Formação da Sociedade Brasileira." *Ciência e Trôpico* 29, no. 1:33–59.

Bento, Maria Aparecida Silva. 2000. "Igualdade e Diversidade no Trabalho." In *Ação Afirmativa e Diversidade no Trabalho: Desafios e Possibilidades,* ed. Maria Aparecida Bento Silva. São Paulo: Casa do Psicólogo.

Berkovich, Alicia. 1991. "Considerações Sobre a Fecundidade da População Negra no Brasil." In *Desigualdade no Brasil Contemporâneo,* ed. Peggy Lovell, Belo Horizonte: UFMG.

Berquó, Elza. 1990. "Como se Casam Brancos e Negros no Brasil." In *Desigualdade no Brasil Contemporâneo,* ed. Peggy Lovell, Belo Horizonte: UFMG.

Bertulio, Dora Lucia. 1996. "O Enfrentamento do Racismo em um Projeto Democratico: A Possibilidade Jurídica." In *Multiculturalismo e Racismo: O Papel da Ação Afirmativa nos Estados Democráticos Contemporâneos,* ed. Jessé Souza, 189–208. Brasília: Ministério da Justiça.

Blau, Peter, Terry C. Blum, and Joseph E. Schwartz. 1982. "Heterogeneity and Intermarriage." *American Sociological Review* 47:45–62.

Blumer, Herbert. 1965. "Industrialization and Race Relations." In *Industrialization and Race Relations,* ed. G. Hunter, 220–53. Oxford: Oxford University.

Bobo, Larry. 1989. "Keeping the Linchpin in Place: Testing the Multiple Sources of Opposition to Residential Integration." *Reme Internationale de Psychologie Sociale* 2, no. 3:307–25.

Boston Globe. 1999. " 'Fake Minorities' Re-Hired by City." February 8.

Bourdieu, Pierre, and Loïc Wacquant. 1999. "On the Cunning of Imperialist Reason." *Theory, Culture and Society.*

Bowen, William G., and Derek Bok. 1998. *The Shape of the River: Long-Term Consequences of Considering Race in College and University Admissions.* Princeton, NJ: Princeton University Press.

Boxer, Charles. 1969. *The Portuguese Seaborne Empire, 1415–1825.* London: Hutchinson.

Braga, Julio. 1999. "*Candomblé* in Bahia: Repression and Resistance." In *Black Brazil: Culture, Identity and Social Mobilization,* ed. Larry Crook and Randall Johnson. UCLA Latin American Center.

Brasil Ano 2000: O Futuro Sem Fantasia. 1969. Rio de Janeiro: Biblioteca do Exército Editôra.

Brown, Diana de G. 1994. *Umbanda: Religion and Politics in Urban Brazil.* New York: Columbia University Press.

Bruce, Tom. 1998. "Can You Prove You're a Minority?" *Seattle Times,* May 26.

Brysk, Allison. 1995. "Acting Globally: Indian Rights and International Politics in Latin America." In *Indigenous Peoples and Democracy in Latin America,* ed. Donna Lee Van Cott. New York: St. Martin's Press.

Burdick, John. 1998. *Blessed Anastacia: Women, Race, and Popular Christianity in Brazil.* London: Routledge.

Burns, E. Bradford. 1970. *A History of Brazil.* 2d ed. New York: Columbia University Press.

Butler, Kim D. 1998. *Freedoms Given, Freedoms Won: Afro Brazilians in Post-Abolition São Paulo and Salvador.* New Brunswick, NJ: Rutgers University Press.

Caetano, André. 2001. "Fertility Transition and the Diffusion of Female Sterilization in Northeastern Brazil: The Roles of Medicine and Politics." Paper presented at the 25th General Population Conference of the International Union for the Scientific Study of Population, Salvador, Brazil.

Caldeira, Teresa P. R. 2000. *City of Walls: Crime, Segregation and Citizenship in São Paulo.* Berkeley: University of California Press.

Cano, Ignacio. 2002. "Racial Bias in Lethal Police Action in Brazil." Unpublished manuscript.

Cano, Wilson. 2002. *Questão Regional e Política Econômica Nacional.* Paper presented at the Session on Brazilian Development. Banco Nacional de Desenvolvinento Ecônomico e Social, Brasilia.

Cardoso, Fernando Henrique. 1962. *Capitalismo e Escravidão no Brasil Meridional: O Negro na Sociedade Escravocrata do Rio Grande do Sul.* Ph.D. dissertation, University of São Paulo.

Cardoso, Fernando Henrique, and Octavio Ianni. 1960. *Côr e Mobilidade Social em Florianópolis.* São Paulo: Companhia Editora Nacional.

Carneiro, Sueli. 2001. "The Conference on Racism." *Correio Brasiliense,* July 2, 2000.

Carvalho, José Murilo de. 2004. "Elite and People in the Formation of Brazilian Identity: 1822–1870." Presentation at UCLA. February 28.

Carvalho, Olavo de. 1999. "Só preto, com preconceito." *República* 3, no. 32.

Carvalho-Silva, Denise R., et al. 2001. "The Phygeography of Brazilian Y-Chromosome Lineages." *American Journal of Human Genetics* 68:281–86.

Castro, Claudio de Moura. 1985. *Ciência e Universidade.* Rio de Janeiro: Zahar.
———. 2001. "Educação Superior e Eqüidade: Inocente ou Culpada?" *Ensaio: Avaliação de Politicas Públicas em Educação* 9 (30):109–22.

Castro, Hebe Maria Mattos de. 1995. *Das Cores do Silêncio: Os Significados da Liberdade no Sudeste Escravista—Brasil Século XIX.* Rio de Janeiro: Arquivo Nacional.

Castro, Nadya Aráujo, and Antonio Sérgio Alfredo Guimarães. 1992. "Desigualdades Raciais no Mercado de Trabalho: Examinando a Indústria Moderna em Salvador." Paper presented at the Latin American Studies Association meetings, Sept. 24–27, Los Angeles.

Cavalleiro, Eliane. 2000. *Do Silêncio do Lar ao Silêncio Escolar: Racismo, Discriminação, e Preconceito na Educação Infantil*. São Paulo: Editora Contexto.

Cavalleiro, Eliane dos Santos. 2000. "Discursos e Práticas Racistas na Educação Infantil: A Produção da Submissão Social e do Fracasso Escolar." In *Educação, Racismo e Anti-Racismo*, ed. Jócelio Teles dos Santos. Salvador: Novos Toques.

Cherlin, Andrew. 2002. *Public and Private Families*. Boston: McGraw Hill.

Cohen, Anthony. 1994. *Self Consciousness: An Alternative Anthropology of Identity*. New York: Routledge.

Cornell, Stephen. 1996. "The Variable Ties that Bind: Content and Circumstances in Ethnic Processes." *Ethnic and Racial Studies* 19, no. 2 (April):265–89.

Correio Brasiliense. 2002. "Entrevista com José Jorge de Carvalho." February 27.

Costa, Emilia Viotti da. [1985] 2000. *The Brazilian Empire: Myths and Histories*. Chapel Hill: University of North Carolina Press.

Costa, Haroldo. 1982. *Fala, Crioulo: Depoimentos*. Rio de Janeiro: Record.

Curtin, Phillip. 1969. *The Atlantic Slave Trade: A Census*. Madison: University of Wisconsin Press.

D'Adesky, Jacques. 2001. *Pluralismo Étnico e Multiculturalismo: Racismos e Anti-Racismos no Brasil*. Rio de Janeiro: Pallas.

Damasceno, Caetana. 2000. "Em Casa de Enforcado não se fala em Corda: Notas sobre a Construção Social da Boa Aparência no Brasil." In *Tirando a Máscara: Ensaios sobre o Racismo no Brasil*, ed. Antonio Sérgio A. Guimarães and Lynn Huntley, 165–99. São Paulo: Paz e Terra.

Da Matta, Roberto. [1978] 1991. *Carnivals, Rogues and Heroes: An Interpretation of the Brazilian Dilemna*. South Bend, IN: Notre Dame University Press.

———. 1996. "Notas sobre o racismo à brasileira." In *Multiculturalismo e Racismo: O Papel da Ação Afirmativa nos Estados Democráticos Contemporâneos*, ed. Jesse Souza. Brasília: Ministério de Justiça.

Darity Jr., William A., and Patrick L. Mason. 1998. "Evidence on Discrimination in Employment: Codes of Color, Codes of Gender." *Journal of Economic Perspectives* 12, no. 2:63–90.

Davis, Darien. 1999. "Afro-Brazilians: Time for Recognition." *Minority Groups International*, December.

Davis, F. James. 1991. *Who is Black? One Nation's Definition*. University Park, PA: Pennsylvania State University Press.

Davis, Kinsley. 1941. "Intermarriage in Caste Societies." *American Anthropologist* 43:358–95.

Degler, Carl N. [1971] 1986. *Neither Black nor White: Slavery and Race Relations in Brazil and the United States*. Madison: University of Wisconsin.

Dulitzky, Ariel E. 2000. "Assessment of the International Human Rights Law Group: Brazil Mission." Washington, D.C.: International Human Rights Law Group.

Durham, Eunice Ribeiro, and Simon Schwartzman. 1989. "Situação e Perspectiva do Ensino Superior no Brasil: Os Resultados de Um Seminário." Working paper, Nucleo Sobre Ensino Superior, Universidade de São Paulo.

Dzidzenyo, Anani. 1999. "African-Brazil: Ex-African Semper Aliquid Novi." In *Black Brazil: Culture, Identity and Social Mobilization*, ed. Larry Crook and Randall Johnson, 105–42. Los Angeles: UCLA Latin American Center.

Encontro Nacional de Parlamentares Negros. 2001. "Carta de Salvador". July 26–28.

Erikson, Erik H. 1968. *Identity, Youth and Crisis.* New York: Norton.

Escóssia, Fernanda da. 2001a. "Determinar quem é negro vira polêmica na lei sobre cotas do Rio." *Folha de São Paulo,* November 16.

———. 2001b. "Analista acha difícil adoção no Brasil." *Folha de São Paulo,* August 25, A13.

Evans, Peter. 1979. *Dependent Development: The Alliance of Multinational, State and Local Capital in Brazil.* Princeton, NJ: Princeton University Press.

Farley, Reynolds. 1984. *Blacks and Whites: Narrowing the Gap?* Cambridge, MA: Harvard University Press.

Farley, Reynolds, and Walter Allen. 1987. *The Quality of Life and the Color Line in America.* Oxford: Oxford University Press.

Fernandes, Florestan. 1965. *A Integração do Negro na Sociedade de Classes* [The Integration of Blacks into Class Society]. São Paulo: Dominus Editora.

Fix, Michael, and Raymond J. Struyck. 1997. *Clear and Convincing Evidence: Measurement of Discrimination in America.* Washington, D.C.: The Urban Institute.

Folha de São Paulo. 1995. "A Cor do Brasilero," p. 5 in *Caderno Especial.*

Folha de São Paulo. 1999. " Os dez mais brasileiros." April 11, section 5.

Folha de São Paulo. 2001. "A Política de inclusão do negro e a penal: Entrevista com Hedio Silva Jr." July 9.

Folha de São Paulo. 2001. "Governo e Delegação do Brasil divergem." August 31.

Folha de São Paulo. 2001. "Rio dá a negros e pardos 40% das vagas." October 10.

Folha de São Paulo. 2001. "Ministério de Justiça Cria Cotas Para Negro, Mulher e Deficiente." December 20.

Foner, Eric. 2003. "Diversity over Justice." *The Nation* 277, no. 2 (July 14):4–5.

Frazier, Franklin E. 1942. "Some Aspects of Race Relations in Brazil." *Phylon* (3rd quarter):287–95.

French, John. 2000. "The Missteps of Anti-Imperalist Reason: Bourdieu, Wacquant and Hanchard's Orpheus and Power." *Theory, Culture and Society* 17, no. 1.

Freyre, Gilberto. [1933] 1986. *The Masters and the Slaves: A Study in the Development of Brazilian Civilization.* Berkeley: University of California Press. Published in Portuguese as *Casa Grande e Senzala.*

———. 1937. *Nordeste: Aspectos da Influência da Cana Sobre a Vida e a Paissagem do Nordeste do Brasil.* Rio de Janeiro: Jose Olympio.

———. 1945. *Brazil: An Interpretation.* New York: Knopf.

———. 1962. "Forças Armadas. Outras Forças." Recife: Imprensa Oficial.

Fry, Peter. 1977. "Feijoada e Soul Food." *Cadernos de Opinião* 4:13–23. São Paulo.

Furtado, Celso. 1961. *Formação Econômica do Brasil.* São Paulo: Companhia Editora Nacional.

Galap, Jean. 1991. "Phenotypes et Discrimination des Noirs en France: Question de Methode." *Intercultures* 14 (Juillet):21–35.

Gans, Herbert. 1999. "The Possibility of a New Racial Hierarchy in the Twenty-First Century United States." In *The Cultural Territories of Race: Black and White Boundaries,* ed. Michelle Lamont, 371–90.

Gaspari, Elio. 2002. "O Pais." *O Globo,* August 12.

Gazeta Mercantil. 2001. "Duas Versões do Racismo." June 25. www.investnews. net.

Gilroy, Paul. 2000. *Against Race: Imagining Political Culture Beyond the Color Line.* Cambridge, MA: Harvard University Press.

Global Justice Center. 2000. "Torture in Brazil." In *Global Justice Center Human Rights in Brazil 2000.*

Goffman, Erving. 1959. *The Presentation of Self in Everyday Life.* New York: Doubleday.

Goldani, Ana Maria. 1989. *Women's Transitions: The Intersection of Female Life Course, Family and Demographic Transitions in the Twentieth Century Brazil.*" Ph.D. dissertation, University of Texas, Austin, TX.

——1999. "O Regime Demográfico Brasileiro nos anos 90: Desigualdades, Restricões e Oportunidades Demográficas." In *Saúde Sexual e Reproductiva no Brasil,* ed. Loreon Galvão and Juan Diaz. São Paulo: HUCITEC and Population Council.

Goldberg, David Theo. 2002. *The Racial State.* Malden, MA: Blackwell.

Goldstein, Donna. 1999. "Interracial Sex and Racial Democracy in Brazil: Twin Concepts?" *American Anthropologist* 101 (3):563–78.

Gordon, Milton. 1964. *Assimilation in American Life: The Role of Race, Religion and National Origins.* Oxford: Oxford University Press.

Gore, Charles, and José B. Figueredo. 1997. *Social Exclusion and Anti-Poverty Policy: A Debate.* Geneva: International Labor Organization.

Graham, Lawrence, ed. 1990. *The Idea of Race in Latin America,* Austin: University of Texas Press.

Guimarães, Antonio Sergio. 1998. *Preconceito e Discriminação: Queixas de Ofensas e Tratamento desigual dos Negros no Brasil.* Salvador: Novos Toques.

——. 1999. *Racismo e Anti-Racismo no Brasil* [Racism and Anti-Racism in Brazil]. São Paulo: Editora 34.

——. 2002. "Democracia Racial: O Ideal, O Pacto e O Mito." Unpublished manuscript, University of São Paulo.

Guinier, Lani, and Susan Sturm. 2001. "The Future of Affirmative Action." In *Who's Qualified,* ed. Lani Guinier and Susan Sturm. Boston: Beacon Press.

Gutierrez, Enrique Sanchez, and Roque Roldán Ortega. 2002. "Titulación de los territorios comunales afrocolombianos e indígenas en la Costa Pacifica de Colombia." Dirección Sectorial para el Desarrollo Social y Ecologicamente Sostenible de la Oficina Regional de America Latina y el Caribe del Banco Mundial.

Hagopian, Frances. 1996. *Traditional Political and Regime Change in Brazil.* Cambridge: Cambridge University Press.

Haller, Archibald O. 1982. "A Socio-Economic Regionalization of Brazil." *Geographic Review* 72:450–64.

Halloway, Thomas H. 1980. *Immigrants on the Land.* Chapel Hill: University of North Carolina Press.

Hanchard, Michael George. 1994. *Orpheus and Power: The Movimento Negro in Rio de Janeiro and São Paulo, Brazil, 1945–1988.* Princeton, NJ: Princeton University Press.

————. 2003. "Acts of Misrecognition: Brazil and Transnational Black Politics." *Theory, Culture and Society,* 20 (4):5–30.

Harper's Magazine. 2002. "Weekly Review." June 4.

Harris, Marvin. 1952. "Race Relations in Minas Velhas, a Community in the Mountain Region of Central Brazil." In *Race and Class in Rural Brazil,* ed. Charles Wagley, 47–81. Paris: UNESCO.

————. 1963. "Racial Identity in Brazil." *Luso-Brazilian Review* 1:21–28.

————. 1970. "Referential Ambiguity in the Calculus of Brazilian Racial Identity." *Southwestern Journal of Anthropology* 26, no. 1:1–14.

Harris, Marvin, and Conrad Kottack. 1963. "The Structural Significance of Brazilian Categories." *Sociologia* 25, no. 3:203–208.

Harris, Marvin, Josildeth Gomes Consorte, Joseph Long, and Byran Byrne. 1993. "Who Are the Whites?: Imposed Census Categories and the Racial Demography of Brazil." *Social Forces* 72:451–62.

Hasenbalg, Carlos. 1979. *Discriminação e Desigualdades Raciais no Brasil* [Discrimination and Inequality in Brazil]. Rio de Janeiro, Brazil: Graal. Translation of *Race Relation in Post-Abolition Brazil: The Smooth Preservation of Racial Inequalities.* Ph.D. dissertation, University of California, Berkeley, 1978.

————. 1985. "Race and Socioeconomic Inequalities in Brazil." In *Race, Class and Power in Brazil,* ed. Pierre-Michel Fontain. Los Angeles: Center for Afro American Studies, UCLA.

Hasenbalg, Carlos, and Nelson do Valle Silva. 1991. "Raça e Oportunidades Educacionais no Brasil." In *Desigualdade Racial no Brasil Contemporâneo,* ed. Peggy Lovell. Belo Horizonte: UFMG.

Hauser, Robert M. 2001. "Meritocracy, Cognitive Ability and the Sources of Occupational Success." Working paper, University of Wisconsin.

Heringer, Rosana. 2000. "Mapeamento das Ações e Discursos de Combate As Desigualdades Raciais no Brasil." *Estudos Afro-Asiaticos.*

Holtzer, Harry. 2001. "Racial Differences in Labor Market Outcomes among Men." In *America Becoming: Racial Trends and their Consequences,* ed. Neil J. Smelser, William Julius Wilson, and Faith Mitchell, 98–123. Vol. 2. Washington: National Academy of Sciences Press.

Holtzer, Harry and David Newhart. 2000. "Assessing Affirmative Action." *Journal of Economic Literature* 38:483–95.

Hutchinson, Harry William. 1957. *Village and Plantation Life in Northeastern Brazil.* Seattle: University of Washington Press.

Ianni, Octavio. [1970] 1987. *Raça e Classes Sociais no Brasil.* Rio de Janeiro: Civilização Brasileira.

Instituto Brasileiro de Geografia a Estatística, Conselho Nacional de Estatística. 1961. *Contribuições Para O Estudo da Demografia do Brasil.* Rio de Janeiro.

Instituto Ethos de Empresas e Responsabilidade Social. 2000. *Como As Empreseas Podem (e Devem) Valorizar a Diversidade.* São Paulo.

Instituto Sindical Interamericano pela Igualdade Racial. 1999. *Mapa da População Negra no Mercado de Trabalho.* São Paulo: DIESSE.

Instituto Sindical Interamericano pela Igualdade Racial. 2002. "Brasil e as Ações Afirmativas." Unpublished.

Jackman, Mary D. 1994. *The Velvet Glove: Paternalism and Conflict in Gender, Class and Race Relations*. Berkeley: University of California Press

Jacobson, Cardell K., Yaw Amoateng, and Tim B. Heaton. 2001. "Inter-racial Marriages in South Africa." Paper presented at the annual meetings of the American Sociological Association, Anaheim.

Jenkins, Richard. 1998. *Rethinking Ethnicity: Arguments and Explorations*. London: Sage.

Johnson III, Ollie A. 1996. "Black Participation in Brazilian Politics." *Journal of Interamerican Studies and World Affairs* 40, no. 4:97–118.

Kahlenberg, Richard. 1996. *The Remedy: Class, Race and Affirmative Action*. New York: Basic Books.

Kahn, Tulio. 2002. "Atrás das Grades: Radiografia e Alternativas ao Sistema Prisional." Unpublished manuscript.

Keith, Verna, and Cedric Herring. 1991. "Skin Tone Stratification in the Black Community." *American Journal of Sociology* 97:760–78.

Klein, Ruben, and S. C. Ribeiro. 1991. "A Pedagogia da Repetência." *Estudos Avançados* 5, no. 12:7–22.

Kottack, Conrad Phillip. 1995. *Assault on Paradise: Social Change in a Brazilian Village*. New York: Random House.

Lam, David. 2000. "Generating Extreme Inequality: Schooling, Earnings, and Intergenerational Transmission of Human Capital in South Africa and Brazil." Paper presented at the annual meetings of the Population Association of America, May.

La Pastina, Antonio C., Dhaval S. Patel, and Marcio Schiavo. 2004. "Social Merchandizing in Brazilian Telenoveles." In *Entertainment—Education and Social Change: History, Research and Practice,* ed. A. Singhal, M. Cody, E. Rogers, and M. Sabido. New Jersey: Lawrence Erlbaum Associates.

Lazo, Aida C. G. Verdugo. 2001. "Nupcialidade nas PNADs—90. Um Tema em Extinção?" Unpublished paper. Escola Nacional de Ciencias Estatísticas (ENCE), Rio de Janeiro.

Lee, Sharon M. 2001. "Using the New Racial Categories in the 2000 Census." The Anne E. Casey Foundation and the Population Reference Bureau, March.

Leeds, Anthony. 1974. "Housing Settlement Types, Arrangements for Living, Proletarianization, and the Social Structure of the City." In *Latin American Urban Urbanization,* ed. Wayne Cornelius and Felicity M. Trueblood. Beverly Hills: Sage.

Lesser, Jeffery. 1995. *Welcoming the Undesirables: Brazil and the Jewish Question*. Berkeley: University of California Press.

———. 1999. *Negotiating National Identity: Immigrants, Minorities, and the Struggle for Ethnicity in Brazil*. Durham, NC: Duke University Press.

Light, Ivan, and Stephan Gold. 1999. *Ethnic Economies*. San Diego: Academic Press.

Lombardo, Paul A. 1996. "Medicine, Eugenics and the Supreme Court: From Coercive Sterilization to Reproductive Freedom." *The Journal of Contemporary Health Law and Policy* 13 (Fall):1–25.

Lopes, Juarez R. Brandão. 1989. "Um Estudo Socioeconomico da Indigência e da Pobreza Urbana." Unpublished manuscript.

Lovell, Peggy. 1989. *Income and Racial Inequality in Brazil.* Ph.D. dissertation, University of Florida, Gainesville, FL.

Maciel, Marco. 1996. "Joaquim Nabuco e a Inclusão Social." In *Anais do Seminario Internacional Multiculturalismo e Racismo: O Papel da Ação Afirmativa nos Estados Contemporâneos Democráticos,* ed. Jessé Souza. Brasilia: Ministry of Justice.

Maggie, Yvonne. 1991. *A Ilusão do Concreto. Análise do Sistema de Classificação no Brasil.* Ph.D. dissertation, Universidade Federal do Rio de Janeiro, Rio de Janeiro.

———. 2000. "Movimento de Prevestibulares para Negros e Carentes." Unpublished paper.

Marques, Luiz. 2002. "Why Can't They Read?" Braudel Papers. São Paulo: Fernard Braudel Institute of World Economics.

Martinez-Alier, Verena. 1989. *Marriage, Class and Colour in Nineteenth Century Cuba: A Study of Racial Attitudes and Sexual Values in a Slave Society.* Ann Arbor: University of Michigan.

Marx, Anthony. 1998. *Making Race and Nation: A Comparison of the United States, South Africa and Brazil.* Cambridge: Cambridge University Press.

Massey, Douglas, and Nancy Denton. 1994. *American Apartheid: Segregation and the Making of the Black Underclass.* Cambridge, MA: Harvard University Press.

Mattory, J. Lorand. 1999. "The English Professors of Brazil: On the Diasporic Roots of the Yòrubá Nation." *Comparative Studies in Society and History* 41 (1):72–103.

Merrick, Thomas W., and Richard Graham. 1979. *Population and Economic Development in Brazil: 1800 to the Present.* Baltimore: Johns Hopkins University Press.

Merton, Robert. 1941. "Intermarriage and the Social Structure." *Psychiatry* 4:361–74.

Mínistério da Justiça. 1996. *Programa a Nacional de Direitor Humanos.* Brasilia, Brasil.

Mínistério da Justiça e Mínistério das Relações Exteriores. 1996. *Décimo Relatório Periódico Relativo à Convenção Internacional Sobre a Eliminação de Todos as Formas de Discriminação Racial.* Brasilia, Brasil.

Mínistério da Justiça, Grupo de Trabalho Interministerial para Valorização da População Negra. 1997. *Realizações e Perspectivas.* Brasil. May.

Mitchell, Michael. 1985. "Blacks and the Abertura Democratica." In *Race, Class and Power in Brazil,* ed. Pierre-Michel Fontain. Los Angeles: UCLA Center for Afro-American Studies.

———. 1999. "Scientific and Legal Discourses in Brazil and the United States." Paper presented at the Third Meeting of the Network of Brazilian Legal Professionals to Combat Racial Discrimination, Florianópolis, May 24–27.

———. 2002. "Anti-Discrimination Litigation and Judicial Reform in Brazil." Paper presented at the American Political Science Association, Boston, August 29–September 1.

Mitchell, Michael, and Charles Wood. 1998. "Ironies of Citizenship: Skin Color, Police Brutality and the Challenge to Democracy in Brazil." *Social Forces* 77 no. 3:1,001–1,020.

Moises, Jose Alvaro. 1997. "A Cultura Brasileira Hoje." *Correio Braziliense,* September 15.

Moreira, Diva. 2002. "The Possibility and Limits of State Intervention in Promoting Racial Equality: The Experience of the Department for Black Community Affairs, Belo Horizonte." Unpublished manuscript.

Morley, Helena. 1948. *Minha Vida de Menina: Cadernos de Uma Menina Provinciana nos Fins do Século XIX.* Rio de Janeiro: José Olympio.

Motta, Roberto. 2000. "Paradigms in the Study of Race Relations in Brazil." *International Sociology* 15, no. 4.

Nascimento, Abdiasdo. 1950. *Relações de Raça no Brasil.* Rio de Janeiro: Quilombo.

———. 1978. *O Genocídio do Negro Brasileiro.* Rio de Janeiro: Editora Paz e Terra.

Nobles, Melissa. 2000. *Shades of Citizenship: Race and the Census in Modern Politics.* Stanford, CA: Stanford University Press.

Nogueira, Oracy [1955] 1995. *Tanto Preto Quanto Branco: Estudos de Relações Raciais.* Sao Paulo: T.A. Queoroz.

O Dia. 2002. "Racismo Hipocrita." August 22.

O Globo. 2002. "UERJ e UNEF Terão Cotas para Negros e Pardos." March 6.

Oliveira, Iolanda. 1999. *Desigualdades Raciais: Construções da Infância e da Juventude.* Niteroi: Intertexto.

Oliveira, Lucia Elena Garcia de, Rosa Maria Porcaro, and Teresa Cristina N. Aráujo Costa. 1983. *O Lugar do Negro na Força do Trabalho.* Rio de Janeiro: Fundação Instituto Brasileiro de Geografia e Estatistica.

Oliveira, Marcelo. 1999. "Juiz veta outdoor considerado racista." *Folha de São Paulo,* July 30.

Oliver, Melvin L., and Thomas M. Shapiro. 1995. *Black Wealth, White Wealth.* London: Routledge.

Omi, Micheal, and Howard Winant. 1986. *Racial Formation in the United States: From the 1960's to the 1980's.* New York: Routledge and Kegan Paul.

Ortiz, Renato. 1978. *A Morte Branca do Feiticeiro Negro.* Petropolis: Vozes.

Pacheco, Moema de Poli Teixeira. 1989. "As Desigualdade Raciais em Dois Tipos de Família." *Estudos Afro-Asiáticos* 16:198–226.

———. 1987. "A questão da cor nas relações raciais de um grupo de baixa renda." *Estudos Afro-Asiáticos* 14:85–97.

Pães de Barros, Ricardo, Ricardo Henriques, and Roseanne Mendonça. 2001. "A Estabilidade Inaceitavel: Desigualdade e Pobreza no Brasil." IPEA discussion paper no. 150 (June).

Park, Robert. [1938] 2000. "The Nature of Race Relations." In *Theories of Race and Racism,* ed. Les Back and John Solomos. London: Routledge.

Pastore, José. 1982. *Social Mobility in Brazil.* Madison: University of Wisconsin Press.

Pastore, José, and Nelson do Valle Silva. 2000. *Mobilidade Social no Brasil.* São Paulo: Makron Books.

Pena, Sérgio P. J., Denise R. Carvalho-Silva, Juliana Alves-Silva, Vânia F. Prado, and Fabrício R. Santos. 2000. "Retrato Molecular do Brasil." *Ciência Hoje* (Abril):17–25.

Pereira, Amauri Mendes. 1998. "A Marcha que Mudou o Movimento Negro." *Jornal Questões Negras* 1 (November):6.

Petruccelli, José Luis. 2001. "Seletividade por Cor e Escolhas Conjugais no Brasil dos 90." *Revista de Estudos Afro-Asiáticos* 23, no. 1.

Pettigrew, Thomas. 1979. "Racial Change and Social Policy." *Annals of the American Academy of Political and Social Science* 441:114–31.

Pierson, Donald. [1942] 1967. *Negroes in Brazil: A Study of Race Contact at Bahia.* Carbondale IL: Southern Illinois University Press.

Pinto, Luis A. Costa. [1953] 1998. *O Negro no Rio de Janeiro: Relações de Raças em uma Sociedade em Mudança.* Rio de Janeiro: Editora UFRJ.

Pinto, Regina Pahim. 1996. "Classifying the Brazilian Population by Color: Underlying Problems." In *Brazilian Issues on Education, Gender, and Race,* ed. Elba Siquera de Sa Barreto and Dagmar M.L. Zibas. São Paulo: The Carlos Chagas Foundation.

Piovesan, Flavia, James Louis Cavallaro, Jamie Benvenuto Lima Jr., José Fernando da Silva, Luciano Oliveira, and Valdenia Brito. 2001. *Execuções Sumárias, Arbitrárias ou Extrajudiciais, Uma Aproximação da Realidade Brasileira.* Recife: Companhia Editora de Pernambuco.

Prandi, Reginaldo. 1995. "Raça e Religião." *Novos Estudos* 42 (July).

Queiroz, Delcele Mascarenhas. 2000. "Desigualdades raciais no ensino superior: a cor da UFBA." In *Educação, Racismo e Anti-Racismo,* ed. Jócelio Teles dos Santos. Salvador: Novos Toques.

Raeders, George. 1976. *O Conde de Gobineau no Brasil: Documentação Inédita.* São Paulo: Secretaria da Cultura, Ciência e Tecnologia, Conselho Estadual da Cultura. First printed in French in 1934 as *Le Conte de Gobineau au Brésil.* Paris: Nouvelles Editions Latins.

Rascussen, Seth. 2000. "Race, Nation and Justice: Punishing Prejudice in a Racial Democracy." Paper presented to the Latin American Studies Association meeting, Washington, D.C., September 6–8.

———. 2003. "The Ideology of the Brazilian Nation and the Brazilian Legal Theory of Racial Discrimination." Paper presented to the Latin American Studies Association, Dallas, March 27–29.

Ravazzolli, Simone. 2002. "Cotas Para Negros." *Correio Brasiliense,* May 12.

Reis, Elisa P. 2002. "Perceptions of Poverty among Brazilian Elites." Paper presented at the International Sociological Association meetings, Brisbane, Australia, July.

Reis, Fabio Wanderbey. 1996. "Mito e Valor da Democracia Racial." In *Multiculturalismo e Racismo: O Papel da Ação Afirmativa nos Estados Democraticos Contemporâneos,* ed. Jessé Souza. Brasilia: Ministério de Justiça.

Reis, João. 2002. "Slavery in Nineteenth-Century Bahia." Paper presented at UCLA, May 19.

Resnick, Barbara. 1998. *The Realities of Affirmative Action in Employment.* Washington, D.C.: American Sociological Association.

Revista Tudo. 2001. "A Vergonha do Racismo." November.

Ribeiro, Luiz Cesar de Queiroz, and Edward E. Telles. 2000. "Rio de Janeiro: Emerging Dualization in a Historically Unequal City." In *Globalizing Cities,* ed. Peter Marcuse and Ronald van Kempen. London: Basil Blackwell.

Ribeiro, Neli Góes, and Paulino de Jesus F. Cardoso. 1997. "Racismo, multiculturalismo e currículo escolar." In Ivan Costa Lima and Jeruse Romão (eds.) *Negros e Currículo.* Florianópolis: Nucleo de Estudos Negros.

Ricupero, Rubens. "Racial Hegemony in Brazil." *Washington Post,* August 30, 1993.

Ricupero, Rubens. 1998. "A Africa Civiliza a America." *Folha de São Paulo,* March 28.

Rocha, Sonia. 1993. "Renda e Pobreza nas Metrópoles Brasileiras." In *Globalização, Fragmentação e Reforma Urbana,* ed. Luiz Cesar Ribeiro. Rio de Janeiro: Civilização Brasileira.

Rodrigues, João Jorge Santos. 1999. "Olodum and the Black Struggle in Brazil." In *Black Brazil: Culture, Identity and Social Mobilization,* ed. Larry Crook and Randall Johnson, 43–52. Los Angeles: UCLA Latin American Center.

Rolnick, Raquel. 1989. "Territórios Negros nas Cidades Brasileiras: Etnicadade e Cidade em São Paulo e Rio de Janeiro." *Estudos Afro-Asiaticos* 17:29–41.

———. 1999. *Territorial Exclusion and Violence: The Case of São Paulo.* Woodrow Wilson Intermedial Center for Scholars. Washington, D.C.

Rosemberg, Fulvia. 1991. "Segregação Espacial na Escola Paulista." In *Desigualdade no Brasil Contemporâneo,* ed. Peggy Lovell. Belo Horizonte: UFMG.

Rosemberg, Fulvia, et al. 1993. *A Classificação de Cor no Brasil.* Unpublished manuscript.

Russell-Wood, A.J.R. 1982. *The Black Man in Slavery and Freedom.* London: MacMillan.

Sansone, Livio. 1993. "Pai Preto, Filho Negro: Trabalho, Cor e Diferenças Geracionais." *Estudos Afro-Asiaticos* 25:73–98.

———. 1996. "Nem Somente Preto ou Negro. O Sistema da Classificação da Cor no Brasil Que Muda." *Afro-Asia* 18:165–88.

———. 1997. "The New Politics of Black Culture in Bahia, Brazil." In *The Politics of Ethnic Consciousness,* ed. Cora Govers and Hans Vermuellen, 227–309. New York: St. Martin's Press.

———. 1999. *From Africa to Afro: Use and Abuse of África in Brazil.* Amsterdam: South-South Exchange Program for Research on the History of Development (SEPHIS).

———. 2003. *Blackness without Ethnicity: The Local and Global in Black Cultural Production and Race Relations in Brazil.* New York: Palgrave.

Santa Anna, Wania. 2001. "Desigualdades Étnico/raciais e de Gênero no Brasil— As Revelações Possíveis do Índice de Desenvolvimento Ajustado por Gênero," *Proposta* 88/89.

Santa Anna, Wania, and Marcello Paixão. 1997. "Desenvolvimento Humano e População Afro-descendente: Uma Questão de Raça." *Proposta* 26, no. 73.

Santos, Jocelio Teles dos. 2000. *O Poder da Cultura, a Cultura do Poder: A Disputa Simbólica da Herança Negra no Brasil.* Ph.D. dissertation, Department of Sociology, University of São Paulo, São Paulo.

Scheper-Hughes, Nancy. 1992. *Death Without Weeping: The Violence of Everyday Life in Brazil.* Berkeley: University of California Press.

Schnore, Leo F. 1965. "On the Spatial Structure of Cities in the Two Americas." In *The Study of Urbanization,* ed. P. M. Hauser and L. F. Schnore, 347–98. New York: Wiley.

Schuman, Howard, Charlotte Steeh, Lawrence Bobo, and Maria Krysan. 1997. *Racial Attitudes in America: Trends and Interpretations.* Cambridge, MA: Harvard University Press.

Schwartz, Lilia Moritz. 1993. *O Espectáculo das Raças: Cientistas Instituições e Questão Racial no Brasil, 1870–1930.* São Paulo: Companhia das Letras.

Schwartz, Stuart. 1974. "The Manumission of Slaves in Colonial Brazil: Bahia 1684–1745." *The Hispanic American Historical Review* 54, no. 4 (November):603–35.

———. 1992. *Slaves, Peasants and Rebels.* Urbana: University of Illinois Press.

Schwartzman, Simon. 1999. "Fora de Foco: Diversidade e Identidades Étnicas no Brasil." *Novos Estudos CEBRAP* 55 (Nov.):83–96.

Sheriff, Robin E. 2001. *Dreaming Equality: Color, Race and Racism in Urban Brazil.* New Brunswick, NJ: Rutgers University Press.

Silva, Hedio, Jr. 1998a. *Anti-Racismo: Coletânea de Leis Brasileiras (Federais, Estaduais e Municipais).* São Paulo: Oliveira Mendes.

———. 1998b. "Crônica da Culpa Anunciada." In *A Cor do Medo,* ed. Dijaci David de Oliveira et al. Brasília: Universidade de Brasília.

Silva, Nelson do Valle. 1978. *White-Nonwhite Income Differentials: Brazil.* Ph.D. dissertation, University of Michigan.

———. 1985. "Updating the Cost of Not Being White in Brazil." In *Race, Class and Power in Brazil,* ed. P.-M. Fontaine, 42–55. Los Angeles: UCLA Center for Afro-American Studies.

———. 1987. "Distância Social e Casamento Inter-Racial no Brasil." *Estudos Afro-Asiaticos* 14:54–84.

———. 1999. "Desigualdades Raciais e Ciclos de Vida." In *A Cor da Desiguldade: Desigualdades Raciais no Mercado de Trabalho e Acão Afirmativa no Brasil,* ed. Rosana Heringer, 31–37. Rio de Janeiro: Instituto de Estudos Racias e Etnicos (ICRE).

Skidmore, Thomas. 1974. *Black into White: Race and Nationality in Brazilian Thought.* New York: Oxford University Press.

———. 1985. "Race and Class in Brazil: Historical Perspectives." In *Race, Class and Power in Brazil,* ed. Pierre-Michel Fontain. Los Angeles: UCLA Center for Afro-American Studies.

———. 1993. "Biracial U.S.A. vs. Multiracial Brazil: Is the Contrast Still Valid?" *Journal of Latin American Studies* 25:373–86.

———. 1999. *Brazil: Five Centuries of Change.* New York: Oxford University Press.

Slenes, Robert W. 1999. *Na Senzala, Uma Flor: Esperanças e Recordações na Formação da Família Escrava-Brasil, Sudeste, Século XIX.* Rio de Janeiro: Nova Fronteira.

Smelser, Neil, William Julius Wilson, Alfred Blumstein. 2001. "Race and Criminal Justice." In *America Becoming: Racial Trends and Their Consequences,* ed.

Neil J. and Faith Michell, ch. 2. Vol 2. Washington D.C: National Academy Press.

Sorj, Bernardo. 2000. *A Nova Sociedade Brasileira.* Rio de Janeiro: Jorge Zahar.

South, Scott, and Steven F. Messner. 1986. "Structural Determinants of Intergroup Association: Interracial Marriage and Crime." *American Journal of Sociology* 91, no. 6:1409–30.

Souza, Jessé. 1996. "Multiculturalismo, Racismo e Democracia: Porque Comparar Brasil e Estados Unidos?" In *Multiculturalismo e Racismo: O Papel da Ação Afirmativa nos Estados Democráticos Contemporâneos,* ed. Jessé Souza. Brasilia: Ministério de Justiçia.

Sparks, Alistair. 1990. *The Mind of South Africa.* New York: Knopf.

Spitzer, Leo. 1989. *Lives in Between: The Experience of Marginality in a Century of Emancipation.* Cambridge: Cambridge University Press.

Staley, Austin. 1959. *Racial Democracy in Marriage: A Sociological Analysis of Negro-White Marriage in Brazilian Culture.* Ph.D. dissertation, University of Pittsburgh.

Stam, Robert. 1997. *Tropical Multiculturalism: A Comparative History of Race in Brazilian Cinema and Culture.* Durham, NC: Duke University Press.

Steinberg, Stephen. 1991. *The Ethnic Myth: Race, Ethnicity and Class in America.* Boston: Beacon Press.

Stepan, Nancy Leys. 1991. *The Hour of Eugenics: Race, Class and Nation in Latin America.* Ithaca, NY: Cornell University Press.

Stephens, Thomas M. 1989. *Dictionary of Latin American Racial and Ethnic Terminology.* Gainesville: University of Florida Press.

Supremo Tribunal Federal. 2001. Commissão Especial de Litigação Concorrência N° 3/2001.

Tannebaum, Frank. 1947. *Slave and Citizen: The Negro in the Americas.* New York: Vintage Books.

Telles, Edward E. 1992. "Residential Segregation by Skin Color in Brazil." *American Sociological Review.*

———.1993. "Racial Distance and Region in Brazil: The Case of Marriage among Color Groups." *Latin American Research Review* 28:141–62.

———. 1994. "Industrialization and Racial Inequality in Employment: The Brazilian Example." *American Sociological Review* 59:46–63.

———. 1995. "Race, Class and Space in Brazilian Cities." *International Journal of Urban and Regional Research* 19:395–406.

———. 1996. *Promoting and Integrating Race/Ethnic Diversity in Brazil.* Ford Foundation Consultancy Report.

———. 2002. "Racial Ambiguity among the Brazilian Population." *Ethnic and Racial Studies,* May.

———. 2003. "U.S. Foundations and Racial Reasonings in Brazil." *Theory, Culture and Society,* 20 (4):31–45.

Telles, Edward E., and Nelson Lim. 1998. "Does it Matter Who Answers the Race Question? Racial Classification and Income Inequality in Brazil." *Demography* 35, no. 4:465–74.

Telles, Edward E., and Stan Bailey. 2002. "Políticas Contra o Racismo e Opinião

Publica: Comparações entre Brasil e os Estados Unidos." *Opinião Publica* 8 (1):30–39.

Thomas, W. I. 1922. *The Unadjusted Girl*. Boston: Little Brown and Company.

Tienda, Marta, Kevin Lecht, and Kim M. Lloyd. 2002. "Before and After Hopwood: The Elimination of Affirmative Action and Minority Student Enrollment in Texas." Paper presented at the annual meeting of the Population Association of America, Atlanta.

Todorov, Tzvetan. 1993. *On Human Diversity: Nationalism, Racism and Exoticism in French Thought*. Cambridge, MA: Harvard University Press.

Turner, J. Michael. 1985. "Brown into Black: Changing Racial Attitudes of Afro-Brazilian University Students." In *Race, Class and Power in Brazil,* ed. Pierre Michelle Fontaine, 73–94. Los Angeles: UCLA Center for Afro-American Studies.

Turra, Cleusa, and Gustavo Venturi, eds. 1995. *Racismo Cordial: A Mais Completa Análise Sobre O Preconceito de Cor no Brasil*. São Paulo: Editora Ática.

Twine, Francine Winddance. 1998. *Racism in a Racial Democracy*. New Brunswick, NJ: Rutgers University Press.

United Nations Development Programme. 2001. *Human Development Report 2001*. Oxford: Oxford University Press.

U.S. Department of Justice. 1997. Bureau of Justice Statistics.

Vainner, Carlos B. 1990. "Estado e Raça no Brasil: Notas Exploratórias." *Estudos Afro-Asiáticos* 18:103–18.

Van den Berghe, Pierre. 1967. *Race and Racism*. New York: Wiley.

Veja. 1992. "Arruaça na Areia," 28 (Oct. 25):44.

Ventura, Myriam. 2000. "Estratégias para Promoção e Defesa dos Direitos Reprodutivos e Sexuais no Brasil." Consultancy to the Ford Foundation.

Vianna, J. J. Oliveira. 1922. *O Povo Brasileiro e Sua Evolução do Brasil 1920*. Rio de Janeiro.

Viera, Frei Domingos. 1871. *Grande Diccionario Portuguez ou Thesaura da Lingua Potugueza*. Rio de Janeiro: A.A. da Cruz Cutinho.

Wacquant, Loïc. 2001. "Deadly Symbiosis: When Ghetto and Prison Meet." *Punishment and Society* 3 (1):95–134.

Wade, Peter 1993. *Blackness and Race Mixture: The Dynamics of Racial Identity in Colombia*. Baltimore: Johns Hopkins University Press.

Wagley, Charles. 1952a. Introduction to *Race and Class in Rural Brazil,* ed. Charles Wagley. Paris: UNESCO.

———. 1952b. "Race Relations in an Amazon Community," In *Race and Class in Rural Brazil,* ed. Charles Wagley. Paris: UNESCO.

Warren, Jonathan. 1997. "O Fardo de Não Ser Negro: Uma Análise Comparativa do Desempenho Escolar de Afro-brasileiros e Afro-norte-americanos." *Estudos Afro-Asiáticos*.

———. 2002. *The Politics of Anti-Racism*. Durham, NC: Duke University Press.

Willems, Emilio. 1949. "Racial Attitudes in Brazil." *American Journal of Sociology* 54 no. 3:402–408.

Wilson, William J. 1978. *The Declining Significance of Race: Blacks and Changing American Institutions*. Chicago: University of Chicago Press.

Wilson, William Julius. 1996. *When Work Disappears: The World of the New Urban Poor.* New York: Alfred A. Knopf.

Winant, Howard. 2001. *The World Is a Ghetto: Race and Democracy Since World War II.* New York: Basic Books.

Wood, Charles. 1991. "Categorias Censitárias e Classificações Subjetivas no Brasil." In *Desigualdade Racial no Brasil Contemporâneo,* ed. Peggy A. Lovell, 93–114. Belo Horizonte: Universidade Federal de Minas Gerais, Centro de Desenvolvimento e Planejamento Regional.

Young, Michael D. 1958. *The Rise of Meritocracy, 1870–2033: An Essay on Education and Equality.* London: Thames and Hudson.

INDEX

abolition, and difficulty of blacks in job market, 165–66

Additional Protocol for the American Convention on Economic, Social and Cultural Rights (San Salvador Protocol), 245

adoption, 157

advertising, and use of black or brown models, 156

affirmative action in Brazil, 1, 16–17, 248–50; and abuses of quotas for blacks, 263–66; and arguments against race-conscious policies or in favor of universalist or class policies, 256–59; backlash from by 2003, 74–75; beginnings of, 58–61; and Brazilian popular support for quotas, 260–61; and collective rights actions, 247; and comparison to U.S., 249; constitutional basis for, 257–58; and debate at 1996 Multiculturalism and Racism conference, 56, 57–58; and determining racial classification and self-identification, 263–66; and education, 121; education of public about necessity of, 258; and elimination of racism, 269; and greater legal permanence and enforceability, 268; and initial embrace of explicit race-based public policies, 56; in labor market, 255–56; and local government programs following Durban conference, 73; and nongovernmental organizations, 58; overall benefits of, 256; post- Durban transformation regarding, 72–73; precedents for, 258; present relationship in Congress to, 60–61, 268, 292n.52; and quotas and meritocracy, 259–60; and regionalization, 266–67; and universities, 61, 72, 73, 74, 251–52, 253–54, 267, 292n.51, 52; and World Conference on Racism of 2001, 71

affirmative action in United States, 1, 16–17, 249; effectiveness of at professional level, 254–55; and false self-identification, 264; and intersection of

gender and race, 268; and university admissions, 254

Afonso Arinos law of 1951, 37–38

African culture: Brazilian ties to, 101; lack of direct North American contact to, 234; promoted as part of Brazilian national culture, 233–34

Africans: declared inferiority of racial category, 26; taken into slavery, 24–25

Afro-Brazilian culture: in Salvador based on racial isolation, 212–13; shared across society rather than racially separate realms, 234

"Afro-Brazilian" or "Afro-descendent" as term, 23

Afro-Brazilian religion, 101–3; not represented in Brazilian media, 155; and residential self-segregation, 207

Afro-Colombian communities, 249

age, and racial classification, 100–101

AIDS, 247

Alberto, Luiz, 51

Allen, Walter, 132, 197

Allport, Gordon, 153

Almeida, Wallace de, 246

Alves, João, 51

Amado, Jorge, 36, 155, 190

Amaral, A. J. Azevedo, 32

amarelo, 81

Americans with Disabilities Act (ADA), 266

Amnesty International, 246

ancestry: as definition of race, 1; and racial classification, 91–95; and self-classification, 92–93

Andrews, George, 271n.11, 273n.29

ANPOCS [Associação Nacional de Pos-Graduaçao em Ciencias Sociais (National Association of Graduate Studies in the Social Sciences)], 55

antiracism laws, 50, 239–40, 253; application of, to only most blatant forms of racism, 243–44; and collective rights, 246–47; convictions on basis of, 52–53;